Writing Well

BOOKS BY DONALD HALL

Books of Poetry
Exiles and Marriages, 1955
The Dark Houses, 1958
A Roof of Tiger Lilies, 1964
The Alligator Bride: Poems New and Selected, 1969
The Yellow Room: Love Poems, 1971
The Town of Hill, 1975
Kicking the Leaves, 1978
The Happy Man, 1986
The One Day, 1988
New and Old Poems, 1990

Books of Prose
Remembering Poets, 1978
Ox-Cart Man, 1979
To Keep Moving, 1981
The Weather for Poetry, 1982
Fathers Playing Catch with Sons, 1985
The Ideal Bakery, 1987
Seasons at Eagle Pond, 1987
Here at Eagle Pond, 1990

BOOKS BY SVEN BIRKERTS

An Artificial Wilderness: Essays on Modern Literature, 1987
The Electric Life: Essays on Modern Poetry, 1989

Writing Well

Seventh Edition

Donald Hall

Sven Birkerts
Harvard University
Expository Writing Program

HarperCollins*Publishers*

Sponsoring Editor: Constance Rajala
Manuscript Editor: Hope Rajala
Project Editor: Robert Ginsberg
Art Direction/Cover Coordinator: Heather A. Ziegler
Text Design Adaptation: Heather A. Ziegler
Cover Design: Circa 86, Inc.
Cover Art: Helen Frankenthaler. *Lush Spring.* (1975).
             Acrylic on canvas. 94.5 × 119.5 inches.
             Collection of Phoenix Art Museum.
Production Administrator: Beth Maglione
Compositor: TCSystems
Printer and Binder: The Maple-Vail Book Manufacturing Group
Cover Printer: New England Book Components, Inc.

For permission to use copyrighted material, grateful acknowledgement is made to the copyright holders on pp. 463–466, which are hereby made part of this copyright page.

Writing Well, Seventh Edition
Copyright © 1991 by Donald Hall and Sven Birkerts

Library of Congress Cataloging-in-Publication Data
Hall, Donald, 1928-
    Writing well/Donald Hall, Sven Birkerts.–7th ed.
      p. cm.
    Includes index.
    1. English language–Rhetoric.   I. Birkerts, Sven.   II. Title.
PE14098.H312   1991
808'.042–dc20   90-41456
                                                                      CIP

ISBN 0-673-46224-2 (Student Edition)
ISBN 0-673-53334-4 (Teacher Edition)

90 91 92 93 9 8 7 6 5 4 3 2 1

Contents

7

FORMS FOR THE ESSAY: RHETORICAL PATTERNS IN EXPOSITION 257

8

ARGUMENT AND PERSUASION   287

9

WRITING RESEARCH   321

10

A BRIEF REVIEW OF GRAMMAR, PUNCTUATION, AND MECHANICS   367

Prefaces to the Seventh Edition

D. H.:

When I make a new edition of *Writing Well*, I need continually to consult and reaffirm the premise from which I started. It remains my intention that *Writing Well* not only recommend good prose but exemplify it.

Some composition texts describe correct prose in language stiff, drab, passive, shallow, boring, and trite. But we learn by observing actions not by memorizing advice. "Do as I say, not as I do," fails in child raising as it does in composition teaching. A textbook that praises "effective communication" resembles a father who screams at his son: "DON'T RAISE YOUR VOICE!"

In *Writing Well*, I mean to teach correctness and originality at the same time. It is nasty to teach the correctness of cliché; it is pointless to teach expression without the correctness that allows readers to understand what is being expressed. Good writing makes passages from one human being to another. To carve a passage we require both correctness and originality.

A naive view proposes that invention precludes revision, or that revision negates invention. Experience shows that we need both, and both continually. As I put it elsewhere: "Writing is acquiring material (the floating memory, the rapid daily writing) and it is also ordering and cutting that material. The writer must be a paradoxical combination of opposites, the big spender and the miser." In the process of writing, these two qualities sometimes come in sequence: invention followed by revision. More often, in the reality of composition, the writer goes back and forth between revision and creation so rapidly that it is hard to tell the one from the other.

We combine these opposites in order to open passages to the reader—and audience is at the heart of everything. Teaching a vigorous and combative class of composition, we meet this defense of the cliché: "But it's *exactly* what I mean!" The answer to this defense brings audience in. If the purpose of writing is to make passages to other people, the narcissistic defense—". . . what *I* mean . . ."—is irrelevant. As with bad mechanics, bad style obscures. The trouble with trite expressions, passives, dead metaphors, vague intensives, jargon, and modish words is that these stylistic mistakes block the passage from person to person.

Writing to Write

It is commonplace to notice that when we enter college, these days, we lack experience in writing. We don't write thank you notes to our grandparents; we use the telephone instead. Someone fluent in speech may remain stiff and inhibited in writing, for reasons that are virtually physiological. We are not illiterate but lacking practice we lack fluency. The neural path from mind to mouth is open and clear from constant use; the path from mind to the small muscles of the fingers is dusty, cobwebbed, narrow, and unused.

Continual application of pen to paper is the first necessity in a composition course. The student who makes one theme a week is practicing writing for only a few hours, and the muscles do not develop. Writing resembles athletic skill; it comes more naturally to some people than to others, but it always and only improves with practice.

Metaphysics of Organization

Writing Well begins with a chapter that introduces its values and methods, using for example mostly essays of personal reminiscense. The new second chapter speaks of reading, and reader response, sketching the relationship between language and audience. The third chapter presents ideas of process, the practicalities of essay writing, and tells the life story of one composition.

In its crucial center, *Writing Well* goes from small to large—from words to sentences to paragraphs. Most readers find "Words" the best part of *Writing Well*. Some teachers follow a different order, going to patterns of rhetoric before they enter the world of the verb and the modifier; teachers must consult their own passions. However, my small-to-large ordering exists for reasons, and I would like to argue the point.

The baby in the crib makes noises that are pleasing to him, autistic utterance without discernible message. Then he begins to associate sounds with responses: "mm" brings milk; another sound gets his diapers changed. Later, the articulation of words becomes the magic of naming, and the magic mind of the child thinks metaphorically because that is the way it knows of thinking. The child sees the leg of the table as a leg like his own or his father's. The table might run away if it wanted to; it stands still, as if under a spell.

Mother Goose and fairy stories perpetuate magic and transformation, sometimes by sheer incantation, as in the great poem:

Ba, ba, black sheep,
Have you any wool?
Yes, sir, yes, sir,
Three bags full,
One for the master,
One for the dame,
And one for the little boy
That lives down the lane.

Here to autistic pleasures of the mouth we add pleasures of dance and rhythm. The muscles of the leg begin to move, whether we notice it or not.

And sometimes, as the level of discourse moves *toward* that of the grownup, we have sequences or stories, but stories in which the nightmare and the seer's dream find embodiment in a beauty or a beast, or a boy who plants a seed and confronts a giant. Words have extended into narration without losing their transformative power.

We are educated to take part in civilization and education puts down the magic world, as people rising in social class are ashamed of clothes or accents that give away their origins. And so instead of incorporating the old uses of language—which have inherent power and intuition—into our new use of language for reason, for conscious control of environment, for order, and for shape, we bypass the primitive modes of thinking entirely. This bypass creates a profound problem in our use of language; that is, in our feeling and in our thinking. It has created the mess we have made of technology and civilization.

No sane man thinks he will accomplish anything by doing away with lightbulbs and appendectomies. The man who substitutes an oil lamp for a lightbulb merely replaces a newer invention with an older one. We do not need to junk civilization to recover a part of the powerful intuition we lost when we disavowed our primitive past. We can go beyond; we can include both; the wisest men have been doing it for years. Creativity requires returning—in part—to the magic of the crib.

I once met a woman who had taught grade school for many years and was concerned, like Wordsworth, with the diminishing imagination of the growing child. She told me—more or less: I must paraphrase—that if you asked a nine-year-old to do a report on Magellan, he might begin, "Magellan got eaten by cannibals!" If you asked the same child, at eleven, for a report on Magellan, the child knew better; the report would begin, "Magellan was born in 1480 in Portugal."

Conventional order has won out over the order of intensity. After chronology come the forms of logic and argument, all creations of the cerebral cortex, strongly suppressing messages from the world of nursery rhyme and fairy story. "That was when I was a kid."

In telling a story, whether true or false, the order of chronology is often the most appropriate order; in persuasion, logic is a component of argument. But no reasonable idea of order satisfies or expresses the whole complex of human thought and feeling. It expresses a portion of human potential, and it would be ridiculous to ignore it. But it is equally and tragically ridiculous to ignore the order of color and intensity: "Magellan was eaten by cannibals!"

As a painter at the turn of the century, when he finished art school, had to set out by forgetting what he had learned, so I think most of us need to build our prose again from the start. Ultimately, shapeliness—the general order within a piece of writing, or the focus I talk about in the first chapter—is part of the style we must reach for, but this order says only: Exclude everything that is not really to the point! Know thyself, and know thy point. The ultimate shapeliness, of the finished essay or the finished Chinese pot, depends on the ingredients we bring to the shaping. In writing, the first ingredient is always the word.

To attempt in a composition textbook to reconstruct growing-up-with-language is doubtless overambitious. We cannot undo and redo, in four hundred pages, twenty years of experience. But perhaps we may set an example for *rethinking* writing: otherwise, we merely give rules and suggestions, Hall's Helpful Hints; otherwise, we avoid the fundamental issues of writing well. No one can emphasize too much that good writing depends on abilities, thoughts, and feelings which are the difficult but available sources of psychic and social health.

ADDENDUM 1991

So I put it in 1988. For the seventh edition, I turned to a collaborator. I am fortunate that Sven Birkerts brings to this venerable textbook his young and energetic mind, as well as the prose style he has developed in his critical essays. Sven brings to this book not only his experience in writing, and his intelligence, but also his active engagement in teaching composition to American students of the 1990s. Sven's new ideas for this volume have extended my own—and then some.

Donald Hall

S. B.:

Donald Hall and I agreed that a two-part preface would be the most appropriate way for us to mark this first collaboration. The "I" of the first six editions *has* become a "we," but this collaborator felt that a familiar use of the plural pronoun would bestow too much unearned credit. *Writing Well* is still overwhelmingly Donald Hall's book. Its beliefs and principles, set out so clearly in the preceding preface, govern the whole. Indeed, in bringing forward my changes and additions, I have tried above all to keep faith with the originating and ongoing vision of the book. The greatest compliment I received was from an anonymous reader who, upon reviewing a largely new chapter, responded that he was glad that the decision to take on a collaborator had been abandoned.

Donald Hall and I worked closely together on every part of the revision. Bulky envelopes traveled back and forth between Danbury, New Hampshire, and Arlington, Massachusetts, for the better part of one year. We had remarkably few disputes, and any that arose were happily resolved.

The reader familiar with the sixth edition will see that the fundamental structure of the book has not been changed. Within the frame, however, there have been abundant additions and alterations. The chapters on Reading (2) and Argument (8) have been substantially rewritten. The chapters on Words (1), Sentences (5), and Paragraphs (6) now include samples of student writing and student writing in process, with commentaries from their instructors. Finally, I have altered something on nearly every page of the text. These changes include materials brought up to date, new examples and exercises, as well as the thousand-and-one modifications that are inevitable when two opinionated sensibilities take a fresh look at one text.

Here, then, is the seventh edition of *Writing Well*. The authors of the separate prefaces join together in hoping that the reader finds challenge, instruction, and pleasure in these pages.

Sven Birkerts

Authors' Notes

People from whom we derive our ideas of style are the writers whose work we love. We quote many of these writers here, so that they may speak in their own voices, and need not depend upon the articulation of admirers. We do not quote them all. We owe our senses of style, as well as some ideas about it, especially to modern writers we grew up reading and imitating: Ernest Hemingway, Ezra Pound, Marianne Moore, George Orwell, Gertrude Stein, James Joyce.

In earlier editions of *Writing Well*, Donald Hall benefitted from the help of many people. Because their help persists in this edition, we mention them again. At Little, Brown, first publisher of this volume, many people helped in the earlier editions: Margaret Zusky, Rab Bertelsen, Jan B. Welch, Dale Anderson, Elizabeth Philipps, Donna McCormick, and David W. Lynch. Lawrence Russ and Rosemary Yaco helped Donald Hall in Ann Arbor. Some of the teachers whose suggestions informed earlier editions were Donald Butler, Terrence Collins, Steven V. Daniels, H. Ramsey Fowler, Neita Gleiker, Federick Goff, Richard Larson, Thomas Lux, Russell J. Meyer, Marcia Stubbs, M. Elisabeth Susman, Barbara Wicks, and Peter T. Zoller. Fifth edition helpers included Sally Crisp, Mark Halperin, Carol Hayes, Celeste Martin, Alan McKenzie, and Barry Weller. In the fourth, fifth, and sixth editions, the editorial assistance of Linda Howe was extraordinary. Traveling around the country, Donald Hall profited from many conversations with teachers of Freshman English, and with directors of writing programs; particularly important were visits to Ball State University, to Oakland University in Michigan, to the University of Wisconsin at Stevens

Point, to the University of Vermont, to Syracuse University, to Orange Coast College, to Macon Junior College, to the University of Pittsburgh at Bradford, to the C. W. Post Campus of Long Island University, to the University of Wisconsin at Eau Claire, to Jamestown Community College, to Behrend College, to Mercer College, to the University of Utah, to Lynchburg College, and to the Poynter Institute. It is impossible to list the names of everyone who helped, but here are a few: Thomas Carnacelli, Peter De Blois, William Hiss, Frederick Bromberger, Joann Mercer, Diana Anderson, Charles Berger, Muriel Allingham-Dale, Doug Carlson, Lynn Matson, Lawrence Mobley, Margaret Woodworth, Richard Lindner, John Coates, Joseph Trimmer, Susan Bartels, Mary Jane Dickerson, Sally Ronsheim; and Sandra Donaldson and Celia B. Diamond who spoke by letter. With the sixth edition we noted the help of Lisa Ede of Oregon State University and David Skwire of Cuyahoga County Community College.

We have profited from many suggestions we have received from Thomas Adler, Linda Albright, Robert Aldridge, Nell Altizer, Nancy G. Anderson, Maureen Andrews, David Baker, Barry Bakorsky, Anna M. Barnes, Richard Bausch, J. Charles Berger. William W. Betts, Jr., Dorothee Bowie, Margaret Brady, May Brown, Carl Brucker, Ingrid Brunner, Nancy Bunge, Edward Byrne, Harriet Carr, Fern Chertkow, T. L. Clark, Jerry Coffey, Steve Connolly, Mary Copeland, Edward Corbett, Gary Culbert, Paul Dameen, David Dawson, Miriam Dow, Helen Dunn, Oliver Durand, Anne Elam, Mary J. Elkins, Thomas Elliott, Richard Fine, Gala Fitzgerald, William T. French, Michele Giannusa, Peggy Gledhill, Robert M. Gorrell, Barbara Griffin, Richard Grounds, Mark Halperin, Norman Hane, Joan C. Haug, David R. Hauser, Joyce Hicks, Kathryn Holmes, D. Howard, M. Huyser, Walter Isle, Thomas Johnson, Paul Kameem, Sighle Kennedy, Sharon King, Opal A. Lanett, Jim Ledford, Karen B. LeFerre, Merrill Lewis, Sherry McGuire, Alan T. McKenzie, Peter W. Mackinlay, Lynne McMahon, Ann Maioroff, Andrew Makarushtra, Silvine Marbury, Doreen Maronde, Timothy Materer, Celest A. Martin, Michael Martin, Paul F. Michelson, Sr., Jean Michaupt, Patricia Moody, Jim Moore, C. R. Moyer, Fred Muramunco, Helen Naugle, Kenneth Newman, Richard O'Keefe, Steve O'Neill, Janice Philbin, Adele Pittendrigh, George Pittman, Martha Rainbolt, Kate Reavley, Kenneth Requa, Elizabeth G. Richards, Chris Rideout, Florence Roberts, Judy Rogers, Monroe Roth, Sherod Santos, Charlotte W. Sargeant, Ted Schaefer, Michael Sexon, Susan Simpson, Harriet Susskind Spiegle, Sandra Stancey, Diane Stege, J. Stege, Pamela Stith, Margaret A. Strom, Sharon Stuut, Kathleen Sullivan, J. C. Taylor, Charles L. Tilgham, George J. Thompson, Darlene Unrue, Linda Venis, Lucien A. Waddell, Ricki Wadsworth, Nancy Walker, Martha S. Waller, James Watt, Richard Widmayer, Diane Williams, Louis Williams, Thomas Wilson, and George Wymer.

Students who mail in completed questionnaires help us to revise this text for future students. From the second edition through the sixth, Donald Hall was helped by Clayton Hudnall of the University of Hartford. In all editions, Donald Hall must acknowledge his debt to the late Richard Beal, of Boston University, who supplied strengths in the areas of his own weaknesses, who was tireless and good-natured and relentless and kind. In all editions, he remains grateful to his former editors—Charles Christensen, Carolyn Potts, and Joe Opiela—and to Constance Rajala who has worked with Sven Birkerts as well as Donald Hall on the seventh edition. Mention should also be made of several editorial assistants: Virginia Pye, Adrienne Weiss, Amy Johnson, Nan Upin, and Jennifer Lonoff. Mike Moran of the University of Rhode Island has helped us, and from the same institution Robert Schwegler has contributed mightily to the changes made in the sixth edition and in the seventh. Especially helpful to Sven Birkerts, in making the seventh edition, have been Constance Rajala, as editor, Hope Rajala, as copy editor, and a host of teachers of English composition, who criticized our old editions and suggested improvements. These invaluable helpers include James Peterson, Alan Jacobs, Joanne Charbonneau, Ralph Latham, Sarah Gallagher, Ed Silva, Richard Johnson, John Pahl, Carol Long, Kelly Dobyns, Tony Magistrale. Special thanks to Richard Marius, Nancy Sommers, Pat Hoy, Gordon Harvey, Jonathan Aaron, Sue Lonoff, Norm Katz, William Corbett, and the rest of the Expository Writing Department at Harvard.

Donald Hall
Sven Birkerts

1

Introduction: Writing, and Writing Well

WRITING TO MAKE CONTACT

Students write essays and answer questions on tests, scientists write reports on their work, teachers write evaluations of their students, people make lists to remember what they must do, some of us keep diaries to remember what we have done, executives address reports to their fellows, salespeople write messages from the field to the office, and we write notes and letters to keep in touch with relatives and friends. There are practical reasons for writing. The reasons for writing well are practical also.

But not at first. First comes the spoken message: *I want milk.* As our brains develop, our messages become more complicated. We give emphasis to out-loud messages by gestures and facial expressions. Learning to write well is harder than learning to talk, but it can bring pleasures deeper than the satisfaction of immediate needs. It can bring us the pleasures of discovery and of contact; writing well, we must think clearly; writing well, we must understand both feelings and ideas; writing well, we reach across the space of our difference and touch other human beings.

A good writer uses words to *discover,* for we use words to think with. We do not first have a thought and then find words to express that thought; we think in the act of finding words—accepting some and rejecting others. Our thought is incomplete until we find a language and a shape by which we can transmit our thought to other people. An essay reflects the shape of our thought; its sentences develop thought and carry it across to others. We write well when our prose gives pleasure

1

while it carries knowledge. That pleasure-carrying knowledge comes from understanding, which includes self-understanding, and creates understanding in the minds of others.

Here is a passage from a student essay about registering for freshman courses:

> Hey, I got a hard time all over the gym, a totally unbelievable experience, and a bad way to begin anything as important like college.

This writer has problems in mechanics, in levels of diction, and in generality of language. A message comes through, but inferior writing garbles the faint sound of complaint. The words may express something for the writer, and maybe it was a relief to utter them, as it is a relief to cry out when we feel pain. But the words do not reach out to make contact with readers. Later in the term, the student rewrote the passage.

> There were long lines at every table, during registration at the gym. It took me one hour to find out that a class was closed and I could not take it. Some teachers didn't know the rules for their own departments. After half a day of feeling frustrated, I went back home and told my mother I wasn't sure about going to college after all.

This version gains clarity through detail, through improved mechanics, and especially through the writer's developed sense that he writes for someone who reads him. He does not merely cry out; he gives examples and pictures by which his reader can locate the source of the complaint. Any reader will respond to stories of institutional incompetence. A short version could have read:

> Registration took a long time and I felt frustrated.

This version is brief and correct, better than the first version, but not good enough. Because it only *tells* us a feeling but does not *show* us anything, it will not create the feeling in the reader. It is not constructed by the writer with the reader's response in mind. Details *shown*, like illustrations, carry feeling from writer to reader; the mere names of feelings, *told* in summary, carry no feelings at all. The short version tells its message abstractly, making a message purified of character and feeling, like a slice of bread purified of nutrition and taste.

When we write, we make a contract: *my words are addressed to the outside world; I construct sentences in order to reach someone else.* Too often we write as if we ourselves were our only reader. If we leave out punctuation or use a cliché, then, it does not matter—*we* know what *we* mean. But neither the first version with its errors and its vagueness nor the third version with its meagerness tells enough to someone besides the writer. The middle version quoted, however, is sociable: it enters the world of other people, and by using detail and conventional mechanics, it speaks to an audience.

Writing well means making contact with an audience. Every piece of advice in this book—about argumentation and about commas, about paragraph structure and about spelling, about avoiding clichés and about inventing transitions—helps the writer make contact with the reader.

THE IDEA OF AN AUDIENCE

Writing well is a social act.

The better our language, the more we may connect with other people whether by speech or by writing. Although we may communicate *something* with a grunt, although we may give tone and feeling by gesture or facial expression, on the page we have words alone, and we require every resource of good writing to cross the space between people, to make contact. Writing well, as well as *Writing Well*, exists for a social purpose.

In writing and revising, writers face a thousand choices that they resolve by *the idea of an audience.* It helps to pinpoint an audience in the mind, as we write, the way a lecturer may pick out one face to address, as if everything were intended for the one face only. Sitting at a desk alone, with no listening face to remind us, we need imagination to sustain the idea of an audience. In other contexts we constantly imagine audiences: walking alone, or driving, most of us daydream encounters and conversations; we invent speech and counter-speech; we imagine contact and communication. For that matter, think about how we talk on the telephone. Even though our listener may be a thousand miles away, and even though we communicate for ear contact alone, using only variations of pitch, volume, and rhythm to get our point across, we still tend to *gesture* as if we had the person in front of us. We gesture, smile, frown, raise eyebrows, and make faces. We do these things not because we forget that our friend cannot see us but because we communicate more thoroughly when we imagine complete contact. *The idea of an audience generates contact.*

When we write words on a page we cannot raise and lower the volume of our speech, or make faces, but by keeping the idea of an audience steadily in the forefront of our minds, we use the gestural resources of language to make contact with another person across the space of our difference.

HONEST AND DISHONEST EXPRESSION

An idea of an audience implies that we have something to say to someone else—and that it is something worth saying. Alas, much human language seems to serve the purpose not of making contact, or revealing, but of concealing or of providing the appearance of communication instead of the real thing. Much language serves dishonest purposes; and much of this dishonesty is unintended. The phrase *honest expression* implies an opposite, dishonest expression, which no one admits to but which we sometimes see clearly in others. We are all aware of honest and dishonest expression. We have grown up on the false laughter of television, the fake enthusiasm of advertising, the commercial jollity and condolences of greeting cards, and the lying assertions of politicians. If some falsity has not entered our prose, we are made of aluminum.

We can be false in a thousand ways. We do it with handshakes and we do it with grunts. We do it by saying outright lies and we do it by keeping silent. But in these instances we understand our own falsity. When we fool *ourselves* we are in more trouble. We fool ourselves with words that can mean almost anything. How much have we said when we call someone *liberal?* We fool ourselves when we avoid blame by leaving *I* out of the sentence, as when we knock over a lamp and claim, "The lamp was knocked over" or "The lamp fell," as if it acted by itself. We also fool ourselves by using clichés, trite expressions that have become meaningless substitutes for feeling and thought:

impressionable age	bottom line
startling conclusion	name of the game
a vital part of our future	get a point across
made it what it is today	a changing society

Clichés are little cinder blocks of crushed and reprocessed experience. When we use them in writing, we violate our agreement to construct sentences in order to reach someone else. We appear to make contact, but the appearance is not a reality. Clichés are familiar and comfortable; they seem to mean something. Indeed, when they were first coined, as phrases or figures of speech, they were often memorable expressions. But excessive usage has drained the life from them. We hear the familiarity but the original force of meaning is lost. When I tell you that the *bottom line* is the *name of the game,* and *just what the doctor ordered,* I am telling you very little. Clichés substitute false contact for true.

Every profession—medicine, law, theater, business—has its own clichés. We call the clichés that belong to a profession its *jargon.* One set of clichés appears especially at graduations, from primary school through graduate school:

the future belongs to you.
the challenge of new . . .
in today's world . . .
responsibility, good citizenship, service to the community. . .

The university, in fact, is a great source of jargon. Here are two paragraphs from a letter addressed by a newly elected college president to his faculty.

> Dear Members of the State College Community:
> I am deeply honored and challenged by the opportunity to join State College as its seventh president. The hospitality and spontaneous warmth of everyone we have met has made both Barbara and me feel very welcome. We look forward to making State our home as quickly as we can arrange an orderly transition from our current responsibilities.
> State College is rich in tradition: it is an institution with a past, and, more importantly, it is a College with a future. Building on its heritage, and maximizing its resources, State College can continue to achieve distinction by providing educational opportunities for young men and women.

This is the language we expect from officials—from politicians and bureaucrats, from the presidents of colleges and the presidents of corporations. It says nothing, and it says it with maximum pomposity. It took this man years to learn the trick of empty jargon, the style of interlocking cliché. Every phrase is trite, and the phrases are stuck together with mortar like *is* and *and* and *with*. The edifice is reprocessed garbage:

deeply honored
challenged by the opportunity
spontaneous warmth
making . . . our home
orderly transition
current responsibilities
rich in tradition
building on its heritage
maximizing its resources
achieve distinction
providing educational opportunities

One should mention as well the trite and meaningless contrast between the past, as in *heritage*—a word as hokey as *home*—and *a college with a future*. The contrast says nothing. Unless the collegiate doors are closing tomorrow, of course it has *a future*. The word *future*—like *heritage* and *home*—carries vaguely positive connotations. A candidate for president of the United States used as a slogan *The future lies before us*, trying to associate himself with this positive connotation; no one found the slogan offensive, but he lost.

In the college president's letter, the smoothness of the masonry is exceptional, but the passage is almost without content. If we call the paragraphs insincere, it is because they express only conventional notions, not anybody's own ideas or feelings. Of course the author did not *intend* insincerity, nor did he feel that he was lying.

We must look closely at the notion of sincerity; all too often it is a cover for its opposite, insincerity. The worst liars sincerely say, to themselves and to the world, that they are the most honest. Yet sincerity can be a valuable idea if we think clearly about it, and sincerity has everything to do with the reasons for writing well. Peter Elbow says:

> I warn against defining sincerity, as telling true things about one-self. It is more accurate to define it functionally as the sound of a writer's voice or self on paper—a general sound of authenticity in words. The point is that self-revelation . . . is an easy route in our culture and therefore can be used as an evasion: it can be function-ally insincere even if substantially true and intimate. To be precise, *sincerity is the absence of "noise" or static—the ability or courage not to hide the real message.*

The static is the distance between what the words say and what we sense lies behind them. The person with a pose of sincerity fixes us with his eyes, saying, "I am going to be wholly honest with you. I am a bastard. I cheat on my girlfriend and I steal my roommate's toothpaste." The real message has designs on us: "Love me, I'm so *honest.*"

The distance between the meaning (the apparently stated) and the expression (the really implied) ruins the statement and prevents real communication between people. The one exception might be the *ironic* statement, where the speaker trusts that her listener will feel the dis-tance and pick up her point all the more acutely. A mother walking into the war zone of her daughter's bedroom might say: "This is lovely. I see that you heard what I asked you to do this morning." Most children will pick up the meaning behind the expression. Here, the real meaning gets through—and therefore there is no insincerity. On the other hand, triteness and insincerity prevent true contact by substituting false con-tact. In the college president's letter, the meaning has something to do with expressing pleasure in a new task; the expression is an exhibition of academic smoothness; it is a little dance performed by a well-trained educationist seal. It says, "Look at me. Admit me to your ranks. I am one of you."

We cannot accept sincerity as a standard if we are going to take the writer's word for it. We can take it seriously if we listen to his *words* for it. Sincerity is *functional* (Elbow's word) if we believe it, if we hear the voice of a real person speaking forth in the prose—whether of speech or of the written word. We must speak in a voice that sounds natural to reach the ears of other people. But finding this natural voice is not easy; the natural voice is usually not the spontaneous voice, for when we write without examining our words we often speak words that are trite and ordinary or even institutional. Writing well requires self-criticism, hard thinking, and analysis. It is worth it. Socrates made the commitment: the life that is unexamined is not worth living.

PLAGIARISM

We have been talking about the kind of dishonesty in writing that anyone can slide into without meaning to. This falsity resembles the social lie, or exaggeration, when we act enthusiastic in order to seem agreeable. Although this falsity is forgivable, surely we do best as moral beings, as citizens, as bosses, or as employees when we learn to say what we mean. But there is also the deliberate dishonesty of plagiarism, which we should speak of early in our approach to writing: stealing someone else's good writing is not an acceptable form of writing well.

Plagiarism is stealing the words or ideas of others and presenting them as our own. It is like cheating on tests; it is trying to steal a better grade. Obviously plagiarism is self-defeating because we cannot learn if we use somebody else's accomplishments as a substitute for our own endeavors.

It is also wrong.

Now I call it deliberate dishonesty and it is usually just that: the plagiarist props open a book beside the typewriter and copies word for word. However, some people come to college unsure of what plagiarism is. We are so accustomed to hearing and using other people's words that we forget where the lines are drawn. The matter is simple. The printed word is a form of private property—and the use of that property without proper acknowledgment (or, in some cases, permission) is theft. In our society theft is punished. Every year, it seems, we read of cases of high-ranking politicians or scholars losing their positions and suffering embarrassment because they plagiarized.

When we consult any printed source, on any subject we write about, we should take a note of that source (book, encyclopedia, magazine, newspaper, radio program, television show) and list this source when we hand in our paper. (See the pages on documentation late in this book, 329–335.) If we quote from a source, we should use quotation marks *and* identify the source. But also, *if we use an idea—or sequence of ideas—from a source, even though we put it in our own words, we must always give the source of the idea.* If we take these precautions, no one can ever accuse us of plagiarism.

Some people need to be especially careful not because they are criminal sorts but because they have good if unconscious memories and tend to mimic or repeat whatever they hear or read. Some of us, hearing a joke from friend A, find ourselves repeating it almost word for word when we tell it to friend B. Others who repeat a story will make it over into their own words. There is nothing better or worse about these different personalities; but the apt repeater or mimic is the one who must *be on guard, always, against unconscious plagiarism.* If this person writes a theme about cigarette smoking in public places, he or she might repeat ideas and even phrases from a newspaper editorial, read a week earlier, without being aware of it. But once this is said, ignorance is no excuse.

NEVER REPEAT ANYBODY ELSE'S IDEAS OR WORDS WITH-OUT ACKNOWLEDGMENT.

EXAMINING THE WORDS

Writing well can be a starting point for all thinking. Self-examination finds what we have inside us that is our own. Understanding the self gives us a certain objectivity; it allows us to move outside the self, to read, to analyze, to define, and thus to make contact outside the self, with others. Self-examination, which may sound like an egotistical thing, can actually lead to the opposite. Self-examination can provide the basis for moving outside the self; looking inward is the basis for looking outward; writing is a social act that begins in privacy.

Of course we are stuffed with clichés—we have been exposed to them all our lives—but clichés are not "our own." We have swallowed everything that has ever happened to us: we dropped the bottle to the floor at the age of eight weeks and cried for the lack of it; the telephone did not ring last week, and we cried for the lack of it; the toy shines under the tree, the toy rusts behind the garage; the smell of bacon, the smell of roses, the smell of kittens and the litter in their box; the flowers and the beer cans emerging from the snow. Everything that ever happened to us remains on file in our heads. As a professor at MIT put it: the human brain is a big computer made of meat. The one difference is that we cannot call everything up just by punching a key. Large portions of what we have stored will only come back if the memory is somehow activated. This is, by the way, one of the real pleasures of reading; language can set off the most surprising and eye-opening chains of association.

If the brain is a computer, we are all engaged in learning how to operate it. For the college president quoted above, the task of writing was simple: he was programmed to write that kind of prose; he pushed the right keys and his brain computer turned out preassembled units of academic jargon. Usually the commencement speaker or the student writing home for money presses other keys for printouts of ready-made pseudothoughts and pseudofeelings. But let us suppose that we are interested in something genuine, the voice without static, the utterance in which expression and meaning are the same. We must learn new ways to use the accumulation of words, sense impressions, and ideas that we keep on disk in the brain. Our words must not make rows of identical houses like the subdivision prose of cliché. "New" is fresh, genuine, ourselves, our own experience. Making it new, we make contact with the reader.

Freshness is not, however, the inevitable result of spontaneity. Writing freely, without pausing for correction, is a good way to practice writing, to learn to flow, and to uncover material you didn't know was in you. It can be important to develop a sense of freedom in writing. But then there is the second half of genuine expression, the half that applies the mapmaker's more objective examination to the new country that has been explored. Examination and analysis, leading to revision, allow the writer to communicate with other human beings. Revising the map, we think of the reader; we revise to make contact with the reader. The idea of an audience must govern us. Writing well is a social act.

REVISING THE MAP

Almost all writers, almost all the time, need to revise. We need to revise because spontaneity is never adequate. Writing that is merely emotional release for the writer becomes emotional chaos for the reader. Even when we write as quickly as our hand can move, we slide into emotional falsity, into cliché or other static that prevents contact. We make leaps by private association that leave our prose unclear to others. We often omit steps in thinking or use a step that we later recognize as bad logic. Sometimes we overexplain the obvious. Or we include irrelevant detail. First drafts remain first drafts. They are the material that we must shape, a marble block that the critical brain chisels into form. We must shape this material in order to pass it from mind to mind; we shape our material into a form that allows other people to receive it. This shaping often requires us, in revising, to reorganize whole paragraphs, both the order of sentences and the sentences themselves. We must drop sentences and clauses that do not belong; we must expand or supply others necessary to a paragraph's development. Often we must revise the order of paragraphs; often we must write new paragraphs to provide coherent and orderly progress.

Good writing is an intricate interweaving of inspiration and discipline. A student may need one strand more than the other. Most of us continually need to remember both sides of writing: *we must invent, and we must revise.* In these double acts, invention and revision, we are inventing and revising not just our prose style but our knowledge of ourselves and of the people around us. Like an artist going over a hastily drawn contour, we revise to get closer to the true perception. When Confucius recommended, "Make it new," he meant that we should keep faith with ourselves by responding honestly—and thus, freshly—to the world around us. He was asking us to live what Socrates called "the examined life." It was a moral position. By our language, we shall know ourselves—not once and for all, by a breakthrough, but continually, all our lives. By our language we connect with other human beings; as we read them (or read their tones and facial expressions) we understand and make contact in reciprocal social exchange—or we don't. The necessity to write well arises from the need to understand and to discriminate, to be genuine and to avoid what is not genuine, in ourselves and in others. Human connection by way of language is not the most important thing: it is the only thing.

THEMES AND REVISIONS

On the first day of class, the assignment was to write for twenty minutes on the topic "How I Came to College." Here is an impromptu theme by Jim Beck.

> Education is of paramount importance to today's youth. No one can underestimate the importance of higher education. It makes us well-rounded individuals and we must realize that all work and no play is not the way to go about it, but studies is the most important part, without a doubt. Therefore I decided when I was young that I would go to college and applied myself to studies in high school so that I would be admitted. I was admitted last winter and my family was very happy as was I. Coming here has been a disappointment so far because people are not very friendly to freshmen and everyone has their own clique and the whole place is too big. But I expect that it will get better soon and I will achieve my goal of a higher education and being a well-rounded person.

Repetition at the end of the impromptu gives it some unity. When Jim says that "people are not very friendly to freshmen," the reader glimpses a real Jim Beck. But through most of the paragraph, the writer is not being himself. You can tell that he is not being himself because he is sounding like so many other people. Doubtless he thinks that he writes for a teacher who wants to hear this sort of language. Therefore in a sense Jim works from an idea of audience. The trouble is, it's a bad idea of audience and, really, he makes contact with no audience at all. Jim is assembling an impromptu from the cliché collection in the why-I-want-to-go-to-college box. When he says *paramount importance,* does he really know what *paramount* means? Does he mean that *today's youth* is genuinely different from yesterday's or tomorrow's? And how far into history does *today* extend? What does *well-rounded* mean? Why say *individual* instead of *person* or *people? Importance* is vague, and saying it twice makes it vaguer. In the sentence of complaint, where the reader briefly senses an actual writer, Jim would have done better to *show* his loneliness in an anecdote, instead of just *telling* us about it. Showing makes contact; telling avoids it.

Later in the term, when he had a free theme, Jim wrote an essay which was not so much a revision of his impromptu as a new start and which *really* told how he came to college.

The Race to College
Jim Beck

It's horrible now, and I don't know if it will get any better. The only people who pay attention to me are the people who are trying to beat me out for the track team. My roommate is stoned all day and gets A's on his papers anyway. I hate him because he hates me because I'm a jock. My classes are boring lectures and the sections are taught by graduate students who pick on the students because the professors pick on them.

But I remember wanting to come here so bad! Nobody from Hammerton named Beck had ever been to college. Everybody knew the Becks were stupid. This went for my father, who never got through high school, and for my grandfather, who died before I was born, and who was the town drunk. It went for my two older brothers who went bad, as they say in Hammerton. Steve got a dishonorable discharge from the Marines and he works on a farm outside town and gets drunk on Fridays and Saturdays. Curt stole a car and did time at Jackson and nobody has heard from him since. My sister had a three-month baby and the town liked to talk about that.

I was different. Everybody told me I was. My mother told me I wasn't a Beck. My father told me I was going to bring back the family's good name. (I never knew it had one.) In grammar school the teachers all told me how much better I was than my brothers. By the time I was in sixth grade my father and the school Principal were talking about the University.

My father isn't really dumb. Sometimes people look dumb because it's expected of them. He's worked at the same grocery for twenty years, I guess. Now that I made it to the University, he wants to be called Manager, because he's the only man there besides Mr. Roberts who owns it. (The rest of the help are—is?—kids who bag and an old lady cashier.) When I went back for a weekend everybody treated me as if I won the Olympics.

I said the Principal and my father were talking about my going to the University. All through junior high I said I didn't want to go. I was scared. No Beck could do that. Bad things kept happening to my family. My father had an accident and totaled the car and lost his license and for a year we didn't have a car at all. He had to walk home two miles every night pushing a basket of groceries. When I said I would quit school and get a job, everybody jumped on me.

It wasn't that I was an A student. It was just that I tried hard at
everything I did. I got B's mostly. Now with B's, the counselors kept
telling me, I could be admitted to the University, but I wouldn't get
a scholarship. I needed mostly A's for that, and then when I got to
the University I would lose the scholarship if I couldn't keep the
grades up. Then my brother Steve, who was a pretty good athlete
once, suggested athletics.

I was too skinny for football, too short for basketball, I could
barely swim and my school didn't have a swimming team anyway.
There is one sport you can practice with no money and no equipment. I started to run when I was in my last year of junior high. It
felt good right away. I ran to and from school. I went over to the high
school and did laps. The high school coach noticed me and asked me
to go out the next year. Running long distances hurts a lot. Sometimes you get a stitch in your left side and suddenly it shifts to your
right side. I didn't exactly mind the pain. I studied it. I studied it in
order to go to the University, the way I studied everything else.

In my Senior year I was all-state and held two high-school records
(600 and half-mile) and I had an athletic scholarship to the University. Now I am here, the first Beck to make it. I don't know why I'm
here or why I ran so hard or where I go from here. Now that I am
here, the race to get here seems pointless. Nothing in my classes
interests me. I study, just as I did before, in order to pass the course
or even get a good grade. I run to win, but what am I running for? I
will never be a great runner. Sometimes when I cannot sleep I
imagine packing my bags and going back to Hammerton. But I can't
do that. They would say, "He's a Beck, all right."

Jim's essay has several important features of good writing: it has
unity, which means the focus, the point, the coming together of many
details; and it has the voice of a real person speaking out of experience
with a minimum of tired phrases or borrowed clothing. It has discipline,
and it has feeling. Although Jim is discouraged and feels aimless and
melancholy, he has made a great stride toward knowing and being able
to present himself. The voice is more unified; we sense that the owner
of that voice has a better grasp of what his experience *really* meant. He
revised, using his own experience in his own language. *And* he was
disciplined; he used tighter sentence structure, and he found a narrative
structure that contained and shaped his thought. Deciding on *what* to
tell and how to tell it gave him a natural sequence. The naturalness
comes across as readability. Therefore he made contact with his readers; and he made contact at least partly because he believed in his
readers. He developed an idea of an audience chiefly from work in class,
where students responded as readers to one another's essays. For Jim the
shape of his thought came from an analogy—the struggle to attend
college compared to a footrace—and this analogy helped him to think,

to embody the shape of his thought, and to reach his fellow-student readers.

This revision was the product of much hard work, of which only a portion went to the actual revision. Jim's daily writing—with which he struggled at first and which he later enjoyed—was a source of improvement. He began to find his own, unpompous voice. He also revised other essays after reading his teacher's comments and after discussing these comments in conferences. Jim Beck also talked with his English teacher during office hours and thought about his writing and his ideas while he ran cross-country in the autumn of his freshman year.

EXAMPLES FROM PRINT

Jim Beck's original essay was impromptu, and the revision printed here came two months later. People who spend their whole lives writing often take longer still and struggle with the same enemies, disunity and evasion. Habitual writers differ from beginners in many ways. For one thing, they know that they are likely to fail at first. Some writers know that they may be weak in details; to succeed they must struggle to generate more of them. Others know that they often generate too many details and lose clarity of organization; to succeed they must pare words and organize. Whatever their problems, professionals learn to be patient. They expect writing to be hard work. They struggle with the same materials as beginners do and strive for a voice that makes contact with others.

People who write well begin by reading well. Reading good prose with close attention, we can acquire the manners that make the good writing we admire. We learn by immersion. The process can be compared to learning a foreign language by living with a family that speaks it. We pick up all kinds of information unconsciously—information that is often available to us when we want to produce certain effects in our own writing. Of course there is reading and reading: different uses of language condition us in different ways.

By way of introduction, take this passage from a book by the anthropologist Margaret Mead. She starts by making a contrast.

> For many people moving is one kind of thing and travel is something very different. Travel means going away from home and staying away from home; it is an antidote to the humdrum activities of everyday life, a prelude to a holiday one is entitled to enjoy after months of dullness. Moving means breaking up a home, sadly or joyfully breaking with the past; a happy venture or a hardship, something to be endured with good or ill grace.
>
> For me, moving and staying at home, traveling and arriving, are all of a piece. The world is full of homes in which I have lived for a

> day, a month, a year, or much longer. How much I care about a
> home is not measured by the length of time I have lived there. One
> night in a room with a leaping fire may mean more to me than many
> months in a room without a fireplace, a room in which my life has
> been paced less excitingly.
>
>   Margaret Mead, *Blackberry Winter*

If we learn to read Margaret Mead, maybe we can learn to write as well
as she does. In the first sentence she contrasts two words as they
function "For many people." Then she spends one long sentence on
each of the two words that she has contrasted. She defines travel as a
positive thing, then as the opposite (*antidote*) of a word (*humdrum*), and
finally combines negative and positive definitions by calling travel the
journey to a *holiday* from *dullness*. This sentence makes a definition by
repetition. When Mead defines *moving*, she uses a similar doubleness.

   All along, we have been held in suspense by the phrase "For many
people" that began the passage. If we hear that a definition is true "For
many people," we are surely going to hear a contrasting definition for
other people. Mead's second paragraph begins with a contrasting "For
me" that provides the transition, or stepping-stone, from one paragraph
to the other. We learn that the words that contrast for many people do
not contrast for Mead. But, conscious that she writes for an audience,
wishing to make contact with that audience, Mead is not content
simply to *tell* us that contradictions disappear for her; she *shows* us by
repeating earlier expressions jumbled together—"moving and staying
at home, traveling and arriving"—and then by detail and example from
her life—"homes in which I have lived for a day."

   Or take another paragraph, from fiction this time. One of the great
prose stylists in American literature is Ernest Hemingway, who worked
carefully on rhythm and sound. When he began writing as a young man,
he studied style and practiced and revised, to learn the way to his own
voice. He believed that the sounds of the words and subtle changes in
the pacing of sentences helped to make the sense, or meaning, more
vivid. A short story called "In Another Country," about some wounded
soldiers in a hospital in Italy during World War I, opens with this
paragraph:

> In the fall the war was always there, but we did not go to it any
> more. It was cold in the fall in Milan and the dark came very early.
> Then the electric lights came on, and it was pleasant along the
> streets looking in the windows. There was much game hanging
> outside the shops, and the snow powdered on the fur of the foxes
> and the wind blew their tails. The deer hung stiff and heavy and
> empty, and small birds blew in the wind and the wind turned their
> feathers. It was a cold fall and the wind came down from the moun-
> tains.

Such a simple style! And if we try to imitate it, we are likely to lace one shoe to the other. Reading it, we may notice that the grammar is simple, yet the length of sentence and clause—the units of rhythm—varies continually. We have to listen, to pay attention. The vocabulary is also simple—*the fall, cold,* and *wind* repeated, *wind* four times in the last three lines—yet expressive. The effect of the whole is hypnotic or dreamy, almost like a child's story; the war is around us, but *we* are not in it. Then the paragraph ends with the corpses of animals, described in loving detail. Look at the word *pleasant*; normally, we might find this word too general and want to ask *how*, exactly, did you feel? But here, in the emotions of the paragraph, the vagueness is an accurate understatement; it embodies the emotional restraint in this removal from war, the tentative acceptance that *we* are alive, unlike the animals outside the shops and the unmentioned combatants among whom *we* used to count ourselves. Though we don't generally think about how these effects are achieved as we react, we nonetheless pick them up. The more we read successful prose, the more likely we are to absorb the different ways that authors give their expression vigor and precision.

DISORGANIZED WRITING, POMPOUS WRITING

For a perverse sort of fun, let us rewrite the Hemingway passage in a couple of bad versions. We can call this exercise *downwriting*, turning something good into something bad. This practice can be instructive as we learn how to write. Mostly, we will try to improve bad writing; but sometimes we will imagine how we might have flubbed the opportunity for good writing that someone else took advantage of.

First, a parody (an imitation of a style, for the sake of mockery: a kind of downwriting) of the disorganized writing that most of us start with:

> September through December, in the fall, at any rate, the war still went on, but we ourselves weren't doing the fighting by this time. It got chilly then in the Italian city of Milan. It started to get dark earlier in the day. When it got dark they turned on the lights. It was nice to look in the windows of stores. There were a lot of dead wild animals outside of the stores. When it snowed it snowed on the animals' fur too. There was a lot of wind and it blew the animals' fur and it even blew the little ones around. It was really cold because the wind was coming down from the mountains, which were cold.

Actually, this parody is better than the prose most of us write at first, because the writer observes real things. Most bad writing omits anything that might be interesting and expressive. The whole paragraph might be reduced to

> It was fall in Milan, Italy, one year during World War I. It got colder and the days got shorter.

But the short version omits all feeling. In the real paragraph, details of image and action carry the scene to the reader. You cannot reduce *War and Peace* to a telegram.

Or we could try it in Pompous Institutional Moderne, the language of the bureaucrat:

> During the autumn, the hostilities continued to ensue, but we personally no longer engaged in them. The daily temperature declined in Milan as the autumn continued, and the hours of daylight gradually contracted. When darkness ensued, lights were illuminated. It was altogether agreeable to promenade and investigate the contents of shop windows. There was considerable unrationed meat available at this particular time, by reason of the prevalence of slaughtered wild animals. Precipitation in the form of snow, as the months progressed, accumulated on the fur of these slaughtered beasts, and the cold breeze that accompanied the snow caused the tails of the animals to wave. Venison was at the present time available, as was small fowl. The extreme cold of this autumn is attributable to the fact that the prevailing winds came from the direction of the mountains which, because of their elevation and the snow which had already accumulated thereon, were lower in terms of temperature than the temperature which normally prevailed in the city.

This last writer, if he or she existed, might be elected chairperson of the Senior Class Gift Committee but would never by such language make contact with another human being. We learn to write well, if we learn, for good reason. If we write with the chaos of the first parody or with the pomposity of the second, we are in trouble in our heads and our hearts, not just in our writing. If we learn to write well, we will sharpen our wits on the one hand and limber up our imagination on the other— both together, or neither at all.

LEARNING TO WRITE WELL

How then do we learn to write well? This whole book tries to answer the question. Here at the beginning let us mention three things, at least. First, we can read well, which helps slowly but keeps on helping; we can think about what we read, in a way that helps our writing. After we have read a page or two, we can pause to consider *how* the author has shown us some portion of experience, *how* the writer has assembled details, organized them, and led us from one thing to another. If we talk in class about essays we have read, either student work or professional models, we can compare our successes and failures of reading; by improving the way we read, we will improve our writing. See the next chapter for more about reading.

Second, we can study writing and think about it and discuss it with others; mostly, we will discuss it in class with a teacher and with other students. Among our friends we may discover one or two willing and able to act as audience for our drafts and revisions. We discover not only by analyzing the finished products of the writing process but by studying the process of writing itself, our own and other people's. (See Chapter 3 for some models of process.)

Third, and most important, we can write and rewrite and rewrite. Because rewriting our own work is most useful, we must have writing to rewrite. We can start by keeping a notebook or a journal. We can also look back to our old themes, or the papers we have written for other courses. In this collection of our own prose, we may find ideas for expanding and rewriting. We might notice, the tenth time we read something, that our writing does better at hiding the truth about some subject than searching out its secrets. After thinking about clichés or paragraph organization or passive verbs, we will find examples in our own prose, and we will see how to revise them. Looking back develops the critical sense; it becomes a path leading forward.

Daily Writing

While we are learning to write, it is essential to write every day. Constantly applying pen to paper will ease the work of writing and will give us a collection of words in which to look for ideas to develop and for sentences to revise. Writing is a skill, like an athletic skill, which comes more naturally to some people than to others but which improves with practice for everyone. Practice is a necessity. Maybe the best method is to write daily dated entries in a notebook. This notebook sounds like a journal, but for most people a journal is like a diary and records merely the day's events:

Had pancakes for breakfast. 9 o'clock boring . . .

Little entries that set out our daily schedule do not help us. Better are memories, whole anecdotes, ideas, and queries. Or it may help to concentrate on the world outside the self. Try describing some common object as accurately as you can—as if no one had ever seen it before. Ask yourself what details a painter's eye might select.

Doing daily writing means writing a page or two a day, every day, seven days a week, working rapidly and without trying to impose a direction on it, without conscious control or focus. Nor should a daily entry be continuous, necessarily. Some days one has apparently unrelated flashes of thought or memory. Some days one seems to have no ideas at all. On such a day, you may let your hand flow over the page with disconnected words and phrases.

Daily writing helps fluency, ease, and supply, but it gives us no practice in making shapes directed toward a reader: our work toward an audience, and our work on organization, will derive from social occasions like classes and conferences and from imagining social encounters. But in the meantime, daily writing will improve the fluency that we will later use for contact with others.

Many lifelong writers keep notebooks. The American poet Theodore Roethke left two hundred and seventy-seven notebooks behind when he died. Some entries were lines and images for poems; some were used, some were not. Others were prose notes to himself about writing poetry and might have been seeds for unwritten essays. At other times, he made a conventional journal entry.

> Today, or tonight, I realized finally at the age of 40, for the first time, that it is really possible for me to think, and even get pleasure from the process. Not that my efforts—or effects—are spectacular. Perhaps four consecutive related thoughts at present is the absolute top of my form—and that only just before falling asleep, or just after eating a fine breakfast, when I'm too lazy to write anything down. But still, even this is a beginning. And such excitement!

The novelist F. Scott Fitzgerald kept a notebook in which he recorded situations, observations, jokes, and anything else. Notice the sharpness of his details and images. The writer is never off-duty.

> Family quarrels are bitter things. They don't go according to any rules. They're not like aches or wounds, they're more like splits in the skin that won't heal because there's not enough material.
>
> Jules had dark circles under his eyes. Yesterday he had closed out the greatest problem of his life by settling with his ex-wife for two hundred thousand dollars. He had married too young, and the former slavey from the Quebec slums had taken to drugs upon her failure to rise with him. Yesterday, in the presence of lawyers, her final gesture had been to smash his finger with the base of a telephone.
>
> Run like an old athlete.

Daily writing can loosen minds. Our minds are made stiff, not by intellect, but by ready-made formulas of thought, by clichés both of phrase and of organization. These are restrictions we can do without. An economics student wrote this entry one day:

> Blue clouds in Arizona. I was hitchhiking last August, at the edge of the desert waiting for a ride that would take me across state. A little tree, a little shade. Sun so hot it melted turtles. Blue clouds of Arizona. Because there were no clouds at all, just blue glaring and

turning white toward the sun. Like an egg only a lot brighter and
hotter. Got a ride with a truck driver. "Never went to college
myself. The war came along and then I had kids, you know. My
daughter's at State." Jiggle. Oil. Hot. We had cheeseburgers in an
airconditioned diner and I never felt so good in my whole life as
when that ice-air hit me. Then the heat outside. Walking into the
oven. [cliché.]

There is no point to his story, or maybe no story. No one said he
had to make a point. All he had to do was write a page. He was practicing. But along the way he found the powerful descriptive phrase "just
blue glaring and turning white toward the sun." Fitzgerald might have
been happy to hit upon such language.

Practice was the first thing for him, sheer practice in putting pen
to paper, letting the words follow each other across the page; if the habit
of writing remains alien to us, we will never learn to write with any
naturalness. Second, he was learning to loosen up. No one was going to
correct his spelling, or argue with his logic, or tell him that his clauses
were not parallel; he felt free to let the images follow each other loosely
by association. Until the last phrase, his loosened mind provided fresh
images. But if he had written a string of clichés, nobody was going to
bother him about it. Earlier in his notebook, before he trusted himself to
loosen up, his prose had been rigid and trite.

Beginning a notebook of daily writing, almost everyone is shy and
stiff, as if this private writing were a public performance. One student
began her notebook:

> I am not "an emotionalist," if such a word exists. I feel as if I'm
> taking a step forward in saying that I tend not to be sincere in my
> writing. From this point forward I shall try to do so. I feel that I'm
> honest with myself, but when I know that others will read my work
> I unconsciously become dishonest as I write.
>
> If I were to write a short essay on any topic and hand it to a person
> to read, I wouldn't stay in the same room while the person read my
> work. Whether this is because of shyness or embarrassment, or
> both, I don't know.

Two months later, her prose was less self-conscious and more relaxed,
and she seemed to enjoy herself more.

> They try to give something special every week. When I read eggrolls
> listed on the menu, I thought, great, my favorite thing in the world.
> But to my dismay, I was shocked at what the Stockwell Cafeteria
> had done. How could they destroy *my* eggrolls? I bit into one of
> them and I noticed *black*, inside my eggroll. Shortly later, I discover
> that *raisons* had been planted in the eggrolls! Raisons! How could
> they! It seemed that they just sat around saying, "What can we put

> in the eggrolls to make them terrible? We can't lose our image!" Of
> all the stupid things. That's enough to start a new war with China!

Nobody leaned over her shoulder, drew a red circle around "raisons,"
and wrote "raisins" in the margin. The student felt the freedom to find a
natural—and believable—sound for her experience. Over the term her
writing improved, perhaps because she wrote ninety-two pages of daily
writing; her spelling stayed about the same.

Everybody who starts daily writing at first fears running out of
material. Really, we have enough memory packed away, by age eighteen, to keep us writing until we are seventy. We gradually discover
tricks that keep the pages coming. We should stop writing while we still
have something to say; it is even wise to make an arbitrary rule: stop at
the bottom of a full page, even in the middle of a sentence, and write
nothing more until the next day. The next day, you will not have to sit
and wait for the words to start.

Many students find that they work best with large categories of
reminiscence, writing many pages—weeks of daily writing—on one
general subject: my six best friends and their families; fishing trips with
my mother; Christmas vacation; jobs I have had; my teachers in grammar school; pets; relatives; the Little League; 4-H clubs; fights with my
brother; learning how to repair my ten-speed bike; my favorite meals;
and my favorite jokes (one student remembered forty pages of jokes!).
Some students interested in science and technology try to write about
science in a language that nonscientists can understand—a difficult and
useful kind of writing.

> I talked with another freshman yesterday who made the same old
> mistake. Arguing about science and history, and what you could
> know for sure, he told me that some physicist had discovered that
> even in science you don't know anything for certain. And I tried to
> tell him about Heisenberg's uncertainty principle, but it's hard to
> explain it when people don't know some mathematics. Heisenberg
> showed that it's impossible to measure, accurately and at the same
> time, both the momentum and the location of a subatomic particle.
> This indeterminacy is totally insignificant with big things like
> baseballs and spaceships, but with an electron or a neutron, for
> instance, Heisenberg proved that knowledge of simultaneous mo-
> mentum and position is impossible.

Giving a clear formulation to a difficult concept like this one brings a
satisfying sense of mental order.

Daily writing is a means and not an end, however. Daily writing
without an audience must prepare us to write for an audience. Our
fluency is the tool by which we search out the shape of our thought, to
reach out and connect with the reader. Unity, clarity, and the discipline

of the sentence and paragraph— all are necessary to move the message from the writer to the reader. Once we have found an idea or an image or a secret lode of language, then we must learn to shape and control in order to communicate.

We need to learn all about language—choosing words, inventing metaphors, phrases, clauses, and sentences, and constructing paragraphs—before we can establish control over our writing. Of course we must try to make whole shapes, like the revision by Jim Beck, from the very beginning, even before we have learned that there are names for the things we are doing. It makes sense to look at what happens when we write an essay, and in Chapter 3 we will investigate the process of writing and look into suggestions for stimulating that process. But first, we must take a look at the more general problems of language and communication. We know that reading and writing are twins. If we investigate what happens when we read, it will help us to understand what should happen when we write.

_____ **EXERCISES** _____

1. Write a page in a notebook, every day, for the rest of the term. Bring your notebook to conferences for your instructor to inspect, but not to correct. Bring it to class, if your instructor asks you to, with a page or a paragraph marked to read aloud. Discuss in class the problems and rewards of daily writing, giving each other suggestions for subjects.

2. Write a brief impromptu essay on the events of your first few days in college. You might write about motives and ideas like Jim Beck, or write a narrative like Marian Hart (see Exercise 12). Work to find unity and focus that will hold your essay together. Use specific details, examples, and anecdotes. Consider the students in your class as your audience.

3. Describe a common object (a lawnmower, a toaster . . .) or action (sewing, shooting baskets) as if you are the first person to have seen it. Pretend, if you want, that you don't know the purpose of the thing or activity.

4. Find a paragraph of description or narration by a stylistically conscious writer like Fitzgerald or Hemingway. See if you can find how the author uses various sentence and clause lengths to add to his meaning. Find an image or descriptive detail that seems fresh to you and try to figure out how the author has achieved this effect. Try writing your conclusions out in a short paragraph

5. Who was the best teacher who taught you in high school? (Do not choose merely the most agreeable but the one from whom you learned most.) How did the teacher do it? What did you learn? Be specific and show what you learned.

6. Pick one sentence from the two paragraphs by Margaret Mead on pages 13–14. *Downwrite* it (see pages 15–16) to achieve one of these failures: disorganization, emptiness or pomposity.

7. We discover ourselves by the language we use. Write a dialogue, or a conversation, in which two people reveal their characters by their language. Consider not only what words they use, but also how they use them.

8. Analyze the language of this essay. Try revising the first paragraph.

My Big Moment

In my humble opinion, after all is said and done, opportunities for people to show what they are made of are conspicuous by their absence at this university. Because of this sad truth, the day I gave my report stuck out like a sore thumb. It was a red letter day. I had spent the entire year at college burning the midnight oil and leading a precarious existence earning my tuition working for a professor who was a veritable mine of information. I was very much interested in the finer things of life. My hopes to do things that would make me stand out from the crowd were usually doomed to disappointment. As I wended my way from class to class each day, and then to the job where I put my nose to the grindstone, I often thought that the events in my life at which I could point with pride were few and far between. But today would be different.

Today I, a rank outsider, would be the center of attention. People would realize that I was smart as a whip. They would listen with bated breath. At ten o'clock I stood as scared as a rabbit before the class. Although I was hungry as a bear because I had not eaten breakfast, I was calm and collected. I stood before them and I told the unvarnished truth about Man's mistreatment of Mother Nature. I explained that the powers that be must sit up and take notice of the fast and furious pace of pollution, and that there was a crying need for immediate action. I viewed with alarm the future of society when the purity of the very air we breathe hangs in the balance. When I concluded my few remarks, there was thunderous applause. I could tell I had hit the nail on the head. I was tired but happy. I had hit one out of the ball park.

9. Earlier you were asked to *downwrite* a passage. *Upwrite* these sentences. Use your imagination if you need to supply details.

   a. The car parked in front of the house was an ugly monster.
   b. We visited the Radio Shack. It was fun. The man talked a lot. He told us all sorts of things.
   c. Swimming lots of lengths in a pool is good for toning muscles but you get tired of the chlorine and I don't like the fact that they are always out of towels at the Y.

10. In *The Atlantic*, a writer criticized certain schools. In one paragraph, he wrote:

> In such places students are taught clichés. In one college a test consisted of stories with blank spaces to be filled with adjectives, the "correct" answers arcane or phony words used by *Time* magazine during the era of Henry Luce (but no longer used even by *Time*). In another college the blanks to be filled were the most hackneyed phrases, so that fires were always "raging," heavy rains always "torrential downpours" and recriminations always "bitter."
>
> *Ben H. Bagdikian*,
> "Woodstein U.: Notes on the Mass Production
> and Questionable Education of Journalists"

Make a short paragraph in which you leave blanks for parts of clichés—usually an adjective or an adverb. Read it aloud in class to see if other students can fill in the "correct" clichés.

11. Here is another "How I Came to College" impromptu. (a) Criticize it for language and for structure. (b) Edit it. Rearrange and rewrite. Avoid clichés. Keep your audience in mind at all times. Be prepared to read the revised version out loud.

> I looked for work waitressing or anything last summer. Not finding anything school seemed like the best thing. Besides my family wants me to go. Learn a trade or skill I guess. So thats how come I am sitting here writing this!
>
> My girlfriend had already gotten in here and so she told me how to do it. I sign up and they tell me what I had to do. Just before I started classes I got the job I was looking for! But my father says you go to school. That's life.
>
> I can't tell yet how I like it or not. But I had a hard time getting here every morning because I don't have a car and, my mother doesn't drive and my father needs it except on Thursdays. My girlfriend has a car, she drives me here MWF. Tuesday I take buses for one hour or so.

12. Here is a better example. (a) What makes it better? (b) In what ways could this student learn to improve her writing? Pay attention to mechanics, to focus, and to word choice. Pay attention to the author's idea of audience and think how it might be improved.

> All my life I have known that I would, some day, go off to school. By the end of my senior year in High School I knew where and when I'd be leaving and spent the summer getting used to the idea. But getting used to the idea was all I did—I did not begin to think or worry about what college was really going to be like. I did not spend hours contemplating the importance of "going off into the big wide world." I did not even speculate what things would be like, what if I hated my roommate, what if the work was too hard, what if I'm unhappy. I did not think about specifics, I had told myself that I would have time to get psyched the week before I left.
>
> But a week before the day I had planned to leave, before I had prepared myself I got a phone call from my father. He had to give a lecture at a convention on the west coast in five days. For him to make it we had to leave that day and he would drop me off in Michigan on his way to

California. I had one hour to pack. One hour to collect all my belongings and somehow fit them into a car that looked like it could not hold half the things I wanted to take. It happened so fast I did not have time to think, I did not even have time to say goodby to my mother who was out shopping. We left in a hurry leaving behind many things I had forgotten to pack and a small note to my mother that simply said good-bye.

If I had more time I'm sure my goodbye to my mother and friends would have been a long, emotional scene. Driving through my town I had no time to look at my Elementary School, my High School, the house of my best friend and get sentimental. It was pouring and concentrating on the driving was all I could do.

The eleven hour drive also left no time for thought. I drove most of the way so that my father could prepare his speech. Every so often he would read parts to me to try them out. Our talk consisted of whether injection-lasers was a hyphenated word or not. (I still don't know).

Then I was here, in the dorm, with my roommate, in my classes. It seemed as if I had been here all my life and the trauma of leaving home was over. I did not even have time to think about it until later and then I could not even remember how it felt to leave home.

13. Here is an impromptu followed by a revision made late in the term. Compare the two essays. Correct the first version. What has the student learned? What is good about the revision? Can the improvements be explained by the writer's attention to an idea of audience? Find places in the revision where the writer could make further improvements. Rewrite two sentences in the revision to make them better.

I always wanted to go to the University because my Dad went here.

I remember how it got started. I had a job as a car-hop in a drive in, an A & W in Flint where I make my home. Business was slack because it was about 3:30 Saturday afternoon so I was talking away with Barb and Karen who were working there too and I knew them from school of course. We had to wear these very tight stretch pants because Boss said it was good for business. A car came in and because it was my turn I picked up a pad and started out for it, then I saw it was my Dad. He jumped out of the car and hugged me. I knew what it was and so did Barb because we were all waiting to hear about admissions. I told him he could open it and he did and that's why he drove out, to tell me. Barb had to wait until she got off, the Boss wouldn't let her go and there was nobody at home to call up.

So! We got here three days ago, in the same car, only loaded to the roof with my stuff. I was petrified with fear. My Dad kept telling me what to do, and then he kept saying he knew it had changed a lot in 25 years. I wished he'd be quiet. My Mom cried. We couldn't find the dorm. Everybody we asked didn't know either. The boys all had pink hair and Nikes and looked exactly the way I expected them too. My Dad hated it. Then when we found my dorm and we found my room my Dad was all out of breath, and mad, and he just pushed the door open with his shoulder and busted in. There was a naked girl standing there, with no clothes on, my roommate (whose very nice, named Terri, but I didn't know that yet) and he made a funny noise and dropped the suitcase and ran back out into the hall.

My Father's Place
Marian Hart

It is about an hour and a quarter from my house in Flint to the dormitory in Ann Arbor. All the way, as we drove here last August to move in, my Dad was talking about the class of 1959. I tried to listen. I had heard him talk about the University since I was a little girl, and since I was a little girl I had wanted to come here to college. But in the car I was shy and frightened. I was going to meet a roommate named Terri who was from Detroit. She would be sophisticated and have long hair. All the boys would be crazy about her. I would be the invisible frump from Flint.

I tried to think about the happy things. I tried to think about how happy I was, as I sat there feeling stupid and ugly. I remembered how happy I was to be accepted. It was a Saturday last Spring when I was working at the A & W, being a car hop in the stretch pants that the boss made us wear "because it's good for business."

It was a slack time of day, and suddenly a car rolled up, parking across two parking places, and rocking with the brakes put on too fast. I picked up an order pad and headed out, and then I saw that it was our car and that my Dad was jumping out at me waving an envelope and grinning. He didn't have to say anything. We hugged and he called me his sweetheart. The three of us went out to dinner that night and celebrated.

Now my mother was sobbing and my teeth were chattering and my father was talking about hula hoops! I groaned a little, and he said—for the twelfth time—that of course he knew that everything was different now, with student rights and politics and ecology and (he gagged a little) co-ed dormitories. But . . . and he was off again. He was as nervous as I was.

When we drove into town my Dad's composure fell apart completely. He didn't know where he was. We asked directions but everyone else was as lost as we were. The whole place had changed, he said; none of the old landmarks were there. And he obviously hated the new land marks. Girls with pink hair and bare feet were throwing frisbees with boys with blue jeans and earrings and pink hair. My father's jaw went tight, and from the back seat I could see the tenseness of his neck that happened when he was worried or angry.

We found the dorm. My father carried the four suitcases. I carried a portable stereo and a box of indispensable records. My mother had three garment bags full of clothes which I knew I would never wear. Of course my room was on the third floor. Every time we passed a boy in the hallway my father's neck, which was red with carrying four suitcases, got tenser.

When we got to the door of my room, he didn't set down the suitcases to knock. Puffing and snorting, he pushed open the door with his shoulder and strode in, me and my mother close behind. Then he dropped all four suitcases, crash, and made a weird little noise. I thought: My God, he's having a heart attack. Then I looked past him and saw a girl standing facing him with her mouth flopped open in surprise—Terri, I thought, even then, and she's *not* too beautiful—and stark naked.

2

Reading, and Reading Well

Recently, in a freshman writing class in Boston, the teacher asked for reactions from his students to a short essay by Phyllis Rose, "Shopping and Other Spiritual Adventures." He began, as he often did with writing examples, by reading the opening paragraph out loud:

> Last year a new Waldbaum's Food Mart opened in the shopping mall on Route 66. It belongs to the new generation of superdupermarkets open 24 hours that have computerized checkout. I went to see the place as soon as it opened and I was impressed. There was trail mix in Lucite bins. There was freshly made pasta. There were coffee beans, 4 kinds of tahini, 10 kinds of herb teas, raw shrimp in shells and cooked shell shrimp, fresh-squeezed orange juice. Every sophistication known to the big city, even goat's cheese covered with ash, was now available in Middletown, Conn. People raced from the warehouse aisle to the bagel bins to the coffee beans to the fresh fish market, exclaiming at all the new things. Many of us felt elevated, graced, complimented by the presence of this food palace in our town.

The teacher expected a few laughs, maybe a show of hands from students with firm views on Yuppies and consumers. What he did not expect was a difference of opinion that divided the group into opposing camps.

Dean Vanelli spoke up first. "She gets it just right," he said. "My uncle owns a food store, and when they renovated and brought in all kinds of new products his customers went wild."

Janet Ong disagreed right away. "Don't you see it? The writer is kidding. She's being tongue-in-cheek. I think she really despises the whole fancy-food craze."

Other hands went up. Both Dean and Janet looked to the teacher for a reaction. But he was curious to see how the discussion would go and gave nothing away. He asked Janet to explain why she thought Rose was kidding. "It's so obvious," said Janet. "Look at the words she uses—'superdupermarket,' for one—and the way she exaggerates. She has people racing around the aisles. She says 'Many of us felt elevated, graced, complimented . . .' That's language that you use when the Pope visits."

Bob Schwegler disagreed. "She's just trying to write in a way that will interest her readers. She is really impressed. Look at the way she lists each different item. She really wants you to think that this is one of the great things about modern life—that you can bring together all these goodies from around the world . . ."

Others joined in with their views, and the discussion went on for a good part of the hour. The teacher did not try to step in to influence opinion one way or the other. He was happy, though, to see such a sharp split in views, for it dramatized the point that reading is a complicated and, very often, subjective activity. The discussion decided him: he would spend the upcoming sessions emphasizing the importance of careful reading. He wanted his students to understand what they were doing when they worked through a particular passage. They would see for themselves how closely reading and writing were connected.

THE READING PROCESS

There is no writing well without reading well. The two activities are intimately connected; they are like sound and echo, body and shadow. For both take place in and through language. Where there is no language there is no thought. (Try having a wordless thought—it's impossible.) When we write we express our thoughts and experiences in language; at best, we arrange our words in logical order on the page. When we read we unravel those strings of words, turning them into an inner stream of thought, sensation, and emotion. Reading is the process of writing in reverse, and writing is the mirror image of reading. The mirror, if we stay with the analogy, is language itself.

This sounds mysterious, and in a way it is: we are, far more than we generally realize, creatures of language. Even in our most private moments we accompany ourselves with an inner sound-track of thoughts, memories, and fantasies, and all of these, to some degree, require words. We may not hear our thoughts distinctly, the sound may be a vague murmur, but the fundamental connection is nonetheless there. It is by way of words and their meanings that we compose the sense of our lives.

Reading, we know, is a relatively recent human innovation, coming after millennia of spoken exchange. And the first readers knew nothing of the silent eye motion that we are accustomed to—they vocalized every mark. Indeed, Saint Augustine (345–430) remarks somewhere in his writings upon the curious sight of a man reading without moving his lips.

Living as we do in an age of information, where quick, silent scanning is the order of the day, it is hard for us to conceive what patient labor was needed to work through the pages of a text. But in fact all of us practice something similar at times. If a work is difficult, or if it has a particular verbal richness, we automatically change out of our rapid-scan habits. We move our eyes slowly and we listen. It is at these moments that we can most truly say that we are *reading* a piece of writing.

When we read this way—slowly, attentively—we translate the black markings of words into sounds. We speak those sounds internally and we try to hear them clearly. Though reading begins with the back and forth movement of the eyes, it only fully takes place when both inner voice and inner ear are engaged. Moving our eyes and listening, we absorb. Ideally, we structure the information and ideas into the clearest possible form so that we can follow and understand.

But we do more than just absorb: we also think our own thoughts and experience our own associations and responses to the words in front of us. These thoughts and associations weave like an ivy vine around the sense of what the other person is saying. For example, the first sentence of an essay by Caroline Bird entitled "College Is a Waste of Time and Money" reads: "A great majority of our nine million college students are not in school because they want to be or because they want to learn." When we read a sentence like this, we first do our best to grasp the logic of the assertion; we absorb and structure the basic information. We understand that a *majority* of college students are *not* in school because they *want* to be.

But even with a sentence this simple, we are probably doing other, more complex things. First, we very likely hear the structure of the whole: it is a negative assertion, telling us what is *not*. We therefore tend to grasp it as a part of an upcoming argument. Our experience as readers and listeners—we have all heard a thousand speeches—tells us that the negative will probably be followed by a positive. Our logical sense creates an expectation: if the majority of students are not in school because they want to be, *then* they must be there because. . . .

But logical expectation makes up only part of our total response. We may also accompany our reading with rapid-fire thoughts and associations like these: *nine million, that's not so many . . . out of . . . what is the population, 250 million? . . . a majority: 5 million, 6? . . . how do they know these things? . . . it's true, though, for some . . . Rick, Sandy . . . True for me? No, it's not that simple, more than just wanting to learn . . .* Obviously this is a slow-motion study of a process that takes place very quickly, and obviously individual responses differ a great deal. But the point does not change: when we read we *absorb*, we *structure*, and, at some level, we *respond*.

READING IS WRITING AND WRITING IS READING

When we read we perform the same acts of organization and association that we perform when we write; we make choices. Reading a sentence like Caroline Bird's, we sound it out to ourselves. If we are Caroline Bird, writing, we do a similar thing: before the words take their place on the page as part of an argument or essay, they pass through the inner ear as if spoken. Some writers contend that the hearing and writing happen at the same moment and are virtually indistinguishable. In any case, try it for yourself: compose a sentence on paper without hearing it. It's impossible. Before, or as, we write we hear our words and test them for sense: we read.

There is another sense in which there is no writing well without reading well. Reading—the experience and memory of reading—is what gives us the back-up for writing. When we read we absorb and store information. But we also absorb and store various structuring possibilities. This learning generally happens unconsciously; we are not aware of many of the things we learn. The same thing happens when we listen to other people talk. We experience and preserve the different ways of making sense, and we draw upon these ways incessantly when we write. If we *didn't* have these different options in our memory banks, we would be hard put to write anything more than the simplest building-block kinds of sentences: "John is thin."

When an experienced reader sits down to write, she has countless patterns in her memory. If "John is thin" does not satisfy her, she changes it. Memory might suggest an analogy—"John is as thin as a greyhound"—or a qualification: "Though he wears loose clothing to conceal it, John is quite thin." Every time a writer makes a decision about expression, it is with an awareness of the possibilities. Different patterns have different effects. The more we read—and the better we read—the larger a store we will have to turn to.

READING AS DETECTION/READING AS CONSTRUCTION

Reading, like thinking, is an extraordinarily complicated operation, and theoreticians write thick books to tell us why. Outwardly it's simple enough. We move our eyes from left to right and down the page, and maybe we mouth the sounds at times—either to clarify the sense or to add to our enjoyment (certain stories and poems beg to be read aloud). The more complex part of reading happens inside, behind the eyes. Here, as a sample, are the first few sentences from an essay by Mary Hood, "Why Stop?":

> There is an essential human ichor of awe, an instinct for reverence, a gracious sap which rises in us seasonally and flowers into devotions and wreaths. "Than longen folk to goon pilgrimages." Goon indeed. Every sap has its sucker. SEE THE CONTINENTAL DIVIDE IN ACTION, the billboard in the Rockies invites. The parking lot is not empty.

The odds are that a quick first reading of this passage will yield more confusion than sense. "Ichor" is an uncommon word; we might need the dictionary to learn that it means "an ethereal fluid supposed to flow in the veins of the gods." The quotation of the second sentence may be obscure as well: it is drawn from the Middle English of Chaucer's *The Canterbury Tales,* and in modern English would read, "Then the folk long to go on pilgrimages."

But Mary Hood is a clever writer with a love of word-play, and even after we understand the references, our minds must shuttle back and forth to weave a coherent meaning. Before we can make any headway, of course, we have to recognize the tone. Hood is looking to have fun; she is leading up to her subject—the lure of unusual roadside attractions—with witty double-meanings. We must be attentive, or we risk missing the humor.

Notice how Hood sets us up for surprise. We have read the fancy (some might say precious or overwritten) first sentence, and the intimidating quotation from Chaucer. Quite possibly we prepare ourselves for a long stretch of high-minded prose. Suddenly we encounter "Goon indeed." Hood forces us to do a double-take; she thwarts our expectations. Is she playing a game with us? She seems to be reading the Middle English spelling "goon"—for goon—as if it were the slang word for someone stupid or inept. Before we can decide how to interpret this new possibility we need more information. We read on.

Every sap has its sucker. Now it seems more likely that Hood has been setting us up, feeding us the lofty prose of the first two sentences in order to pull the rug out from under us. The word "sap" obviously refers back to "a gracious sap" in the first sentence, but the associations of that word and "sucker" suggest that she was just waiting to ambush us. The puns are flying in all directions. The statement literally means that every different sap has a creature that will feed upon it. But a "sap-sucker" is also a bird known for extracting sap from trees with its beak. And a *sucker* is also a slang word for a fool; and a *sap,* too, is a sucker, a fool, possibly a *goon.*

We have read only four sentences, two of them fragment-length, and already we have performed complex mental feats, reading for subtleties of tone, juggling the connotations of words, and cross-checking references from one line to the next. Who will deny that reading can be every bit as demanding as mathematics or chess? As readers (and, implicitly, as writers) we should be aware of this complexity, the better to give our fullest concentration.

We should also keep in mind, with this passage as with many others, that our responses will differ greatly depending upon our associations, our store of background information, and even our tolerance for word-play. A reader familiar with the Chaucerian reference will applaud Hood's cleverness more readily than one who has never heard of Chaucer. One person might laugh at the multiple pun of the *sap/sucker* line—another might, so to speak, gag.

PHILOSOPHIES AND POLITICS

The possibilities for diverse responses among readers are probably greatest with literary works like poems, stories, and novels; poets and fiction writers are more likely to make use of ambiguity and to exercise the more suggestive properties of language. A straightforward description or analysis in a history textbook will probably generate more agreement than dissension, at least about *what* is said. However, we should not assume that any act of reading is simple or that any two readers will ever completely agree about the meaning of a passage.

Our backgrounds and our personal associations to words are not the only things that color our responses to the words on the page. Our political and philosophical beliefs—and biases—influence us enormously. Also, we tend to be unconscious of them, which makes them hard to detect when we revise. Consider this sentence: "Ann is a model wife and home-maker." Your grandmother might read these words without flinching, nodding approval. A veteran of the woman's movement, on the other hand, might feel her blood start to boil. Our politics are by no means limited to Republican or Democrat. All choices and thoughts are conditioned by our beliefs—beliefs, for instance, about human equality, environment, economics. . . .

Words do not exist neutrally, except perhaps on the dictionary page. They occur in context; they pass from speaker to listener, from writer to intended audience. If we read the sentence "Harry comes from a large family," we probably respond to the word *family* as we would to any simple noun used in an informational context. But if we read "Harry believes in family values," "family" has become a loaded word. It calls to mind the rhetoric of election speeches and it implies a range of meanings charged with strong emotional associations. To be a proponent of "family values" is, in our present social climate, to be politically conservative. If Harry is for family values, it most likely means that he opposes abortion and gay rights. We could compile a list of similarly loaded words, words like *motherhood, ecology, nuclear, communist, choice.*

READING TONE

We have seen that words do not exist neutrally, that we all draw constantly upon our unique experience and our often unconscious beliefs as we read and listen; we interpret everything according to who we are. We have seen, too, that meanings shift accordingly. Soon we will look more closely at some issues of interpretation and consensus. But first we need to discuss tone.

Reading or interpreting tone is something we do constantly in the course of conversation. Talking with others, we interpret irony, exaggeration, understatement, mock seriousness, and a dozen other styles of expression. When our co-worker says, "I'll kill you if you're late tomorrow," we understand it as a figure of speech—or *hope* we do. When a friend steps in from a downpour and announces, "It's really nice out," we don't hurry to find our tanning lotion. Indeed, if we think of how most casual conversation is carried on, we will realize that a great deal of it involves communication by way of *tone*. Tone tells us how to interpret the obvious sense of a remark, whether to reverse its meaning, scale down its exaggeration, or take it at face value. In daily life, we are all experts at making these translations.

With reading, however, we face a greater difficulty. We do not have the author's speaking voice to go by. We have to do some guessing. The context—other words—provides our only clues. Sometimes, of course, the context makes our job easy. We turn to the humor column in our newspaper with the expectation that we will find irony there. The writer may begin by stating "I was depressed yesterday. I decided that I would either shoot myself or go shopping." If we didn't know that the columnist was looking to be funny, we could guess as much.

But what about the piece that begins "America is a great country"? Our first impulse is probably to give assent: yes, of course, a great country. But what if the next sentence reads: "It allows more than ten percent of its citizens to live in abject poverty."? Suddenly we must turn our expectations inside out: we hear irony, as the writer suggests that our greatness needs serious questioning. We could find dozens of examples in any newspaper of passages that need to be read with care, passages where the intended meaning depends not just on the words but on the larger verbal context they inhabit.

Reading is not just negotiating the fine point of *what* gets said; it also requires close attention to the *how.* Sometimes—when reading an encyclopedia entry, say—we can relax our vigilance: a reference book insists upon a matter-of-fact assemblage of information. We don't have to screen the words to try to decide the author's intent. Editorials, opinion pieces of all descriptions, speeches—indeed, *any* writing that seeks to persuade—these force us to read with all our faculties on the alert.

CHAOS OR CONSENSUS?

Considering the variables that make up even the simplest act of reading, it is hard to see how any two people could ever be said to read the same piece of writing. Strictly speaking, it's true: not only do different individuals respond differently to the same words, but any one person will probably feel or interpret the words differently at different times. The text of *Walden* that you read in high school for English class is not the same *Walden* that you might take up for pleasure after college or when you retire. Our experience changes us; our understandings and associations are never exactly the same from day to day. As the Greek philosopher Heraclitus once said, "We never step into the same river twice."

This issue of the subjective response of readers is one that literary critics and theoreticians are fond of debating. Indeed, one group of thinkers takes an extreme position, arguing that since every reading of a work of literature is different there can be no correct interpretation. Who will judge between reader *A,* who believes Shakespeare's *King Lear* to be a satire, and reader *B,* who understands it as a tragedy? We cannot call the playwright on the phone to ask him what he meant. And even if we could, would his word be final? We cannot be sure that Shakespeare planned out what his play would mean, that he was not just writing down speeches and scenes as his inspiration dictated them.

In part, of course, this kind of questioning is an academic game. As readers we may not have identical inner reactions, and we may debate points of interpretation, but we tend to agree on the main substance of what we read. Few careful readers of Shakespeare will insist that *King Lear* is a satire. But in considering the *logic* of the extremist view we are brought face to face with the paradox of reading. To put it simply: language reaches our most private and subjective selves, and reading is the most solitary of acts; at the same time, language is a social in-strument—a means for communication. Words isolate, and words bring us together. The philosopher is right in one sense: we cannot step twice into the same river. But the fact is that we do; at least we pretend that we do. We call it the Mississippi or the Ohio or the Kennebec. We draw it on maps and sail our boats down its waters. We read privately, but when we speak or write about what we've read, we look for agreement, for consensus.

Reading and writing are social acts often accomplished in solitude. When we speak or when we pass our writing to another person, we break that solitude and enter the social realm. Our expression becomes communication, which means that our meanings must be shared, carried across to others. For this to happen, there must be agreement—about the meanings of words, the rules governing sentence formation, and so on. There must also be a shared understanding of context. We need to be sure that the other person understands that we are being completely serious or tongue-in-cheek. When these rules are clear, then the paths of communication are open; then we stand a chance of finding agreement, consensus. Consensus literally means *shared sense.*

Soon we will take up some of the practical applications of these ideas. We will see what they mean in a classroom, how they affect us as readers and writers working to master a craft. But first we need to make a few additional points about reading.

WORDS ARE SOCIAL

Most of our thinking about language, especially in a writing course, has to do with words as a means of personal expression. We work to shape our opinions, our ideas; we may, if we are writing more personal essays, attempt to clarify *our* feelings about a person or an experience. As citizens of the world, however, we ought to stop from time to time to ask ourselves about the larger implications of language. For these, too, have bearing on our reading, thinking and writing.

Consider, first, how we know what we know about the social world. We study basic subjects in school, like history, political science, and sociology. We listen to the radio and watch TV, and news about events and trends reaches us. We may turn to newspapers and magazines for a deeper understanding. We also pay attention to what others say—what our parents discuss at the dinner table, what friends remark upon. If we think about it for a moment we will realize that the knowledge we have of our world comes to us largely through language. Needless to say, how that language is used influences much of how we understand our history, our political life, and our place in society. Our understanding, in turn, is what determines our actions. If a presidential spokesman assures us that claims about environmental deterioration "are challenging but await the results of further investigation," we may not be moved to change certain of our habits. If that same spokesman says "This is the gravest crisis we have ever faced, and we must act immediately," our response is different.

George Orwell, in his well-known essay "Politics and the English Language," investigated the ways in which euphemism and imprecise usage infected our public language and our perception of events. He cautioned us all against the empty assurance and the ringing cliché that conceals the truth. "In our time," he wrote, "political speech and writing are largely the defence of the indefensible. Things like the continuance of British rule in India, the Russian purges and deportations, the dropping of the atom bombs on Japan, can indeed be defended, but only by arguments which are too brutal for most people to face, and which do not square with the professed aims of political parties." The political situation of the world has changed since Orwell wrote, but this kind of misuse of language remains constant. We owe it to ourselves, not just as readers and writers but as citizens, to heed most carefully the uses of words. We have to ask ourselves repeatedly about the meaning and truth of what we read and hear.

READING AS RE-READING

Whenever this book speaks of writing it speaks of revision, and not only when it concentrates on process; writing *is* revision. When we become conscious of the act of written revision, we may learn to hear ourselves revise even as we *speak*, even in casual conversation. Almost everyone speaking crosses out one word and substitutes another, saying, "It was a small, I mean *tiny* dog . . . " Sometimes we may say the same sentence over again, repeating it almost exactly but making little changes in word choice, in grammar, or in emphasis by pitch and volume—trying for more exact shades of meaning as we reach out to the listener.

It is less obvious but equally true that reading requires revision.

As writing is revising so reading is re-reading. Even the most experienced of readers will misread on occasion. If we read actively, demanding coherence from the page before us, we will from time to time realize that we have lost this coherence, and we will need to go back to the text and start again. We lose track because our minds wander when we are tired, because a car backfires, or we tune in to a conversation at the far end of the hall. We lose track because of imprecise knowledge of a word, because we miss the force of a grammatical turn or the sense of a transition, or because we do not share an association with the author.

We may misread because we do not share experience with the author. If an Argentinian uses the word *July* with the implication of a frigid climate, we from the northern hemisphere may miss something at first reading. We also misread because of bias or because we do not want to hear something the author wants to tell us. For all these reasons and a thousand more, we need to revise as we read; we must return to the text and question it, stopping to look up the meaning of a word or the date of a battle; we must try to pick up again where we left off. At times it is almost as if we were reversing a film a certain number of frames in order to look at a sequence again.

PUT THE BLAME ON BLAME

People often lose sight of the issues—readings and misreadings—by assigning fault. When we have trouble reading, we often think *either* "This is a stupid/obscure/lousy writer" or "I am stupid/This is not the kind of thing I can read." Casting blame lets us off the hook of a text. Casting blame is a kind of laziness, because it suggests that we are surrendering. As always, of course, there are exceptions. When the writing is thoughtless or imprecise, we may be able to take the author to task: part of reading well is insisting on clarity. But we should not expend our energy on assigning blame; we should try to identify the problem and then move on. Everything is grist for the writer's mill. When we sit down to express ourselves, we will remember the ways that other writers have tripped us up—and we will seek to avoid them.

ACTIVE AND PASSIVE READERS

We must be active not passive readers. Much in our culture encourages passivity. When we grew up watching cartoons on Saturday mornings, we bathed in the glow of animations created to entertain us in order to sell us something. If we felt bored we would switch the channel; therefore no one allowed us to feel bored. If we read the way we watched television, we would never get past Archie comics.

Maybe we should call not merely for active reading but for aggressive reading. We should look the text in the eye; if it will not look back at us we should take it by the scruff of the neck and shake it. Or we should sit on a chair with a thousand-watt bulb and ask our questions: "What are you saying? Why aren't you making more sense?" But we must not merely question a suspect text; if we grill our reading like a detective, we must also be sure to investigate the investigator.

In practice, the active or aggressive reader is a series of detectives, one of them interrogating the text and the rest interrogating the interrogator. Suspect, detective, judge, and jury are all the same—which makes for difficult justice. If we ask the text to confess how it got from *A* to *B*, or why it lacks detail in support of *Z*, we must also ask if the question itself is appropriate. Are we sure that the interrogator is not making the mistake (omitting to notice the connective; missing the support offered) that he accuses the text of making?

The point is to be active not passive, to be aggressive not merely accepting. When we read that E. M. Forster gives two cheers for democracy, we must not simply record the number as a given. After we register the number we must inquire *Why?* Why does Forster use the figure *two* instead of *three* or *one* or *twenty-seven?* Out of our experience we should recollect that the traditional number of cheers is triple—three cheers for the old school—and understand that Forster's approval of democracy implies limitation. But if we merely registered *two cheers* without actively inquiring about the phrase, without questioning the significance of the number—if we had been passive to it—we would have no limitation to look for. We would be missing the point.

The more active or imaginative we are in our reading, the more we tend to make our own essay as we respond to the writer's. This invention is not only inevitable with active readers, it is even a good thing—so long as we recognize what we are doing. Our interpretation, our *subjective* response, should not be whimsically private; we should always keep one eye on the probable consensus. Reading E. M. Forster on "two cheers," the reader may wonder what happened to the third cheer. She may think, "That cheer must be for the English class system!" But that is finally *her* conscious notion, not Forster's. Try to gauge at all times which part of your reaction is private, and which part seeks the more objective view of the consensus.

CLOSE READING

When we have discriminated, as well as we can, the subjective from the objective, we can then analyze the text, reading with utmost care and concentration to see just how the writer has caused our responses. This kind of scrutiny is often called *close reading*. When we close-read we approach a text with full attention. We make ourselves sensitive not just to the meanings and associations of the words and sentences, but we also try to heed the fine points of the author's style. Is the author using different kinds of sentences, different rhythms, to bring a message across? Do the word sounds contribute to the effect of the prose? What about punctuation?

Here, as an example, is a paragraph from the beginning of an essay entitled "The Golden Age, Time Past" by Ralph Ellison. Ellison is writing to evoke the atmosphere of Harlem jazz clubs in the 1940s:

> It has been a long time now, and not many remember how it was in the old days; not really. Not even those who were there to see and hear as it happened, who were pressed in the crowds beneath the dim rosy lights of the bar in the smoke veiled room, and who shared, night after night, the mysterious spell created by the talk, the

laughter, grease paint, powder, perfume, sweat, alcohol and food—
all blended and simmering, like a stew on the restaurant range, and
brought to a sustained moment of elusive meaning by the timbres
and accents of musical instruments locked in passionate recitative.
It has been too long now, some seventeen years.

There is nothing difficult about the sense, or meaning, of Ellison's
paragraph. But if we read carefully, slowly, allowing the phrases to
sound in our ears, we can appreciate just how much the style—the
phrasing, the rhythms, sounds, and sentence lengths—highlights the
meaning.

For one thing, the whole paragraph imitates the feeling of a memory. There are three sentences. The first is short; it does the job of
leading us up to the moment of recollection. The second, by contrast,
shifts and flows, packing together the images and details from all the
remembered nights. Reading it, we get the misty, dissolving sensation
that comes when we think about the past. The third sentence brings us
back, almost as if the author shook his head abruptly, to shock himself
into the present again.

Now look at other fine points. The semicolon in the first sentence,
for example, sets off and emphasizes the "not really." Read it out loud
and you can feel the punch. It would not be the same with a comma, nor
would we get the right effect if the author had tried to make separate
sentences. The memory sentence then makes for a complete change; it
is almost impossible to read it out with a single breath. Ellison forces us
to move through it as if we were walking through a crowded room—
which is, of course, what the memory is about. By the time we reach the
end, with the "timbres and accents of musical instruments locked in
passionate recitative," we feel the same strain of breath that the horn
players must have felt. The short sentence that follows brings a nice
relief.

We could go on and on. We could ask whether the many *s* sounds
in the middle sentence add to the mood; we could analyze the changes
in rhythm that Ellison uses to keep the memory sentence from falling
apart. But I think the point has been made: style and content go hand in
hand. To write well we must constantly try to bring the *what* and the
how of our expression together. The more we close-read, reflecting on
the choices made by other writers, the more choices we will have when
we sit down to write.

READING FOR WRITING

Close reading, then, is an aggressive, engaged kind of reading: we
focus our attention to understand how the writer has caused our responses. When we read aggressively, we follow a path back to writing.

We learn what different uses of language can accomplish; we learn to adopt different strategies for our own purposes. Sometimes we are aware of how we change our writing. Other times—and this is true of all learning—the process happens unconsciously.

Reading and writing are a continual conversation, a transaction sometimes immediate and always potential. Reading old writing is conversation with the dead, almost miraculous; maybe all communication is a miracle. We feel this especially when we get the sense that the author has reached out to us and made a difference in our thoughts. By analysis, by close reading, we decide how well the author has performed. We are the audience. Has the writer reached us? Was the writer aware of us? By making this judgment about the transaction between the writer and ourselves as readers, we develop an idea of audience that ought to help us in our own writing.

Reading and writing are social activities. When we talk about audience, about reader response, about the objective and the subjective, we talk about the *social* use of language, which includes business letters and résumés as much as poems or histories of the world in twenty volumes.

When we interview someone for a club or a job, we form opinions based on appearance, gestures, and accent, as well as on the words the candidate uses. Although these judgments may be poor or superficial, we make them. When we write without the aid of gesture or voice, the words (sentence, paragraph structure, transitions) are all important. They make up the difference. Anyone reading listens to the tone of the transaction. Therefore, when we study our own reading we study what happens when others read us.

PRACTICE IN RESPONSE

A class at a university in Rhode Island practiced and compared its own responses by reading Edward Hoagland's editorial "Walking the Dog" reprinted from the *New York Times*. Beginning the exercise, the teacher identified the essay as an editorial. After all, any reader encountering it under normal circumstances would come to it with such information. She also reminded her class that editorials speak like kings and queens, using *we* where the writer would say *I*. Otherwise, she said to her class, you're on your own.

She asked the class to write a page or so of notes as they read it. She asked them not to read through the whole editorial before beginning their notes, but to write as they went along, pausing after every paragraph to write about what they had just read—and to predict what would come next if they had any notion. She told her students: Don't spend more than ten minutes on this; you don't have to be correct; but be prepared to read it out loud to each other. She reminded them that in such an exercise there are no right answers, though it is always possible to misread. No one would be graded on correctness of response; the point of the exercise was to explore *differences* of response. This exploration, she said, should help us not only as readers in trying to understand our response and discriminate between the more subjective and the more objective, but it should also help us as writers who try to predict the responses of our readers. Here's the editorial she used:

Walking the Dog

We are in favor of cleaning up after them, but we are also in favor of dogs. Manhattan was once the home of whistling swans and seals and mountain lions, and, walking the dog, we remember this in our bones. Walking the dog, we feel occasionally that we are with a living ancestor, as children seem to do also. Children are born with a liking for dogs; and when we are out with the family dog, we seem to remember aptitudes of nose and leg that we no longer have.

For the dog, one purpose of our walks is checking out the gutter— the chicken knuckles and Reuben sandwiches there. As a student of fermentation (wine and cheese buffs have nothing on him), he is immensely cheerful as we go around the block. Also, he marks his territory. You might say it's like the trappings of wolf territoriality without the territory, just as for us it is a walk in the woods without the woods. He looks particularly for irregularities to mark: a shovelful of dirt next to a Con Ed excavation, a clump of grass, houseplants or Christmas trees that have been thrown out but still smell of earth. Males found females by the process, but the other social function—when dogs were wolves—was to reinforce the order of rank and rule within the pack, increasing the pack's efficiency on a hunt.

We are animals too. We confront a cold wind with our backs, and turn grumpy if somebody unexpectedly grabs hold of us while we are bent over a steak. But the spirit of both man and dog is sociable, and most people will never be too old to get a kick out of whistling to a dog and seeing him wag his tail. The point of having a descendant of the Lost Wolf for company is not to crush his spirit but rather to direct it so that he can live in, even delight in, the city. The eagles and wild swans are gone, and we have an idea that dogs and the saving irregularities they look for add life to New York City.

At the next meeting of the class the instructor asked two students to read their responses aloud. Bill Julio read:

This "we" business sounds phony even if it is an editorial. I keep wondering "How does this guy know what *I* think?" City dogs to me mean those small furry balls that you could almost step on if you weren't careful, but I suppose there are police dogs and Great Danes, too. Though I don't agree that all kids are born loving dogs.

My sister cried whenever she got near one. Maybe he's generalizing too much about things. Interesting, though, to think about feeling old human memories in our bones. Do swans whistle?

This confuses me about mountain lions in Manhattan—I thought they lived out West.

He is probably going to come out and say that dogs don't really belong with all this concrete.

Litter, street garbage—it's mostly just disgusting. This writer is showing off when he talks about dogs as "students of fermentation," as if they were wine experts. Con Ed—who is Con Ed? He shouldn't assume we know these things.

We are animals, he says. This is the oldest cliché in the book. The whole point is that we're *not* animals, that we have to keep animals. I start to lose interest. If we are all animals how come we write and read editorials like this? The argument for keeping dogs in the city is stupid—if it's just so that we can remember what we used to be like. What about the poor dogs, locked up in stuffy apartments all day?

When Bill finished reading a number of people raised their hands. Someone said: "Obviously not every kid in the world likes dogs—but there is a definite truth to what Hoagland is saying. Sometimes a writer has to exaggerate to make a point." Bill answered that he agreed, but that he had been trying to put down exactly what went through his mind as he read along. His teacher nodded. Other hands went up. One student said that she agreed completely with Bill's thought about dogs locked up in apartments all day. "That's not what nature intended," she said. "I can't respect a writer who thinks dogs are just there for people." Some others voiced agreement.

The teacher then asked Rachel Goldberg to read from her notes:

Cleaning up after being sick? Shedding hair? What does cleaning up have to do with seals? Is a living ancestor like a grandfather or like a caveman? I can't believe that this is an editorial because it doesn't . . . argue. Is it about our own "aptitude" that this is about? Dogs in Manhattan—pooper scoopers!

I bet this article is from the time when they were passing the law about dog poop on sidewalks.

In the suburbs it's more like telephone poles and mailboxes, not sandwiches and chicken knuckles. Yuk! Chickens have knuckles? Is that what they mean by knuckle sandwich?

He marks off territory. This is by lifting his leg, right? Why can't he say so? Can the N.Y. Times use language like *piss*? For that matter, what's all this about *he*? Why do we always assume everyone and every animal is male? Do lady dogs do their marking in different ways? That might be a funny article. . . .

Grabs steak. Like a kid protecting a popsicle. Natural, I guess. Is it really animal? Or just self-defense? Countries do it, too. They grab other countries, go to war. Maybe we *are* all animals after all. I don't know. He gets to these "big" generalizations awfully quickly.

Rachel's remarks brought another show of hands. "You're right, all these guys are male chauvinists." "Girl dogs and boy dogs pee the same way—don't they?" "This piece only pretends to be about dogs. It's really about people and how they need to be reminded of where they came from." "I still think it's cruel. He says the dog is happy to be sniffing garbage and he sounds so superior. He'd be sniffing garbage too if he'd been locked up all day!" "I think he's really saying how all the wild things have been tamed, and how everything has become civilized."

The teacher let the discussion flow for a while, then signaled for silence. She asked everyone around the room to quickly note exactly what they had pictured when they first encountered the word *dog* in the editorial. Then, pointing to one student after another, she listened to the responses:

> A poodle/"Clarabel," our setter/big dogs, two on a leash/one of those hot-dog type dogs with the little short legs/a German Shepherd/Lassie from TV/a part golden named Gussie/Frank/a whole line of mutts following each other down the street/a spotted dog—dalmation/"Buster"—our collie/Lassie/a friendly mutt/ nothing, no picture/vague kind of city dog/one of those dogs on a dogfood commercial/Grandma's old shaggy dog. . . .

So—said the teacher after a sigh—when you look up *dog* in the dictionary, does what you find have anything to do with what the word meant when you read it on the page? Nobody even tried to answer. Several people shook their heads.

NEGOTIATING MEANING

To continue the work and to look for consensus, after something like discouragement, the instructor divided her class into five small groups dispersed around the room. They passed their notes to each other and compared; they argued a little but mostly they expressed surprise at the differences. From time to time there was laughter.

SIGHT READING

For the next class meeting, the teacher asked for a volunteer to bring in another editorial, so that she herself could read something aloud to the class—trying to speak out her responses as she encountered the sentences for the first time. They would continue their investigation of reader response with the teacher as Exhibit Number Two.

She said that she would leave the room for a few minutes so that the class could decide what to do.

When the door had closed, Cathy Bates took the lead. She told everyone how her mother regularly sent her clippings from a California newspaper. It was a sure bet, she said, that their teacher would not have seen any of them before. Everyone agreed. One classmate cautioned that she should clip away all identifying marks, including the author's name.

On Monday, Cathy presented the teacher with the clipping. She had cut and pasted so that the piece had a title but no author identification. "I'm not sure that this is an editorial," said Cathy. "Does it matter?" The teacher assured her that it was not all important *what* kind of writing was used—the results would be the same. She then explained that she would leave the room again, this time to allow Cathy to read the piece aloud twice. When the class was familiar with the text, then she would return and encounter it for the first time.

When the students let her back in, she read the following text. Here the newspaper material is in regular print, and the teacher's italicized impromptu associations follow each sentence in parentheses and quotation marks:

First she read the title:

Bad Luck Bob and His Dog

("Hey, this might be fun. I expected something dreary about parking laws or merchants' associations. 'Bad Luck Bob' suggests a story, a tall-tale. Simple guy . . . not Maurice or Frederick, but Bob, good ol' Bob. Why 'bad luck'? Because he has bad luck, or is bad luck? I guess we'll find out. As for the dog—well, that's a friendly touch. A guy and his dog. There's something familiar. I sense that I want to like Bob.")

Bob Greene is the kind of guy who, if there were one hole in the ground within a 10,000-mile radius, would fall into it and break his leg. Then, when he got out of the hole and sued the hole owner, he would lose the case and be successfully countersued for falling into an unauthorized hole.

("I was right, this will be fun. The writer has a great sense of humor. He's absurd and exaggerated. But I'm tuning right in, not only because I want to know where the piece will go, but also because I identify. Don't we all sometimes feel that we're Bob. I sure did yesterday—I got two parking tickets. But back to Bob. I'm drawn in, too, because I sense it's going to be about the little guy, the underdog. Lawsuits, countersuits—isn't that just the modern world. I get anxious just seeing the word lawsuit. But I have the feeling, I don't know why just yet, that the piece is going to make me feel better.")

Later he would suffer a deadly deep-hole virus that would cause his hair, his teeth and his fingernails to fall out. He would lose his home and his life savings to medical bills and legal costs, his wife would run off with the hole owner and his carnivorous plant would try to eat him.

(*"I feel a slight sense of disappointment. He's going too far with the exaggerations. I don't feel that it's my life any more. Now it's a shaggy-dog story or something. I still want to know what will happen, but . . . And, speaking of dogs, I've forgotten about the dog in the title. What else? Losing hair and teeth and fingernails. Well, hair is something men have to worry about. My husband—well, never mind, he wouldn't want me telling about his problems. Teeth, though. That's a nightmare I sometimes have. I'm able to reach into my mouth and pluck out my teeth. Horrifying! I guess we all fear old age, the body's collapse. The wife running off, and the plant—those details turn the whole business into a joke. Well, let's see where the joke will go."*)

Believe me when I tell you that misfortune sticks to the man like drool to a baby.

(*"That's nice: I like the casual touch of "Believe me." It's a funny image, drool sticking to a baby. Funny, too, to find it referring to a guy who is older, who has a wife and loses his hair and teeth. Is there a message: are we all babies? No, I guess it's just a figure of speech. The author is trying hard to be memorable. Drool sticking to a baby is pretty good, though. It's kind of . . . universal. The baby can't help it, and neither can Bob, apparently."*)

For those who may not recall Robert Alan Greene, he was arrested last March in Laurel Canyon Park for walking his dog.

(*"Aha! I'm surprised. The writer set me up, and he got me. The piece is suddenly turning around. Robert Alan Greene instead of Bob. The language of official papers, arrests, legal action. Very ominous. Now I don't know at all where this piece is going. Are we supposed to get all serious? Or are we going to jump back to Bad Luck Bob and carnivorous plants? I'm not sure I like being tricked. But it does wake me up. I mean, I am going to read on to find out what is happening. The author is holding me. Now I know that it's from California. Maybe it was a big story there, I don't know. Mostly I'm wondering how I should be responding, if I should relax and enjoy, or if I should be ready for something more disturbing. I do see, though, that the dog has finally appeared. It makes me think back to the title: Bad Luck Bob and His Dog."*)

Forget that the park was probably the worst place on earth to be at the time. Dog owners were battling with children owners over the question of who ought to be leashed, the dogs or the kids, and

Animal Regulation Cops were swarming over the hills like Jewish commandos at an Arab outpost.

(*"More switches. There's enough humor to make me think I should be reading for amusement—the business about dog owners and children owners is clever—but there's a certain amount of uneasiness, too. You can't just joke about the warfare in the Middle East—at least I don't think you can. My reaction now is one of confusion. It's a picture, half humorous, of a kind of battle scene. Dogs are being equated with kids. In some ways that's funny. In other ways, it's too true. I mean: I see mothers at the supermarket yelling orders to kids as if they were just animals that needed to be controlled. And then the part about Jewish commandos—it makes me edgy. I see too many images on the evening news—I can't find the humor there, no matter how hard I try."*)

The teacher stopped reading. "It's a fairly long piece," she said. "It's obvious that I won't be able to get all the way through. But maybe you get the idea. I may be getting paid to teach you writing, and you may be tempted to think that I have the answers, but I'm just another reader. There is no reason to think that my responses are in any way better, more correct, more *any*thing than your own. They are different. I am older, I've had different experiences; I've probably read more, and I've had more practice at finding my responses. Now, tell me who I was reading."

Cathy identified the writer as a columnist for the *Los Angeles Times* named Al Martinez. The teacher praised the selection. "It's a lively piece of writing," she said. "I hope you'll let me take it home and finish it." (See exercise 3 for the complete column.)

A week later, mostly studying other matters, they reviewed the subject of reader response by working together, instructor and students, on another editorial brought to class by one student but unread by anybody else. For the rest of the term, when the class talked about student essays or essays read in a reader, they analyzed their own responses as readers. Writing, they tried to remember the potential responses of others, and to respond to their own writing, and they reread and revised their own work. The teacher was satisfied that the message was sinking in: that there is no writing well without reading well.

_____ EXERCISES _____

1. (a) Here are two passages of writing that are exceptionally attentive to word sounds and rhythms. Choose one passage and practice close reading. Recalling the discussion of the Ralph Ellison passage (pp. 38–39), see how many deliberate effects of rhythm and

word sound you can locate. Heed the shifts of tempo from sentence to sentence as well as the movement of the whole. Make notes about what you find and be prepared to discuss in class.

> I grew up in N.Y.C., where I learned to drift with crowds, to be one shining particle in those streaming currents of phosphorescence that merge and intersect around Fifth and Fifty-seventh, especially on late winter afternoons. As one sparkling corpuscle, I delighted in the speed, the thrust, even the bumps and jolts of those other glittering corpuscles. Black, white, Hispanic, Asian, Native American, we made up one Amazonian bloodstream. In those crowds, I savored my anonymity, that deliciously sensuous private space where I could dream in public, sensing the outermost edges of other people's dreams: that woman striding past me in a green suede coat, lighting up a Mary J—the burned eggplant smell drifted back to me, spreading, smudging the purely olfactory calligraphy of her dream. Long after she disappeared into the crowded distance, her dream flowed from her nostrils, enigmatic, persistent.

—*from "Dreaming in Public: A Provincetown Memoir"* by Susan Mitchell

> I came to reading and writing more or less naturally. As, for example, you might come to swimming early and easily. Which, matter of fact, I did; learning to swim at about the same time I learned to walk. I can very well remember the name of the man (he was the swimming coach at Rollins College near Orlando, where I grew up during the Depression years) who took me as a toddler and threw me off the end of a dock into a deep lake where I had the existential choice of sinking or swimming. And I chose to swim, thank you very much. His name was, I swear, Fleetwood Peoples. Could I forget a name like that? More to the point, could I invent that name? For reading we had all the riches of my father's one great extravagance—an overflowing library of some thousands of books. Books of all kinds in bookcases and piles and on tables everywhere in the house. Everybody read and read. And so did I. I remember reading Kipling and Stevenson and Dickens and Scott sooner than I was able to. And you could earn a quarter anytime for reading any one of any number of hard books that my father thought anybody and everybody ought to read.

—*from "My Two One-Eyed Coaches"* by George Garrett

(b) Write a description of your own that attempts to incorporate something you've learned from one of these passages. Read it to the class and see if others can identify what you have used.

2. Here is the complete column by Al Martinez from the *Los Angeles Times*. Pick up where the instructor left off. Find three or four paragraphs to respond to (they should be in sequence). Try to capture your real reactions by noting not only associations and expectations, but also the ways in which those are played upon by Martinez.

Bad Luck Bob and His Dog

Bob Greene is the kind of guy who, if there were one hole in the ground within a 10,000-mile radius, would fall into it and break his leg. Then, when he got out of the hole and sued the hole owner, he would lose the case and be successfully countersued for falling into an unauthorized hole.

Later he would suffer a deadly deep-hole virus that would cause his hair, his teeth and his fingernails to fall out. He would lose his home and his life savings to medical bills and legal costs, his wife would run off with the hole owner and his carnivorous plant would try to eat him.

Believe me when I tell you that misfortune sticks to the man like drool to a baby.

For those who may not recall Robert Alan Greene, he was arrested last March in Laurel Canyon Park for walking his dog.

Forget that the park was probably the worst place on earth to be at the time. Dog owners were battling with children owners over the question of who ought to be leashed, the dogs or the kids, and Animal Regulation Cops were swarming over the hills like Jewish commandos at an Arab outpost.

Dogcatchers, as a police friend pointed out, are usually people who cannot qualify to be *real* policemen and take out their career frustrations on whoever happens to be in the vicinity during periods of high tension.

Bob Greene, of course, was the one strolling by.

The way Bob tells it, his dog Princess was on a leash. The way the animal cops tell it, Princess was walking next to him *unleashed* and was snarling and looking around for babies to kill.

An officer shouted for Greene to stop, but Bob said he had witnessed the "Gestapo tactics" of the animal cops before and was not about to submit to their torture and humiliation and gruesome death. So he told them that and kept going.

Bad news. Bob fell into the hole again.

"I probably shouldn't have said that," he reflected during a more reasonable moment the other day. "I have a big mouth."

The animal cops thought so, too. Greene says they waited in the bushes, jumped him, beat him and booked both him and the dog. The dog was later o.r.'d, but Greene was charged with resisting arrest and failing to keep his pet on a leash.

He requested a jury trial, acted as his own attorney and, of course, lost.

"I was a fool," Bob lamented.

Somewhere along the way, incidentally, he had mortgaged his house in Laurel Canyon to buy a sign-making business. The business naturally failed and he lost the house.

But wait. We're not finished.

Bob was arrested that first time on March 31. He remembers it because it was Palm Sunday, but that didn't do him any good at all. And it didn't improve his luck or his judgment. Four months later, he went back to the park and this time, he admits, was walking Princess *without* a leash.

"Bob," I asked him as gently as I could, "why in the dog-walking hell did you go *back* to Laurel Canyon after that first incident and not even put the dog on a leash this time?"

He thought about that for a moment, then shook his head sadly.

"I don't know," he said. "I guess it was just bad timing on my part."

Greene is 55 and, as one might expect, divorced. We met in the West Hollywood sign-making shop he once owned and now works for. He sleeps in a tiny room adjacent to the office. Princess and a stray called Barney sleep in the room with him when they are not out hunting babies.

"I'd do some things all over again now if I could," he said. I hope to God he would.

Sparing you the strange details of that second encounter at Laurel Canyon Park, Bob was subsequently charged with abandoning a pet, interfering with a dog officer and threatening a dog officer.

He is to appear in Municipal Court on those charges unless he is already in jail after sentencing on the first set of convictions.

"When I was found guilty," Greene remembered, "the judge gave me a choice of being sentenced right away or of waiting until October. I asked him what he would suggest and he said, 'Well, if I sentence you now, you'll go straight to jail.' So I said I'd wait until October."

Greene and others involved in the Laurel Canyon Park mess insist that he is being punished not for crimes he committed but for twice testifying before the Animal Regulation Commission on the excesses of the dog cops.

Maybe so, but if bad judgment were a felony, Bob Greene might be sitting on Death Row today.

As a final example of his synaptic lapses, I asked if he were going to appeal the first conviction.

"I sure am," he said. "A friend of mine is going to show me how to fill out the papers. I'm doing it myself."

Oh my goodness, oh my soul, there goes Robert down the hole.

Again.

3. Here is another column by Al Martinez. Break up into small groups and take turns reading the piece out loud. The reader should pause after every paragraph to give group members a chance to jot down their responses. Afterwards, work through the notes, looking not only for differences, but for consensus as well. Is there a sense of overall agreement? If not, why not?

Heeding the Winds of Change

His name is Marty. I last saw him at the front of the house, his tan Toyota bulging with the bare essentials of a life he was about to start. At 20, he was heading out on his own, responding to a whisper of independence that was blowing in the wind, a call to see new places and hear new sounds.

I asked him how he felt as we stood together near the large oak that sheltered the driveway, where we had stood so many times before. He smiled slightly and said, "A little nervous, I guess."

"That's pretty normal," I said. "We've all gone through it. But sooner or later a kid's got to leave the nest. It's scary, but we stumble on through somehow. You'll do all right."

"I hope so. I'm going to try."

"I know you will."

We talked for a long time. I was trying to come up with the kind of advice that might do him some good as he began building an adulthood high up at the northern end of California, where the redwoods march to the edge of the sea, where a roaring surf dares the granite cliffs.

But all I could come up with were a lot of rambling basics Marty had already mastered simply by reaching 20. Drive carefully, work hard, be honest, clean your room, keep the music down, do your homework and, for God's sake, leave my clothes alone.

"Your clothes are safe," he said, laughing. "I won't be here, remember?"

So he won't.

That's going to take some getting used to. An empty boy's room with posters on the wall. No rock music rattling the windows. The vacancy. The silence.

Marty!

He had actually decided months ago that L.A. was no longer for him. It wasn't an easy decision. He was torn between the security of life at home and a whisper on the wind that said *be your own man!* That said *spread your wings, boy!* That said *fly!*

The voice in his head was compelling, and in the end he responded to the call that came from beyond the distance, from the shadows of the ridge line, from the sunlight in the glades.

I considered trying to talk him out of the north coast as his destination. Eureka isn't exactly a land of opportunity. The weather isn't ideal.

But I kept my silence because opportunity is what you make it to be, and because someone told me a long time ago that a man grows tall under dark skies, when the storm howls and the rain falls, and I think I know what he meant.

Mart was simply following my lead. I have always loved the open land and have talked about it for years. He must have been listening.

The north coast is honest country. Redwoods dwarf our fussy priorities, and the wild rivers rush down from the mountains with a strength that defies containment. There are lessons there for the young, far beyond what I could teach on the front porch, with only minutes left.

Still, there had to be something I could say, something vital, something important, something to strengthen him in the hard times, to cheer him in the sad times. Something real, something fine. *Something. . . .*

Not that I haven't had the opportunity to do all that before. I have known the boy for a lot of years. It's just that I never got around to it, or maybe I didn't even know what to say then, or maybe I was just too damned preoccupied with writing words and meeting deadlines and responding to the whispers in my own head.

Time is measured by different standards. We had an apple tree in the yard once and I used to promise myself that Mart and I were going to go off somewhere and talk before the apples were all gone. I'd tell him what life was all about and prepare him for the tomorrows which then seemed so distant.

But I never did, not that way, and then one day I'd realize that the last apple had fallen from the tree and it was too late. Time had passed and I hadn't even noticed.

Damn me and damn the days that fly too fast, the years that flicker by like fireflies in the night.

"Well," he said with a mixture of reluctance and anticipation, "I guess I'd better leave."

I nodded. "The traffic shouldn't be too bad," I said.

Is that what I would leave him with?

A traffic report? That's all?

We shook hands, the small hand grown large that I had once held as we walked through the summers of his youth, the hand I had touched as he slept in a crib long turned to kindling, the hand I had taken to pull him up over a hilltop where we hiked.

"So long, Dad."

"So long, Mart."

We hugged, and as we did it suddenly came to me, advice beyond planning, a word drawn from that area within us where all good instincts are born.

I said simply, "Care."

And then my son's car pulled from the driveway, and then it was a disappearing blur of tan down a long and winding road, and then it was gone. I stood there for a very long time, listening to the wind blow.

4. Further exercises may come from your reader, if your class uses one, or from the text of *Writing Well*. For instance, study your responses to paragraphs from "The Insides of Words," pages 87–101, or "Verbs," pages 104–111.

Throughout this book exercises print whole paragraphs for analysis, especially in the chapter about the paragraph, where examples are collected for study of structure. These paragraphs will do as well for investigation of reading habits and as subjects for collaborative learning.

Take any of the paragraphs on pages 253–255. Let the class divide into groups of three to five students and work on negotiating a consensus or a community of meanings, one paragraph at a time. Let each group collaboratively write a one-sentence summary of its consensus on a paragraph. Let each group find two examples of subjective responses that needed correction in the pursuit of objectivity and consensus. If there are significant differences among the consensuses arrived at by different groups, let the whole class try to negotiate a super-consensus.

3

Writing an Essay

"Students write essays and answer questions on tests. . . ." So we began this book, naming an immediate and practical necessity for the student writer. Then we talked about the idea of an audience and other matters essential to good writing. In the second chapter we talked about how we read and about interconnections among reading, thinking, and writing—even their identity. Now we must attend to the most basic part of the writing process: getting the words onto the page. In most composition courses the student is asked to write a complete paper at the very beginning and to write additional complete papers every week or two throughout the term. It is time for some practical advice on writing an essay.

In the first chapter we named some qualities, like focus and unity, that we look for in a paper. Now we must investigate the *process* of writing a paper, how a writer achieves focus and unity, and makes contact with a reader. For many students, daily writing will increase their fluency, and fluency will help them revise their papers. But daily writing—spontaneous, undirected, and uncorrected—is a means to an end, not an end in itself. The end is good writing, and the occasion for good writing in a composition class is the essay. The essay is *controlled*, *disciplined*, and *directed* by the student writer.

A paper has a purpose—to give information, to define or to contrast, to explore, perhaps to persuade. A paper *shows* its purpose, both in its shape and in its statement, or the paper fails. In beginning a paper, we *find* that purpose, often in the act of writing; revising and finishing the paper, we make that purpose *clear* to the outside world.

In a paper we must support our purpose by detail; we must provide sufficient detail, and we must arrange the details into an order that expresses purpose. If we are writing five hundred words we must find a purpose limited enough to be supported adequately in two pages of typing. If we try brief surveys of grand topics— "Nuclear War," "The Problem of Welfare"—our five hundred words will remain abstract and superficial, lacking detail. If we choose a more limited topic—" Recruiting High School Seniors for the Army," "Applying for Food Stamps"—we can organize adequate detail into a shape that reaches an audience. We must limit not only topic but purpose.

Writing an essay we need to use both the critical and the creative sides of our brains. To accumulate detail, we can use the spontaneity we cultivate in daily writing. But to cut and to shape, to narrow and to focus, we need to cultivate other qualities of mind. We must develop a sense for order and shape, a sense by which we understand the whole paper as several units organized to become one larger unit controlled by one purpose. Finally the shape of an essay reflects the shape of our purposeful thought.

We must also understand that our whole paper —from our choice of words for the opening paragraph to our choice of detail for the concluding paragraph—directs itself to the eyes and ears of other people. We do not write for ourselves only. We need to persuade, to inform, to please, to convince, to charm, to arouse, to make an impression on *other people.* By definition a composition class presumes—as much as a newspaper presumes by publishing—that its writing directs itself from inside out, from writer to reader, from individual to world. Acts of language are social acts; it takes two to talk.

Once we understand that writing is directed to an audience—and not inward, where we can be sure that a generous interpretation will accept our intentions—then we can understand the function of good style and even of mere correctness. Good style smooths the passage from writer to reader; good style is a convincing clarity. Mechanical correctness removes impediments to understanding; even a mistaken *it's* for *its* can throw a momentary monkey wrench into the machine of comprehension. We must write well in order to make contact with our readers. We avoid clichés, or extraneous information, or misleading abstractions, or dangling modifiers, or incomplete arguments, *for one reason:* all these flaws, errors, imperfections block the passage between the writer and the reader.

In later chapters, we will look into the choice of words, the making of sentences, the construction of paragraphs, and at the different types of writing a student may undertake. First we must investigate how the whole essay is made. We must look into the process that will be the student's classroom task throughout the term: writing papers single in purpose, integrated in shape, and clear to others.

GETTING IDEAS FOR PAPERS

<u>Writing begins with invention</u>. Many writers find that getting started is the hardest part and feel discouraged about learning to invent. Beginning writers commonly suspect that organization and clarity are qualities that can be learned by study but that originality depends on luck or genius—the inventor's spark of inspiration. Fortunately, however, this common idea is untrue; anyone can learn procedures that generate ideas. We need not be Thomas Alva Edison to invent a good paper: even for a literary genius, inspiration is 99 percent perspiration.

When an instructor assigns a free paper, both topic and organization are up to the writer. When an instructor assigns a general topic like "public transportation," we need to formulate and organize ideas on the topic. When an instructor assigns a form of organization—comparison and contrast, for instance—we need to generate a topic appropriate to the form and an idea by which to organize the topic. Then we must discover and organize the best details. Whatever the assignment, we need to discover details and set them in order.

Maybe the mind feels blank, at first, with an open assignment. Total freedom suggests no starting place. If we do daily writing we can read over the pages and sometimes find a suitable subject to rewrite into a shape that will convey a purpose to the reader. Otherwise, it is a good idea to consult our recent interests, or subjects of discussion or argument in other classrooms, at breakfast with family, or with other students. It is also true that we should simply keep our eyes open: essay topics float around us like motes in the air.

When the instructor assigns a topic or a pattern, the direction simplifies the process of invention. We generate ideas on a topic by narrowing it; reducing "Student Politics" to "Running for Class President" begins the choice of detail. We can call to mind incidents we have witnessed and slogans we have heard. When form is assigned, we must filter possible topics through this special entry-gate: although we could contrast a small college with a large university, do we know enough about life in a large university (or a small college) to provide fair comparison? If we do not, we cannot write a decent comparison and contrast paper on this topic, which therefore fails to pass through the gate. If we are to analyze a process and think of writing a recipe for spaghetti sauce, can we really generate enough detail for a paper? Hot pepper and chopped carrots are not enough. And even if we add oregano, we may fail to keep our readers interested.

The true beginning of the essay waits for desk and paper, concentration on the task. Writers find many ways to begin, and in a moment we will look at several of them. First, we must emphasize how *not* to begin: <u>*do not sit down with a few notes and a vague notion of topic and form to write the paper.*</u> Many papers fail because beginners try to improvise the final paper at first sitting, attempting to find ideas at the same time as they organize and shape them. Too often, vaguely aware of shortcomings but despairing of making large changes, the writer merely copies this rough draft—improving only mechanical matters like spelling and capitalization—and hands in a messy, disorganized, incoherent paper.

Time spent in preparation is time well spent. It is wise to figure how much time we have and allot half to preparation and half to execution. When we begin by writing a whole draft, we start without a full supply of detail. If we go back later with the idea of adding detail, we all too often try to squeeze in material that doesn't really belong. Detail should grow into place naturally; it should not feel taped-on. Of course if we have the time and energy, we can look at a premature first draft as raw material, take it apart, rewrite and reorganize it thoroughly. But it takes less time and effort if we prepare patiently and thoroughly before attempting a draft. A <u>delayed draft</u> is more likely to generate the material and a complete and coherent final revision. The longer we brood over an idea, the more details we are apt to accumulate.

Any advice on writing a paper, however, must recognize that different writers follow different processes. Indeed, the same writer, at different times, may find different procedures useful. Some writers, or maybe all writers on some occasions, will find it best to begin by writing several pages before the plan of the paper becomes clear, in order to generate material. Some people think best in the act of writing. Later, they must return to what they have written in haste, to mine this material for the real essay. Attitude is important. <u>If we do not wait, think, and plan before attempting the paper, we must use much of our writing time to generate raw material.</u> We must not write expecting merely to polish this material into a final draft. Revision more radical than polishing will be necessary.

Whatever procedure we follow, two things are worth knowing. First, it helps to know that we can go about writing a paper many ways, to be aware of the many options. Second, we must acknowledge that however we go about writing a paper, it will always take *work*—we will not get it right, or close to right, the first time we try.

Here are some ways to prepare for writing an essay, ways to get ideas, develop them, examine them, analyze them, and expand them. Later we will mention ways to select and organize these ideas.

Brainstorming

To <u>brainstorm</u> is to list ideas and details rapidly, without self-criticism, without attending to formalities or parallelisms or mechanical considerations—and without worrying about being silly: no one else need see the product. When we brainstorm we fill a blank sheet of paper with fragmentary notes that we hope may lead to ideas on a topic. We write rapidly and uncritically, receiving the brain's topical snow flurries without trying to make sense or to give shape. The uncritical mind generates good ideas and bad ones together with a broad generosity.

Suppose the topic is comparing and contrasting bicycles and cars at a residential campus. Sitting down with a blank sheet, a student might list:

> bikes quicker no parking trouble
> but bike theft—chains and combinations
> healthy, keep in shape
> but carrying groceries?
> more car accidents; more serious?
> bikes ecology, energy saving
> winter ugh salt jeans
> bike cheap car expensive
> insurance gas parking fines
> car status symbol
> kind of car?
> old car repairs
> vans, hearses, old buses

When the mind compares and contrasts, it brainstorms ideas by flipping back and forth like a Ping-Pong ball—bikes are healthier, *but* you don't carry a lot of groceries on bikes; bikes save energy, *but* riding them in winter can be unpleasant. These alternatives are good raw material, but if we wrote an essay that swung from side to side so rapidly, the to-and-fro would only confuse the reader. After we list alternatives, we can organize coherently, often putting like with like—the advantages of cars in one paragraph perhaps, and the advantages of bicycles in another.

It is useful after brainstorming to look back at the list and circle ideas that need thinking out. The creator lists; the critic reads the list and responds to it. We may put question marks by some notes to acknowledge that we are only guessing; are we really more likely to have an accident driving a car than riding a bicycle? To make such an assertion, we would need the authority that comes from research. Sometimes we find an item, like "car status symbol," which can head a list for further brainstorming:

> car status symbol
> rich students—rich-seeming?
> money and parents

some earn own money
but—doing errands for others
weekends? not on campus—
getting away!
sports cars, antiques, clunkers

When we brainstorm, we list a few words, sensing that if we needed to, we could expand any item. Each phrase stands for something possible to develop. We are generating material for later expansion, generating the seeds from which we will cultivate our sentences and paragraphs. Often we begin with a general area for investigation, and as we investigate we generate possible ideas and purposes. This usually involves some narrowing down of the subject. When we glimpse a purpose for a paper—perhaps to demonstrate the superior utility of the bicycle—purpose will allow us further brainstorming. After we have accumulated much material, we could try organizing our notes and writing a draft—but chances are we will do better if we continue to delay the first draft, preparing further. Many professional writers make a practice of such stalling. They know that *once they have come up with an idea,* that idea will work like a magnet, drawing forth details from memory. The more we learn to trust ourselves as writers, the more faith we put in the capacities of the unconscious mind.

Sprinting

Sprinting—or free associating—is another technique for loosening the mind into discovery or invention; we can use it instead of brainstorming or in addition to it. Sprinting, we write a quick paragraph on our topic, writing as fast as we can for five minutes or so, beginning with the first thought that occurs to us and hurtling forward by association of ideas without pausing for logic or correctness. The results at times resemble (or *are*) nonsense, but every so often—often enough to make it worthwhile—some unexpected connection opens up a whole new set of possibilities. Even when it doesn't bring fresh insight, the process is a useful way to loosen up for writing. Before beginning an essay, we may try sprinting on our essay topic for our daily writing.

Sprinting resembles the method Peter Elbow calls "looping," writing a series of ten-minute passages, each loop circling out of the passage before it. This technique is especially appropriate for endeavors longer than a weekly paper. We may follow Elbow and loop a second sprint onto our first one. Pausing to look back at our spontaneous prose, we should extract the essence of what we have written. Do these sentences lead toward something in particular? Is there a leading idea? Trying to answer such questions, we should write one more sentence that captures the best or most interesting idea of our paragraph. And next, using this sentence as our beginning, we should sprint again. Often a brainstorming list provides an initial range of topics, and a sprint or two will generate detail within the narrowing topic. Sprinting on the topic of cars vs. bicycles during an in-class exercise, one student came up with: "Funny how when I drive I hate bikers, when I ride I hate drivers . . ." Her spontaneous expression made her realize that she had two different attitudes about the subject. She later made the idea of a double perspective the core of a short weekly theme.

Cross-examining

There are questions we need to ask ourselves when we gather materials for writing. If we cross-examine our notes and ideas before we begin a draft, we will save ourselves revising time. Not all questions will apply to all topics. But usually an array of questions directed at the topic undertaken will generate new ideas, details, and directions.

The Journalist's Six. Anyone who writes for a newspaper or takes a journalism course learns to answer six questions at the beginning of a news story: <u>Who? What? When? Where? Why? How?</u> Here is how a news story in a Detroit daily begins: "A Grosse Pointe systems analyst missed out on a $1,000 first prize at a Pontiac radio station yesterday because he could not remember the lyrics of 'America the Beautiful.' " *Who?* "A Grosse Pointe systems analyst"; *What?* "Missed out on a $1,000 first prize"; *Where?* "At a Pontiac radio station"; *When?* "Yesterday"; *Why?* "Because he could not remember the lyrics of 'America the Beautiful.' " (*How?* does not fit without some stretching.) The journalistic formula anticipates the questions any reader might ask; newspapers cannot afford baffled audiences.

Although essays for freshman English are seldom news stories, if we ask the six questions before we begin to write, they will help us make contact with our audience. If we write about the old television series *Hogan's Heroes*, we may find ourselves easily telling what it was, why it was the way it was, how it formulated itself—but we may forget to tell when it was on the air, which will leave a question hanging for our readers. If we remember to answer the six questions, we will satisfy our audience's curiosity.

Questions of Form

Later, in Chapter 7, we will discuss rhetorical patterns in some detail, but a quick preview might be useful here. Rhetoric, simply put, is the study of effective speech and argumentation. Rhetoricians long ago found that most presentations of material were organized according to certain basic patterns. These rhetorical forms can be as useful as the journalist's six questions. They, too, can be turned into basic interrogations—an idea-generating exercise that finds six new ways of asking "Is it bigger than a bread-box?"

We can phrase *comparison and contrast* by asking: What is it like or unlike? *Definition* asks: What is it? *Division:* What is it composed of? What are its parts? *Classification:* What kind of thing is it? *Process:* How does it work? *Cause and effect:* What causes it? What effect does it have? The same questions can help us to develop paragraphs when we revise (see Chapter 6).

Thus, if we were preparing to write about leaves changing color in autumn, consideration of rhetorical forms might lead us to write about the chemical *process* by which chlorophyll drains from the maple tree, or about the temperature-related *cause* of the change, or about the *classification* of different maples, or about the *comparison and contrast* between two parts of the country or two kinds of maple tree. Considering these forms, not unlike the journalist's six questions, allows us to consider alternatives for the structure of our paper. We may choose a rhetorical form for our whole paper—*comparing and contrasting Hogan's Heroes* and *M*A*S*H* or *defining* the national debt—or we may simply use *analysis* or *classification* in a paper; calling something a "situation comedy," we classify a form of popular entertainment.

More Hints for Inventors

Always begin thinking about a paper early, because much of our best invention happens after we have chosen a topic but when we are not consciously thinking of it: sometimes in dreaming sleep, more often in daydreams while we are lightly occupied driving a car or walking from parking lot to class, or—let us admit it—while we are attending a lecture in another course. The brain never stops its unconscious activities, and if we have planted a seed—or posed a provocative question to ourselves—there's no telling when answering ideas might start to sprout.

Internal dialogue can become an exercise of mind and imagination, for we can talk things over, not just with a friend or a roommate, but with the ideal listener/critic that we keep inside ourselves.

This invisible voice can embody a teacher, a whole stable of teachers, a priest, an aunt, or friends back home or at other colleges. It is, in a sense, our writer's conscience, and in many ways it knows better than we do. If we slack off, contenting ourselves with a cliché or a generality, chances are that this voice will caution: *That's a dumb way to say it!* Or *I just can't see it.* We may not always hear it or pay attention, but the voice is usually there. The more we train ourselves to read and respond—to others and to ourselves—the more audible it will become. As writers, the best thing we can hope for is a crabby, insistent voice—and when it argues we should listen carefully. It is the closest we can come to taking an audience inside, an internal critic whose opinions help us to see what we have not said or what we have said badly.

Even at an early stage, the idea of an audience may generate further ideas. If we have not thought of whom we address, that thought may bring to mind special responses that we may expect from our audience, and therefore generate material shaped to meet these responses.

Selecting Detail

Invention generates detail; next we must select and organize what we have generated. To write a good paper, we have to organize details in the best order, and we must leave out any details, however attractive, which do not contribute to the whole. The whole essay embodies our purpose in writing it. The essay's shape is the shape of our thought, and focus or concentration is the architecture of purpose. The idea of focus, in Chapter 1, is perhaps the most important *structural* idea in making a paper, unless it is the related idea of a thesis. With many essays it is possible to boil our purpose down to a single sentence that states a thesis: a summary or kernel of purpose, which our detail and argument support. A single governing thesis allows us unity and focus.

Sometimes—before we write or during revision—we find ourselves oppressed with too much detail. Writing is acquiring material (through brainstorming, sprint-associating, and rapid daily writing), and it is ordering and cutting that material. The writer must be a paradoxical combination of opposites: the big spender and the miser, the exhibitionist and the recluse. Cutting can take place when we organize our notes before writing, or it can come later. When we start to write, it is often hard to know which details are going to prove relevant. Many writers consciously write too much in their first drafts, knowing that they do not yet know what will be useful and knowing that they will later cut for focus and form, often with the help of a discovered thesis directed to a specific audience.

Suppose you describe a particular day. At the end of a vacation, you had a perfect (or perfectly horrible) day. On that Thursday, when you woke up, it was 8:35. You ate scrambled eggs with catsup. These details could be relevant, or they could be mere padding. Cut what does not contribute to the whole. But first, you must have a whole. The point of your paper could be a triviality of your day: a dog barked, the mail was junk, nobody was home when you telephoned your friends. The point is to have a point. Find one—or even make one up. The truth we want is truth-to-feeling; we are not under oath in a court. If we are remembering a sequence of events—A, B, C, and D—we can rearrange the sequence to make a piece of writing true to the feeling we want the whole to give. If event B happened second, but we see in retrospect that it was the emotional climax, we can change the sequence in order to tell the emotional truth. We can use C, A, and D in that order and save B for last. We are still writing out of our own life. We are telling the truth in a serious sense. Within the limits set by credibility, we can even combine different events into one, or different people into the same character. Suppose in a family anecdote two uncles move in and out of a story, doing approximately the same things. In telling the anecdote, it might be more shapely and pointed—and just as true—to turn them into one person. This advice does not apply, of course, when the writer's relationship to audience—a report to a committee investigating a problem, a journalist's account of an event—implies a contract to tell the literal truth.

To make a point, and to give our writing a shape, we must limit our material. Here we are back to unity. If we try to write about a whole summer, we are most likely to write disjointed paragraphs and be boring and superficial. We should find one event, or one unifying device (a place, a person, an automobile, a time of day, a kind of food), to tie together different details. Contrast can make a glue as adhesive as similarity. We must find the detail and form that combined will embody the summer's spirit.

When Jim Beck (Chapter 1) decided to make a theme out of his drive to attend college, he knew that he had accumulated detail in his daily writing. In fact, he had too much detail. At first, when he looked over thirty-six pages of undisciplined writing, he felt elated because he had so much to write about; then he felt depressed because he had too much to write about. Should he tell about his father's parents? The story of their troubles was background to his father's lack of self-confidence. Should he tell about his brother Steve's dishonorable discharge? In two pages of daily writing, he had told only half the story, but he suspected that Steve's life story contributed to local opinion of the Becks. In a way, it belonged.

Of course *everything* belongs. Everything that ever happened to us contributes to how we are, how we act, and how we feel at this moment. But because Jim had to condense his idea into three pages, he had to narrow his topic. He had to focus on his purpose, to seek out the proper order for his thoughts. The idea of focus helped him begin to narrow. In this paper, the topic was his personal feelings; he realized that he had to concentrate on himself and keep his family at the side, mentioning his parents and his brothers only so far as details about them promoted his purpose. The essay's shape was the shape of his thought, and his thesis used the analogy of a footrace to express the struggle of getting to college; his disillusion as he begins college only emphasizes that struggle to get there.

Reading over his daily writing, he listed the topics covered, as if he were outlining a chapter in his reading. When he crossed out the topics he did not require, he found focus. Right away, he could cut thirty-six pages down to eight or ten. The rest of the cutting came when he chose details that would most affect a reader. He decided that accounts of races by which he won his athletic scholarship would mean little to a reader. He decided with regret to omit an anecdote about a vice-principal. He let the larger focus dictate his choices.

WRITING THE DRAFT

To write the draft, we first try <u>setting our notes in order, notes derived from brainstorming, sprinting, or cross-examining</u>. Orderly notes resemble an informal outline, reminders of what we need to say in the best order of saying. Writing a first draft, we waste time if we worry about finding the perfect beginning. If we do not immediately know how to begin our paper, we should plunge ahead anyway and worry about the introduction later.

What matters is the paper's shape-of-thought: *the shape we give the paper, like the motion in the paragraph, is the structure formed by our thought.* Our matter and our purpose determine our way of proceeding—or they ought to. An anecdote or a historical summary or an explanation of a process must use chronological order. In an argument that advances a thesis, the paper's order embodies persuasion—accumulating detail, proceeding by logic, and using various forms of persuasion or argument.

Our purpose is reflected in our paper's order of development. A different order of ideas can make a different statement, even when the ideas or details remain the same. In a reminiscence, if we begin with pleasant associations and move to horrid ones, we leave the reader with a negative impression; if we move from horrid to pleasant, we leave the reader feeling positive. We could accumulate identical details for each paper but make a different impression by our organization. We have to decide on the point we want to make. There are important associations that result from the order we give details. In a history paper, one student wrote:

> The rainfall in the Southern provinces is approximately two inches a year. On the average. What this means is that most years the country people starve in a drought; one year in five, they drown in a flood. However, the combination of surviving Indian ritual, and a

local brand of Roman Catholicism, keeps the people remarkably cheerful and content.

For the same assignment, writing from the same source, another wrote:

Indian rituals which still survive, combined with a peculiar indigenous Catholicism, keep the natives of the South apparently contented. However, the climatic conditions are deplorable. The rainfall averages two inches a year. This means that the peasants parch for several years in drought, and are drowned in floods the next one.

Both students' original notes for this passage were, approximately,

Catholicism and Indian stuff
happy
rainfall
floods
starvation, drought

The two students were heading in different directions—the first toward an expository essay on daily life in the tribe, the second toward an argument for public works such as irrigation and flood control—but they started from the same information, which they organized or pointed in different ways. Their paragraphs embody the different shapes of their different thinking.

We need to make an order that is lucid and expressive. Too often, essays lack lucidity because they lack orderly development. One sentence should lead into another and lead the reader to follow the track of thought. Lucidity and expression carry our thought, writer to reader; we are not expressive if our message is garbled by repetition, by lack of transition, or by afterthought. We need orderly progress in all our writing in order to engage the reader. We must always assume that the reader cannot second-guess our intentions; a lucid structure makes intentions clear.

The development in Jim Beck's paper is deceptively simple. He started with a paragraph telling us how much he hated college, with details to make sure the reader understood the feeling.

It's horrible now, and I don't know if it will get any better. The only people who pay attention to me are the people who are trying to beat me out for the track team. My roommate is stoned all day and gets A's on his papers anyway. I hate him because he hates me because I'm a jock. My classes are boring lectures and the sections are taught by graduate students who pick on the students because the professors pick on them.

But this would not be news. Lots of people are unhappy in college. So Jim constructed his second paragraph to make a contrast to the first. He not only told us how much he wanted to come to college, but gave us reasons.

> But I remember wanting to come here so bad! Nobody from Hammerton named Beck had ever been to college. Everybody knew the Becks were stupid. This went for my father, who never got through high school, and for my grandfather, who died before I was born, and who was the town drunk. It went for my two older brothers who went bad, as they say in Hammerton. Steve got a dishonorable discharge from the Marines and he works on a farm outside town and gets drunk on Fridays and Saturdays. Curt stole a car and did time at Jackson and nobody has heard from him since. My sister had a three-month baby and the town liked to talk about that.

In the third, fourth, and fifth paragraphs, his writing made us understand his separateness from the rest of his family and from his hometown, and then the easy and appropriate order of chronology began to organize the paper. Jim began a paragraph speaking of athletics in general and moved on to his own ambitions as a runner; he carried us with him, right up to the paper's conclusion, with ease and clarity.

> I was different. Everybody told me I was. My mother told me I wasn't a Beck. My father told me I was going to bring back the family's good name. (I never knew it had one.) In grammar school the teachers all told me how much better I was than my brothers. By the time I was in sixth grade my father and the school Principal were talking about the University.
>
> My father isn't really dumb. Sometimes people look dumb because it's expected of them. He's worked at the same grocery for twenty years, I guess. Now that I made it to the University, he wants to be called Manager, because he's the only man there besides Mr. Roberts who owns it. (The rest of the help are—is?—kids who bag and an old lady cashier.) When I went back for a weekend everybody treated me as if I won the Olympics.
>
> I said the Principal and my father were talking about my going to the University. All through junior high I said I didn't want to go. I was scared. No Beck could do that. Bad things kept happening to my family. My father had an accident and totaled the car and lost his license and for a year we didn't have a car at all. He had to walk home two miles every night pushing a basket of groceries. When I said I would quit school and get a job, everybody jumped on me.
>
> It wasn't that I was an A student. It was just that I tried hard at everything I did. I got B's mostly. Now with B's, the counselors kept telling me, I could be admitted to the University, but I wouldn't get a scholarship. I needed mostly A's for that, and then when I got to the University I would lose the scholarship if I couldn't keep the grades up. Then my brother Steve, who was a pretty good athlete once, suggested athletics.

I was too skinny for football, too short for basketball, I could barely swim and my school didn't have a swimming team anyway. There is one sport you can practice with no money and no equipment. I started to run when I was in my last year of junior high. It felt good right away. I ran to and from school. I went over to the high school and did laps. The high school coach noticed me and asked me to go out the next year. Running long distances hurts a lot. Sometimes you get a stitch in your left side and suddenly it shifts to your right side. I didn't exactly mind the pain. I studied it. I studied it in order to go to the University, the way I studied everything else.

Jim had what was for him a new experience while he was writing these paragraphs. He tried describing it to his teacher. "It was like catching fire," he said. "All of a sudden the words and sentences were coming at me as fast as I could get them down. I had a good feeling—that things were finally right." Jim experienced what some writers have called "the gift state." Every so often we fall into the right relation to our subject. We know the details, the order; we have a clear sense of what we want to say. All of a sudden the usual barriers fall away—it is as if the pen, or typewriter, or word processor knew more than we did. The more we write, the more often we'll catch fire: hard work has its rewards.

Beginnings

When considering structure we have to think hard about beginnings and endings for papers. Beginnings are like first meetings: they leave all-important impressions. And as with people, so with writing—there is nothing harder than overcoming a bad first impression. We are bored by vagueness, exhausted by pointless detail, and angered when we feel that our time is being wasted. Try, while writing, to imagine how your reader would respond. Ask yourself: would I really like to read an essay that begins like this? Sometimes we overexplain at the beginning of a paper and begin too far back. Trying to talk about something that we did last weekend we realize that it resembled something we did last summer; then we realize that last summer's feelings were like the feelings we had at age five when we started kindergarten or at age three when we moved to a new town. All these details may be valid, but to include them all would destroy the paper's shape. The bridge into the country of last weekend would be longer than the country itself. With enough self-questioning, we could begin every autobiographical paper with "I was born," or "My grandparents emigrated from Lithuania in 1905," or "Life for my peasant ancestors in medieval Turkey must have been difficult." Too much detail prevents the reader from perceiving the shape of thought.

Long bridges curse not only autobiography; the same malady can afflict all writing. In discussing how World War II began, we can begin with the fall of the Roman Empire. Or else we can fall victim to what might be called the closing funnel approach. Setting out to write about the disappearing whale, we begin the paper with the general topic of man's destroying his environment, narrow it to his destroying species, narrow it to his destroying whales, and then narrow it to the decline in population of one type of whale. The last category is the paper's focus; if we are not careful, we can spend three-quarters of our paper walking the bridge to our topic.

The good, sharp beginning narrows the topic. When we understand our writing's purpose, we can begin with reference to that purpose, or with a thesis we propose to explain. We can begin with something that arrests the reader and points to the main topic.

> Humpbacks are mammals, as all whales are; they breathe into huge lungs, bear live young, which they nurse for the better part of a year, and have vestiges of hair. . . .

In this research paper, the author catches our attention immediately with facts that will interest almost anyone, probably because they interested her and she shows it: *huge lungs, for the better part of a year.*

Editors of magazines sometimes refer to hooks, beginnings (or *leads*) to articles constructed to grab the reader by the hair. *Time* is good at hooks. Here are two opening sentences from one issue.

> The United States was founded on a complaint.

> When the young Chinese woman heard a mysterious voice asking, "What's under your pillow?" she felt sure that the answer was a "biological radio apparatus" put there by a special agent who suspected her of crimes against the state.

In the *Saturday Review*, Gordon Lish began an article:

> Like every interesting American, I live in New York City—

All immediately involve our interest, and none has a preamble. Two begin by startling us. A short sentence makes an unconventional assertion that arouses our interest. We will read the next sentence because we want to see what the writer will do. We are *hooked.* At other times a definition of the subject may be essential before we can begin.

> In its widest possible extension the title of this book—*Adventures of Ideas*—might be taken as a synonym for The History of the Human Race. . . .
>
> A. N. Whitehead, *Adventures of Ideas*

Whitehead builds a swift bridge into his topic. He is free to get right to his point.

Purpose and context determine the kind of beginning. But in any piece of writing, the beginning focuses our writing; it requires special attention, and it requires brevity and incisiveness. Some information we need quickly; information which may be pertinent but not wholly necessary should be held back; information which is both pertinent and necessary but which might take a tedious beginning can often be put off until later in the essay, when its relevance becomes obvious and it ceases to seem tedious.

One kind of opener, the overt announcement of what is to be done, is often boring: "I am going to show that the government of the United States is split into three branches, the executive, the legislative, and the judicial." Papers may be constructed analytically by delineating parts, but they should show and not tell. The paper that begins with the sentence above will probably take a paragraph each for the three branches and end, as boringly as it began, "I have shown that the government of the United States is comprised of the executive, the legislative, and the judicial branches." It is structure for people who have difficulty following the story line of a Disney movie.

Once he had discarded the thought of beginning with his grandparents, Jim Beck tried several opening sentences.

> When I was daydreaming about college it scared me, but I didn't have any idea how I would hate it. I thought that it might be too hard but I never suspected that it would be horrible. It's horrible now, and I don't know if it will get better. . . .
>
> Since I first came to the university, I haven't slept more than four hours in a row. . . .

Giving up on getting the beginning right in his first draft, he went on to the rest of his paper. When he looked at his draft the next day, he decided to start with the third sentence of his first attempt:

> It's horrible now, and I don't know if it will get any better.

principally because he thought it would arouse curiosity in his reader.

Endings

Endings are every bit as important as beginnings. The same kinds of caution therefore apply. They give the last impression, the taste that the reader carries away from the banquet. But we often make them too long, summarize facts that are already obvious, reargue a point already established, say abstractly what we have shown concretely—and by all these methods dilute the intensity our conclusion should have. Our endings often drag and decline into blank space, dwindling instead of concluding. This diminishment is bad organization. Usually the dwindling can be cut, just as most bridges at the beginning can be removed. If the dwindling qualifies the conclusion, the qualification should come before the conclusion.

Endings, like beginnings, must serve their purpose. In a long complicated argument, we may be pleased to find at the end a succinct summary of the author's argument. It is like seeing an aerial photograph of country we have just walked through. But the short paper—the kind in which we are most interested in this book—rarely profits from summary and often withers by it. We should point the whole essay toward the last sentence, and when we have written it, stop writing. Often we conclude an essay and then continue writing. The essay writer must develop the confidence to let facts and arguments stand by themselves without epilogue. We should trust the intelligence of the reader. If the point has been clearly made, there is no gain from repeating it. People who moralize at the end of a story or summarize at the end of an argument are the same people who kill jokes by explaining them. In a report about Tracy Kidder's *The Soul of a New Machine*, which recounts the invention of a computer called "Eagle," a student concluded:

> Kidder makes an adventure story out of unlikely materials, the marriage of business and technology, the interrelationships of a corporation and its research engineers. Both in the book and in the marketplace, the Eagle flies.

Unfortunately, this student felt the need to continue after her conclusion:

> *The Soul of a New Machine*, by Tracy Kidder, is a book that tells a story both unusual and exciting.

Her paper improved when, at her instructor's suggestion, she revised by crossing out her final paragraph.

Usually we should conclude a topic without seeming to draw attention to the conclusion. Part of a paper's unity is the resolution it comes to, all details organized toward an end. But this resolution can be violated by obviousness; anything that feels tacked on destroys a sense of unity.

Joan Didion, in an essay called "On Going Home," writes about the fragmentation of American family life. Visiting her parents in the house where she grew up, she encounters familiar details of her old life. She feels that she was "born into the last generation to carry the burden of 'home'" and clearly finds a value in the burden. Her feelings are complex, and she ends her essay not by summarizing her feelings or reducing them to abstraction, but by turning to her own child and allowing her mixed feelings to show directly.

It is time for the baby's birthday party: a white cake, strawberry-marshmallow ice cream, a bottle of champagne saved from another party. In the evening, after she has gone to sleep, I kneel beside the crib and touch her face, where it is pressed against the slats, with mine. She is an open and trusting child, unprepared for and unaccustomed to the ambushes of family life, and perhaps it is just as well that I can offer her little of that life. I would like to give her more. I would like to promise her that she will grow up with a sense of her cousins and of rivers and of her great-grandmother's teacups, would like to pledge her a picnic on a river with fried chicken and her hair uncombed, would like to give her *home* for her birthday, but we live differently now and I can promise her nothing like that. I give her a xylophone and a sundress from Madeira, and promise to tell her a funny story.

> Joan Didion, in *Slouching Towards Bethlehem*

When Jim Beck first drafted his essay, he had no title and no ending. His last paragraph trailed off.

Sometimes when I cannot sleep I think about going back to Hammerton but I can't do that. Sometimes I think about getting a gold medal in the Olympics. Both of them are happy dreams except that I *know* I'm not Olympic class and if I went home it would be a disgrace to everybody. So all I am doing is sticking it out and hating every minute of it and hoping that things will get better sometime.

When he reconsidered his essay in terms of focus and thesis, he discovered his title by turning his actual running into a metaphor for his drive to get to college. Then he saw that by cutting and shaping his original last paragraph, he could make the paper's ending strike the reader and refer to the beginning without being obvious about it.

In my Senior year I was all-state and held two high-school records (600 and half-mile) and I had an athletic scholarship to the University. Now I am here, the first Beck to make it. I don't know why I'm here or why I ran so hard or where I go from here. Now that I am here, the race to get here seems pointless. Nothing in my classes interests me. I study, just as I did before, in order to pass the course or even get a good grade. I run to win, but what am I running for? I will never be a great runner. Sometimes when I cannot sleep I imagine packing my bags and going back to Hammerton. But I can't do that. They would say, "He's a Beck, all right."

Reading these last words we feel a satisfying sense of completion—or closure—which is partly determined by the echo of what we recall from the beginning. A subtle hint is all it takes, though; if the connection is made too obvious we may feel that we are being manipulated.

Revising and Invention

Usually it takes several drafts to arrive at an essay that is worth finishing. Later in this chapter we will follow a student through typical changes. We have already looked at Jim Beck proceeding from an impromptu to a finished essay. Often we will need to revise our first draft in major ways, for focus and clarity, removing some paragraphs and adding others, altering the order of details or paragraphs, developing and expanding. Finally, if we are persistent, we will accomplish a draft which is almost there—a roughly finished object which we may now polish and perfect.

In the next chapters we will concentrate on words, sentences, and paragraphs, providing tools for final revisions. But in this chapter on Writing an Essay, we must anticipate some advice. In revising, as in composing, we must invent. But in order to revise we must find fault with what we have written, and it is difficult to find faults that we have just committed. As the cliché would have it, we can't see the forest for the trees. If we have started writing our paper early enough, we can put time between the latest draft and the final revision; nothing is so helpful as a night's sleep.

First, we should check the drafted paper against the teacher's assignment; it is easy to drift away from original intentions. Second, it helps if we make a checklist of our own typical errors—we can collect them from our teachers' corrections on old papers so that we can be on guard against them. Spelling? Look up every word that seems doubtful. Incomplete sentences? Comma splices or run-on sentences? Parts of sentences not going together? Check the review chapter (pp. 367–406). Examine the length of your paragraphs. Have you denied your reader the pause of paragraph breaks? Or have you made your paragraphs too short, only three or four lines long? Look at your paper for its sentence structure. Many beginners make their papers boring by using too many simple or compound sentences in a row; their prose can start to sound childish. Vary sentence length and complexity. Try reading your words out loud to see what kind of rhythm they make. Would a longer sentence with subordinate clauses (see pages 152–153) offset the staccato sound of simple assertions? The ear, like the mind, must be kept alert. Experiment with different possibilities.

At the suggestion of your instructor, it may be useful at this time to get together with one or two other members of the class, to read each other's drafts and criticize each other. You can provide examples of audience for each other—models, anticipations.

Finally, look closely at your prose for clichés and empty expressions. Summon the Critic Inside for internal dialogue. A cliché discovered is an opportunity for new invention. If you have written that

something is the *basic foundation* of something else, and you detect the
cliché *basic foundation,* consider what kind of building-base you are
talking about. Is the *basic foundation* made of granite? Concrete block?
Cinder block? Frozen baloney? Empty expressions give us the same
opportunity. If you have written that a teacher was *awfully nice,* as
critic you should cross it out; then as inventor you should fill the empty
space. You should invent, out of memory, a detail or a story or a fresh
expression or some quoted speech that *shows* the quality which *awfully nice* tried to *tell.*

A Note on Impromptus

This survey of essay writing emphasizes preparation over several
days and advises sleeping on ideas, brainstorming, sprinting, cross-
examining, daydreaming, drafting, and revising. It is good to have the
time to follow these steps. But sometimes in the real world we are
required to write thirty-minute essays on final exams or to put a letter
in the mail by five o'clock—or to write an impromptu paper in an
English class with only forty minutes for invention, drafting, self-
criticism, and revision. We are unlikely to be able to sleep on an impromptu, much as we might like to. Nor are we able to spend much
time brainstorming, sprinting, or consulting the Critic Inside. This
chapter's advice is still useful, however, even when time is short.

The components of invention, organization, drafting, and revision
remain the same whether we have a week or a quarter hour. If our time
is brief, all components are reduced in length, and we must remember
to follow our habitual methods *in proportion.* If we have learned to
spend half of our time in preparation and half in execution, we should
keep the same proportion when we find ourselves with forty minutes
instead of four days. Many beginners make the mistake of changing
their methods entirely, feeling so cramped for time that they try to
write a final draft right away. The result is panic, and a messy product.

If we have forty minutes, we should spend twenty minutes
thinking and organizing and twenty minutes writing and correcting.
Try brainstorming a list; try sprinting one small paragraph; circle the
most inventive idea, make another list, and organize it into an informal
outline. Try daydreaming the Critic Inside for a minute or two. Try
remembering the responses of other students to your earlier writing; if
there were ways you missed your audience earlier, these are ways to
watch out for. We should do everything we would do at our desks over
an optimal period—only squeeze the time.

Writing an impromptu in the time remaining, we should write
slowly and deliberately, crossing out and correcting—but be legible. If
we write on alternate lines of lined paper, when we spend the last

minutes revising we can add missing phrases or sentences in the blank lines.

BIOGRAPHY OF A THEME

Frank Rodriguez took composition in the second term of his freshman year in 1989, doing daily writing, exercises in and out of class, and an essay a week. His first grades frustrated him: a C minus, a D, and a C minus minus. When he was assigned a fourth paper, he decided to get an early start and try the suggestions for getting ideas and for inventive revising that his teacher had made and that he found in his textbook.

Frank's instructor assigned the paper on a Monday, due one week later. This time, the instructor said, his students should write about something besides their own experiences. They had been writing personal narratives, trying to make their own actions and feelings clear to an audience. For this paper they should attempt more objectivity; in pursuit of that objectivity, their instructor asked them to write a five-hundred-word essay making use of comparison and contrast.

The class asked questions. The instructor referred his students to a definition of comparison and contrast (pp. 269–273). He reminded them that an essay must be governed by its purpose and that therefore they must find a comparison which could legitimately make a point, fulfill a purpose. Frank raised his hand; if they were not to write out of personal experience, he asked, how were they supposed to know what they were talking about? His instructor replied that the assignment did not prohibit writing about something they had experienced; the challenge was to be objective about it, to avoid subjectivity or autobiographical narrative. Don't tell us your feelings about the election of 1990 or what you did on Election Day; tell us what happened in the election of 1990.

Frank walked from class to dormitory to kill an hour before lunch. He started jotting ideas for paper topics on the inside cover of his daily writing notebook:

> Hot Dogs Boiled and Grilled
> McDonald's versus the Hamburger

He must have been hungry. In the dormitory lounge, someone was playing solitaire. Frank's list continued:

> To Cheat or Not to Cheat at Cards—or Solitaire?

He opened his daily writing and glanced over the twenty-four filled-up pages about hitchhiking to Arizona, about playing defensive tackle in high school, about an old girlfriend, about a poly sci class, about rock climbing, about loyalty, friendship, and two old friends. All of it was autobiographical. Maybe he could write objectively about rock climbing. . . . But comparison and contrast? He tried rapidly brainstorming a list:

> washouts
> vegetation: don't grab!
> Arizona vs. Massachusetts
> equipment: shoes
> seasons
>   fall
>   summer
>   spring
>   winter tough
> park rangers
> bear tracks
> other animals

Lunch was approaching fast; he closed his notebook, aware that most of this list led to personal anecdotes out of his own experience. . . . Possibly *"Arizona vs. Massachusetts"* could lead to an objective comparison and contrast of terrain, difficulty, and equipment needed. He circled *"Arizona vs. Massachusetts."*

After lunch he did a two-hour chemistry lab, and while he performed mechanical tasks, his mind returned to rock climbing and flitted over several other topics as well, like the *objective* boredom of Chemistry 101. When the lab was over, he stopped in the lounge again before going up to his room. The television set was on, one student watching late afternoon reruns on a UHF channel. He was surprised to see the old situation comedy *Hogan's Heroes* still on the air. Frank saw Colonel Klink humiliate Sergeant Schultz and suddenly found himself thinking how different *Hogan's Heroes* was from *M*A*S*H*—and pulled out his chemistry notebook to take notes for five hundred words of comparison and contrast on two television comedies with a background of war.

> *Hogan* childish
> unrealistic
> watching after school with Kenny
> *M*A*S*H* real war, blood, death
> *Hogan*—no dead?
> *M*A*S*H* real
> *Hogan*—beautiful women spies
> Germans WWII/Koreans

Germans always stupid, play tricks on
in *Hogan* everybody same
M∗A∗S∗H characters change
Audience *Hogan* kids? *M∗A∗S∗H* grown-ups?
Hogan impossible

When he ran out of thoughts, it was almost time for supper, and then Frank studied for a history quiz and played Ping-Pong for an hour. Just before going to bed, he looked at his notes again. He felt uncertain that he could compare the shows at all—they were so different. Did he have anything to say? Was there any purpose to comparing them? He did not know. How could he find a thesis or focus when he chose to compare marshmallows with circuses? He did not know. He went to bed telling himself that he would look at his notes in the morning.

In the morning before breakfast, he opened his daily writing note-book and wrote for five minutes without pausing to think:

> *Hogan's Heroes* was a rerun when I first heard of it—1973? I was five—when I came in from playing after school it was on at four-thirty or so and I watched it every afternoon with Kenny who was about three and a half or four and we both laughed at it until we were sick, Shulze (?) especially who Hogan always convinced of anything he wanted to, and Klink was just as stupid as Schultz—like recess!! G.I. Joe doll on TV ads. It's lousy when you think about it that kids got an idea of war from *Hogan's Heroes* . . .

After breakfast and poly sci, in the library before chemistry lecture, he read over his rapid paragraph and circled "like recess" and the word "war." Then he wrote one final sentence: "Instead of the reality of war, *Hogan's Heroes* was just like babies." Then he tried sprinting on *M∗A∗S∗H*.

> I never saw the movie *M∗A∗S∗H*—it's the TV show I'm comparing *Hogan* to. No comparison? *M∗A∗S∗H* is funny, not mostly about the war but you never completely forget that the war is there all the time, with all the blood in the operating room. The people are real. Realistic. They don't just say funny things all the time. People die on it, in the hospital and off-camera in accidents or the war. Its still going so I can watch it this week, maybe reruns too. They all want to get home—guy who wears women's clothes? Klinker?—Always two plots going at once.

That night he set aside an hour to work on his paper. In his second paragraph, he circled "Always two plots" and "People die" and wrote this sentence: "Using two plots at once helps *M∗A∗S∗H* be real, with real ups and downs, death and comedy." Then he wrote another five-minute sprint:

M∗A∗S∗H is more serious than most sitcoms I guess. There
are always (?) two stories flipping back and forth in every episode,
maybe one of them more serious and the other one just funny. They
always have the other plot to fall back on when things get too
serious or sad. But it is funny. I remember watching it every afternoon for two weeks on vacation and laughing myself silly. I think
the *words* are funny in *M∗A∗S∗H*, I mean not just what you see but
the way they say things. How to compare the two things? *Hogan* is
all one way, all jokes like the Three Stooges—The only thing not
jokey is the danger—will they get away with it again?—and even
when you're a baby you know that they will. In *M∗A∗S∗H* you don't
know because sometimes somebody dies—a patient or once the old
Colonel in a plane crash . . .

He circled "*Hogan* is all one way" and "two stories flipping back
and forth." He hoped he might be coming to a focus for his paper. Trying
to make the point in one sentence, he wrote:

Hogan's Heroes is childish and simpleminded in its humor but
M∗A∗S∗H tries to bring in more of life in all it's complexity.

He tried again.

In *Hogan's Heroes*, a whole show serves one purpose which is
comedy appealing on a low level but *M∗A∗S∗H* is adult and tries to
show the dark side of life as well as . . .

He tried again.

M∗A∗S∗H is comedy for adults, because although it is funny it
tries to show the complexity of war and human feelings. *Hogan's
Heroes* is simply comedy, with no attempt to be realistic about war
or . . .

He stopped because he realized he was about to begin a draft of his
paper, and he did not feel ready to begin. For one thing, although the
contrast was clear and becoming clearer, he was not sure that he had
found a purpose for making the contrast. How could he find a thesis to
support or a single focus to develop? He could contrast apples and
oranges—clearly enough—but what good would it do? Yet he had the
notion that if he continued to think he would discover a purpose.

He tried the journalist's six questions: Who? What? When?
Where? Why? How? *Who* should include the names of characters. *What*
was the body of his paper, to define the programs by comparison and
contrast; should he say what a situation comedy is? *When* was the dates
of programming, which he must somehow discover; or it was the set-
tings of World War II and the Korean War. *Where* seemed irrelevant,
except as Germany and Korea, which were also *When. Why* was difficult; how could he decide the motives of television networks? Maybe

Why would be a clue to his purpose. *How* was like *What*—how the plotting and structure of each series contrasted.

He decided to try to organize his ideas by listing topics he might cover, in some sort of order—an informal outline. Then he realized that he lacked information he needed—especially dates—and decided that he should gather everything together before trying to organize. Consulting a television schedule he discovered reruns of *M*A*S*H* on the same channel showing *Hogan's Heroes;* he could do his research in the dormitory lounge any afternoon. Watching reruns he could record the correct spellings of characters' names, and could use plots or lines of dialogue as details for his paper. But how could he discover the dates when the comedies started to broadcast, or when *Hogan's Heroes* stopped? He knew *approximately* when. If *Hogan's Heroes* was already a rerun by 1973, it must have started earlier, maybe in the sixties. Because he was occasionally allowed to stay up for the regular show, he remembered that it was still being broadcast new when he was in second grade; and he remembered staying up to watch *M*A*S*H*—he was almost positive—when he broke his arm in the sixth grade, in 1980. But being "almost positive" was not going to satisfy his English teacher; the word *vague* would fill the margin of his paper with red ink. He wondered if some encyclopedia could tell him what he needed to know.

For a moment it seemed that he might have to abandon a good comparison and contrast just because he lacked a couple of dates. Then he had a bright idea. The UHF channel broadcasting these reruns was only a few miles away. Frank looked up the call letters in the paper, found the channel listed in the telephone book under its call letters, and telephoned it. An obliging woman in public relations left the phone for a moment and returned to tell him that *Hogan's Heroes* had run from 1965 to 1971, and *M*A*S*H* had started broadcasting in 1972. Frank had seen its last program in February 1983. The woman at the TV station also answered his surprise by telling him that *Hogan's Heroes* still appeared regularly as of 1989 in every major American market on UHF; so did shows that started and ended on regular network television even earlier, like *I Love Lucy* and *The Honeymooners.*

Now he was ready. Using the lists and paragraphs he had generated, Frank sketched a preliminary organization for his paper.

1. Sitcoms, war comedies, network
2. Watching *Hogan*, watching *M*A*S*H*
3. Definition of *Hogan*
4. Definition of *M*A*S*H*
5. Similarities
6. Obvious differences

7. Wars
8. Attitudes to war
9. Kinds of humor
10. Characters
11. Plot
12. Examples
13. Conclusion—childhood and maturity?

He put numbers in the margins of his notes that corresponded with the numbers on his informal outline. He set his notes on his desk in a semicircle around a fresh pad of paper and began writing a first draft.

> The situation comedy television show gets its humor from a continuing set of characters in the same place with a plot which begins and ends in each episode.
>
> When I was about seven I watched a situation comedy called *Hogan's Heroes* every day when I came home from school. For a long time I thought it was the funniest thing I had ever seen, it was slapstick like a cartoon more than it was like a movie, with Germans being fooled all the time by Americans in a prison camp. My brother who was only three and a half laughed as much as I did, which shows the level it was on.
>
> I don't remember when I saw *M*A*S*H* first. I think it was partly over my head when I first saw it, because it was about things that are over your head when you are ten years old. But as I got older— and it was on reruns in the afternoon—I got to love it and really appreciate it . . .

Frank stopped writing. He realized he was describing himself, not *Hogan's Heroes* or *M*A*S*H*, and this paper was supposed to be objective. It was a false start. Even the first paragraph, which was at least objective, was a waste of time; to compare two television shows, he did not really need to define *situation comedy* any more than he needed to define *television*. He decided to start again on a fresh page.

Two War Shows

> Two television situation comedies have war in the background. *Hogan's Heroes* was on from 1965 to 1971. *M*A*S*H* was in 1972 and only stopped in 1983. Each of them is funny although there backgrounds are killing. The two programs sound just alike but they are totally different in every way.
>
> All you have to do is watch *Hogan's Heroes* once or twice and we can tell what will happen next. An American in a prison camp makes a fool out of the Germans. They believe everything he says. He gets away with it every time and he never gets caught.
>
> *M*A*S*H* is different. It is in the Korean War. Its stars are doctors and nurses. Its got two plots usually in each episode. Something like

life and death contrasted with something silly. *M*A*S*H* is called a comedy but it has everything in it, all kinds of feelings.

Hogan's characters are always the same and the German officers are always stupid. *M*A*S*H*'s humor is not childish but wise-cracks.

In *Hogan's Heroes* war is an easy game which the good guys always win. In *M*A*S*H*, war is hell and the show's stars hate it.

Frank stopped without an ending. At least he had started.

He picked up his draft a day and a half after putting it down.

It was terrible. It was too short. It was thin. It said nothing. His paper had no hint of a purpose. As his teacher had written about his earlier papers, it was vague and general, without detail or development. It had no shape of thought, he decided, because it had no thought. As for audience, he had not even thought about it. Discouraged, he was tempted for a moment to give up, just to copy it out and hand it in. But he hated to give up like that. With a deep sigh, he picked up what he had written and started to read it over slowly. This time as he read, he pretended to be his own teacher, the Critic Inside, and wrote in the margin his own nasty comments to himself. *What movie!* he wrote beside the first paragraph. Next to "they are totally different in every way," he wrote, *Says nothing.* When he found himself saying both "you" and "we" in the second paragraph, he wrote, *Make up your mind. Thin*, he wrote halfway down the page. When he read the third paragraph, he wrote, *What's M*A*S*H mean? What's it about?*

Beside every paragraph he questioned himself on detail. *Who? Like what?* He changed punctuation here, altered a word there—but concentrated mostly on structure and detail. When he came to the end, he wrote a new paragraph that just entered his head:

> The differences between the two shows must be because of one thing in particular. *Hogan's Heroes* started before most Americans even knew about the Vietnam War. By the time *M*A*S*H* started in 1972, after the protest movement in the United States, Americans were ready for a television show that was against the war.

He sat back: he did not yet have a paper, but he had thought of an answer to the journalist's *Why*. He had found a purpose for his comparison and contrast, and as soon as he recognized it, he realized that it had been there all the time, waiting for him to see it. He always knew that his high school course Social Issues in Contemporary History would come in handy.

Now Frank began his most difficult draft. He had assembled and roughed out his material; he had a comparison and contrast which led to a conclusion, which served a purpose. Now, with the help of his critical notions about his first draft, he would write a version that would do what he wanted it to do. He would concentrate on detail, on organization, and on making better sentences.

This time he wrote in less of a hurry, because he was more confident of where he was going. This time when he found a sentence going wrong, he crossed it out and tried again before he went further. When he needed to move from one subject to another, he experimented with transitions. Slowly, with much rewriting, searching for detail and color, trying to move gracefully between his two subjects, Frank drafted his theme. He did not rewrite his first draft so much as to write the theme over again from start to finish, with the Critic Inside's marginal questions as reminders. When he had finished this draft, he set it aside again; then on Saturday he revised yet again. Again the Critic Inside made marginal comments: *trans., fragment, Germans 3 times, more detail, parallel.* He repaired to satisfy the Critic Inside. Then he checked over the margins of his three earlier essays to list errors he was likely to make: comma splices, apostrophe with *it's,* repeated simple sentence structure, transitions, lack of detail, lack of color imagery. He made the list and returned to his essay—correcting, replacing, changing compound sentences into complex ones, adding an adjective, making a noun or a verb more particular. He had used *fool* twice as a verb for what Hogan did to his captors. He looked up *fool* in his *Roget's Thesaurus* and found "deceive, beguile, trick, hoax, dupe, gammon, gull, pigeon . . ."—and in a series of words and phrases near the end of the entry discovered for his purposes either *outwit* or *outsmart.*

On Sunday he went over his manuscript one more time, checking for mechanical errors and for spelling. Then he typed a clean copy, checked over his typing, and on Monday handed in his paper.

On these two pages are Frank Rodriguez's next-to-final draft, with the Critic Inside's marginal comments, and, on pages 82–83, his finished essay, on which he received his first A in freshman English.

	Two War Comedies	*boring title*
	Two television situation comedies, which	
unclear	are still seeable on afternoon re runs, have	
	war as a background. *Hogan's Heroes* orig-	
	inally showed in seasons from 1965 to	*awk.*
	1971.[footnote] *M*A*S*H* premiered in 1972	
short	and only stopped in 1983. Each makes	
sentences	jokes out of war. The two programs sound	
	similar. But they are as different as kinder-	
trans.	garten and college.	
	All you have to do is watch a few episodes	
you/we	of *Hogan's Heroes* and we can predict	
	a plot. An American colonel named Bob	
	Hogan is in a German prison camp during	

*German
3 times*

*longer
sentences*

trans. It?

not stars

how?

*detail
parallel?*

repeats

*revise
parallels*

rewrite

*trans.?
repeats—
"Changing
channels—"*

logic?

World War II. He makes a scheme against the Germans. With other American prisoners, he fools the Germans. He flatters them and they believe him. Then something is going to spoil his plan—he wants to blow up a bridge for example—but he manages to get past the trouble and win. Every time.

But *M*A*S*H* is unpredictable. It stands for Mobile Army Surgical Hospital and it takes place during the Korean War. Its stars are doctors and nurses. When a doctor works over a wounded soldier, he may not live. *M*A*S*H* has two plots usually in each episode. Something like life and death contrasted with something like bathwater. *M*A*S*H* is called comedy but it mixes comedy and sadness, horror and laughs. In this mixture *M*A*S*H* shows its grown up.

Hogan's characters are always the same stereotypes. Hogan's flattery fools the German officers who are always stupid. We laugh as they trip and fall, or as Klink hits his head. We laugh at people as predictable as cartoons. In *M*A*S*H* on the other hand, there is a nurse we don't like because she is all for No. 1. But then we see she is human after all. *M*A*S*H*'s humor is not childish but wisecracks. Somebody tells a soldier who is toying with his dinner, "Don't pick at your food. It will never heal."

Perhaps the greatest contrast lies in realism. *Hogan's Heroes* uses war as a playground, with no sense of the horror of World War II—genocide and saturation bombing. On the other hand, *M*A*S*H*'s operating tables are covered with blood. In *Hogan's Heroes* war is an easy game which the good guys always win. In *M*A*S*H*, war is hell and the show's stars hate it.

The dates of the two series show why they are different. In the seven years between *Hogan's Heroes* of 1965 and *M*A*S*H* of 1972, America made its major commitment of troops to Vietnam. Tens of thousands of our soldiers died in the jungles. As a result, this country was torn apart by protests—many of them led by college students who grew up on *Hogan's Heroes*.

*more
particulars*

fragment

*make one
sentence*

*clarity
ambiguous*

*it's!
word?*

*so what?
other word?*

details

*more
detail*

names?

*what kind?
war*

heroes?

*one
sentence?*

*do you
know?*

Two Comedies, Two Wars, Two Worlds

You can watch reruns of both in the same afternoon, in many cities—two situation comedies with a background of war. Hogan's Heroes was produced from 1965 to 1971; M*A*S*H premiered in 1972* and only stopped filming in 1983. Each recounts humorous plots, in dialogue interrupted by ''canned'' laughter, although the reality behind each is tragic. Thus described, the two programs sound similar; but they are as different as kindergarten and college.

After we have seen a few episodes of Hogan's Heroes, we can predict each plot. An American colonel named Bob Hogan, incarcerated in a German prison camp during World War II, conceives an intrigue against his captors. With the aid of other allied and American prisoners, he outwits a stupid sergeant and a vain colonel, often by flattering them. Some accident seems to thwart his intention (for stealing plans, for blowing up a bridge) but he overcomes adversity and succeeds—in every episode.

The plots of M*A*S*H on the other hand are unpredictable. The show's initials stand for Mobile Army Surgical Hospital, it takes place during the Korean War, and its heroes are doctors and nurses. When a surgeon struggles to save a wounded soldier, we are not certain that the soldier will live. Usually, M*A*S*H works two plots against each other in each episode, something as serious as a soldier's life contrasted with something as frivolous as the availability of bathwater. Although M*A*S*H is called a comedy, it mixes laughter and tears, horror and happiness; in this mixture M*A*S*H shows its maturity and realism.

Hogan's characters never change, and its humor comes from exploiting stereotypes. Hogan's flattery manipulates the vain Colonel Klink and the gullible Sergeant Schultz to act against their own interests. We laugh as an officer of the Gestapo bumps his head; we laugh at characters as simple as cats and mice in Saturday cartoons. In M*A*S*H, on the other hand, we feel compassion for an apparently overambitious nurse (''Hotlips'') when she reveals her vulnerability. Humor in M*A*S*H is not childish slapstick but verbal wit; a surgeon (''Hawkeye'') speaks to a soldier (''Radar'') who is depressed and toying with his dinner: ''Don't pick at your food. It will never heal.''*

Perhaps the greatest contrast lies in the realism of the war used as backdrop. In Hogan's Heroes, World War II is a playground; there is no genocide, no saturation bombing. Switching channels, M*A*S*H's operating tables are red with American and Korean blood. In Hogan's Heroes the good guys always win and no one dies. In M*A*S*H, war is hell and the show's protagonists hate it.

* Dates supplied by public relations at Channel WYBS.
* Heard on rerun, February 3.

Perhaps the dates of the two series reveal the reason for the difference. In the seven years between the start of <u>Hogan's Heroes</u> in 1965 and M*A*S*H in 1972, America committed a huge army to Vietnam, tens of thousands of our soldiers died in the jungles, and this country was torn apart by antiwar protests—many of them led by college students who must have watched <u>Hogan's Heroes</u> as children.

—— **EXERCISES** ——————————————————————

1. In class, imitate collectively how we choose a subject and narrow a topic. Narrow these general subjects into topics.

drug testing	environmental pollution
the plight of the aged	alternate energy sources
the Saturday-night special	women's athletic programs
coming to college	college admissions policies

Some subjects are broader than others, but all can be narrowed further.

2. In class, brainstorm details for a paper on a recent local controversy. (Look at the editorial page of the local paper for some ideas.) Then try to organize the details, using the blackboard. Or take the details home and elaborate and organize them for the next class.

3. Write a paragraph rapidly (sprint) in class, taking as a starting point one of the topics listed in question 1. Read the paragraph aloud for class discussion. Which sentence or phrase would profit from expansion and development?

4. (a) On your own, work up an idea that might be developed into a theme. (b) Accumulate details, brainstorming or sprinting if you wish. (c) Organize details, eliminating those which seem irrelevant, tailoring your material to your purpose. (d) Bring all material to class. Students can read their material one at a time for general discussion. Or the instructor may want to collect the material and copy some of it to use in the next class meeting.

The instructor may also ask one student to outline his or her topic for the rest of the class. Students will then have twenty minutes to sprint impromptu paragraphs. These may be compared and discussed.

5. Here is a student essay. (a) Does this essay answer the journalist's six questions? (b) How well does this student accomplish comparison and contrast? Might questions of form have helped this student revise? Does the theme show a purpose? Is it addressed to an audience? (c) Pretending that you are a teacher, correct this paper in the margins. Give it a grade. (d) Revise and improve one of the paragraphs of this essay.

Night and Day
Betty Hampers

There is a small ski area about five miles away from my home town of Easthampton, Massachusetts, called the Mt. Tom Ski Area. Besides its excellent slopes and trails, Mt. Tom is the only ski resort in my neighborhood that offers both night and day skiing. Although night skiing is convenient and fun, there are many advantages to skiing during the day.

One annoying problem that can be avoided by skiing during the day is the large crowds. In the daytime, most people are in school or working and therefore, aren't able to go skiing. That means the parking facilities are less crowded and the lift lines are shorter, giving you more time on the ski slopes. Usually the conditions of the mountain are best during the daytime. The surface powder is still deep and fluffy. At night, the slopes often become icy because the deep powder has been worn away.

Also, feeling the sun's warmth as you glide down the slopes makes daytime skiing quite enjoyable. When the sun is warm, you can shed some of those layers of clothing. Who knows, maybe you'll even get a suntan!

With all that daytime skiing has to offer, there are still some disadvantages. For example, because your friends are either in school or working, you have to ski alone. Skiing just isn't as much fun unless you have a friend to fall down and look like a fool with! The view when riding the chairlift is much more glamorous at night than in the day. The bluegreen and white lights you see from above look like the flashing eyes of some Hollywood monster.

However, I still haven't mentioned safety, the most important advantage to skiing during the day. In the daytime, the trails are much more visible. At night, they are dimly lit and can be dangerous if you're not careful. In case of injury, it is much easier to locate an emergency telephone than it is at night. For these reasons alone, I feel that daytime skiing is best.

6. Which of these beginnings are interesting and which seem potentially boring? Why? How might different purposes be served by different beginnings?

   a. When the United Nations met in September, its members were already agitated, anxious, and almost apoplectic.
   b. The origins of the missile crisis are already well known to the informed reading public.
   c. Bang!
   d. When I was born I lived in Cleveland. Then my family moved to Akron when I was two years old. After that we moved to Muncie, Indiana.
   e. The goat had three eyes.

7. Revise this beginning:

Every Easter we drove to my great Aunt's house in Troy to eat a ham for Easter dinner. Even when my father was a little boy, they had gone to Troy for Easter. Sometimes it would snow and we would be late. Once we blew a tire about half way, and the spare was soft, and we took at least an hour and a half to get it fixed.

Last year was my Senior year in high school, and my great aunt thought graduating from high school was a big deal, so I knew I would get a lot of attention when I got there. We have to pack because we actually stay over Friday and Saturday nights. Fortunately, for some reason, I packed my tennis shoes and my jeans. If I hadn't, I wouldn't have been able to play touch football decently, I wouldn't have wound up in the emergency ward, and I wouldn't have met Linda.

8. Consulting the margins of essays your teacher has returned with corrections, make a checklist of repeated errors. Bring it to class or conference to see if your instructor agrees with your self-assessment. Use your revised list when you write your next paper.

9. Correct Frank Rodriguez's draft on pages 78–79.

10. Here is another essay in two drafts. The next-to-last draft is followed by the last draft. Notice differences between the two versions. Is the last draft better? Why? Find faults in the earlier draft that are repaired in the final. Is the final perfect, or can you find ways to improve it? Consider the two versions, thinking of purpose and audience.

Two Wheels Are Better Than Four
Sharon Rustig

Bikes are better than cars, at least on this campus. Although cars protect you against bad weather, and take you on long trips, they cannot compare with bikes for practical daily use. You can pedal from dorm to class, lock up outside the door, and backpack your books upstairs—ten minutes from bed to classroom! If you have an hour's break between classes, you can go back to your room instead of wasting your time hanging around the hallways. Or you can zip downtown and do an errand and zip back to your next class.

But with a car, you would get to class half an hour late, because you couldn't find a place to park. If you park legally, you feed a meter. If you park illegally, you feed more than that. If your car is towed away from a no-parking area, you may pay as much as thirty dollars to get it back again. And not only parking is expensive, in connection with cars. Automobile insurance if you are student age will cost you practically as much as tuition. Gasoline has become expensive and is liable to get more so by the end of the year.

Bikes are better, not only because they are more efficient in getting you from place to place, and not only because they are cheaper, but because they're good for your body. They give you good exercise, especially if you live on a hill. Most students don't do much exercise, and just sit around getting flabby, so a bike is good for your health as well as everything else. The only bad things about bikes are their habit of getting stolen, but this works out for health too. You toughen up your neck muscles by riding around with a ten pound bike chain for a necklace.

But I haven't said the most important reason that bikes are better than cars. Cars use up petroleum which is in short supply. Bikes use up nothing but the bike riders' excess fat. Car exhaust pollutes the atmosphere and causes respiratory diseases. Bicycles exhaust nobody except the rider. Ecology makes the final reason why a bike is better than a car.

Two Wheels Are Better Than Four—Number Two
Sharon Rustig

On a large residential campus, like the University of Michigan's, bicycles suit the needs of students more than automobiles do. Buicks and Chevrolets are useful for long trips, or as protection against bad weather, but the daily advantages of Schwinn or Raleigh are far greater. Bicycles save students time; from dormitory to classroom, bike rack to bike rack, will take only five or ten minutes. If students have an hour between classes, they can pedal to the library, lock up, and spend forty minutes in a book on Library Reserve. Or they can do an errand at a nearby store, and return to the classroom in time for the next lecture.

On the other hand, if students were driving an automobile, these alternatives would not be available. Parking makes the difference. Starting out for class, they would need to allow an extra half hour to look for a parking space. They would need to walk to the library or the store, because they would not be able to count on finding a second or a third parking space. On this campus, cars parked illegally are ticketed and towed, which wastes the student not only time but money. The bicycle, which saves the student parking fines, saves the cost of gasoline as well, and the immense expense of insurance. The practicality of bicycles includes the economy of student finance, as well as the economy of student time.

There is also the economy of student health. Most students work hard at their books, and relax by sitting with their friends at taverns. The student body gets no exercise at all. But the bicyclist uses muscles otherwise unused, and adds to health while subtracting the waste of money and time. The only waste connected with bicycle riding is the epidemic of bicycle thievery; a stout chain prevents theft—and, worn around the neck, contributes to the health of the rider's neck muscles.

Finally, automobiles are detrimental to the health, not only of the sedentary student, but of everyone in the community. It is clear that bicycles are preferable to cars on this campus for purely practical or utilitarian reasons. But we should always ride bicycles, or walk, whenever we can, if an automobile can be avoided. Not only is the world's supply of energy diminishing, requiring us to conserve what energy we can, but the expense of that energy in car exhaust is a present danger to everyone alive. Pollution from carbon monoxide causes respiratory disease. Conservation and ecological danger make it imperative that all of us make use of two wheels rather than four.

4

Words

THE SMALLEST UNIT

When we study writing we learn to swim by jumping into the lake; some of us swallow much lake water before we paddle to shore. How do we learn to write a paper of five paragraphs when we don't know what a paragraph is? How do we write a paragraph out of seven sentences when the concept of "sentence" remains fuzzy? With writing as with many endeavors, we start at the end because it is the only place where we can make a beginning. We must try everything at once. After we have made a start, only then is it possible to return to beginnings. Now we attend to words, sentences, and paragraphs. Presumably the student comes to this section after writing several essays. In this section we look at the smaller units of writing with the notion that, having sketched out some larger shapes, we can concentrate on language for a while.

THE INSIDES OF WORDS

Words Themselves

It may seem difficult, at first, to think of words apart from contexts; *salt* does not stand alone; it is part of "salt and pepper" or "Please pass the salt." Words seem like drops of water in a stream that has its own wholeness and its own motion. But when you write well, each word is accurate and honest and exact in itself, and contributes its special history to the wholeness of the stream of meaning.

The writer must be able to feel words intimately, one at a time. He must also be able to step back, inside his head, and see the flowing sentence. But he starts with the single word. He starts with tens of thousands of these units, and he picks among them. He may end by writing a passage like this account of man's first sleep on the moon:

> It was almost three-thirty in the morning when the astronauts finally prepared for sleep. They pulled down the shades and Aldrin stretched out on the floor, his nose near the moon dust. Armstrong sat on the cover of the ascent engine, his back leaning against one of the walls, his legs supported in a strap he had tied around a vertical bar. In front of his face was the eyepiece of the telescope. The earth was in its field of view, and the earth, "like a big blue eyeball" stared back at him. They could not sleep. Like the eye of a victim just murdered, the earth stared back at him.
>
> Norman Mailer, *Of a Fire on the Moon*

Until the end, this exposition seems simple and straightforward. Simple and straightforward it is, with the power of visual exactness, "his nose near the moon dust," and the unexpected detail, "a strap he had tied around a vertical bar." Mailer cements each word in place exactly and inevitably, with the help of rhythm and sentence structure. For now, just look at how he prepares for the last, emotional image with related words.

This passage, and much of Mailer's book, is about man and machine. The machinery is sophisticated, complex, overwhelming. Men are frail in comparison. The language begins to embody this idea by repeating the names of parts of the body: *nose, back, legs, face.* We have become accustomed to the jerking motions of the puffed-up spacesuits, as if we were watching robots. Now suddenly we see *nose* and *face.* We might be a mother looking at a sleeping child. From *face* we move to the must vulnerable and necessary of sense organs, the *eye,* first by way of a telescope's *eyepiece,* then by a visual comparison, easy to follow, of the earth to a *big blue eyeball,* which stares. We have departed from the astronauts' bodies and moved on to the emotional crux: the earth is dead, murdered by the astronauts who leave it behind for another destination, beginning the exploration outward, into the stars. Mailer makes his point not by telling us about it overtly, but by his control of language, his understanding of the insides of words, so that the movement from *nose* to *face* to *eyepiece* and *view* to *victim just murdered* —in each case a distancing movement—has an inner and emotional necessity.

> All the warm night the secret snow fell so adhesively that every twig in the woods about their little rented house supported a tall slice of white, an upward projection which in the shadowless gloom

of early morning lifted depth from the scene, made it seem Chinese, calligraphic, a stiff tapestry hung from the gray sky, a shield of lace interwoven with black thread.

John Updike

This sentence begins a short story called "The Crow in the Wood." Updike exercises the possibilities of our language in rhythm, in variety of sentence structure, and in observation that is dreamy and precise at the same time. He does it with words. Instead of looking at everything he does, let us look at two words that stand out. *Adhesively* is a word we all know, from the noun or adjective *adhesive*, as a longer way of saying *glue* or *sticky*. Here the snow "fell . . . adhesively." Snow really cannot fall like glue, and so we have something apparently inaccurate; yet it is right, because the context prepares us. It is a *warm night*; the snow will be damp. And using *adhesively* rather than *stickily* shows that the snow is not gooey to the fingers, but will readily adhere to something. What's more, the word's four measured syllables give us a sensation of slowness—we can feel the steady downward motion of the snow. *Adhesively* by its unusualness draws the right attention to itself.

Then look at the word *slice*: "every twig . . . supported a tall slice of white." Most of us would have said something about snow *piling* or *accumulating* on branches. But a "tall slice of white," besides being pleasing to the ear, is a brilliant image; the sharpness of *slice*, together with the image of whiteness, nearly dazzles the eye. With the word *slice* is an unspoken knife, just out of sight. And I think we have a moment's vision of an upright piece of white-frosted cake.

We could pick many more words for praise in the passages from Mailer and Updike, and maybe for blame as well (we will do that later). But the excellence here is perhaps like all excellence. These writers are *original, as if seeing a thing no one else has seen*; yet they report their vision in a *language that reaches the rest of us*. Here, again, we find the opposites we must combine. For the first quality, writers need imagination and freshness of perception; for the second, skill. Without both qualities, they could not write such a passage. Imagination without skill makes a lively chaos; skill without imagination, a deadly order.

4 No Synonyms

To appreciate the word—the *eyepiece*, the *eyeball*, the *slice*, the *adhesively*—writers and readers must first realize that no words can be exact synonyms. Some words are close to each other in meaning, close enough to reveal that they are not the same. Writers must know not just the surface definitions of words; they must go deeper and realize the families of contexts into which words have extended their associations—like *slice* with *knife* and even *cake*. These families are the connotations of the word and the associations we make with its denotation. We use *denotation* to mean the explicit or literal meaning of a word, *connotation* to mean a word's implications. The verb *to stagger* denotes an unsteady or irregular motion; one of its connotations is drunkenness. Associations are different from connotations. *Pepper* is not a connotation of *salt*, but an association of it. Because we use the whole family, it does not matter that we discriminate connotation from association. But we must know the insides of words; we must be a friend of the family.

The verbs *to emulate, to imitate, to copy,* and *to ape* are synonyms by definition, but when we use them in a sentence, they carry slight differences in meaning. *To emulate* sounds fancy; also, it usually implies that the imitation involves self-improvement. *To imitate* is neutral, except that everyone knows that an imitation is not the real thing; inferiority shadows the word. *To copy* is to reproduce exactly; like *to imitate*, it states a lack of originality. *To ape* is mimic, and to be comical or mocking about it. If you wanted to say that a young pianist imitated a famous virtuoso, but you carelessly used *ape* instead of *imitate*, you would grant her style the grace of a gorilla. Context is all; the inside of a word must reinforce or continue the force built by the context. When a sportswriter wrote that one middle linebacker aped another middle linebacker, he was being witty.

Dictionaries of synonyms and other books, especially *Roget's Thesaurus*, list words that resemble each other. Experienced writers can sometimes use a thesaurus to joggle their brain to find not a *synonym*, but the *right* word. They will be aware of the insides of the words they discover. The thesaurus can be useful not for supplying words never heard before (we know words only when we have met them in sentences; some dictionaries supply examples of words in use), but to remind writers of words known in the past, but not remembered when needed.

Sometimes an unsophisticated writer finds disaster in such a book. A thesaurus supplies us with words that *resemble* each other, but we must recognize the *differences* among them. When I look up *imitation* in my pocket *Roget*, I find under Verbs:

> imitate, copy, mirror, reflect, reproduce, repeat; do like, echo, re-echo, catch, match, parallel; forge, counterfeit.

> mimic, ape, stimulate, impersonate, act, etc. (drama), 599; represent, etc., 554; parody, travesty, caricature, burlesque, take off, mock, borrow.

> follow in the steps (or wake) of, take pattern by, follow suit [colloq.], follow the example of, walk in the shoes of, take after, model after, emulate.

The editors separate the verbs into three categories of association, which ought to help the cautious writer, but it is difficult sometimes to defend their sorting out. Why does *forge* or *counterfeit* belong among the closer synonyms in the first group and *emulate* among the phrases in the third group? Why is *represent* among the comic or belittling words? Putting *ape* with *travesty* and *parody*, however, reminds us of the comic insides of *ape*. Beginning writers should certainly be wary of a thesaurus, because if they believe too wholeheartedly in synonyms, they can produce a prose that means something completely different from what they intend. The sentence

> I walked in the flowers that bordered the garden, sniffing the sweet
> airs of spring.

could become

> I peregrinated in the flowerets that flounced the orangery, sniffing
> the saccharine ventilation of the vernal equinox.

Spoken by W. C. Fields, the second version could be perfect for its context, but otherwise it only makes sense as an example of how people misuse a thesaurus.

Using dictionary synonyms, you can test your sensitivity to the insides of words. Put the adjectives *false, fake, phony,* and *insincere* with the noun *laugh*. Everyone has heard laughs that were unreal, laughs for the sake of flattery, laughs that express the laugher's nervousness, or laughs at jokes that are not funny. If we wrote a description of such a laugh, we might want to write, "His laugh was false," or "His laugh was fake," or "His laugh was phony," or "His laugh was insincere." Each time the exact meaning differs. "His laugh was false" sounds direct and serious, a stern and objective judgment. "His laugh was fake" sounds harsher, a strong indictment of the laugher; it implies that the falseness was deliberate. "His laugh was phony" tells us more about whoever wrote the phrase. The choice of *phony* over *false* or *fake* or *insincere* makes the speaker imply something like, "I am relaxed enough to be slangy." On the other hand, "His laugh was insincere" sounds slightly pompous in its moral judgment—partly pompous, partly naïve.

These attempts to name the associations that words gather, without setting the context that story or essay bestows, are speculation; but, whatever the context, the words would all be different. Slightly, but genuinely, different. Katherine Anne Porter announced in 1961 that she had discovered "a law" that she put into "a little axiom":

> There is no such thing as an exact synonym and no such thing as an
> unmixed motive.

Literalness and Metaphor

Another way to become sensitive to the insides of words is to take them as literally as you can. When you read "Fog enveloped the city," try seeing a gigantic gray-brown envelope enclosing Los Angeles. You can see some silliness in literal images—but it is a silliness that can increase your sensitivity to words. Puns are another form of useful silliness. Punning is a relaxed playing with the sounds that sense is made of: words have meaning, but words also *halve* meaning.

Literal-mindedness, like all exercises that can improve your writing, can improve your reading as well. Literal-mindedness exposes mixed metaphors, careless phrases comparing things that are comic or gross or inappropriate when brought together. Metaphors usually become mixed when a writer uses the kind of clichés called "dead metaphors" without noticing their original meanings. Sometimes people write, "The door yawned open"; the would-be comparison of door to mouth is dead from overuse. Sometimes people write, "The door beckoned," and the dead metaphor has the door turn into a hand that gestures an invitation. Once a student wrote in a paper, "The door yawned and beckoned." Two clichés make a mixed metaphor, if we are carefully reading the insides of words: first the door is a huge, gaping mouth; suddenly an arm materializes between rows of teeth and motions us to enter.

When we take words literally, we respond to metaphor. We see the fog *compared* to an envelope. A metaphor is a comparison made without being stated. We *state a comparison* as a simile—"like a big blue eyeball"—and we *make* a comparison when we leave out *like* or *as*. Hamlet in his soliloquy wonders if he should "take arms against a sea of troubles," rather than against troubles as vast and overwhelming as the sea. It is futile to fight with the ocean. The futility is what Shakespeare had in mind. If you take the words literally, you might see an armored knight wading into the surf and slashing at the waves with his sword. The image shows an emotion that the abstract word *futility* would only name. The picture—which we receive by literal reading—gives us the emotion without losing the idea.

Sense Words

Words that carry feeling most strongly convey pictures and smells and touches and tastes and noises. Images are details of sense. The more sensuous words are, the more they reach us and move us. Updike embodies feelings of cozy shelter, and of precise observation of the outside world. He does not tell us how to feel, but he arranges the sense details so that we will supply the inner response ourselves. Mailer does something similar with ideas. He does not abstract them from the actions. When he gives us an exact visual image of the astronauts trying to sleep on the moon, he gets us to feel their cramp and discomfort without ever using those words. In the next paragraph, Mailer writes about the failure to sleep, and he writes ideas, but he uses images as well.

> It used to be said that men in the hour of their triumph knew the sleep of the just, but a modern view might argue that men sleep in order to dream, sleep in order to involve that mysterious theater where regions of the unconscious reach into communication with one another, and charts and portraits of the soul and the world outside are subtly retouched from the experience of the day.

"Theater," "charts," "portraits . . . retouched"—Mailer uses images to make his concept clear by a comparison. Not all writing can be sensuous and figurative—not every occasion will call for it—but most essays benefit tremendously from such attention. Of course, it is always possible to be safe and boring by stating only the facts, without images and feelings. Mailer could have said that the astronauts arranged themselves to go to sleep but couldn't, perhaps because so much had happened that day. Updike could have said that when his characters woke up, they discovered that it had snowed while they slept.

In his essay "Once More to the Lake," E. B. White needs to let his audience know that his son lacked experience of lakes; he therefore speaks of "my son, who had never had fresh water up his nose and who had seen lily pads only from train windows." Sense words *always* reach the reader with more strength than words of generality, like "lacked experience of lakes." The phrase "had fresh water up his nose" probably wakens a sharp sensation-memory in every reader.

Sense words carry feeling, and they fulfill purposes appropriate to different kinds of writing: for Mailer, the sense words embody a speculation; for Updike, they convey sensation to enhance the illusion of fiction. For Jane Addams, in this passage from *Twenty Years at Hull House*, images explain a scene at the same time as they express outrage over poverty in Victorian London:

> . . . On Mile End Road, from the top of an omnibus which paused at the end of a dingy street lighted by only occasional flares of gas, we saw two huge masses of ill-clad people clamoring around two hucksters' carts. They were bidding their farthings and ha'pennies for a vegetable held up by the auctioneer, which he at last scornfully flung, with a gibe for its cheapness, to the successful bidder. In the momentary pause only one man detached himself from the groups. He had bidden on a cabbage, and when it struck his hand, he instantly sat down on the curb, tore it with his teeth, and hastily

devoured it, unwashed and uncooked as it was. He and his fellows
. . . were huddled into ill-fitting, cast-off clothing, the ragged finery
which one sees only in East London. Their pale faces were domi-
nated by that most unlovely of human expressions, the cunning and
shrewdness of the bargain-hunter who starves if he cannot make a
successful trade, and yet the final impression was not of ragged,
tawdry clothing nor of pinched and sallow faces, but of myriads of
hands, empty, pathetic, nerveless, and workworn, showing white in
the uncertain light of the street, and clutching forward for food
which was already unfit to eat.

Notice that our sense of outrage, almost without exception, comes
from the images chosen; we are not *told*, except when she writes, "that
most unlovely of human expressions"; we are *shown*. If Addams used
only abstractions like *degradation* and *extreme poverty*, we could forget them easily; we do not forget the man who devours the cabbage
unwashed and uncooked or the hands clutching at inedible food.

Misusing the Insides of Words

Just as we can learn to embody feelings and sensations by being
aware of a word's associations and connotations and by using language
that appeals to the senses, so we can misuse words to fool ourselves and
other people. By misusing the insides of words, we are insincere. The
poet W. B. Yeats wrote, "The rhetorician would deceive his neighbors, /
The sentimentalist himself." A rhetorician, in his usage, is something
like a propagandist—one who manipulates words to achieve some end.
Sentimentality means cheap or exaggerated feeling, emotion that is not
genuine. Usually, the rhetorician who wishes to deceive others must
first become a sentimentalist who deceives himself. In the advertising
business, it is common wisdom that you have to *believe* in your product, so that grown people ride the commuter trains believing that Acme
is superior to all other toothpastes. To con others, you begin by conning
yourself, or you end that way.

Some propagandists deceive by will. The conscious manipulator
sets out to change minds by slanting words to *seem* objective and yet to
carry a disguised subjective content. News magazines (*Time, Newsweek, U.S. News & World Report*) generally serve specific corporate or
political interests. They are not neutral—what besides the naked fact *is*
neutral?—and often convey subtle editorial comment within their reporting. Newspapers do the same, though the best editors try to keep
the editorials editorial and the news objective. But even when you
appear objective, you can select with bias. One photograph of candidate
Y looks flattering; another makes him look like an ass.

We will never destroy bias, but we can learn to see bias, and not be deceived by reporting that is really editorializing. A few years back, one news magazine blatantly supported one presidential candidate. It openly supported him editorially. And in its news stories it supported him subtly, using the associations of words. Candidate A, it said, "in his rumpled suit slouched into the gleaming limousine." Candidate B, on the other hand, "strode smiling into his black sedan."

Now, a sedan may sound expensive, but it may also seem to suit the dignity required of a candidate for high office. *Gleaming limousine* is more lavish, more gloatingly rich. *Rumpled suit* and *smiling* are obvious contrasts. The most telling use of the loaded word is the contrast between *strode* and *slouched*. Who would vote for a man who slouched when he could pick one that strode instead? Yet in all fairness, can we say that the *news* in each sentence is different? In the flattest language, the sentence would read, "The man got in the car." The rhetoricians of the news magazine, playing upon the separation between meaning and expression, flash us the sign: "Vote for B!" Because they pretend to objectivity, their use of sense words to influence opinion is underhanded.

Rhetoricians and propagandists—"spin doctors" as they are sometimes called—manipulate language and images for a living. We know their motives. But what about the thousand-and-one deceptions we all practice in daily life, and the loaded words we kid ourselves with? We use euphemism to persuade ourselves that one thing is really another; a *janitor* cleans floors, but it sounds more lofty to call him a *custodian*. When we say that someone is *wealthy*, we avoid the plainer word *rich*, which has acquired overtones of vulgarity. If a real estate agent shows you a two-room shack converted from a chicken coop, he does not call it a *house*, he calls it a *home*. A Cadillac is never a *used car*; it is *previously owned*.

Often, a euphemism is more abstract or general than the plain word. The euphemism not only sounds fancier (mortician/undertaker; route salesman/milkman), but it has less color or imagery. H. L. Mencken, in *The American Language*, gave some historical background to American euphemisms.

The tendency to engaud lowly vocations with names presumably dignified goes back to the Revolution, and has been frequently noted by English travelers, beginning with Thomas Anburey in 1779. In 1784 John Ferdinand Dalziel Smyth observed that the smallest American shopkeepers were calling their establishments *stores*, which indicated a large place to an Englishman. "The different distinct branches of manufacturers," he said, "such as *hosiers, haberdashers, clothiers, linen drapers, grocers, stationers*, etc., are not known here; they are all comprehended in the single name and occupation of *merchant* or *storekeeper*." By 1846 the American barbershop had begun to be a *shaving salon* and by 1850 a photographer was a *daguerrian artist*. By 1875 barbers were *tonsorial artists* or *tonsorialists*, and in the early 80s presentable saloon keepers became *restauranters* or *restauranteurs*. By 1901 the *Police Gazette* was carrying on a campaign for the abandonment of the lowly *bartender* and the adoption of either *bar clerk* or *mixologist*.

But euphemism is not only comical. We employ euphemism, frequently, when we want to conceal something painful. When we have a tomcat castrated, we hesitate to admit that we have cut off his testicles or even that we have castrated him; we have had him *altered*. We have a tooth *extracted*; it would be more painful to have it *pulled*.

Politics and political acts of destruction always bring forth the worst in our prose, as we struggle to justify ourselves. Hitler euphemistically labeled his genocide of Jews "the final solution." The most massive outrage ever perpetrated is cloaked in the tidy neutrality of an abstract phrase. One of the finest essays on the deeper implications of style is George Orwell's "Politics and the English Language," written in the 1940s. He says:

> Millions of peasants are robbed of their farms and sent trudging along the roads with no more than they can carry: this is called *transfer of population* or *rectification of frontiers*. People are imprisoned for years without trial, or shot in the back of the neck or sent to die of scurvy in Arctic lumber camps; this is called *elimination of undesirable elements*. Such phraseology is needed if we want to name things without calling up mental pictures of them. Consider for instance some comfortable English professor defending Russian totalitarianism. [George Orwell was English and was writing after Stalin's execution of the Kulaks and the mass murders of the Soviet purges of the late thirties.] He cannot say outright, "I believe in killing off your opponents when you can get good results by doing so." Probably, therefore, he will say something like this:
>
> "While freely conceding that the Soviet regime exhibits certain features which the humanitarian may be inclined to deplore, we must, I think, agree that a certain curtailment of the right to political opposition is an unavoidable concomitant of transitional periods, and that the rigors which the Russian people have been called upon to undergo have been amply justified in the sphere of concrete achievement."

Meanwhile, the bullet enters the back of the head. Always be suspicious—as Orwell advises—when the words do not call up a picture. "Terminate with extreme prejudice" does not call to mind the prisoner bound, blindfolded, kneeling, the pistol at the back of his head, the sound, the rush of the body forward, the splatter of brains and the blood.

Avoiding Self-Deceit

Sometimes, then, we use abstractions or euphemisms to avoid or suppress feeling. And sometimes we use sense words in underhanded ways, not so much to evade feeling as to twist it. *Slouched* and *strode* are both verbs of action that make us see. We must decide, by using our brains and our sensitivity, whether the difference between two images is literal description or an emotional nudge disguising itself as objective description. We do not complain that emotions *show*; we complain that the emotions are *disguised*. We do not object to laughter or to anger. We object to laughter that hides anger, expressing gaiety while it means hostility. We can learn to sense the falseness in language—our own or that of others—by heeding the particulars of every expression. This means listening and *hearing*, and checking what we hear against what we know. Take nothing for granted; the examined life demands it.

If we ourselves have strong opinions or biases, we must be wary, in both reading and writing. If we react instantly to a cliché like *the military-industrial complex*, we are not thinking about it, and we can manipulate ourselves or be manipulated by others. We must become aware of our habits of opinion. We need not alter our convictions; we need only open them to the air—and to our own conscious minds. When we hear a phrase like *iron-curtain countries*, we must not respond like an automaton to a pressed button, but like a human being, and decide what the phrase means, if it means anything, in its current context. Contexts, we might recall, have a way of changing around us.

Like most of the advice in this book, these notions apply equally to writing and to reading. The more intense our convictions, reading or writing, the more vulnerable we are to self-deceit.

Collecting Words

We must watch our words to see if we are using them with respect for honest expression. It helps to love words, and a love of words is something that we can develop. The growing writer finds pleasure in becoming a word collector, picking up, examining, and keeping new words (or familiar words seen suddenly, as if for the first time) like seashells or driftwood. Think of the richness in *hogwash* or the exact strength in *rasp*. English abounds in short, strong words. You can collect words from books, of course, but you can also find them in speech; a sense of lively speech adds energy to the best writing. A writer listens to speech—others' and even his own—with a greedy ear. Primitive people and children love words as things in themselves and collect them as ornaments. To become a better writer, rediscover some of the pleasure from words-as-things that you had in your childhood but have probably lost along the way. Patrol the miles of speech looking for words like *flotsam*.

Dictionaries can help, too. A thesaurus or a list of synonyms has the limitations mentioned earlier (p. 91). Brief dictionaries have brief definitions, and though they may light up a dark patch in our reading, they often give such a limited definition for the word, so empty of context, that we may misuse the word when we try to say it in a sentence. Good-sized college dictionaries carry more information, and can be a pleasure to read. The more information, the better. The biggest dictionary in the language rewards investigation. Sometime, when you are in the library, take down from the shelves one of the thirteen volumes of the *Oxford English Dictionary* and browse a little. The English poet and novelist Robert Graves says only one book is indispensable to the writer's library: the *OED*. In the thirteen volumes of the original, the editors tried to make the most precise possible map of the English language. They left out only recent coinages and words considered unprintable at the time of publication. There is a photographically reduced edition that includes all the pages of the original dictionary, making a two-volume set out of the original thirteen. The price of the two-volume set puts this great dictionary within many people's reach. In 1989, Oxford University Press published a completely revised edition in 20 volumes. The price, alas, will keep it off most students' shelves.

It is not the *OED*'s completeness that makes it so valuable; it is the context given for each word. The editors try to supply a context for the earliest example of each shade of meaning for every word; for each word in the language the dictionary provides a small biography, or *etymology*. Words, like individuals and nations, have complex and fascinating histories. Suppose we look up the word *vegetable*. More than three columns of small print chronicle the life of the word, which began as an adjective meaning "having the vegetating properties of plants; living and growing as a plant or organism endowed with the lowest form of life." The earliest example is from 1400. The poet John Lydgate, a couple of decades later, wrote of the wind (spelling modernized): ". . . that is so comfortable / For to nourish things vegetable." When Andrew Marvell wrote "To His Coy Mistress" two and a half centuries later [1687], he used the adjective in the same way: "My vegetable love should grow / Vaster than empires and more slow." Six examples (complete with small context) come between Lydgate and Marvell.

Meanwhile, the noun *vegetable* got started in 1582, when an author named J. Hester spoke of "the Hidden Vertues of sondrie Vegitables, Animalles, and Mineralles." The reader can discover thirty-six contexts for the word *vegetable* as a noun from 1582 to modern times—

and many shades of meaning. If you take pleasure in words, you will find your sensitivity to the insides of words increasing as you know more about the history of words. Meanings keep changing, of course, but old meanings live on as part of a word's connotative or associative life. So much of our history, external and internal, global and psychic, is coded into our words. The more you know, the more you respect the integrity of the word. (Integrity, as we find out when we check the dictionary, originally meant wholeness.) A word's wholeness includes all its possibilities: its family, its insides.

Words as Blanks

A frequent failure in our language, spoken or written, is our use of words that can mean anything the context requires. These words are like blanks for the reader or listener to fill in. Words of vague praise or blame—*lovely, nice,* and *terrible*—are frequent blanks. *Great. Terrific.* What does "nice hair" look like? Is it red or blond or white or black or brown? Long or short? Liveliness is specificity. Obscenities are common words as blanks, used without attention to their literal meaning. Vogue words are usually blanks also. *Awesome, wicked, psyched. Fink* was popular some years ago as a vogue word of contempt, no more precise than the *jerk* or *creep* of earlier generations. Yet once *fink* meant something exact: a man employed to join a labor union and spy for bosses. Words of complex history suddenly come into fashion and lose all color. *Funky* moved from black American speech into television—and no longer has anything to say.

Words and Associations

Words used as blanks get in the way of writing and thinking and feeling. Words mean things only by our agreement. If we start using *April* to mean *sunset* or *anything pleasant,* it will not be of use to us anymore. Our agreements about words are coded into dictionaries, which of course change as the words shift gradually in meaning because of historical change and the way that literary genius adapts old words to new conditions. Our agreements about words are also coded into the dictionary from which we really make our sentences—the dictionary (the computer) of the brain. This mental collection is even more complicated and useful for our writing than the dictionary on the shelf. The innumerable associations of the word *April* are stored in it, waiting to be used in the right way at the right time. The inside of a word is a huge room of possibilities, limited—because *April* does not include *August* or *catsup* for most of us—but multiple: flowers and showers, Easter, spring, seeds, vacation from school, Chaucer and Browning and Eliot for readers of poetry, ploughing or manure-spreading for farmers.

Someone might associate April with catsup or cats or soup or a girl in the first grade who had that name. These associations are private. The few phrases I listed at the end of the preceding paragraph, on the other hand, are public or general. Other people can share them. A moment's thought will usually reveal to the writer, at least in revision, whether he is using a word privately or generally. "Tulips like catsup" would be a grotesque and inappropriate simile for most of us—despite the real color—though it might be a spontaneous expression of the writer who privately associated April with catsup. A writer must learn to suppress the highly private, because writing must get through to an audience; you are talking to someone besides yourself; you have climbed out of the pure self-involvement of the crib and are trying to make human contact.

Words and Audience

But we must also remember, in choosing words, that an audience is not *everyone*. The larger the audience we try to reach, the fewer associations we can take for granted and the more limited our room of possibilities. If we are writing for a big newspaper, we probably do not assume that most of our readers associate April with Chaucer, Browning, and Eliot. An idea of the audience is crucial to our choice of words. Everyone makes this sort of choice in conversation: we use words with our best friend that we do not use with our grandmother; if we hitch a ride with a white-haired man wearing a blue suit, our words differ from those we would use if the driver wore reflecting sunglasses and an earring. If our vocabulary stays the same, chances are that we are being nasty in the sacred name of honesty.

To adjust our vocabulary to our audience is honest and not hypo-critical; we do not speak of adjusting our opinions or beliefs. Our minds contain multiple possibilities of expression among which we choose. If we do not try to make contact with another, the notion of honest speech is meaningless: for speech is speech only when it reaches another person.

In writing we make the same choices. If we write a letter to the college newspaper, we choose the words from a collection different from the one we choose from when we write a thank-you letter to an aunt. A term paper in business administration requires a vocabulary different from the one for a term paper in literature.

The difficult, necessary task is to adjust your vocabulary to your audience with tact, humility, and appropriateness—but without hy-pocrisy. Sometimes it is merely a matter of common sense. If you are writing for an audience from the southern hemisphere, you must remember that April connotes autumn and leaves falling, not green and seeds sprouting. But common sense is easy, compared to the difficulties in learning the difference between appropriate tact and gross hypocrisy. When Jim Beck wrote his first essay, the one about "well-rounded individuals" and so on (p. 10), he was writing for a faceless audience— an audience that enjoyed clichés and formulas. In other words, he was not writing for anybody at all. Probably at that moment he did not believe that he could write with honesty for an audience that was a teacher or a fellow student. Probably Jim had no vocabulary to fall back on at that moment but that of high-minded hypocrisy or that of the boys in the locker room or the dorm, which can be just as hypocritical and one-sided as graduation oratory. But little by little, by becoming aware of the insides of words, he learned a lot about the insides of Jim Beck; and he learned to make the inside outside— to make connection with other people, to use words for social purposes, to *write*.

Revising Words

From the first notes for an essay to its final typing, words are the material we work with. When we brainstorm or sprint, we use the associations of words. When we develop ideas, when we expand generalities by detail, our focus on individual words generates more words. But our local concentration on language increases as drafts come closer to the final draft. It may be far along before we discover that *wage* may be more appropriate for our context and audience than *salary*. It may take a final draft before we excise the blank word *aspect* and find a useful substitute. At the end we check our sentences both to remove error and to find better language: more exact, more particular, and more original—in a word.

—— **EXERCISES** ——————————————————————

1. Here are three lists of words similar in meaning. Discuss the varieties of meaning within each list. Write a short sentence using each word accurately. Or else insert the words from each list one by one into the context of a single sentence and note how the connotations of the statement change.

> ostentatious, showy, conspicuous, exhibitionistic, show-offy, pretentious
>
> preserve, maintain, keep up, support
>
> disease, illness, sickness, infirmity, disorder, indisposition, debility

2. Using a thesaurus, rewrite this passage by substituting a "synonym" for each of the words in italics. See the example on page 91.

> I *remember sitting* with my *foot* up on *pillows* on the edge of my *bed* in my *room*, gazing at my *freckled face* in a *hand mirror*. My *face embarrassed* me most of the time and I couldn't *get a comb* through my *mass* of *unruly, tangled red hair.*
>
> *Shirley MacLaine, Don't Fall off the Mountain*

3. Look past these thesaurus words, and find the proverb:

  a. It requires an entirety of species to fabricate a cosmos.
  b. Precipitousness occasions depletion.
  c. The sum total of matter that scintillates is not necessarily bullion.

4. Here are some headlines or sentences quoted from daily newspapers. Try the tests of "Literalness and Metaphor," page 92. Which writers of the following phrases were conscious of what they were doing? Were any, in your opinion, being deliberately comic?

  a. Unmasked as a faceless automaton, he toyed with her affections, and a stormy argument ensued.
  b. Auto Show Fans Bask in Cream of City's Crop
  c. A gush of poetic language cushions these pivotal events until they are nearly—but not quite—camouflaged.
  d. Mushrooming insurance and energy costs represent a double-barreled shotgun pointed at New England ski areas.
  e. PTA Opens Fire on TV Violence
  f. Off the top of her head she claimed that grass roots were the bottom line.

5. On page 93 is E. B. White's phrase informing us that his son lacked experience of lakes.
  (a) Using his sentence as a model, and using sense words, think of two more particulars that could express the same information. You could write "My son, who caught minnows in a sieve. . . ."
  (b) Recall a powerful physical sensation from your own experience and try to present it as vividly as possible in two or three sentences.

6. When prose gets out of control, there is often more than one thing wrong with it. In these passages of bad prose, find words used as blanks and as euphemisms. If you notice other faults, name them.

  a. Thank you for the information you recently provided in connection with your request for Gulf Travel Cards. The information contained in your communication, along with other data developed, has enabled us to reverse our previous decision regarding your Travel Card application.

b. We will be experiencing a development of shower activity.

c. The purpose of this program is to provide opportunities for
teachers at undergraduate colleges and universities and at
junior and community colleges to work in their areas of
interest with distinguished scholars in their fields and to
have access to libraries suitable for advanced study.

d. The evidence developed was not corroborative of the allegation on which it was predicated.

7. Read several articles in a national newsmagazine (*Time, Newsweek,* etc.) and see if you can discover any instances of subtle (or
not-so-subtle) bias. Your instructor might want to copy a single
such article for everybody to read. Come to class prepared to discuss
your findings.

8. In this paragraph, underline three words that the author uses
with special skill—the way John Updike uses *adhesively* and
slice—and be prepared to defend your choices in class.

> The top of the hill, pasture for one straggly cow, was clear of brush
> except for patches of dark juniper, in spreading flat circles ten feet
> across. Around the tumbled stone walls tall pines and maples held off
> an advancing army of small gray birch. At one side, by the bouldery
> path that had once been a town road, a little family graveyard lay on
> slightly tilted ground. A deer trail ran right through it, bright and
> twisted between the slate stones, and a birch had fallen and rotted out
> of its bark, leaving a print like a white hand.
>
> *Thomas Williams, Town Burning*

9. Underline the sense words in this passage from a magazine
article. How effective are they? Does the author have the insides of
words under control? When he perceives "ten million persons . . .
hustling in the . . . carpet," what does he compare them to?

> A blinding splendor sparkling in lazy rhythm to the whine of retard
> ing jet engines welcomes you to Mexico City. The surreal glow seems
> to extend to the end of the world and it's not hard to believe some ten
> million persons are rising for the day, hustling in the brilliant carpet of
> light below.
>
> *Sergio Ortiz, "Mexico" (Playgirl)*

10. Underline examples of euphemism in these passages from a
speech about the public relations business:

> So confident were we that a breakthrough was imminent that it
> became popular to think of changing our name from public relations
> specialists to communications specialists.

What is new is the role the public relations consultant is beginning to play in relation to the social crises which no one foresaw 10 or 20 years ago. In these new assignments—which represent a small but rapidly growing part of his business—he is no longer primarily a communicator; he is a sort of moderator whose job it is to try to prevent the crisis from getting out of hand. He may still use the same tools, but the measure of his performance is not how effectively he gets his clients' message across, but how successful he is in avoiding a flare-up which can stop the machinery of his clients' business, how he can help his clients conduct their business in a way that is responsive to the new demands made by concerned scientists, environmentalists, consumerists, minority leaders, underprivileged segments of the community, the young generation.

David Finn, "Modifying Opinions in the New Human Climate" (Public Relations Quarterly)

Rewrite the passage without using any euphemisms at all.

11. (a) Pick one of the following words—chemical, comb, shield, car, slave, table—or a word from a list your instructor gives you. Read the complete entry for that word in the *OED (Oxford English Dictionary)* and write a short report on its origin and later history. Compare the earliest usage with the present sense of the word.

(b) Look through the *OED* and find your own word to trace. Prepare a history to present in class.

VERBS

Action, and the Choice of Style

Verbs act. Verbs move. Verbs do. Verbs strike, soothe, grin, cry, exasperate, decline, fly, hurt, and heal. Verbs make writing go, and they matter more to our language than any other part of speech.

Verbs give energy, if we use them with energy. We could have said, "Verbs are action. Verbs are motion. Verbs are doing." But if we had written the sentences in this second way, we would have written dull prose. We could have gone even further into dullness and written, "Verbs are words that are characterized by action."

Try to use verbs that act. Yet sometimes you will need to write verbs that are less than active. Just as there are no synonyms, there are no two sentences that mean the same thing but are different only in style. A change in style, however slight, is always a change in meaning, however slight. Is it, therefore, possible to make a stylistic generalization at all?

Generalization does remain possible, with explanation and with room for exception. Both explanations and exceptions will follow in the sections on verbs and nouns, but let us start with a general explanation. Most of the time, passives and weak verbs evade precision and commitment. Examples follow, in which weak verbs add static to statement and in which passives avoid being wrong by evading definite statement. These habits fuzz our prose with bad brain fuzz. To recommend that we use active forms of active verbs is to recommend energy and clarity, definite statement and commitment. Style is morals.

Verbs with Nouns and Adjectives

Usually, a lone verb is stronger and better than a strung-out verb-and-adjective or verb-and-noun combination. People say, "I am aware of this fact," or "I am cognizant of this situation," when they could have said, "I know it." In these examples, we have a weak verb and adjective followed by a noun that means little, but appears to end the sentence, to give the verb an object. The phrases mean something different from "I know it," but the difference is mere pomposity. "I am aware of the fact" differs from "I know it" because it shows us that the speaker thinks well of himself. "I am cognizant of the situation" is so pompous it may sound ironic; it would usually drip from the lips, or leak from the pen, of someone nervous about his intellectual status, like a television executive.

Look out for the verbs *be, is, are,* and *has, have* combined with nouns and adjectives. See if you do not gain by using the verb itself, clear and clean. Edit your writing to simplify your verbs. "He looked outside and became aware of the fact that it was raining" revises easily into "He looked outside and saw that it was raining" or, more simply, "He looked outside. It was raining." Instead of "We had a meeting," try "We met." The meaning is different, slightly, but if the second phrase is accurate, it is better—we save three syllables and add energy to our prose; when we cut to the essential motion, we add vitality. Instead of "They were decisive about the question of . . . ," try "They decided to. . . ."

Now "to be decisive"—if we look at the insides of words—means something quite different from "to decide." The person who "is decisive" has vigor and intellectual intensity; he cuts through the uncertainties that surround a question and makes a choice firmly and quickly. If you are describing a committee meeting in which, after long discussion, the members reached a consensus or took a vote and decided to do something, "they decided" is the clearest phrase to use. "They reached a decision" wastes words, probably; it does imply that it took some work "to arrive at the decision," which by itself would imply more ease, and less struggle, than *reached.* If you feel that the meaning requires *reached* or *arrived*, use the accurate word. But, certainly, in writing about the committee meeting described above, "they were decisive about . . . " would be misuse of words. They weren't decisive at all. They decided. Most of the time, when we use a wordy noun-adjective-verb phrase, we are merely trying to *sound* more complicated. Most of the time, the shade of meaning in *reached* or *arrived* is not needed. We use the longer phrase just to *seem* to be considering fine points. The sensible rule: use the shorter, more direct verb ("they decided") except when the longer variation has a precision that your meaning requires. "They talked for two days about lowering the voting age, without coming to a conclusion. Then Senator Jensen returned from a junket. He spoke briefly. He was decisive. The measure carried by a two-thirds majority."

Verbs with Participles

The same advice applies to phrases that use verb forms ending in *-ing* (present participles). "They were meeting to discuss" can often become "They met to discuss," and "He is clearing his throat" becomes "He clears his throat." But the participle is different in meaning—it marks a different sort of time—and therefore can be useful when that difference is important. "She'll be comin' 'round the mountain" has more continuous motion in it than "She'll come 'round the mountain." Participles imply continuing action. But be sure that you *intend* the difference and are not just lazy. To say that the group "was deciding a topic" implies that it took some time; if you use this verb phrase, be sure that you mean to use it instead of *decided.* Apparently the mind finds it easier to be pale than to be colorful. Or maybe the mind finds it easier to avoid the extra vocabulary of verbs, sticking to *be* and *has* with nouns and adjectives. Whatever the reason, when we add little words like *is* and *has* to participles, adjectives, and nouns, usually we thin our prose into invisibility.

Verbs in the Passive Voice

A verb is in the passive voice when it acts upon the subject; for instance, "The passive voice *is used* when the subject *is acted upon* by the verb."

When writers use the passive, they usually subtract meaning from their prose. We say, "A message was received," instead of "They [or *I* or *you* or *he* or *she*] received a message." We suppress identity, which is a particular, and we put hazy distance between implied subject and definite action. The passive voice avoids responsibility. We might claim that "A dish was dropped in the kitchen" rather than name ourselves as the dropper. Omitting a doer diminishes a sentence. It can be politically useful: "PLO enclaves were bombed yesterday." Or, as the President said when profits from secret arms sales were covertly diverted to a guerilla army, "Mistakes were made." Many inquired: Who made them?

Sometimes we use the passive from shyness, or modesty, or false modesty, or all three. It waters the soup. We sound as if we wrote labels for medicine bottles: "Doses may be administered three times daily. Dosage recommended for adults is. . . . " A depressed writer might say, making an argument: "It can be assumed that someone in college is fairly mature. It might be objected that. . . . " Here, the passive makes invisible dialogue, a pale argument between people who are not there. Scientific prose uses the passive by convention, establishing an impersonal tone. Sometimes writers on nonscientific subjects achieve a pseudo-scientific tone by using the passive. "Crest has been shown to be a decay preventive dentifrice. . . . "

Occasionally the passive is right or unavoidable. Passives are used in a textbook whose author generally advises against passives.

> The author uses passives in the textbook.
> The textbook uses passives.
> Passives are used in the textbook.

In some contexts, the third sentence is best. The second is most terse, but it involves a hidden metaphor—the text must be compared to a person, if it "uses" something—which may weaken the sentence. The first correctly says that the author does the using, but it would be intrusive and wordy in some contexts to state the subject when the subject is perfectly obvious. The passive might be the least of three evils.

Sometimes the passive is useful because we do not know the identity of the doer. The passive (especially if we use it sparingly) can imply this ignorance, which may be part of the meaning of the sentence. Suppose this were the start of a story:

> He walked into his bedroom. Clothes lay in heaps on the floor. Dresser drawers lay upside down on the rug, their contents scattered.

This paragraph describes a scene, mostly in the active voice, with inanimate objects (clothes, dresser drawers) doing active things (lay, lay upside down). It is terse, but it implies no reason for the scene and no response to it. The active voice in this passage is less meaningful than the passive would be:

> He walked into the room. Clothes were heaped on the floor. Dresser drawers were dumped on the rug, and their contents had been scattered.

The scene is the same. We still don't know who did it. But the passives (after the first sentence, which is active) imply that someone else, unknown, has done the damage. They only *imply* it, not *state* it, but the implication is real and further implies shock. The second and third sentences suggest what happens in his mind as he enters the room: "I've been robbed!" To make this last sentence active would sound artificial: "Someone has robbed me!" The writer would be taking as absolute the advice to avoid the passive, which is only a sensible, general rule.

Good writers use the passive for variety in sentence structure, too. Rarely, but they do. In a paragraph about two groups taking opposite sides on an issue, in which all sentences have the active voice, the author looking for stylistic variety might insert the sentence "Arguments were put forward, on both sides, which would make a goat blush." When you use a passive for variety, be certain that you are not using it for any of the reasons that make passives bad: shyness or self-consciousness, false modesty, evading responsibility, or imitating scientific respectability.

Particular Verbs

I have been writing all along as if there were two classes of verbs: strong ones and weak ones. Of course language is more complicated than that, and not only because weak is sometimes better than strong, as I have suggested. Some strong verbs are stronger than others. "He moved" is stronger than "he was in motion." But in the right context, we might say with greater strength, "he crept," or "he slid," or "he hurtled." We would almost always want to say, "he crept" rather than "he moved, creeping." (A difference of meaning might, in some instances, make the second phrase useful.) The first verbs I listed in the paragraph that starts this section are general verbs: *do, move, act.* The second series is particular and more colorful.

Invisible Verbs

In the prospectus for a dissertation, a Ph.D. candidate wrote this sentence in which he misused verbs; in fact, he managed to write almost *without* verbs.

> Illustrative of what Kornhauser means by constraint imposed on professionals in organizations are the findings of Leo Meltzer in a survey of 3,084 physiologists in the United States.

The sentence has no strong and active verbs. *Means* is the closest. *Illustrative* is an adjective substituted for a verb. *Imposed* is a past participle that suppresses responsibility. *Are* is boring.

To rewrite the sentence in a language not far from the original, but with more vigor and clarity, we can simply cut and rearrange. Edited in revision, the passage could read:

> Leo Meltzer questioned 3,084 physiologists in the United States; his findings demonstrate Kornhauser's contention that organizations constrain professionals.

Maybe *surveyed* is more accurate than *questioned*, but *surveyed* smells of jargon.

The last phrase of this revision may not mean what the original author had in mind. Did he mean that the institution imposed the constraint or that something else, unnamed, chose professionals in organizations, rather than others, to impose restraint on? The ambiguity in the original passage is real and serves no function; it is merely unclear. The second version is clearer, though without context it still raises questions. What is this constraint? What desires are held back? Does the author mean "constraint" as restraint or as compulsion? Does he mean all organizations—like YMCAs, universities, corporations, fraternities, bridge clubs, and nations—or specifically professional ones, like the American Association of University Professors, the Modern Language Association, or the American Medical Association? We must make sure that our sentences leave no unanswered questions. The more straightforward our presentation, the easier it is—for us and the reader—to be sure of the sense. Clarity comes from vigor combined with detail. Verbs are the most vigorous parts of speech; by particularity, they add detail.

False Color in Verbs

The search for particularity and color can become obvious, and the prose look silly. In the examples that follow, the faults do not lie in the verbs alone, but in the whole style. Verbs are at the center of the action in our prose, however, for good or for ill. In the play *The Owl and the Pussycat*, a would-be novelist reads the first page of his manuscript to the girl who has invaded his apartment. When he starts by saying the sun *spat* on his protagonist, she flies into a rage. And so should we whenever we see language being abused. Men's action magazines are full of Methedrine prose, violence done to language in the name of violence. In a thriller called *A Clash of Hawks*, the author's second sentence reads:

> The 200-foot-high derrick was a black, latticed steel phallus raping the hot, virginal blue sky.

If an author needs these overblown images to describe an oil rig, we have to wonder what language-tortures he will resort to when he gets to a sex scene. But tough or sadistic writing is not the only kind of bad overwriting. Pretty writing may be worse.

> Songbirds trilled out my window, vines curled at the eaves, and Spring drenched the day with gladness.

Often a beginning writer tries to make the verbs describing dialogue too exaggeratedly active: *he whimpered, she snapped.* Almost always it looks too strenuous. We should use *said*, or nothing at all, most of the time. The emotion should be in the dialogue itself, in the speaker's words; if the reader has to be told, the emotion is not there. The trick is to convey energy with appropriateness. We may need to learn to do too much before we can learn to do the right amount. Newly wakened to verbs, one student wrote this passage:

> The train slammed to a stop in the station. Steam vomited from all apertures. Passengers rushed through the barriers and hurtled into the night.

It was a useful exercise, because the student was searching through his mental dictionary for energetic verbs. But the color was more vivid than necessary, to the point of distortion. Steam gushing out at the base of an engine is not like vomiting; *vomiting* is too sick and unpleasant and bad-smelling a word; the writer used it only for its power, not for what it contributed to the picture. Though the general advice—choose color over pallor, energy over lethargy—holds true, one matter overrides all others, in any discussion of style, and that is appropriateness: context is all.

Fancy Verbs

Some verbs are too fancy for normal use. Writers use them when they think their prose ought to wear fancy clothes or when they don't fully trust what they're saying. *Depict* is usually inferior to *paint* or *draw* or *describe*. "He depicted a scene of unparalleled magnitude." Maybe that means, "he painted a big picture," or "he told a good story," or half a dozen other things, but its real meaning is its would-be fanciness. Of course, *depict* is not the only culprit here—"A scene of unparalleled magnitude" sounds like something W.C. Fields might conjure up in an inspired moment. Indeed, the whole sentence is busy admiring itself in the mirror. *Emulate* would usually be fancy for *copy*, *ascertain* for *make sure*, and *endeavor* for try.

Made-up Verbs

Then there are the made-up words, neologisms, which sound fancy to the people who use them. When we are tempted to say *finalize,* we would do better to say *end* or *finish; make personal* is more accurate than *personalize.* In general, we should avoid verbs made of an adjective and an -*ize.* Advertising and politics have created many crude verbs, often using nouns as bases instead of adjectives. Some good old English verbs end in -*ize. Scrutinize,* deriving from the noun *scrutiny,* is a useful verb. *Finalize,* on the other hand, is used to sound fancier than *finish* or *end,* to give false complexity to a simple act. Therefore it is bad style, pretending to be something that isn't; it is a form of euphemism, a way of overdressing plain usage. The writer should search the language for the simplest and most direct way of saying and expressing, not make up a new word when an old one will do.

Revising Verbs

The section headings of these pages (Verbs with Nouns and Adjectives, Verbs with Participles, Verbs in the Passive Voice, Particular Verbs, Invisible Verbs, False Color in Verbs, Fancy Verbs, Made-up Verbs) can form a checklist for revising the draft of an essay. Scan your prose to see how you have been using verbs. See if you can't find substitutions that make your style stronger, more honest, and more precise.

_____ **EXERCISES** _____

1. Underline the weak verbs (verb-noun or verb-adjective or verb-participle combinations, invisible verbs, verbs lacking particularity) in these sentences. See if you can substitute strong verbs for those you underline. When you make a substitution, does the meaning of the sentence vary? Can you think of reasons for preferring the weaker verb combinations in any of the sentences?

    a. She made the observation that German had been her minor in college.
    b. We have endeavored to reach a conclusion that will be satisfactory.
    c. We were just starting to sing when the door opened.
    d. The committee has been meeting every day for a month.
    e. I am trying to be healthy so that I will be playing tennis when I have arrived at eighty.
    f. We had gotten around to the subject of getting good grades and got into an argument.
    g. A different way of expressing the same idea is that having no commitment to activity, we are engaged upon a course of activity lacking purpose.
    h. We were in action right away, moving out into the field on our stomachs until we got to the river.

2. These five sentences contain passives. Underline the passive verbs, and then consider if any are necessary or useful. When the passive is objectionable, figure out why, and revise the sentences so that passive becomes active.

   a. Arabella was understood by her neighbors to have cornered the market in soybean futures.
   b. People committed to excellence are sought after in the business community.
   c. At the picketing sites on North Campus, GEO members were not allowed to use the restrooms.
   d. My canoe tipped over, I was thrown out into the water, and I saw the McDonalds ahead of me.
   e. Remembering August with Emily in Poughkeepsie, and rereading her letter which arrived this morning, I gradually realized that I had been deceived.

3. (a) Write three sentences of description without using *is, are, was,* or *were.* (b) Find verbs to describe the way wind moves in the leaves of a tree. Perhaps wind *ripples* in leaves or *surges* through them. What else? (c) Write a vivid passage describing a crowded city street; let the verbs do the work.

4. Here are some fancy verbs. Find simpler verbs that would usually do better.

masticate	disseminate
cogitate	substantiate
commence	estimate

5. Here is a list of verbs chosen for varieties of tone and degrees of color. With each of them, find alternatives, close synonyms, which might work better in a specific context. For an example, remember the differences among emulate/imitate/copy/ape discussed on page 90. Make up a context for five of the verbs—listed and discovered—in which the verb feels appropriate.

clutch	communicate
exterminate	rasp
rattle	split
cook	decide
act	recommend

6. Here are four passages. Underline the verbs and decide in class how well each author uses them.

   a. When it comes to the actual methods of consumption, asparagus eaters seem to be roughly divided into two groups. There are those who assume a crouching position and attack the vegetable with knives and forks. Lined up against this faction are those who believe the only way to eat asparagus is to throw back the head, grasp the stalk between thumb and forefinger and lower it slowly into the mouth, chewing steadily.

> *Diane White,* "The Noble Asparagus"
> (*The Boston Globe*)

b. A machine gun lashed at him from across the river, and he ducked in his hole. In the darkness, it spat a vindictive white light like an acetylene torch, and its sound was terrifying. Croft was holding himself together by the force of his will. He pressed the trigger of his gun and it leaped and bucked under his hand. The tracers spewed wildly into the jungle on the other side of the river.

> *Norman Mailer, The Naked and the Dead*

c. The service shall be delivered in the following manner: Immediately before commencing to serve, the Server shall stand with both feet at rest behind the base line, and within the imaginary continuation of the center mark and side line of the singles court. The Receiver may stand wherever he pleases behind the service line on his own side of the net. The Server shall then throw the ball into the air and strike it with his racket before it hits the ground. Delivery shall be deemed complete at the moment the racket strikes the ball.

> "How Service Is Delivered," *Official Tennis Rules*

d. Weighing the half-pounds of flour, excluding the scoop, and depositing them dust-free into the thin paper sacks held a simple kind of adventure for me. I developed an eye for measuring how full a silver-looking ladle of flour, mash, meal, sugar or corn had to be to push the scale indicator over to eight ounces or one pound. When I was absolutely accurate our appreciative customers used to admire: "Sister Henderson sure got some smart grandchildrens." If I was off in the store's favor, the eagle-eyed women would say, "Put some more in that sack, child. Don't you try to make your profit offa me."

> *Maya Angelou, I Know Why the Caged Bird Sings*

NOUNS

Particularity and Choosing a Style

Nouns are the simplest parts of speech, the words least tricky to use. Nouns are the names of things, *things* in the broadest sense: *table, elm, Nancy, rain, noun, Centerville, nation, hunger, nine o'clock.* If verbs supply the energy that makes prose go, nouns are the body of prose. Without nouns, nothing would be doing the going.

Many of the generalizations that apply to verbs also apply to nouns. We prefer as a rule the specific, the sensuous, the strong, the simple, and the colorful over the abstract, the general, the polysyllabic, and the fancy. We prefer *elm* to *tree, Nancy* to *girl,* and *nine o'clock* to *evening.* The more particular the noun, the clearer the pictures we make, and the more accurately we can represent feelings. Pictures carry feelings from writer to reader, as abstract idea-words do not. Particulars make contact. A student wrote,

> I remembered the flowers that grew on some land near a relative's house. . . .

and revised it to

> I remembered a path of daisies that grew on a meadow near my Cousin Annie's farm. . . .

and the particularity is all gain. The first example was not bad style, but it was pale prose. The second by comparison is vivid.

But we also need to generalize, and we must express reservations. Sometimes the more general noun is more accurate and honest than the specific one. From a distance, you see *a man* or *a woman,* not *a sophomore* or *a mechanic. Town* may be more appropriate, in the right context, than *Centerville,* though it is less specific. We must keep in mind the advice to be specific; but, as ever, we must be wary that our rules do not lead us into absurdity. A student revised some daily writing into

> On Tuesday afternoon, October thirteenth, I read a sentence halfway down the first page of *War and Peace* which. . . .

Maybe in a particular context, such extreme specificity would be useful, but usually it would sound overly precise.

Also, we must remember again that the advice to cultivate one kind of style, at the expense of another, means thinking or seeing things in special ways. *A change in style, however slight, is always a change in meaning, however slight.*

Although most writing improves as particularity increases, there are exceptions to this rule. If we are philosophers seeking generality *tree* might be preferable to *elm* and *humanity* to *Nancy* and *David.* For scientific summary, injunctions to *Be particular!* and *Avoid abstraction!* are useless.

> At first cats would not seem to offer a likely clue to human history. Yet when one considers that the writing of adequate histories of human populations began scarcely 200 years ago, that writing itself dates back only about 6,000 years and that for many populations historical, linguistic and cultural records are inadequate or nonexistent, cats appear in a different light. They have been associated with human beings for a long time, but they have never had any economic significance and only rarely have they had much social sig-

nificance. Genetically they, unlike other domesticated animals, have been left largely to themselves. The study of the population genetics of cats is therefore rewarding not only for what it reveals about the evolution of cats but also for what it suggests about the movements of human populations.

Neil B. Todd, "Cats and Commerce"
(*Scientific American*)

Todd writes a vigorous expository prose, which must be abstract and concrete by turns to impart the necessary facts and perspectives to his readers.

The wise advice is simply to be as particular as the context allows us; when we are as concrete as possible, we have a better chance of connecting with our audience. Too often, we are vague and general, when we would say much more by discovering the concrete. Instead of saying

When it got cold the animals looked for shelter.

we could convey much more by a particularity:

In October there was frost, and the sheep huddled in one corner of the barn for warmth, the cattle in another.

Abstract and Particular Nouns

Degrees of difference separate the noun at an extreme of abstraction from the noun at an extreme of particularity. S. I. Hayakawa, in his book *Language in Thought and Action*, speaks of moving up a ladder of abstraction, climbing from the most particular level, gradually discarding particularities, and arriving into the thin air around the highest abstraction. The number of rungs on this ladder is limited only by our ingenuity, but we can usefully distinguish three main degrees—the abstract, the general, and the particular.

Beginning with the abstract, we can move by degrees toward greater particularity. Take "animal, dog, spaniel." One might become still more particular by adding an age and a color and by naming a breed of spaniel: "a five-year-old rust-colored cocker spaniel." On the other hand, one might become more abstract than the general *animal* by climbing the ladder into the thin air of *organism*. Or one might remain general by defining *dog* in scientific classification as *canine* and *quadruped*.

The more abstract a noun, the more difficult it is to use well. Words like *emotion* (or *love*, for that matter) or *courage* or *hatred* or *responsibility*. To make these nouns work, you must provide a context with anecdote or analogy; you must put flesh on the bones. Usually an adjective in front of an abstraction does not do the work. The abstraction is lazy, retrieved by the writer from the attic of Big Ideas, and the adjective strives to do all the work; but adjectives themselves often are weak, and so we have two weaklings failing to budge the door that one strong noun could burst open.

Take the word *love* again. *Love* is thin and airy; it is pretty, but what is it about? Our affection for a pet salamander? The feeling of a grandfather for his granddaughter? Bert's obsession with the character of Charles Dickens? Mark and Nancy in the Oldsmobile? Married affection? *Love* is a grab bag of possibilities, only a bit less abstract than *emotion* or *feeling.* If we modify it with the adjective *intense,* we narrow its possibilities a little, but we do not really localize it. If we speak of *young love,* we are more particular—and yet we move toward cliché. Many clichés are adjective-noun combinations in which the adjective is a desperate, though habitual, attempt to rescue a bland abstraction; *blind faith,* for example.

Abstractions are usually lazy. The writer finds it easier to label the general category of a feeling than to search out the particulars that embody the feeling. Sight, taste, smell, touch, and hearing carry feeling from writer to reader—concepts don't. (And most writers using abstractions, we notice instantly, are not using concepts with the precision of a philosopher but vaguely and inaccurately.) Usually, we talk best about *love* when we do not use the word at all. If we use *Nancy,* and *Centerville,* and a 1989 Pontiac, and *rain,* and *nine o'clock,* and connect them with strong verbs, the reader may know what we mean by the big hazy word *love*—in this time and in this place.

Time and *place* are abstractions. Are they used appropriately here? Sometimes the abstract affords a setting for the concrete, as a black velvet background shows up diamonds. In other contexts, instead of *time* and *place* we would want to use more specific words—*end of high school, summer night, elm, Long Lake Road.*

Abstract Nouns: Beginnings and Endings

An abstraction can be explained by context, by analogy, or by anecdote. Some abstraction or generalization is necessary to any conceptual or argumentative writing. Only fiction, poetry, and autobiography can be free of it, and they do not always stay free. When we revise an essay, we should look most carefully to eliminate abstractions at two points—beginning and ending. Frequently, we introduce a subject with an abstraction—"I am going to tell a story that illustrates inequality"—and then we tell a story that illustrates inequality. If the illustration is clear, the introductory abstraction was unnecessary; what is more, it was probably distracting. When you announce that you are going to tell a funny joke before you tell it, you take the humor away. Let the idea of inequality arise in the reader's mind—by name or not—from your anecdote, and it will be much more powerful. Telling the reader the meaning of what he is going to hear bullies him; he is likely to resist.

Similarly, we often write anecdotes that trail off with an abstraction. Having told a perfectly clear story, we end, "which is an illustration of the inequality so prevalent today." Don't nudge your reader in the ribs, saying, "In case you didn't get it, this is what I mean." We summarize abstractly because we lack confidence in our own writing and in the reader's intelligence. Of course some stories need interpreting; that usually makes them less valuable. But if the road is clear, do not put up road markers; they are good only for stumbling over.

Invisible Nouns

So far, we have been talking about degrees of particularity and color, and we have admitted that some prose needs abstractions. The Preacher could not have said, "All is vanity," if there had been an enforced commandment against abstractions. But some nouns are almost always useless. These nouns are invisible. When someone says, "The snow is gray in color," what is the phrase *in color* doing? It doesn't do anything for meaning or particularity. Maybe it contains a message informing us that the speaker is pompous.

Words like *nature* and *character*, which have perfectly good uses, also turn up invisibly in pale prose. Probably the snow was gray in color because of the urban nature of the environment, and the frigid character of the weather. Probably it would have seemed too ordinary to speak of gray snow in the cold, dirty city.

We use invisible nouns with adjectives—much as we use invisible verbs like *be* and *do* and *has* with adjectives or nouns—to make a sentence *sound* grander than it really is, or because we lack the vocabulary. Whatever the reason, we abuse the language. Some other nouns we render invisible: *sense, kind, action, situation, respect, regard, case,* and *element.* Look at this piece of prose from the annual report of a large corporation:

> The President is pleased to report that, despite the unusual nature of the fiscal situation in the past twelve months, earnings have risen substantially above the margin foreseen by the Treasurer's Report of March, 1981. In a marketing sense, the profitable character of the corporation proved itself under trying circumstances.

Circumstances is another invisible noun—at least as it is used here. Sensible writers avoid these words unless their contexts provide visible meanings. For instance, a *case* holds papers, *characters* speak parts in plays, and there are five *senses.* Edit invisible nouns out of your prose when you revise.

Making Bad Nouns from Verbs

The sensible writer also chooses the plain noun, if it is adequate, over the fancy one, and he chooses the old noun rather than making up a new one. On pages 110–111 we mentioned the verb *finalize,* which had been wrenched out of an adjective. It has been wrenched further into a noun: now and then we run across *finalization* when *end* or *finish* or maybe *finality* would do. Bad stylists will go to any lengths to complicate things. *Scrutiny* is a fine noun; *scrutinize* is a necessary and traditional verb. But recently a young man wrote on an application form that he submitted documents "for your scrutinization." The word means nothing more than *scrutiny;* it must have sounded more respectable to this writer.

Or maybe his vocabulary failed him. He remembered the verb *scrutinize* but forgot the noun *scrutiny.* And so he made up a new noun out of the verb. When you are tempted to make a new noun from a verb, go to the dictionary first. You know *unify;* when tempted to create *unifization,* go to the dictionary and you will find *unity* and *unification*—and clearer, more eloquent prose.

Fancy Nouns

Reading bad prose, we find thousands of examples of pomposity or fanciness, either neologism (new words generally invented, when old ones would do, out of a failure of vocabulary) like *scrutinization* or polysyllabic alternatives to simple words like *domicile* for *house* or *cessation* for *end.* These words parallel verbs like *masticate,* substituted for *chew.* The fanciness may arise from lack of confidence or ignorance or pretension or whatever. Probably we are more often lazy than insincere and simply settle for what we first think of. Whatever our motive or our failing, the result is the same; fanciness separates the thing described and the mental act of perceiving it. Feelings are kept at a distance. Fancy abstractions and clichés enable Orwell's Communist professor to discuss without feelings the murder of innocent people.

Revising Nouns

In revising, we should look to remove the lazy abstraction, as well as the invisible noun, the neologism, and the merely fancy noun. Cutting such a word leaves a hole, which we can fill with another noun or a phrase, to specify and bring down to earth the airy word we started with. Lazy abstractions are like clichés and jargon—and the three are usually discovered together—because they are instantly available to the tongue; they lie heaped together with clichés and jargon in the foreroom of the brain; we do not have to search for them with our intelligence or dream for them with our imaginations. Here is a passage from an essay.

> Financial problems were coming to a head in my family last spring and we didn't know if my sister and I could have the benefit of higher education. Then my grandfather got the surprise of his life when a large amount of money came his way when he least expected it. He got a sum from the VA, which he didn't know was coming to him. Through his generosity, we were enabled to arrange payment for tuition.

As usual with faulty prose, the faults do not lie in one part of speech alone. Some hunks of cliché are ready-made—*financial problems, coming to a head, benefit of higher education, surprise of his life, when he least expected it, arrange payment*—and combine with a dozen other signs of lazy thinking and evasion of feeling. Think of the emotional reality—the anxiety, the sudden jubilation—these phrases obscure with their familiar haze. Instead of *financial problems,* let us forget euphemism and talk about being in debt, or having no money, or losing a job, or payments coming due; *anything* more particular. The ultimate particularity would probably sound as cold as a balance sheet (outstanding indebtedness $27,429.31; assets . . .), but we know a median lies between the bland, evasive euphemism of *financial problems* and the sterile figures. The median is actual circumstances and anecdotes; the median comes closer to the truth than the extremes.

Certainly *go to college* or *go on in school* is preferable to *have the benefit of higher education.* Then instead of speaking generally of *surprise*—an abstraction that takes the surprise out of surprise—why not show it happening? Describe the grandfather opening the envelope or picking up the telephone. Use dialogue. Or use some new analogy to express his feelings, instead of a useless cliché. How much is *a large amount of money* or *a sum?* Both seem genteel evasions for saying a specific figure, like *a check for $5,000.* But perhaps it seems crass to the writer to name the figure. Then at least some phrase could give a better idea of the numbers, so the reader can place the figure between five hundred and five million dollars or judge the amount of money by what it can do: "enough money to send us both through school."

The phrase *through his generosity* includes an unnecessary, labeling abstraction. We do not need to be told that he is generous. When we are bullied with the notion, we resist it. Maybe the old man just wants to boast that his grandchildren go to college. Finally, the last part of the paragraph has a pair of general nouns and a fancy verb in place of simpler and more natural language. It is pretentious to write, "we were enabled to arrange payment for tuition," when we could write "we were able to pay for college."

The student, in fact revised the passage.

> My family was so far in debt last spring that we didn't think my sister and I could go to college. My father had borrowed money to get a fish and chips franchise, and lost it all in six months. My sister and I both took jobs in the summer. I was working twelve hours a day in the mill, and when I came home at night I was so mad and tired I just drank beer and watched the box. Then my grandfather telephoned my father and I saw my father suddenly start crying. The VA had just sent my grandfather a check he didn't know was coming, and it was enough to pay for us both. That night, we bought a bottle of Four Roses.

He changed verbs and other parts of speech, but the revision of his nouns is most useful of all.

_____ **EXERCISES** _____

1. Write a paragraph with a highly abstract title—*love, idealism, education, boredom, naïveté, courage*—which does not contain the title word, but which describes a particular occasion that embodies the word. For instance, you might describe someone's apartment so that the reader would understand the loneliness of the tenant. Read your paragraph aloud in class, and see if the class recognizes the abstraction.

2. Take each of these nouns and find two other words to go with it, one more general and one more specific. If you can't find a word, use a short phrase.

rodent	cat
student	butter
lily	book
day	spaghetti
business	sports car

3. Collect four or five clichés that combine an abstract noun with an adjective, like *blind faith, basic needs*, and *conflicting desires*. Look in the newspaper for accounts of political speeches, or read magazine advertisements. See how many alternatives you can find for each, always realizing that a different context will require a different substitute for these filler phrases. Thus, *basic needs* in different contexts might be revised into distinctly different

phrases—like *minimum nutrition* or *attention and support*. Provide brief contexts, if you need them for clarity.

4. In these sentences, unde _ne the nouns that fail by invisibility, imprecision, fanciness, neologism, or overabstraction. Invent substitutes that improve the sentences.

   a. I chewed the food without swallowing it.
   b. What is the nature of your complaint?
   c. Religion, says Harvey Cox, has undergone privatization.
   d. When I think about my high school, I remember the love I felt for my Spanish teacher and the other feelings I felt for other people.
   e. Precipitation in the form of a thunderstorm situation is expected.
   f. Different aspects of the case of migrant laborers need discussion.
   g. Relationships are a matter of togetherness.

5. Underline the nouns in these passages, and label each as abstract or general or particular, according to the context. In class, compare your judgments with those of other students. Be prepared to argue. These distinctions are often tenuous, but discussing the distinctions will sharpen your eye for the insides of words.

   a. I myself, to come right down to it, have never been in love from afar, except perhaps for a handful of fleeting moments when a flickering shot of Wallace Reid driving over a cliff would make me feel queer. I know of women who have really mooned, and for years, over some such glamorous shadow, and it is highly possible that my own immunity is due to my sensual satisfaction, even vicarious, in such things as potato chips and Beluga caviar.

   M.F.K. Fisher, "Once a Tramp, Always"

   b. At 15,000 feet, its best operating height, the Kittyhawk IA could fly at a maximum speed of only 354 mph and climb to that height in 8.3 minutes, a longer time than the AGM2 Zero took to reach 20,000 feet. Empty weight was 6,350 pounds, normal loaded weight 8,280 pounds, which was the load carried in combat without drop tank or bombs, and maximum permissible weight was 9,200 pounds. Service ceiling was 29,000 feet. The IA climbed best at lower altitudes, but its best rate was only about 2,100 feet per minute at 5,000 feet.

   John Vader, Pacific Hawk

   c. It is a very small office, most of it taken up by a desk. The desk is placed smack in front of the window—not that it could have been placed anywhere else; this window looks out on the daylight landscape of Bergman's movies. It was gray and glaring the first day I was there, dry and fiery. Leaves kept falling from the trees, each silent descent bringing a little closer the long, dark, Swedish winter. The forest Bergman's characters are always traversing is outside this window and the ominous carriage from which they have yet to escape is still among the properties. I realized, with a small shock, that the landscape of Bergman's mind was simply the landscape in which he had grown up.

James Baldwin, Nobody Knows My Name

6. (a) Describe your room—its furnishings, decorations, objects— as precisely as you can. Avoid all generalities and try to give each thing its most accurate designation. (Instead of couch, say *bright blue convertible sofa . . .*).

(b) Look out the window and describe every form of activity that you notice. Again, be as precise as you can; make your verbs *work*.

MODIFIERS

Qualities and Choosing a Style

Modifiers—adjectives, adverbs, participles, and sometimes other words—give quality to nouns and verbs. "The *huge, green* lion leapt *slowly*. Adjectives and adverbs *modify* nouns and verbs. Participles, and sometimes nouns, work in the same way: "the *grinning* lifeboat," "the hypothesis *constructed* on Thursday," "*rock candy* mountain," "*mouse* music." Used well, modifiers create distinctions in meaning and add particularity to the particular. They discriminate and promote precision.

But modifiers give us the greatest trouble of all parts of speech. A writer using clichés assembles prepackaged combinations of nouns and adjectives. A beginning writer, when he tries to write colorfully, may stuff his style into obesity with a fatty diet of adjectives.

Overuse or misuse of adjectives and adverbs makes prose weak and lethargic. Because they are qualities rather than actions or things, adjectives and adverbs are inherently weaker parts of speech. Yet once more, choosing a style *means* something. *A change in style, however slight, is a change in meaning, however slight.*

To choose vigor in writing is usually to work with fewer modifiers. A few great writers, like Faulkner, use as many adjectives as any beginner—but use them well and with great originality. Most of the best writers use them sparingly and then make them count. We are not saying that adjectives are unimportant to writing. They are important. But verbs and nouns carry the sentence; if they take charge properly, they liberate adjectives, adverbs, and other modifiers to do their proper work: to make the exact final discriminations necessary to honesty and fullness.

Using Modifiers Well

Ernest Hemingway is known for using adjectives and adverbs sparingly. Let us look once more at the passage that begins "In Another Country."

> In the fall the war was always there, but we did not go to it any more. It was cold in the fall in Milan and the dark came very early. Then the electric lights came on, and it was pleasant along the streets looking in the windows. There was much game hanging outside the shops, and the snow powdered on the fur of the foxes and the wind blew their tails. The deer hung stiff and heavy and empty, and small birds blew in the wind and the wind turned their feathers. It was a cold fall and the wind came down from the mountains.

Hemingway says *the war*, not *the long war* or *the distant war* or *the bloody, maiming, killing, useless, horrid, revolting war*. He uses *always* and *any more* as adverbs in his simple predicates. *Cold* is an adjective in the second sentence; *electric* is necessary to lights, at a time when electric lights were new; in a country at war they seemed especially unwarlike; *pleasant* is an adjective as restrained as the verbs *was* and *go*. Then the eye of the paragraph turns away from restrained thoughts of war and looks at the dead animals that substitute for dead soldiers; right away the verbs and nouns become stronger and more particular: *foxes, shops, powdered*. Then the adjectives, exact and strong, come marching in: *stiff and heavy and empty*. The last is especially vigorous. The adjectives used sparingly are used strongly and well.

Let us apply the same standards to the passage quoted before from a story by John Updike.

> All the warm night the secret snow fell so adhesively that every twig in the woods about their little rented house supported a tall slice of white, an upward projection which in the shadowless gloom of early morning lifted depth from the scene, made it seem Chinese, calligraphic, a stiff tapestry hung from the gray sky, a shield of lace interwoven with black thread.

Updike is sometimes condemned by critics for overwriting, for self-indulgence in description, for too much prettiness. Can you find anything here to back up such a charge? We can admire a writer, or a passage of his writing, and still find flaws.

What good does the word *secret* do us? It adds a little to the meaning—a kind of coziness—but the word seems there mostly to be pretty and because its *s* sound chimes nicely with that of snow. We might like the line better if it read, "All the warm night the snow fell so adhesively. . . ." *Warm* is connected to *adhesively*, but *warm* would be a stronger adjective if it were more isolated, if the next noun, *snow*, did not carry its adjective also. Then later, in one phrase after another, each noun takes one adjective, and although each adjective is defensible in itself, the effect is monotonously pretty: *tall slice, upward projection, shadowless gloom, early morning.* The mixture tastes too sweet. Rearranging clauses, putting an adjective after a noun instead of before it, putting two adjectives with one noun and none with the next—any number of minor reworkings could improve the passage.

The modifier in exposition or argument can help you or hurt you, just as in poetry and fiction. E. B. White, in a brief essay on schools, says that he always went to public ones; by contrast, he says, "my wife was unacquainted with public schools, never having been exposed (in early life) to anything more public than the washroom of Miss Winsor's." The sentence includes several modifiers—*unacquainted, public, exposed, early,* and *public* again—and yet it has vigor and clarity. The words express light disdain for the snobbism that White associates with private schools. The verb phrase *was unacquainted with* is preferable to alternatives like *knew nothing about* because *acquainted* is a word we use in more formal social contexts: "No, I am not acquainted with that person." In the small world of White's sentence, the past participle wears a monocle and looks down at the peasants. *Exposed (in early life)* suggests that public schools are a contagious disease, like measles. And the parenthesis (*in early life*) has a mock formality that agrees with the medical metaphor.

But the adjective with which White plays the best trick is *public*, which he uses twice: first with *schools* and then in the phrase "anything more public than the washroom of Miss Winsor's." *Public* then becomes associated with public lavatories; we wrinkle our nose in disdain. At *Miss Winsor's*—the name sounds upper class (maybe we think of the British royal family)—of course the lavatory would be spotless and relatively private. What's more, it would not be a lavatory, john, W.C., or even bathroom; it would be a *washroom*. By a turn on the adjective *public*—from describing schools to implying lavatories—White makes his point most clearly.

In expository prose, adjectives usually narrow a noun's generality, to make the statement more specific. But if we do not watch ourselves carefully, we'll let the adjective drift into one of its characteristic errors. Here is a passage of exposition from a student essay.

> If you approach the shore of a rocky island in your kayak you must
> paddle slowly and cautiously. Even a gentle breeze may crush the

kayak against a sharp rock and sink the traveler, his vehicle, and all his very precious equipment.

Let us examine the modifiers. *Rocky* is necessary. *Slowly and cautiously* might become only *cautiously*, because *slowly* seems included in the idea of caution. *Sharp* is useful to make the threat more particular. But *very precious* is not so useful; is the equipment any more precious by being called so? Does *very* do anything at all? The sentence would end more vigorously as three nouns in a series: " . . . the traveler, his vehicle, and his equipment."

One adjective in the piece makes a palpable cliché, *gentle breeze.* Yet the writer clearly wants, and needs, to tell us that the winds that can cause this accident need not be gale force. "Why not use 'gentle breeze,' " says the beginning writer, "because 'gentle breeze' is exactly what I mean?" But the problem is not *what I mean*, but *what gets through:* the problem is communication. All problems of writing are problems of audience, of the responses of readers. *Gentle* together with *breeze* simply repeats a commonplace, and the reader is unmoved. We would do better simply to alter the expectation slightly and speak of a *faint breeze, slight breeze,* or *tiny breeze.*

Take another passage:

> The November meeting at the Union League Club was widely reported in the press, which saw evidence of high enthusiasm and sober purpose in the proceedings. A period of feverish activity now ensued. Legal documents were drawn and redrawn (mostly by Choate), potential trustees were sounded out, and advice was solicited. On January 31, 1870, the first board of trustees was elected. The ingredients of this twenty-seven-man founding board were predictable—a pomposity of businessmen and financiers, a clutch of lawyers, a nod of city officials, and a scintillation of writers and architects; less predictable, perhaps, was the inclusion of four practicing artists—the painters John F. Kensett, Frederick E. Church, and Eastman Johnson, and the sculptor J.Q.A. Ward.
>
> Calvin Tomkins, *Merchants and Masterpieces*

Usually a careful writer, Tomkins sounds fatigued. Commonplace combinations of adverb and verb, or adjective and noun, make much of the prose tedious, wordy, and wasteful: *widely reported, high enthusiasm,* and *feverish activity.* The clichés of color are there too: the *ingredients* of the *board* were *predictable.* Other modifiers are decent qualifications, like *November meeting* and *legal documents.* The author moves into vivacity at the end with unexpected and inventive nouns, "a pomposity of businessmen and financiers, a clutch of lawyers, a nod of city officials, and a scintillation of writers and architects."

The Modifier and the Cliché

Beginning writers often misuse modifiers, especially as portions of clichés. In our minds we associate adjectives and nouns in pairs. Our minds are not only computer dictionaries, they are junkyards of cliché. Thus the clichés listed in Exercise 3 on pages 120–121 consist of adjective-noun combinations like *blind faith* and *basic needs*. *Gentle breeze* is another such combination. Often nouns seem to imply adjectives, and if an adjective is implied by its noun, we should not use the adjective. If we think *grass*, we probably think *green*. We move in worn tracks. If we think *snow*, we think *white*. These weary associations are not really thinking; they are automatic responses to stimuli. When the reader encounters a cliché, his mind shuts off, even if only briefly. The point of writing is to keep the reader engaged at every moment. To do this we have to be engaged ourselves, first as human beings, then as writers. The more we can be ourselves, the less we will resemble a machine. If we remember more closely the grass and the snow we are describing, we will describe them precisely, out of our own memories, not out of the sad memory bank of other people's words. We might find an unexpected adjective for grass that is accurate for the grass at that place and that time. We might think of *harsh grass*. Or we might not describe the grass at all, or we might describe it in a clause or in a whole sentence. But we must avoid familiar associations; only the distinct particular takes our attention. Green snow is news.

Other nouns summon their cousin adjectives by bookish associations. Some of these combinations become comical from overuse or inherent absurdity, like *inscrutable Oriental*. Others have sources not so bookish: *responsible citizen, gracious living*. Whenever you use an adjective that sounds habitual to its noun, try omitting the adjective or recasting the phrase. In avoiding cliché, we have to *think*. We have to decide what we mean by a phrase like *fundamental truth*.

The Modifier That Weakens the Noun

An adjective gives us the noun's quality or type: *white* snow. An adverb relates to a verb in the same way: he grinned *happily*. But each of these examples would be bad style in most contexts. In each, the modifier diminishes the word it should strengthen. *Snow* is whiter than *white snow*. *Snow* is white in the brain's computer-dictionary, so why color it, unless to suggest its opposite? To say *white snow* brings to mind snow that is gray with dirt. This suggestion might be just what the writer wanted. "White snow fell, that morning, on the trash of the old city." The contrast is part of the meaning; *white* takes its place, modifying *snow*, because of the later words *trash* and *city*. But most of the time, when a writer adds *white* to *snow*, he subtracts from his sentence. He adds *white* in an uneasy search for particularity; he lacks confidence in the insides of *snow*. The adjective over-insists on a quality already firm in the word.

If we know that the character grinned, must we be told that he *grinned happily?* It can only bring to mind that he *might* have grinned unhappily, which is a nasty thought; the author reassures us that this supposition is not so, but without the reassurance there would have been no supposition.

A beginning writer often goes through stages with adjectives, and different people have different problems with them. With some beginners, all adjectives are predictable.

> It was a long trip from the high mountains of the frozen north to the desert wastes of sunny Arizona, but it was highly educational and well worthwhile.

Or remember Jim Beck's original impromptu on going to college.

> Education is of paramount importance to today's youth. No one can underestimate the importance of higher education. It makes us well-rounded individuals and. . . .

The problem is not primarily adjectives and adverbs, but thinking (or not thinking) in the old tracks.

Modifiers as Weak Intensives

We often misuse adjectives and adverbs as weak intensifiers. We say, "she moved gracefully," when we might say with more gusto that "she danced" or "she swept" or "she glided." We may use vague adjectives in place of specific ones or in place of clauses that could add color and precision. We say, "a tremendous amount," when *amount* is vague and *tremendous* is a weak and unspecific intensifier, or *really huge,* when we might say, *ten million,* or *as long as a supertanker.* Here the specific number of the comparison carries color; the accuracy is one of feeling, not of dimensions.

Automatic Modifiers

Another misuse of adjectives and adverbs, a more advanced or sophisticated misuse, appears when writers suddenly appreciate bright colors in writing, especially when they try their hand at stories and poems. In this misuse, the symptom is not cliché but multiplicity. Nearly every noun carries its adjective, like a tote bag, and every verb wears an adverb for a cape. The style is flashy and overdressed. Here is part of a poem written by a student in a creative writing class.

> I woke suddenly from a ghost-ridden dream
> of old women, to find myself wandering vaguely
> on the far edges of the raw city where white skulls tipped crazily
> in the western sky, and dirty children ran by
> to the cave shelters of abandoned cars. . . .

The lines are improved by mechanically stripping them of modifiers. Should any be kept? Yes. *Abandoned* is necessary to the emotion in *abandoned cars*. If it is merely *cars* that are *shelters*, they could be the kind of comfortable, middle-class vehicles one drives to the supermarket. The *abandoned* makes the children take *shelter* in something more suggestive of a dump.

Certainly *old women* is different from *women*. The phrase is altered by leaving out the adjective; perhaps we should restore *old*. But the other modifiers are best exterminated. When revised, the poem read:

> I woke from a dream
> of old women, to find myself wandering
> on the edges of the city
> where skulls tipped
> in the sky, and children ran
> to the shelters of abandoned cars. . . .

Here only two modifiers remain from the thirteen in the original version. Certainly the spare version is better writing, and it was accomplished wholly by deleting modifiers.

Nouns as Modifiers

In the phrase *cave shelter*, *cave* was a noun used as a modifier. Writers use participles and nouns as modifiers—*sheltering cave*, as well as *cave shelter*—with the same dangers, and the same opportunities, which attend the use of plain adjectives. Keep the same cautions in mind.

It is an advantage of the English language that its grammar is not rigid. In some languages, a noun would have to undergo respelling before it could be used as an adjective. English accepts change. And because it accepts change, in speech and writing, the writer or the speaker can make shades of meaning more precise. Using nouns as modifiers, we can say, *house party, religion committee, death wish*.

We can also say, "this type grammar," or—as in Bergen Evans's example of tediously multiplied nouns-as-modifiers— ". . . he absconded with the River Street fire house Christmas Eve party funds." Because English lacks grammatic rigidity, it is subject to abuses which can lead to chaos and disorganization. *Type* is frequently a filler-noun, and when we use it as a modifier we make even less sense than we normally do. With Bergen Evans's example, as with too many sentences that are seriously intended, the proliferation of nouns as modifiers creates heaviness and awkwardness. Here a longer, complex sentence would be preferable: "He absconded with the funds that the River Street fire house had collected for its Christmas Eve party." The noun-modifiers in "River Street fire house" and "Christmas Eve party" are reasonable, and they are not heaped upon each other.

Be careful when you use nouns as modifiers. Sociologists are often prone to abusing this device. One hears of the "city group research effort." By the third of these noun-modifiers, the reader begins to feel afloat in a sea of possibilities. What will go with what? It is as if one were wandering inside a Chinese sentence, with no inflections, with no connectives, with no tense or number. Avoid afflicting your reader; confine yourself to no more than two noun-modifiers in a row.

Revising Modifiers

When you revise your prose, question the need for every adjective and adverb. Can I do without these modifiers? Does the noun (like *postulate* in *basic postulate*) or the verb (like *run* in *run quickly*) do the job without the modifier? Or can I find an exact noun or verb to do the job in one word? Do I avoid a succession of adjective-noun combinations, the monotonous pairs? Do I create a cliché by joining two words that are commonly used together? Do I, on the other hand, use the necessary modifier to make the discrimination, or to add the expressive color?

Edit out all unnecessary modifiers; add necessary, useful, colorful ones.

_____ **EXERCISES** _____

1. Here are five simple nouns and five simple verbs. Make up ten sentences, using one of the words in each, and try to come up with fresh adverb and adjective choices. Try, also, to let your context make the modifier work: "We bask in the warm concern that radiates from Roger."

cut	sand
scramble	humility
search	concern
waver	hut
bask	scholar

2. In these sentences from student essays underline adjectives and adverbs that are useless, either because they are redundant (like *white snow* or *basic postulate*) or because they are weak intensives (like *very cold*).

   a. The cat slinks quietly into the room, its sharp claws ready for instant combat.
   b. It was a very long examination, with huge one-hour questions to answer completely, and I didn't have the slightest idea how to prepare for it.
   c. Whenever a large supertanker approaches a coastal port, concerned environmentalists take special notice.
   d. We got to know each other real soon and she is real nice.
   e. The forthcoming encounter between these two great teams promises to add luster to the annual classic.
   f. It was a spooky horror movie, and we were awfully happy when it finally ended and we could go back home.

3. In these passages from student essays, underline all modifiers. Then see if you can improve the passages by cutting some of them or by substituting other modifiers.

   a. Traveling is a great way to learn history. After seeing important places like Bunker Hill and the Smithsonian Institution, national history takes on new and significant meaning.
   b. Twenty-four separate and distinct pieces of glass in a metal frame make windows that open outward and dull the landscape with layers of dirt. The factory metal window frame is rusting through the yellow, chipped, peeling paint.
   c. Side by side, the swimmers skimmed across the water like swift hydroplanes. The crowd was frantic as it cheered the racing swimmers on.
   d. It was a perfect day for skiing, except that the snow was so bright and shiny that it hurt my eyes.
   e. Social Security is a regressive tax, harming the old and the poor as much as it helps them.
   f. George Washington crossed the Delaware in a rowboat.

4. Underline adverbs and adjectives in these passages. Can you criticize or praise the author's use of modifiers? Isolate specific examples and write short comments.

   a. After the age when hunting was done by males and the gathering of vegetables and small animal food by females—always with close cooperation between men and women—the discovery of planting and herding and then of the animal-drawn plow assured a steadier food supply, which underwrote male enterprises: conquest, the building of cities, trade, and *the stratification of society*. But women's role continued to be circumscribed by childbearing; whatever a women did she had to do near home.

Margaret Mead, "Needed: Full Partnership for Women"
(*Saturday Review*)

b. The needs of a society determine its ethics, and in the Black American ghettos the hero is the man who is offered only the crumbs from his country's table but by ingenuity and courage is able to take for himself a Lucullan feast. Hence the janitor who lives in one room but sports a robin's-egg-blue Cadillac is not laughed at but admired, and the domestic who buys forty-dollar shoes is not criticized but is appreciated. We know that they have to put to use their full mental and physical powers. Each single gain feeds into the gains of the body collective.

Maya Angelou, "Mr. Red Leg"

c. Nick looked at the burned-over stretch of hillside, where he had expected to find the scattered houses of the town, and then walked down the railroad track to the bridge over the river. The river was there. It swirled against the log spiles of the bridge. Nick looked down into the clear, brown water, colored from the bubbly bottom, and watched the trout keeping themselves steady in the current with wavering fins. As he watched them they changed their position by quick angles, only to hold steady in the fast water again. Nick watched them for a long time.

Ernest Hemingway, "Big Two-Hearted River"

d. Personal consideration of various and sundry matters of considerable importance has led numerous observers to ultimately conclude that the final end of Western civilization is certainly closer to a realistic possibility than might earlier have been tentatively assumed.

e. All girls in this period of American Victorianism suffered in an environment that utterly discouraged the healthy development of their emotional lives. However, at least some enterprising girls with a full measure of curiosity were less ignorant—perhaps less virginal—than the popular mythology supposed.

Cynthia Griffin Wolff, A Feast of Words

5. You might make more exercises out of the five examples above. Here are some possibilities. (a) Discuss in class the modifiers in each passage. (b) In each passage, look at the verbs and nouns. Are they used well? (c) In example c, put an adjective with every noun that lacks one and an adverb with every verb. Make the additions as apt as you can, and see what you have done. (d) Try to rewrite passage a, omitting adverbs and adjectives. How much, and what, do you lose?

6. Pick one of the passages in exercise 4 and write a paragraph to follow it. Stay as close to the author's style as possible; use similar kinds of adjectives and adverbs.

ORIGINAL WORDS: COMPARISONS

The Need for Originality

When we put words together—adjective with noun, noun with verb, verb with object—we start to communicate. We begin to show our own minds, or we show a dull copy of someone else's mind. Originality depends upon clarity and vigor. One source of originality in language is comparison. To talk about metaphoric writing and originality, we must go over some old ground.

Formulas or clichés or trite expressions substitute for the originality that each of us can attain. A girl who was mourning the death of her grandfather wrote, starting her first term paper of the term, "A tragedy recently occurred in my ancestral home." In a conference with her instructor, the girl wept over the death, she was pale, her hands shook. Moved by her obvious unhappiness, her teacher was sympathetic. At the same time he recognized that her prose style was not adequate to the depth of her feeling. Her body showed her wretchedness, but her prose showed her reading of a weekly country newspaper. He saw no grief in her phrasing, only the set phrases of headlines or lead sentences in obituaries. Perhaps the formulas came to her pen so that she could avoid the pain that comes with the real feeling. Or perhaps they came because she did not know the difference, in words, between the formula that communicates nothing and the originality that communicates feeling. No feeling reaches her reader. Her audience, instead of feeling moved, is bored. Her teacher felt that writing about her grief might help her to understand it, might help her through her mourning. By asking sensitive questions he helped her to criticize her own expression of grief. He suggested that *A tragedy occurred* is a formula that denies the tragic and compared this formula to others, like *a catastrophe was averted* and *a blessed event took place.* The journalistic familiarity, and the detached passivity of the construction, block off any believable expression of emotion.

A phrase becomes a formula or a cliché not just because it is used commonly, but because it prevents feeling. The phrase *rain fell* is more common than *a tragedy occurred,* yet we do not think of it as a formula because we do not use it to keep feelings down. A psychiatrist described clichés as "the lies we tell ourselves, that we *want* to hear." When the student wrote, "A tragedy recently occurred at my ancestral home," she was not lying overtly or intending to lie. It was not like saying that she did not chop down a cherry tree when she really did. The lie was internal, the lie of using language to avoid difficult reality, the lie of euphemism.

Overhearing Your Own Originality

Listen to yourself as you daydream or think idly. Are you reciting newspaper formulas or greeting-card verse? If you overhear yourself, in your own head, thinking trite sentimentality about your love, something is wrong. Find out what your real emotion is. Make it new. *Invent.* This does not mean that you should make up something that you haven't experienced—only that you should push yourself to discover the true specifics of your feeling. What is really there behind those bland formulas of affection?

In general, trying to *overhear* yourself is a good idea. On some days, you can listen to the dreaming voice easily; on other days, that voice seems mute; it is more likely that you are deaf. The dreaming language is clichés sometimes, sometimes puns or phrases with crazy originality. Sometimes the voice hums the tune from a song; when you remember the lyrics, a coded message is there. You may hear a country-western song about an abandoned lover, when you are feeling lonely or abandoned, or when something inside you feels that you will be lonely soon. The puns and crazy phrases are codes, too. Look at them closely. They have information for you. They are spoken by your original self, which is looking for attention from your conventional self, the self trained by parents and school and television to think like a train on a track. The crazier the phrase, the more devious the pun, the deeper the source in the self. It's not for nothing that psychiatrists often ask their patients to free-associate: associations are like arrows pointing to the real. When the dreaming voice talks in clichés, the train track is getting in the way of the real voice, because the real voice would tell us a truth that we might find painful.

Overhear yourself to know yourself. Then you can farm your daydreams for original verbal images that express feeling. The crazy image and the pun do not make good writing in themselves—though often they can be the leaping-off point in daily writing—but they do give clues to feelings that the conscious mind can follow. Here is an unrevised passage from a student's daily writing.

> I was taking out the garbage this morning and I heard (in my head) Fanny Davis's voice talking. She has a funny way of talking, Englishy but not really, and I knew it was her. She was saying, "I like to use the word 'to intimate' without any regard for its actual meaning." I kept stuffing the garbage bags into the cans, wondering why I

made that up, and why I chose Fanny's voice. It's always sounded affected to me. But that wasn't the sort of thing she says. She talks about her family and the home on the lake up North and going skiing in Switzerland. I was feeling blue. Bob had gone to New York and I knew that Sally was there, his old girlfriend, and I worried about that. Then I started laughing, right at the garbage, because I saw that "to intimate" and "too intimate" are close, but "to intimate" is a long way from the meaning of "too intimate." I was blue because I was too close to Bob, and I could get hurt.

The girl had uncovered something—which she almost knew already—by overhearing a daydream pun and by figuring it out. We may start dreaming, we end up thinking. Now she might be ready to examine her feelings about Bob or her feelings about her past.

When you discover something new by subjective scrutiny, paradoxically this inward-look allows outward-expression; for an audience of readers will respond to what is new—and often material that comes from *your* insides will speak to *their* insides. Of course you have to work it over and revise it so that it will make itself clear to an audience.

Looking for Originality

We can try to activate the daydreaming mind. We will not always succeed. The girl who wrote the paper beginning "A tragedy occurred" returned to the subject many times. The week after her initial paper, she wrote, "A month ago my grandfather died," and went on for a few rather dry sentences. Though the prose was colorless, it communicated more than her sentences about tragedies occurring at ancestral homes. Still, it had no images, no pieces of *sense*, no particulars.

Later, thinking about things she could associate with her grandfather, she wrote about *farm implements* that were *unused* and "hanging on the wall of the barn." Then she changed *farm implements* to *rake and hoe*. Then she revised the sentence again and added an image that could come only from the imagination guessing into the unseen. "His hoes and rakes hang from pegs in the barn. Spiders will spin webs there while the iron turns red with rust." She had farmed the dreaming part of her self, with a selective intelligence, and wrote two sentences that, in their details and associations, began to embody her melancholy and loss.

Simile and Metaphor

Images are groups of words that give an impression to the senses. Most images are visual, but we can also make images of taste, touch, hearing, and smell. Images communicate feelings and locate them firmly, really making contact between writer and reader. Comparisons in simile and metaphor mostly use images; they become ways for us to show emotions and illustrate ideas.

Similies are comparisons that use *like* or *as*, little words that announce a comparison. Metaphors omit the announcement. We write, "Her face bloomed with affection," and the word *bloomed* compares the girl to a flower; the face-flower is pretty, it is coming into its maturity, and it is associated with spring or summer. The writer may wish to go on talking about the girl in similes that use garden images. Perhaps her dress *rustles like leaves* and her skin is *as soft as petals.* The difference between similes and metaphors is small—a signal is there or not there—but it is real; the simile, because it announces itself, is more reasonable, more conscious of what it is doing.

For clarity, we must distinguish this brief comparison from the word *comparison* as we used it in the last chapter, discussing comparison and contrast as a structure used in exposition. We must also distinguish it from the grammatical sense—the *comparison of adjectives.* A comparison between the gross national products of Greece and Turkey, or between *less* and *least*, is not like comparing an old cheese to an untidy hog.

Creating a new, verbal comparison—simile, metaphor, and analogy—is our most original act of speech; the originality comes from the dreaming part of the self. Although we cannot always manufacture metaphors at will, we can learn to be alert for comparisons, and we can stimulate their coming. The dead grandfather's funeral had happened during a thunderstorm. When the girl tried to write about it, she encountered the trite associations of thunderstorms and death. She began simply.

> The funeral was 2 P M He was laid out in the front parlor, which was always closed except for weddings and funerals. Fifty people were there, some crowded into the parlor, others backed into the living room. The minister talked a little and read scripture. Then the sky turned dark.

The prose is simple and direct but it lacks energy. "The minister talked a little and read scripture" would probably be better if it included direct and indirect quotation. "Then the sky turned dark." *How* dark? How did she *feel* about the sky turning dark? We have the sense reading this prose that the feelings (which she earlier misrepresented in journalistic clichés) are still restricted, held back, reserved.

Suppose the sky turned "as dark as" something. If it turned "as black as the ace of spades," we would be nowhere. What does the ace of spades have to do with her grandfather or her feelings? Even if she had told us that the old man was a poker-playing farmer, the simile is so hackneyed that no one will see the black of the playing card when she says it. The useful comparison has to be new. But to say "the sky turned as dark as the soot from a factory chimney" would seem inappropriate; what would a factory have to do with a farm? The comparison must be more than new, it must relate to the context: to her memories of the man, to the funeral, to the idea of death. "The sky turned black as my grandmother's dress" would be a better direction; but maybe that's too black, or the texture is wrong. Or she might want to compare it to something she remembers and associates with the dead farmer. "The sky turned black, like inside the barn after milking." "The sky turned dark as a blueberry."

Sometimes one phrase will not be adequate. You want your comparison to go on longer than that. "The sky turned dark. I could see a black round storm cloud coming. I remembered leaning over the open well, staring down into the round black eye of the water." Here, we find a comparison within the comparison; the water is an *eye*, and the reader alert to the insides of words might reconstruct the dead metaphor: *the eye of the storm*—and revive it—although (or because) the author has not stated it.

Originality and Memory

To find the right comparison, we must draw on memory and daydream; imagination newly combines old things remembered; it is always present and often hard to discover. Our memory does not consist only of things memorized, but of everything that ever happened to us, which we can summon from the storehouse in our minds. We must learn the path to this treasury. Memory is crucial to our writing, thinking, and feeling. By scrutiny of the retained past, we begin to understand and to express that understanding. In the floating world, we connect feelings in the present to feelings about the past. We express these connections mostly by making comparisons. In our own uniqueness we can each find something that the sky grew as dark as.

In speaking of originality and memory, we do not imply that originality applies only to autobiographical writing. Whether we write about grandfathers or the gross national product, dinosaurs or television programs, we need original comparisons to make our prose lively enough to make contact with an audience. In an essay on economics called "the Technostructure," John Kenneth Galbraith contrasts *the man of intelligence* with his opposite; he could have used the abstract noun *stupidity*, parallel to *intelligence*; probably we would have remained content. But instead, he chose to brighten his prose with a figure: " . . . the same for the man of intelligence and for his neighbor who, under medical examination, shows daylight in either ear."

Galbraith remembers a familiar exaggeration of stupidity, as in *airhead*, and rewrites it in his own language by introducing a doctor's office. As we read his complex essay on economics, we are tickled momentarily by his comedy; it keeps us attentive.

Analogy

We use the word *analogy* for a comparison that makes or illustrates a point at greater length than a metaphor or a simile. An analogy can be extended into a whole essay; ministers' sermons are sometimes analogies—life is like the hundred-yard dash: birth is the starting gun, death is the tape, God is the judge. A whole book, or system of thought, can be based on analogy. Oswald Spengler, in *The Decline of the West*, at the beginning states an analogy that a civilization is an organism, is born, grows old, and dies; then he writes a long book to make a factual case for his analogy.

Analogy often works best within a unit no longer than the paragraph. Frequently, it illustrates the intent of an abstraction. Analogies may make points; they don't prove them; they show how you feel, or they clarify your use of an ambiguous or all-inclusive word. Suppose we were tempted to support the stick-figure philosophical assertion "Love is better than hate." We would not get far with such a proposition, because it is too vague for support, but we would at least put eyes and ears on our stick figure if we went on, "It is a meadow in the country compared to an alley of garbage and broken glass."

An analogy often runs through a paragraph like a thread in tweed, not separated into patches of assertion followed by comparison, but interwoven. James Thurber wrote this paragraph about working with the editor of *The New Yorker*, Harold Ross:

> Having a manuscript under Ross's scrutiny was like putting your car in the hands of a skilled mechanic, not an automotive engineer with a bachelor of science degree, but a guy who knows what makes a motor go, and sputter, and wheeze, and sometimes come to a dead stop; a man with an ear for the faintest body squeak as well as the loudest engine rattle. When you first gazed, appalled, upon an uncorrected proof of one of your stories or articles, each margin had a thicket of queries and complaints—one writer got a hundred and forty-four on one profile. It was as though you beheld the words of your car spread all over the garage floor, and the job of getting the thing together again and making it work seemed impossible. Then you realize that Ross was trying to make your Model T or old Stutz Bearcat into a Cadillac or Rolls-Royce. He was at work with the tools of his unflagging perfectionism, and, after an exchange of growls or snarls, you set to work to join him in his enterprise.
>
> James Thurber, *The Years with Ross*

Thurber begins by announcing his subject, "Having a manuscript under Ross's scrutiny," departs from it for the rest of a long sentence, returns to the manuscript for a sentence, then in the final three sentences develops his analogy, makes it funnier, and makes his point about Ross as an editor. He sharpens his points by contrasts: *mechanic* not *engineer*; not *automotive engineer* but *guy*. He then develops his analogy into impossibility (repairing a Model T into a Cadillac), exaggerating it out of all touch with reality; the customer joins with the mechanic to rebuild his torn-up machine. The analogy expresses feeling, it is witty, and it is a pleasure to read. Consider this alternative, omitting the garage and substituting abstraction and generality for analogy:

> Having a manuscript under Ross's scrutiny was an edifying if terrifying experience. He was a skilled editor, not an academic, but a practical man. When you first gazed, appalled, upon an uncorrected proof of one of your stories or articles, each margin had a number of queries and complaints—one writer got a hundred and forty-four on one profile. You beheld all your work torn apart, and it seemed impossible to put it together. Then you realized that Ross was trying to make ordinary prose into prose of the highest order. He was using his editorial skills with unflagging perfectionism, and, after an exchange of growls or snarls, you set to work to join him in his enterprise.

This gutted version is slightly shorter, but the cutting loses rather than gains: the paragraph diminishes in energy and expression.

The Unintended Comparison

With analogy as with other forms of comparison, you must be wary of the dead, the mixed, and the inadvertently comic. Often a writer will trap himself in an unconscious analogy expressing an attitude that he really feels but denies to himself. The disparity is as slapstick as a top-hatted man with his trousers missing. Here is an English critic, writing about American music in the London *Times Literary Supplement*. He writes in attempted praise of American energy and vitality, but other messages come through his bad prose.

> The American composer is neither enriched nor shackled. He had nothing to start from but old rags and bones of European culture that, imported to a new environment, soon lost their savor. Then gradually, in the pulping machine of a polyglot society, the rags and bones began to acquire a taste of their own.

Look at the main analogy, rags and bones. When they were imported here, they "soon lost their savor." Did the gentleman actually expect rags and bones to taste good? His idea of the American stew expresses his distaste: the analogy suggests eating the product of something like a paper factory: "in the pulping machine . . . the rags and bones began to acquire a taste of their own." The writer expressed his feelings, but he expressed feelings he didn't know he had. He appears to believe that he likes American music, but the unacknowledged Critic Inside is holding his nose.

For another example, we could look at a headnote I (D. H.) wrote in a textbook. Speaking of Virginia Woolf, I wrote, "Handicapped by her sex . . . she persevered against prejudice to refine and develop her abilities." Professor Sandra Donaldson, of the University of North Dakota, wrote me an inquiring letter about my "most puzzling remark." "Did she wear a brace on her arm to help her develop her ability to write, thus overcoming this handicap? Or are there pills women can take, to overcome this curse? Or did she follow a regimen of exercises?" Of course I *intended* to imply that the handicap was male chauvinism; but in my *unintended* comparison, I revealed my hidden bias. Perhaps my consciousness had been raised, but my unconsciousness nevertheless compared being female to being crippled. I had not paused to examine what I really said.

To express a feeling without examining it is dangerous. Originality combines opposites. we dream—with our eyes open; we are inspired—then we scrutinize and revise. Scrutiny provides the motive for revision. We need to look at words—to see the connection between *rags and bones, savor,* and *taste*—and we will sometimes discover feelings we had not wished to acknowledge. Then we can revise ourselves or our prose or both. We must again float on daydream and memory for new words, and then put the new words under scrutiny again. Only by developing all these mental abilities—and this discipline—can we begin to be honest. The paradox is that to be sincere we must struggle; we must struggle to be spontaneous, and then struggle to revise, refine, and order our spontaneity, in order to reach an audience other than ourselves. To speak our most intimate selves into the ears of others, we must revise.

One way to cultivate our sensitivity to the insides of words is to develop an ear for the unintended comparison. (The unintended comparison is often an overt, and sometimes extended, version of the dead metaphor.) On a Monday night football broadcast, Howard Cosell said of a new quarterback that he "walked in the wake" of a great predecessor. In this example, the unintended comparison approaches blasphemy.

The mixed metaphor is, of course, another consequence of thoughtless analogy making. *The New Yorker* regularly cites examples as humorous filler. Here is one of their findings:

Saint Audrey and her board puppets have royally ripped their britches trying to ram more and higher taxes down our throats. Indeed, they have danced around the budget Maypole for too long. These same supervisors should now retreat, rethink, and re-program. The time has come to fish or cut bait.

Looking for Analogies

We can think out an analogy more easily than we can create the lone metaphor, which, to most writers, seems a gift from the god within us, an inspiration. Suppose you are discussing what makes a love affair succeed. Suppose you decide that it takes a lot of work. The word *work*, itself a metaphor nearly dead, can lead you into analogy. What kind of work is it like? Is it like a nine-to-five job? You can make an analogy in the negative: "This work is no nine-to-five job." Is it like building a house? Rebuilding a destroyed city? Making the sets for a play? Sculpting a life-sized elephant out of used bubble gum?

Revising writing in order to reach an audience, we can use our clichés as clues to lead us toward inventing new analogies and meta-phors. If we can learn to identify the worn out, we can create the original. Suppose that when we look over the draft of an essay, we discover the cliché of *clues* used above. By heeding our sense of the insides of words, we can discover a mystery story buried in the dead metaphor: clichés are the smoking guns that reveal the murderer—and oddly enough "the murderer" we discover in this analogy will become our original, invented comparison. If we convict the murderer of being a new metaphor, we have won our case. The defense rests.

The liveliest prose moves from analogy to analogy without strain. It takes practice to learn how to invent, and practice to learn when to stop inventing. When analogy shifts abruptly, the effect is usually ridiculous, and comic writers can use these sudden shifts to their ad-vantage; if in one sentence you compare tennis with big-game hunting, do not compare it in the next sentence with knitting unless you want a laugh. Often a sentence or a paragraph of general summary or narrative separates passages of differing analogies, keeping them from clashing.

Here Edward Hoagland begins an essay called "The Courage of Turtles" with a bizarre comparison and goes on to make others.

> Turtles are a kind of bird with the governor turned low. With the same attitude of removal, they cock a glance at what is going on, as if they need only to fly away. Until recently they were also a case of virtue rewarded, at least in the town where I grew up, because, being humble creatures, there were plenty of them. Even when we still had a few bobcats in the woods the local snapping turtles, growing up to forty pounds, were the largest carnivores. You would see them

through the amber water, as big as greeny wash basins at the bottom
of the pond, until they faded into the inscrutable mud as if they
hadn't existed at all.

(A *governor*, as Hoagland uses the word, is an automatic device attached
to an engine to limit its speed.) Hoagland compares a turtle to a bird
exactly because the comparison seems impossible. When he provides
the bird-turtle with a mechanical device appropriate to tractor-trailers,
he makes another impossibility. But by comparing the incomparable,
Hoagland shocks us into seeing something freshly: both turtles and
birds observe the world with an alert nervousness. When Hoagland goes
on to speak of *virtue rewarded*, he makes ironic comparison of turtles
with downtrodden humans. He follows with a straightforward but unexpected connection of turtles with bobcats and ends extravagantly by
comparing turtles to metallic kitchen utensils which have the power to
disappear. The prose's energy derives from its quick assembly of details
and outrageous, but accurate, comparisons.

Revising for Comparison

First, check your sentences to make sure that you are controlling
the comparisons you make. Make sure that you do not inadvertently
turn a quarterback into a deity or an art form into a bad smell. Second,
see that you have not made cliché comparisons that no longer function,
like "black as the ace of spades."

Then do the more difficult. *Add* simile, metaphor, and analogy.
Most of us in our first drafts lack energy and feeling. Our prose resembles the pale version of Thurber, after the analogy was deleted. The
prose is too plain to reach the reader with excitement and precision.
Float on memory and daydream to invent; scrutinize with critical
intelligence to cut and to improve. Ask yourself if your invention is
new, if it is appropriate, if it does not clash with anything else. In a
paragraph of exposition, think if you can clarify by analogy. If you find a
cliché or a dead metaphor, remake the old into something new. What
was it like, to have your prose edited by Ross? What was it like, the day
your grandfather died?

Revising Words

Cheryl Lewis, the student who had tried without success to write
about her grandfather's death, eventually found another way to approach her subject. When her teacher assigned a short descriptive
theme later in the term, Cheryl decided that she would try to describe
her grandfather as she remembered him. Her first attempt began:

> My grandfather was a big man. He was over six feet tall and had white hair. But he did not look old. He was strong from working all his life and he stood very straight. His face was like leather. When he smiled or frowned, his wrinkles showed clearly. He usually wore overalls and a shirt, but sometimes he would walk around the house in his long underwear. Then you saw that even though his face and hands were brown, his feet were completely white. He liked to sit in the kitchen like that early in the morning, reading the paper and drinking coffee.

Several days later, Cheryl had a conference with her teacher. He praised her determination, her desire to master the subject and the emotions it aroused; he also agreed that this draft was better. She let her emotions show indirectly by allowing the description to speak for itself. *But,* he said, he still had some problems with this presentation. The picture in the reader's mind was not clear enough. "Let's look at the opening," he said. "If you can solve that you'll probably see what to do with the rest."

The teacher told Cheryl that she was not making use of some of the writer's best tools. "Precision tools," he said, "like images, adjectives, and adverbs." He reminded her of subjects they had covered in class discussions. Cheryl nodded. She said that she knew there was a lot she could do in the way of fine tuning. "I wanted to get my general impressions down first," she said. "If I spend too much time getting the first few sentences right, I freeze up." Her teacher acknowledged that perfectionism often led to writer's block, especially in the beginning stages of composition. But now that she had the essential shape, he added, she could turn her attention to more precise detailing. He reminded her that specific images and concrete words were the best way to make a connection with an audience.

Cheryl and her teacher talked about the opening passage. The teacher asked her a number of questions. "You say he was big," he said, "how big? Tell me so that I can see. Was he fat?" And: "He worked, but what kind of work did he do? What were his overalls like—rumpled, neatly pressed, dirty? Is there a better, less trite, image than leather for his face? What about those wrinkles? Is there some way you can describe those white feet? Can you compare them to anything?" Cheryl scribbled notes on her paper, but at that last question she looked up with a smile. "Albino fish," she said. *"What!"* Cheryl then explained how her grandfather had joked about his own feet—*he* had compared them to albino fish. "Perfect," said the teacher.

Cheryl finished making notes and looked up. "I think I'm starting to see what you're after," she said. "It's as if you want to *be* there." The teacher nodded. Then he made a suggestion. Cheryl was to sit down at home with her opening paragraph and try some of the brainstorming and sprinting exercises used by the class earlier in the term. She was to bring a page of ideas and images to class. "Check your memories," advised the teacher. "Try to reach back for some associations. Put down anything that comes to mind." Two days later Cheryl handed in her list:

> Grandma's kitchen, gramps leaning to get through the door
> reading the paper in longjohns (already mentioned)
> silvery hairs on his chest
> big belly—but hard
> Santa Claus?
> "A man needs to eat, needs energy."
> standing up and patting belly
> teasing grandma all the time
> loves jokes, loves to laugh
> boom, boom, boom—the whole kitchen rattles
> wrinkles tighten when he smiles
> I thought cheeks would break in half
> dressed he looked so brown, years in the sun
> but his feet—what a surprise!
> "albino fish" and how he wiggled his toes when he pointed to
> them

On the bottom of the page Cheryl had written, in exasperation, "Too much to tell!" When her teacher handed the sheet back the next day, her remark was circled. Beside it he had written "Better too much than not enough!" In smaller letters: "Much better. Use some of these. Try to make every detail and action precise."

When rewrites were collected the following week, Cheryl passed in a much expanded essay. She was happier with the whole piece, but she especially liked her new beginning.

> My grandfather was a big man. He was tall enough to have to stoop coming through the kitchen door, and though he was not hugely fat, you could see that his weight made him do extra work. Sometimes at the end of a long day of driving the John Deere or mending fence he would come puffing from the barn. My grandmother was always after him to go on a diet. But he had an answer for that. "How can I work if I don't have energy? Where does energy come from?" Or else he might stand up tall, stick out his chest, and slap his belly hard with his palms. "Pure muscle." Standing there in his longjohns, barefoot, he was a sight. He was like two different people put together to make one. His face and hands were dark, penny-brown, from working in the sun. The skin was hard, too. When he smiled I thought his cheeks might crack open. But what a shock it was to look down at his feet. "Like two albino fish," he would say, wiggling his toes furiously.

The teacher was pleased with the rewrite. He asked Cheryl if she could feel the difference herself. She could. "I also enjoyed the process of writing much more," she said. "It took a long time, but I felt *there*, really close to the farm and my grandparents."

"A few mere words," said her teacher. Then he took two minutes to point out the parts of Cheryl's description that he found especially successful. He praised the precision of the second sentence. Cheryl had managed to suggest the man's height, get him into motion, and introduce the kitchen setting; she had also given a sense of his girth. "I like your adverb *hugely* there," he said. "It tells us that he was big, *too* big, but that he stopped short of obesity." The next sentence helped the reader picture the kind of work he did—naming "John Deere" instead of writing "tractor" was good—but the focus, the real weight, was on the participle *puffing*. "Another nice choice," he told her. "Your words are starting to do the job they were meant to do."

"What else?" Cheryl's teacher said that he very much liked the sentence: "Or else he might stand up tall, stick out his chest, and slap his belly hard with his palms." The separated phrase defined the stages of the action very clearly, he explained. But it was the crisp emphasis, the clean word-sounds of "slap his belly hard with his palms" that registered most vividly. *Slap* as a verb, *hard* as an adverb, and *palms* as a noun that was far more precise than *hands*. Palms, he said, forced the reader to visualize the action; the word established the position of the hands in space.

"I singled out a number of things here," said Cheryl's teacher. "I wanted you to know where you succeeded, and why. You turned a vague, somewhat lazy piece of writing into something that begins to live on the page. You didn't do it by magic or voodoo, but by tuning in to every sentence. You made sure that you had something to say, and that you said it as vividly and accurately as you could. You've got adjectives and adverbs working to sharpen your perceptions; you have in the cracking cheeks and those albino fish a pair of wonderful images. The playful sense of the toes wiggling *furiously* adds pleasure. And the *penny-brown*. . . ."

EXERCISES

1. (a) Here are six common comparatives. Taking any three, write sentences in which you make a new simile. Make up comparisons that derive from their subjects. For instance, "The 747 looked as long as the runway of my hometown airport." "The book's cover was as bright as a fresh idea."

as long as	as green (or any color) as
as bright as	as sour as
as wet as	as heavy as

(b) Pretend that you are walking through a dark woods late at night. Find three similes that might express your feelings. Pretend now that you finally see the lights of your destination in the distance. Describe those lights using three different metaphors or analogies.

2. In the Hoagland passage, underline verbs, circle nouns, and draw oblong boxes to enclose modifiers. How do the parts of speech work together—adjective with noun, subject with verb? Do his metaphors and comparisons make use of all parts of speech?

3. These clichés began life as new metaphors. Think of them as they must have sounded when somebody first made them up, when "glued to the spot" implied a puddle of Elmer's in one's chair seat. Then invent a new metaphor that does what the cliché no longer does. Instead of "glued to his chair," say "stapled to his desk."

toe the line	a golden opportunity
an axe to grind	it dawned on me
chip on his shoulder	bathed in sunlight

4. In these passages, underline analogies, metaphors, and similes. Choose three examples that you particularly like, and explain your reasons for preferring them.

a. But his position was weak. Like a cougar, the army was constantly perched above him, ready to pounce.

> *John Gerassi, The Great Fear in Latin America*

b. After thousands of years we're still strangers to darkness, fearful aliens in an enemy's camp with our arms crossed over our chests.

> *Annie Dillard, "Strangers to Darkness"*

c. Many of us grow to hate documentaries in school, because the use of movies to teach us something seems a cheat—a pill disguised as candy—and documentaries always seem to be about something we're not interested in.

> *Pauline Kael, "High School and Other Forms of Madness"*
> *(in Deeper into Movies)*

d. I lay down on a solitary rock that was like an island in the bottom of the valley, and looked up. The grey sage-brush and the blue-grey rock around me were already in shadow, but high above me the canyon walls were dyed flame-colour with the sunset, and the Cliff City lay in a gold haze against its dark cavern. In a few minutes it, too, was grey, and only the rim rock at the top held the red light. When that was gone, I could still see the copper glow in the piñons along the edge of the top ledges.

The arc of sky over the canyon was silvery blue, with its pale yellow moon, and presently stars shivered into it, like crystals dropped into perfectly clear water.

Willa Cather, The Professor's House

e. . . . Women have served all these centuries as looking glasses possessing the magic and delicious power of reflecting the figure of man at twice its natural size. Without that power probably the earth would still be swamp and jungle. The glories of all our wars would be unknown. We should still be scratching the outlines of deer on the remains of mutton bones and bartering flints for sheepskins or whatever simple ornament took our unsophisticated taste. Superman and Fingers of Destiny would never have existed. The Czar and the Kaiser would never have worn their crowns or lost them. Whatever may be their use in civilised societies, mirrors are essential to all violent and heroic action. That is why Napoleon and Mussolini both insist so emphatically upon the inferiority of women, for if they were not inferior, they would cease to enlarge.

Virginia Woolf, A Room of One's Own

5. Make up three paragraph-long analogies that express what it is like to go to school. Thurber's version of Ross as mad mechanic provides an example. Could you construct an analogy from work with a computer? From building a house? Work collectively on this exercise during the class hour. Be ready to read your best paragraph out loud to the class.

5

Sentences

STYLE AND THE SENTENCE

A sentence is a group of words with a period, exclamation point, or question mark at the end. But no definition of the sentence is likely to help us much in writing one. Sentences—the spoken kind—happened first, grammarians named them later. We learn sentence structure by speaking and listening, by reading and writing, more than by studying types of sentences. Still, after studying sentences we can listen more carefully, read more closely, speak more eloquently, and write more clearly. We can learn to *control* the style of our sentences to express feelings and ideas—to make contact with our reader and to hold our reader's interest. We can learn to make sentences that hang together, cohering part with part, achieving unity in the service of clarity. We can learn as well to *vary* our sentences.

PARTS OF SENTENCES

Before we look into the types of sentences, we need to know something about the parts of sentences and the names of those parts. For convenience we will use standard names for the parts—like *subject* and *predicate*. Once learned, the names will save time; *elbow* is both clearer and less wordy than *that joint in the middle of the arm*.

Sentences have two main parts, subjects and predicates. The *subject* is what we make a statement or ask a question about. Usually the subject is a noun, or a pronoun like *she* or *who*; but on occasion the subject can be something else that substitutes for a noun, like a clause or a phrase. (Even a verb can be a subject: "*Is* is a verb. *Is* is the subject of these sentences.") In these sentences, the subjects are in italics:

> *The frogman* dived.
> *The theory* was valid.
> *Who* committed this brutal crime?
> *Whoever committed this crime* must be insane.
> *Watching pinball machines light up* gave him a headache.

In the following sentence the *simple subject* is *woman,* and the *complete subject* is *the woman in the blue house by the river:*

> The woman in the blue house by the river wrote bizarre sentences on the walls.

The *predicate* is the verb along with its modifiers and complements. The predicate is what the sentence says about the subject; most often, the predicate is the action that goes on in the sentence. In these sentences, the simple predicates are in italics:

> The frogman *dived.*
> The theory *was* valid.
> Who *committed* this brutal crime?
> Watching pinball machines light up *gave* him a headache.

The *simple predicate* in the next sentence is *wrote;* the *complete predicate* is *wrote on the walls with invisible liquids.*

> The woman in the blue house wrote on the walls with invisible liquids.

Objects come in four forms: direct objects, indirect objects, objects of prepositions, and complementary objects.

The *direct object* is the part of a sentence that the predicate acts upon. Here, the direct objects are in italics:

> She designed the *atomic reactor.*
> The president washed the *dishes.*
> *What* did the elephant say?
> Underline the *predicates.*

An *indirect object* usually comes before a direct object and tells us to whom or for whom (or to what or for what) the predicate acts.

> She gave the *team* a case of beer.
> Sam wrote *her* a new song.

Most of the time, the indirect object replaces a prepositional phrase using *to* or *for.*

> She gave a case of beer *to the team.*
> Sam wrote a new song *for her.*

In the last two sentences *team* and *her* are *objects of prepositions*, nouns or noun substitutes that a preposition relates to another word or word group. Here are more prepositions followed by objects:

> When you are defenestrated you are thrown *out a window.*
> Hulk Hogan was barred *from the premises.*

Another construction has two objects, in which the second modifies or describes the first. The second, or *complementary object*, may be a noun or an adjective. In these examples the complementary object is in italics:

> They made her *bartender.*
> He called her a *humbug.*
> Margaret painted the tree *purple.*

Complements follow linking verbs like *is* and *become* and *appear.* When they modify or describe the sentence's subject, we call these words *subjective complements.* These words can be adjectives or nouns:

> She's an *artist.*
> They appeared *pretty.*

A *phrase* is a group of words which work together as a unit, but which lack a subject and a predicate. There are several kinds of phrases, defined by the word introducing them:

Prepositional phrase	The bat *in the attic* is not a vampire.
Verbal phrase	More and more people *will be buying* sub-compact cars as gasoline prices again rise.
Infinitive phrase	Hockey fans tend *to enjoy violence.*
Gerund phrase	*Establishing a fascist state* requires ruthlessness and ambition.
Participial phrase	*Doubting the medical assumptions of his time,* Pasteur sought further knowledge about what causes disease.

A *clause* is a group of words that contains a subject and a predicate. A clause may be *main* (also called independent) or *subordinate* (also called dependent). A *main clause* can be a simple sentence in itself.

The thin dog barked.

A *subordinate clause* is not a complete sentence and cannot stand by itself; rather, it works as a noun, as an adjective, or as an adverb within a sentence.

Noun clause	*Whether the new league will flourish* is a question that no one can answer with certainty.
Adjective clause	The cricket, *which appeared to be wearing a tiny tuxedo*, did not answer his naïve questions.
Adverb clause	She ordered the troops to attack *when it became apparent that to delay any longer would be suicidal.*

Each of these last two clauses is a *modifier*. A *modifier* is any word, phrase, or clause that functions as an adjective or adverb. It quite literally *modifies* or changes the meaning of the noun or verb in question.

The bat *in the attic* is not a vampire.

Here the prepositional phrase *in the attic* does something to, *modifies*, bat; it tells us *which* bat. If we say *the vampire bat is in the attic*, then the word vampire is an adjective that modifies *bat*.

The vampire flew slowly around the room after he assumed the form of a bat.

Here we have three modifiers, all acting as adverbs. One modifier tells us about the way the vampire flew: the single word *slowly*; then a prepositional phrase tells us where: the vampire flew *around the room*; then a subordinate clause tells us when it happened: *after he assumed the form of a bat.* Manner, place, and time; how, where, and when.

Now that we have the names of parts, we can examine types of sentences.

TYPES OF SENTENCES

Simple Sentences

A sentence is simple as long as it remains one clause, containing one predicate. *John laughed* is a complete, two-word sentence, simple and common in its structure: subject/verb. We could add modifiers, *Big*

John laughed loudly, or a prepositional phrase, *John laughed at her,* and the sentence would remain simple.

A sentence can be quite long and yet still be simple. This sentence is simple, but elaborates the predicate with prepositional phrases:

> *Phil runs/with his wife/at Waterman Gymnasium/before classes.*

We can add as many modifiers as we wish; the sentence will remain simple unless we add a subordinate clause.

A subject can be long, too.

> *The ape-man in the gray loincloth, a wooden spear in his hand,* attacked.

Either subject or predicate can be compounded and the sentence remains simple.

> John *and his zebra* cried.
> John *laughed and cried.*

Or the verb can be elaborated.

> The ape-man *attacked swiftly, with a sharp cry, from behind the rocks.*

Or we can have a direct object, and the object can be elaborated.

> The ape-man attacked *the sluggish warriors, those intruders tired from their lengthy searching.*

Or the simple sentence can have all its parts elaborated and remain simple.

> The ape-man in the gray loincloth, a wooden spear in his hand, attacked the sluggish warriors swiftly from behind the rocks, the boulders shining in the hot sun.

The basic sentence is still *The ape-man attacked,* though by this time we have more definition for each of the parts, more information, and too many adjectives.

Compound Sentences

A compound sentence has two or more main clauses, each containing a subject and a predicate, each describing an action complete in itself. Compound literally means "put together" or "added together." The clauses in the compound sentence are joined by a connective—*and, but, or, nor, yet, for,* or *so*—or by a semicolon or colon.

> The economy stagnates and prices rise.

> We can lower the price of admission or we can stage fewer plays.

He never went to the snake house again; he had been revolted by the alligator.

The clauses in each of these sentences are independent. Each sentence could become two sentences, with minimal change in meaning.

The economy stagnates. Prices rise.

We can lower the price of admission. We can stage fewer plays.

He never went to the snake house again. He had been revolted by the alligator.

In the compound sentence, notice that the two complete clauses are nearly equal in importance, or *coordinate*. A compound sentence, of course, can have more than two parts.

Clemens pitched a curve, the runner on first sprinted toward second, and Barrett ran to cover the base.

But a string of coordinate clauses is usually boring.

There was more crime in the street, the criminals were running around free, the judges were letting people go, nobody was safe in the streets, criminals were out on bail, murderers were on parole, and nobody did anything.

Complex Sentences

If, however, one part of the sentence depends on the other—if the one is the cause of the other, for instance—we have a complex rather than a compound sentence. We call the clause that depends upon the other for explanation or completion the *subordinate clause*. A complex sentence would be

Because the economy stagnates, high-priced items find few buyers.

The first clause in this sentence is subordinate. It cannot stand alone.

We can vary sentences even when we use only simple clauses and compounds of equally complete clauses. But the complex sentence provides further variety and allows us to emphasize the relationship of ideas to others in the same sentence. If we combine the two simple sentences

We were good friends. We saw each other only in the summer.

alternately into two different complex sentences, the results have different meanings:

We were good friends, although we saw each other only in the summer.

Although we were good friends, we saw each other only in the summer.

Complex sentences allow us to establish a precise relationship among ideas.

Clauses introduced by relative pronouns, *that, which,* or *who*—sometimes called *relative clauses*—are subordinate to a main clause; they depend on it.

Do you remember the face of the man *who sold you this ticket?*
The king executed the horse *that had thrown him.*

In other sentences, we attribute cause or sequence, and we do it by a conjunction like *because* or *after.*

Because the Girl Scouts had proved to be unscrupulous, the neighbors destroyed the cookies they had purchased.

After the movie ended, everyone in the audience left.

Many other conjunctions—like *although, after, if, since,* and *when*—can introduce subordinate clauses, each with its own precise meaning to be used by the careful writer.

Compound-Complex Sentences

Sometimes we can combine compound and complex sentences, using at least two main clauses and one subordinate clause. In each sentence below, the clause in italics is subordinate; the main clauses are in roman type.

The young heiress jumped under the covers *when her uncle walked in wearing his gorilla suit,* and she refused to come out.

If you had only proofread the article more carefully, Mr. Crumbly would not have been so insulted, and we wouldn't have this lawsuit on our hands!

Incomplete Sentences

Another type of sentence commonly used is the incomplete sentence, or fragment. It is incomplete because it lacks a subject or a predicate. *John laughed* is a brief but complete sentence. Neither *John* nor *laughed* would be complete by itself, but we could use either word alone in the proper context.

She thought about whom she might ask to the picnic. Harry? Harry was too grubby. John? John.

> When she saw him she covered her mouth and, though she tried to suppress it, laughed. Laughed. He could not believe it.

Often the incomplete sentence is a phrase or a clause of several words.

> The essay by Ellsberg shows control of sentence variation. Like the variety in his first paragraph.

Although this combination of sentence and sentence fragment makes sense, we should revise it if we intend to write formal prose. We have several ways of working the meaning of *Like the variety in the first paragraph* into a longer sentence:

> Ellsberg's essay shows control of sentence variation, an attribute obvious in his first paragraph.

> As we can observe reading his first paragraph, Ellsberg's essay shows control of sentence variation.

The incomplete sentence is informal and we should usually avoid it when we write essays. Often we use it in speech, where tone of voice or facial expression or gesture completes meaning. But when we write, only the marks on the page carry meaning for us. As writers we must make connections for the reader, fixing meaning with word choice, word order, and punctuation. Frequently the incomplete sentence leaves the reader baffled. But not always. We use the incomplete sentence with many common phrases like *No comment, Not at all, Of course*, and *But not always*.

Student writers usually make sentence fragments accidentally, without noticing that their sentence lacks a main verb. Such fragments creep up on us even when we think we are paying attention.

> Among my favorite foods, English muffins, hot from the oven, dripping butter and honey.

> When I climb onto my moped and drive out of town, away from the noisy dormitories and the silent library, onto the dusty back roads.

> Which she often does, although I don't approve.
> While I was growing up.

These sentence fragments hang in air. They give information which goes nowhere, which holds something back from the reader. They leave unanswered questions: *why, where, what?* Each can become a whole sentence when we supply what was missing.

> Among my favorite foods *are* English muffins, hot from the oven, dripping butter and honey.

> When I climb onto my moped, *I* drive out of town, away from the noisy dormitories and the silent library, onto the dusty back roads.

She drove home last night, which she often does, although I don't approve.

I fell down and skinned my knees all the time while I was growing up.

The first rule is clarity.

Students who have difficulty identifying fragments, and who write them unknowingly, should look carefully at the review of sentence fragments, pages 368–370, and do the exercises there.

Another common problem with incomplete sentences is that they tend to avoid committing themselves. If we take notes on a history lecture, using fragments rather than sentences, we may look at them a month later and read something like *Too many wars. Bad economy.* Unless we remember the context, these phrases may leave us puzzled. They could imply that the number of wars, at some time in history, destroyed a nation's economy. Or they could imply that bad economy created the wars. Or both. With neither a verb nor the expected order of subject and object to complete the action, the meaning is left vague. Of course it is ambiguity—uncertain meaning—which appeals to the part of our mind that likes to absolve itself from responsibility.

> The recession put everybody out of work in Flint. All those rich people in Cadillacs driving past the homes of the unemployed.

Here the sentence fragment avoids the responsibility of explicit connections and leaves the meaning unclear; an incomplete sentence leaves the thought illogical. Are the rich people responsible for the unemployment? Should the rich people take detours to avoid the workers' parts of town?

We must remember, at the same time, that writers *can* use the sentence fragment *when they know what they are doing.* If the prose is informal enough, the sentence fragment allows yet another possible variation in rhythm and structure. It isolates a fragment in time, because the period creates a pause longer than the pause inserted by a comma or a semicolon.

> We were going to be consumed by fire once more, and once more the world would let it happen. As usual. What was true yesterday will be true tomorrow.
>
> Elie Wiesel, *A Beggar in Jerusalem*

We must be careful to use the incomplete sentences only in an informal context, or deliberately, like Elie Wiesel, to establish pause and emphasis. A careless writer may make clauses into sentences (with periods and capital letters) without purpose, and with choppy results.

> He was a writer. Which is a difficult profession.
> She looked tall. Although she was really only 5'3".

Avoid incoherent sentences like these. These sentences need to become complex, with commas replacing periods.

> He was a writer, which is a difficult profession.
> She looked tall, although she was really only 5'3".

———— EXERCISES ————————————————————

1. In these sentences, identify subjects, predicates, objects, indirect objects, and objects of prepositions:

   a. The Empire State Building is no longer the tallest building in New York.
   b. When we sent three rock stars into space, we opened the way for new imagery in pop lyrics.
   c. Which of the fifty states spends least on education?

2. In these sentences, identify phrases as prepositional, verbal, infinitive, gerundive, or participial:

   a. Remembering the tradition of the Old South, Rhett was unable to dishonor his name.
   b. The senator from Arkansas tried voting the way he felt.
   c. In the morning, the sun will be drying the dew off the grass.

3. Combine each of these groups of simple sentences into one compound or complex sentence. In the resulting long sentences, discern any differences in meaning from the originals. Try both compound and complex; is one more effective than the other? Why?

   a. The hurricane struck the island at four yesterday afternoon. Mr. Potts couldn't find his Lear jet.
   b. Henry ironed his shirts. He ironed pillowcases. He ironed his thumb and a small corner of the wall above the ironing board.
   c. The ram was named Chauncy. He butted Mrs. Grace. She carried a bag of groceries. The freezer is now full of mutton.
   d. A boa constrictor slowly emerged from the piano. It played a Bach concerto. It went to sleep on the keyboard.
   e. Their mother bought Crunchy Bits every Saturday. She went shopping. Crunchy Bits is the only cereal with an inflatable bowl in every box.
   f. His shoes squeaked on the linoleum as he walked. Ten people in the library looked up. They frowned angrily.
   g. Television antennas bristled from every roof. Pigeons perched on the antennas. They were a nuisance.
   h. They met at a party last Saturday night. He likes anchovy pizza. She prefers pepperoni and sausage. They think they have a lot in common.

    i. Paul turned white. He gasped. He coughed. He ran into the street.

4. Identify each sentence as simple, compound, complex, compound-complex, or incomplete. Rewrite each sentence into one of the other types. Decide whether each revision is more or less effective than the original.

    a. Because Margaret had brought the elephant into the house, Sandy had to take her sculptures down to the basement.
    b. Rose ordered an apricot sour although she had been drinking daiquiris, and winked at her companion as she did.
    c. This sentence, for example.
    d. Rocking back and forth on her heels, the professor lectured.
    e. Although the rainfall is minimal, irrigation waters the valley and nourishes the corn.
    f. Australopithecus reasoned, he cooperated, he hunted in large bands, and he used tools.
    g. The man in the Foster Grants strolled down the crowded street, a beret on his head, a cane in his hand.
    h. Always cheerful, Mr. Sputter the mailman smiled, although a German shepherd hung by its teeth from his sleeve.
    i. Without hesitation, thinking only of the box of jewelry, Branny dashed through the rising flames.
    j. He grabbed the chicken feathers and threw them off the cliff, screaming and dancing all the while, although the rites were not yet due to begin and he, a crazed poet, was forbidden to take part.

5. Here are five contexts, each including an incomplete sentence. Which fragments succeed and which fail? Revise the failures into successes. Try revising a. and b. as an in class exercise, compare results.

    a. Henry Moore was born in 1898, in a country not known for sculpture since the Middle Ages. Son of a coal miner, raised in Yorkshire, trained to be a teacher, when Moore learned that he could attend an art school on an exserviceman's grant.
    b. Nevertheless, advocates of strip mining persist in their rhetoric. We hear of "vast untapped natural resources." It makes strip mining sound like pouring a glass of beer. Instead of destroying the earth.
    c. When I came back from Canada, my friends were all tanned. Everybody. I looked like a pale dime in a pile of rich, copper pennies. And I felt like ten cents.
    d. They looked up and saw it. The second stage of the launch vehicle.

    e. Whenever the Congress decides to tangle with the president, and the people need tax relief or something of that order of magnitude, although the country needs immediate help, and the newspapers are all complaining, except that nothing ever gets done.

6. Here are three passages taken from student essays. What is wrong with the writing? Revise each passage.

    a. We used to eat when my father got up. Because he wanted it that way.
    b. When inflation rises above 6 percent annually, and the consumer can no longer afford essential services, but the rich still get whatever they want.
    c. We looked at the mountain. Four inches of light snow were on it. It was a good day for skiing.

7. In your daily writing or old papers, find and copy examples of these: (a) A simple, complete sentence. (b) A compound sentence. (c) Three complex sentences of two clauses, in which you use different conjunctions. If you do not have three examples, revise until you do. (d) A compound-complex sentence. (e) An incomplete sentence.

CLARITY, COHERENCE, UNITY

To be understandable, our sentences must hang together. *Clarity* and *coherence* are needed in writing at all levels—from words, to sentences, to paragraphs, to essays, to whole books. We start pursuing clarity when we choose the right word; when we bring that word together with a second word, we begin to pursue coherence. Phrases and clauses must cohere; they must show connectedness in the logic of the sentence and in the larger unity of sentence and paragraph.

We first discover clarity and coherence most obviously in the next-to-smallest unit, the sentence. We must make clear sentences before we can make clear paragraphs or clear essays. Unity, clarity, and coherence—we must define these goals before we enumerate ways to reach them.

One way of trying to define a quality—something as abstract as *unity,* as *clarity,* as *coherence*—is to look at its opposite. Here is an incoherent sentence.

> The attention brought to Campus Management's mismanagement of its rental property at 410 Observatory makes a convincing case for the need of a strong and active tenants' organization in Ann Arbor.
>
> From an editorial, *The Michigan Daily*

Nothing holds this sentence together; it lacks unity and sprawls disconnected across the page. When we try to rewrite it, we run into difficulty, because before we revise, we need to know what the writer wants to say. What does he mean when he asserts that "attention" itself "makes a convincing case"? Perhaps he confuses two ideas. (In another chapter, we will look into logic and speak about clarity as it relates to methods of thought. See pages 301–302, 307–308.) Maybe the meaning is something like this: "When we see how this property is mismanaged, we realize that we need a strong and active tenants' organization in Ann Arbor."

Here is another incoherent sentence.

> It seems to be delivering a message right up to the end, but to decipher it, one has to dig deep within his subconscious and then he may not be sure of the nature of the manner in which it has affected him.
>
> From a theater review, *Ann Arbor News*

It is hard to rewrite empty phrases like *the nature of the manner.* Vague, shifty, and incoherent pronouns—*it, one, he*—cause confusion here. Maybe this sentence could become two sentences. If we put a period after "within his subconscious," we could make a sentence like "Even then, one may not be sure how the filmmakers have done their digging."

Or take a sample from a student paper.

> All these shortages are eventually going to put people in a position which forces them either to take some type of action that will level off the population somewhere, or people are slowly going to make life difficult for the whole human race.

Reading this, or the earlier examples, we long for the fresh air of sense. All of these examples have faults in punctuation and grammar—but with one common result: the sentences are unclear. The writers were unable to use language to make their thoughts clear to another person.

When we speak of unity, clarity, and coherence, and later when we speak of variety, we use different words as approaches toward the same goal. It would be difficult to find a clear sentence that was not also coherent and unified. Coherence makes unity, which is necessary to clarity. Varied sentences can help win the reader's attention; but we pursue our three qualities all at once, in the act of writing and thinking. In this book, we discuss grammatical errors and proper grammar mainly toward this end. When you read advice on not misplacing modifiers, or on avoiding the comma fault or the sentence fragment, remember that the goal is not mere correctness but unity, clarity, and coherence—qualities we cultivate in order to make contact with other people.

Unity: Coordination and Subordination

The poet W. B. Yeats said that a finished poem made a noise like the click of the lid on a perfectly made box. Good prose makes that noise too, no less loudly and clearly than poetry. A good passage of prose resolves rhythm, emotion, and idea into a pleasing whole—a unity.

Our tools for achieving this unity are the types of the English sentence. A good simple sentence is direct and clear; but the simple sentence will not always embody a complete thought. Writers can choose among simple sentences, compound sentences, and complex sentences—and variations within each type and a combination of the latter two types. Beginning writers usually run to simple sentences and collections of simple sentences bound together, which become compound sentences. But often we want to express certain exact relations that require the complex sentence. Think of it as using the right tool for the job at hand. Usually, the beginning writer needs to practice the art of the complex sentence, the art of subordination.

Subordination, often using conjunctions, saves words and makes connections between ideas. *Coordination* happens when phrases work together like equals, like *co*-workers.

I climbed the mountain and worshipped the sun.

When we use *subordination*, one clause leads the other; the subordinate clause hangs from the main clause, depends on it, is underneath— *sub*, as in *sub*marine—the main clause.

When I climbed the mountain, I worshipped the sun.

Here, *I worshipped the sun* is the main clause and *When I climbed the mountain* is a subordinate clause. The main clause could stand by itself. *I worshipped the sun* could be a perfectly fine, coherent, simple sentence. *When I climbed the mountain,* all by itself, is only a sentence fragment; it does not stand by itself; it hangs from, it depends on, it is subordinate to a main clause.

We could write:

Hamilton was tired of the game. He took out his doughnut cutter.

These sentences are correct, and they are understandable, but too many of them in a row would be boring, and they might not give us a complete idea. We could write:

Hamilton was tired of the game, and he took out his doughnut cutter.

This version is a compound sentence, two whole and simple clauses joined by *and*. This sentence differs from the earlier version by enforcing, with its grammar, the notion that the two statements are intimately connected. But with a conjunction and a complex sentence, we could make the connection more explicit.

> When he tired of the game, Hamilton took out his doughnut cutter.

> Because he tired of the game, Hamilton took out his doughnut cutter.

Syntax, like words, has insides. Think of syntax as the invisible system of logic—the blueprint—that makes the sentence make sense. Each arrangement of words into a sentence makes a gesture of meaning. The last two examples, with subordinate clauses beginning with *when* and *because,* make alternatives to the simple sentences or to the compound sentence. The subtle logic of the meaning is different in each case. We could also make alternatives to the sentence using a participle.

> Tired of the game, Hamilton took out his doughnut cutter.

In all the examples but the complex sentences, the closeness of the two notions implies a connection between them, but does not state it. The explicit conjunction makes a statement. If we want to emphasize cause, we can use the conjunction *because.* If we want to emphasize the time element, we can use the conjunction *when.*

We must always remember the insides, the implications or connotations, of our syntax. In some contexts, *because* might seem over-insistent or bullying. If we write that Bill's best friend has stolen his wife, ruined his business, turned his friends against him, and hired someone to kill him, it is enough to say, "Bill had grown to hate his former friend." If we write, "Because Sam had done these things, Bill had grown to hate his former friend," we have wasted our readers' time. They are likely to feel that we have slighted their intelligence. We have no way of deciding, without knowing the context, what form of the sentence about Hamilton and his doughnut cutter would be best. In relaxed, informal writing, the participle might feel right. But the participle might leave questions for the reader that conjunctions like *when* or *because* would answer. The writer has to decide, with each sentence, how much to tell the reader, and with what precision.

Subordination: The Correct Conjunction

When we make complex sentences using words that imply sequence, cause, or other forms of subordination, our sentences will be whole and solid only if the context supports the idea we have expressed. We achieve unity only if we are sensitive to the insides of syntax and use conjunctions responsibly. Beginning writers frequently violate this duty, however. If a writer omits something important, the conjunction may appear illogical; with all the information, the conjunction would have made sense. If we read,

> The work was hard; however, John was an extraordinary worker.

the word *however* is illogical. The hardness of the work should not be set in opposition to John's ability. If we read,

> The work was hard; however, the pay was good.

however functions logically: pay is compensation for difficulty. The first sentence omits something like this:

> The work was so hard it was difficult to imagine anyone doing it; however, John was an extraordinary worker and therefore he could do it.

Here the positive assertion of the second half of the sentence (however . . . extraordinary) balances the negative suggestion of the first half (so *hard it was difficult to imagine anyone doing it*). The two parts of the sentence go together, and the conjunction earns its place.

A beer commercial (the brand changed) has an interviewer ask, "As a lawyer, what do you think of Fitz's?" The relationship between the two parts of the sentence is mysterious. The possible sentences in this pattern are without limit. We could say, "As a retired major-league relief pitcher, would you tell me the median rainfall in the Canary Islands?" Really, the beer commercial hides the meaning; its illogic conceals a social statement. Other commercials for the beer include women who don't find beer drinking unfeminine, a black man who identifies himself as a professional artist, and several working-class males. The lawyer finds his way into the series to imply that beer drinking is acceptable among rich chaps, too. He likes beer best after sailing all afternoon in his catamaran. Beer, then, is *not* just lower-class, white, and male, and the interviewer means something by his weird sentence. But he is not allowed to say what he means: "We want to show you that upper-class, professional, chic sailing types drink Fitz's. You are a lawyer who sails. You like Fitz's?" Information is suppressed, and the result is "As a lawyer, what do you think of Fitz's?"

Probably the most important function of conjunctions is to establish relationships and notions of cause and of time. And they save words. Always be careful, however, not to use them falsely, as transitions, when you do not intend such a relationship. The commentary supplied on football games yields an example. The announcer blends two sorts of information into one sentence, with brevity but without logic: "And of last year's graduating class two-thirds went on to graduate school while down on the field O'Leary makes three yards on an end-around.''

Other forms of subordination—without using conjunctions—save words and strengthen sentences. Subordinate phrases and clauses, used as modifiers, give our prose density and variety.

In the *absolute construction,* we omit the connective and the verb, or sometimes a preposition, and modify directly and clearly. The absolute construction is in italics in this sentence:

> *Day done,* he raised his pitchfork to his shoulder.

Here we have cut from "When day was done" or a longer construction.

> *The desk ordered, pencils sharpened, paper blank,* he was ready for a day of combat with the English language.

> The fullback twisted and plunged, *his legs pistons, his head an iron wedge.*

Using an adjective with a prepositional or comparative phrase gives us a construction very much like the absolute.

> Spring air, *thick with odor of lilac,* moved through the gardens of Montgomery.

Similar in effect is the *appositive,* a construction that identifies the word preceding it.

> Joe, *the mailman,* said hello.

The appositive is more direct than the adjective with prepositional phrase and briefer than clausal versions. "Fred the horse thief walked in" is more concise than "Fred, who is the horse thief, walked in." In relative phrases not in apposition we should also omit words when the relationship is clear without them. Any unnecessary word, in writing, makes it more likely that the reader will become bored and inattentive. Say "The flowers she picked were lying on the newspaper," not "The flowers that she picked. . . . " This device is often useful in expository prose. "He had taken a position that was both unworthy and untenable" becomes more forceful when we say, "He had taken a position both unworthy and untenable."

The participle is also helpful. Participles are verb forms used as adjectives, *usually* ending in *-ing, -ed,* or *-en.*

> *Breathing heavily,* he plopped down on the bench.

Breathing modifies *he.*

> The *broken* umbrella was afraid of the rain.

Broken modifies *umbrella.*

> *Impressed* by her credentials, Mr. Jefferson stroked his *unshaven* chin, muttering, "Yes, yes, just what we have in mind."

Impressed modifies *Mr. Jefferson,* and *unshaven* modifies *chin.*

To save words, we can frequently use participles in modifying phrases in place of whole subordinate or independent clauses. Of course in saving words we must be careful not to sacrifice meaning; using a participle, we must make clear what it modifies, which is usually the noun nearest it in the independent clause. Participles can be past or present:

> *Tiring* of the game, Hamilton took out his doughnut cutter.
> *Tired* of the game. . . .

Coordination: Punctuating Compounds

We have concentrated on forms of subordination only because subordination is more complicated than coordination and needs more practice to become habitual. But compound or coordinate sentences form an important part of our prose style. And often when we use coordinate clauses, we find ourselves confused about punctuation.

We use a comma, generally, when the two independent clauses in a compound sentence are long.

> The man wore a green bandanna around his neck, but his wife wore a Brooks Brothers suit and a black silk tie.

Short compound sentences, however, need no commas. "He was fat and she was thin." The contradiction inside *but* often suggests a comma's pause, but it is a matter of ear, of judgment, rather than of rule. "He was thin, but he was tall" draws more attention to the speaker's insistence on two opposed ideas than does the same sentence without a comma—"He was thin but he was tall"—which seems more matter-of-fact, more conversational. Context, as always, determines choice.

Compound sentences are loosely held together; a semicolon can substitute for the connective *and.* The semicolon implies the close relationship between two clauses, which *and* also implies, but the semicolon makes a different rhythm by substituting a pause for a connective word. It is a useful variation, especially in more formal writing. Avoid tacking together random compounds, many clauses all in a row. Prose that repeats the same loose structure comes to feel too lax. We are all familiar with the speaker who cannot pause.

> I saw her and she was carrying a kitten and it had a crooked tail and I think it was part Siamese and . . .

Some of the same boredom afflicts us when the writer multiplies compounds; the redundant rhythm puts the ear to sleep.

I saw her and she was carrying a kitten. It had a crooked tail and it was part Siamese. The cat was making tiny squeaks and struggling in her arms. She smiled and then she let out a shriek. The cat had clawed her and jumped out of her arms and run away.

It is easy enough, without radical change, to introduce variety; we vary the type of sentence, using some subordination, and we vary the punctuation in the compound sentences.

When I saw her she was carrying a kitten with a crooked tail. It was part Siamese. The cat struggled in her arms, making tiny squeaks. She smiled. Then she shrieked. The cat had dug its claws into her, jumped out of her arms, and run away.

The variety we choose can be more or less expressive. In this small anecdote the action in the last sentence may be best expressed by three brief clauses, which were there in the original version. However, the long compound has more effect when it follows the two short sentences—two periods make the rhythm choppy with pause—than it had when it followed other compounds. It is like coming from a dark theater into daylight; the light is brighter because we are used to darkness. The pause between "She smiled." and "Then she shrieked." gives us the surprise we want. In a small way, the grammar and the rhythm add to the feeling, or the expression, which is the meaning.

We use conjunctive adverbs—like *however, still, certainly*—to join independent clauses, and not to join subordinate clauses or phrases. Clauses that follow these adverbs must be complete. Subordinating conjunctions—*although, when, because*—lead to subordinate clauses, and conjunctive adverbs—*moreover, also, finally*—and coordinating conjunctions—*and, but, or*—indicate the equality of independent clauses. When these independent clauses are made up of few words, we usually employ a semicolon before the adverb and a comma after it: "Universal Airlines gained two points yesterday; however, it had lost three the day before."

When we join two or more clauses in a compound, we use a connective word or a semicolon, except on rare occasions when we join brief clauses by commas. The classic example is Julius Caesar's "I came, I saw, I conquered," in which the commas make the pauses appropriately brief. Periods—"I came. I saw. I conquered."—make too much space between these clauses. Remember that if the clauses are long, a comma will not hold them together by itself. We need a comma *and* a connective or a semicolon. In

The hair fell to the floor of the barbershop, the man with the broom was dozing in the corner.

the comma is misleading. The sentence could be made into two sentences. Or a semicolon, which is always a safe choice, could take the place of the comma. Or we could insert the word *and* or *but* after the comma.

The distinction between *long* and *short* in this advice is vague, and must remain so. It is clear that with clauses as brief as

> John blushed, Sara wept, Linda shrieked, the whole class erupted at once.

the commas work. In the bad barbershop example, the comma does not work. When you come to clauses of middling size, you must decide. It could be the comma splice between brief sentences, acceptable in the most informal prose:

> I climbed the hill, Susan climbed with me.

or preferably the semicolon:

> I climbed the hill; Susan climbed with me.

or a subordinate phrase:

> I climbed the hill, Susan with me.

No easy rule will decide among these arrangements. Context and tone as well as audience and purpose should dictate the choice. The writer must become aware of the alternatives, then work to refine his sensitivity to the differences.

Students who make inadvertent comma splices should look at the review section, pages 371–374, which gives advice on how to avoid them and provides exercises.

The insides of syntax and punctuation show themselves in slight differences in meaning. The first version of *I climbed the hill* is rapid and idiomatic and informal. The semicolon in the second example increases the pause slightly and adds formality. A period would make the longest pause and create a choppiness, perhaps even an overly simple tone—that boring monosyllabic simplicity we remember from learning to read in the early grades. (All comments on the implication of these forms are generalities, not rules; a context could make the choppiness rhythmically satisfying.) The final example is closest to everyday speech. The first example, by omitting the connection, is a tighter unit.

We have been talking as if *and, but,* or *or* either takes a comma or doesn't, depending on how long the clauses are or on whether the sense will benefit from a pause. Sometimes when the clauses on each (or either) side are long, we may want to use the semicolon, even when we use a connective. This punctuation allows us to take a longer breath, yet still indicates a close relationship by keeping the two clauses in the same sentence.

> The block was dilapidated, gray, the houses raw and the sidewalks sprouting grass; but he knew he was home.

This semicolon before the connective is more common with *yet* and *so*. We can write:

> The lion was sleeping in the corner of the cage, yet his feeder approached him warily.

But we are more likely to use the greater pause:

> The lion was sleeping in the corner of the cage; yet his feeder approached him warily.

When we use adverbs as connectives—words like *however, therefore,* and *consequently*—we always use a semicolon.

> The lion stirred awake in the corner of the cage; consequently, his feeder threw down the pail of food and ran away.

Notice that the adverb connective takes a semicolon in front of it and a comma after it. Or we can make the two clauses into separate sentences.

REVISING SENTENCES I

In one class, while covering this material on sentences, the instructor asked each student to compose a single descriptive or narrative paragraph. She then photocopied several and passed them out among small discussion groups. She asked group members to apply what they had been studying about sentences to the prose before them. Here is one paragraph.

> In my neighborhood there are a lot of people who work on cars. They have formed a club. They each put in a certain amount of money and then they go to Mike's and buy a junker. Mike also sells all kinds of used parts. Sometimes on Saturdays you can see five or six guys working on a jacked-up car, they've taken the engine apart and pieces are all over the ground. The amazing thing is that they usually manage to get it put back together and working. Tim's dad is a mechanic and he is sometimes there. When the car is finished they all ride around town. They wave at people and give each other high-fives. Usually they sell the car to someone and put the money toward another junker.

The group (which included the writer of the passage) spent part of the hour working individually, each person looking for ways to improve the prose. Then they pulled into a small circle for discussion. The teacher gave some advice on workshop procedure: students should try to be good-humored and tolerant; they should focus more on making helpful suggestions than on pointing out flaws. Everyone in the group agreed that the subject was interesting and that the problems could be solved by making simple changes. "You've got too many short sentences," said one member. "It feels choppy." The others nodded. The writer admitted that he had written his paragraph quickly. He said he knew that the short sentences made the piece feel jerky, but that he wasn't sure where to make long sentences.

"How about combining the first two," suggested one girl. "You can combine the idea of a group of people and a club somehow." A few people had specific ideas. *The kids in my neighborhood who work on cars have formed a club.* Or: *My neighborhood has a club for people who fix cars.* The writer shook his head at the second suggestion. "That makes it sound too formal," he said, "as if there's a club they've all signed up to join. It's just a group of people who like doing the same thing. The first sentence would work, though."

Discussion continued. Two members said that the part about Mike was not clear: is it a junkyard or a shop that he owns? Or is he just a person who has a great many old cars? The writer made a note.

"I have trouble with other information," said a student who had been quiet thus far. "You mention Tim's dad, and you make it sound as if he's right there. But *where* are they? Also, you say that he's a mechanic, but you never come out and say that he helps them. We're supposed to guess? Why don't you nail that down better?"

At that point another student read what he had written in the margin of his copy. *They work in Tim's yard, which is the best spot to be, since Tim's father is a mechanic and sometimes comes over to help or to give advice.* The group was silent. "Well, it was just a thought," said the reader. "I guess it's a bit lumpy."

Other possible changes were suggested, mostly small connections or ways of combining two sentences. Everyone agreed that a semicolon would help the sentence beginning "Sometimes on Saturdays . . ." The group was running out of things to say when the teacher called a halt. She gave the next assignment: everyone was to rewrite his or her own passage for the next class.

The writer of the car paragraph handed in this version.

> The car buffs in my neighborhood have formed a fix-it club. When they have raised enough money—everyone contributes something—they take a trip to *Mike's Cars & Parts* and buy a junker. Several members of the group prowl around the back lot looking for parts: usable starters, carburetors, maybe a clutch assembly . . . Then they head back to Tim's yard and start to work. I've seen them all there on Saturdays, five or six would-be mechanics crawling over and under a jacked-up car. Sometimes they've taken the engine out

and scattered parts all over the place. To an outsider the situation would look hopeless; however, the outsider wouldn't know about Tim's dad, who happens to be a real mechanic. With his help, and with a lot of hard work, the fix-it boys usually get that mountain of scrap humming like a sewing machine. The next thing to do, naturally, is to show off. Look for them on Saturday night, cruising Main Street in a spiffed-up buggy, waving to people and handing out high-fives.

___ **EXERCISES** _____

1. Look at these sentences from student papers for clarity, coherence, and unity. Rewrite each of them. If you have to, make assumptions about the writers' intended meanings.

  a. It is hard for a graduate to hold down <u>both</u> a teaching position and work for their degree.
  b. He takes one student, Mike, who says he can trust anyone and also that he only has acquaintances and no friends since when is unclear.
  c. When a friend of mine, Robert Olds, who I had known for years converted to Christianity in high school and I began to resent him.

2. Make the following sentences more concise.

  a. When he had finished eating the birthday cake, he stretched out on the sofa.
  b. The magnetic pole, which is not the same as the North Pole, governs the compass.
  c. United States Customs destroys tons of food every year. These fruits and meats are illegally imported.
  d. A vacuum-cleaner salesman, who was nearly seven feet tall and who smiled continuously, fell down the cellar stairs.

3. Revise each of these passages into one complex sentence. You will have to make your own assumptions about relations of cause and time. Do more than one version if you can see different meanings.

  a. It was raining. It was about seven o'clock the next morning. The Jeeps sloshed through the street outside the window. We couldn't sleep. We had breakfast. We all felt hungry. All there was was some beans and brown bread left over. We felt better. The sun came out about nine o'clock.
  b. She packed her suitcase. It sat open on the bed. She folded a red sweater. She put the sweater in the suitcase. Her mother stood near the window. She looked out at the stark

trees. Her arms were crossed in front of her. Her face drooped. She was sad.
c. Mark sits at his desk. His electric typewriter is blue. It is a portable. He received the typewriter on his last birthday. His birthday is in March. He types five words. He pauses. He drinks coffee. Suddenly he gets an idea.

4. Analyze two or three of these passages. Decide how each sentence is put together, and identify the variety of sentences in each paragraph. Is the writer using the best tool for the job? Praise or criticize.

a. Down the hall in Apartment 2 the reporter found a very "strong case." There were holes in both the floor and the ceiling, big enough for the biggest rats. Cockroaches crawled up the kitchen wall. A curtain divided off a section of the room for a bedroom, and out from it peeked an old woman. She smiled at the visitors and watched them with interest. Isabel Sánchez, the head of the house, was pointing out some more ratholes. A teen-age girl sat staring at a television set whose screen was filled with a constantly wavering, almost undistinguishable cowboy movie, spoken in Spanish. The reporter walked to the kitchen to watch the cockroaches, and observed that some dishes were sitting on the table that contained the remains of rice and beans.

Dan Wakefield,
Island in the City

b. The greatest sea power in Europe and the greatest land power faced each other in war. The stake was the leadership of Europe. Each was fighting to strengthen her own position at the expense of the other: in the case of the sea power to hold her widely separated empire; in the case of the land power to challenge that empire and win one for herself. Both, as the war began, were uneasily conscious that an important and even decisive factor might be an Asiatic nation, enormous in extent of territory, which had a foothold in Europe and was believed by many to be interested in watching the two chief Western powers weaken and perhaps destroy each other until in the end she herself could easily dominate Europe.

Edith Hamilton,
The Greek Way

c. Many women have given their lives to political organizations, laboring anonymously in the background while men of far less ability managed and mismanaged the public trust. These women hung back because they knew the men would not give them a chance. They knew their place and stayed in it. The amount of talent that has been lost to our country that way is appalling.

Shirley Chisholm,
Unbought and Unbossed

d. There under a spotlight, two Oriental gentlemen in natty blue suits were doing some amazing things with yo-yos. Tiny, neat men, no bigger than children, they stared abstractedly off into space while yo-yos flew from their hands, zooming in every direction as if under their own power, leaping out from small fists in arcs, circles, and straight lines. I stared open-mouthed as a yo-yo was thrown down and *stayed down*, spinning at the end of its string a fraction of an inch above the floor.

Frank Conroy,
Stop-Time

e. The American does not enjoy his possessions because sensory enjoyment was not his object, and he lives sparely and thinly among them, in the monastic discipline of Scarsdale or the barracks of Stuyvesant Town. Only among certain groups where franchise, socially speaking, has not been achieved, do pleasure and material splendor constitute a life-object and an occupation. Among the outcasts—Jews, Negroes, Catholics, and homosexuals—excluded from the communion of ascetics, the love of fabrics, gaudy show, and rich possessions still anachronistically flaunts itself. Once a norm has been reached, differing in the different classes, financial ambition itself seems to fade away. The self-made man finds, to his anger, his son uninterested in money; you have shirtsleeves to shirtsleeves in three generations. The great financial empires are a thing of the past. Recent immigrants—movie magnates and gangsters particularly—retain their acquisitiveness, but how long is it since anyone in the general public has murmured, wonderingly, "as rich as Rockefeller"?

Mary McCarthy, "America the Beautiful"
in *On the Contrary*

6. Take one of the passages above and rewrite it completely using different kinds of sentences. Stay as close to the author's intent as possible. How do the new sentences change the meaning?

Grammatical Coherence

The good prose already quoted exemplifies unity in the structure and arrangement of sentences through agreement, consistency, and the use of coherent conjunctions. But we need to consider further various grammatical areas of agreement and consistency essential to good writing. Disagreement and inconsistency can sabotage even the most interesting ideas and alienate the most attentive reader.

Misplaced Modifiers. Placing modifiers properly is essential to unity in content and construction. We must always be careful that a clause *does* modify the word that its position makes it appear to modify. As we have seen, the dangling participle, with its often comic effect, destroys unity.

> Being six years old and rusted through, I was able to buy the car for a song.

Arranged in this way, the participial phrase *being six years old and rusted through* modifies *I;* it implies that *I* was six years old and rusted through. Here the best solution would be a subordinate stating clause.

> Because it was six years old and rusted through, I was able to buy the car for a song.

A similar mistake is the dangling appositive.

> A good teacher, his superior saw to it that he was promoted.

This order would imply that *his superior* was *a good teacher.* Solutions:

> He was a good teacher; his superior saw to it that he was promoted.

> Because he was a good teacher, his superior saw to it that he was promoted.

Yet another kind of misplaced modifier is the dangling participle introduced by a preposition.

> Tall and strong, the job was easy for him.

> On achieving the age of twenty-seven, his parents threw him out of the house.

The syntactic logic in the preceding sentence forces us to picture twenty-seven-year-old parents expelling a small child—probably not what the author intended.

> Hopefully, this book will be done by late July.

Hopefully is a dangling adverb which is common to everyday speech, but which disfigures formal prose. Does the book really hope? The simplest rewriting would be

> I hope this book will be done by late July.

In all such misreferences, ambiguity is a possible problem; the reader may not be able to tell what we really *did* mean. We lose clarity, we lose coherence. Even if our *intended* meaning is apparent, however, misapplied language is a flaw that cannot be excused as informality. The reader is dismayed by the frayed edge left by incorrect order. We write with correct grammar in order to reach our audience—and grammar (like everything else having to do with language) is a social act.

For the unity of a sentence, nothing is more important than the precise placement of all modifiers. The dangling construction is a common error; everyone falls into it from time to time. We also make mistakes—sometimes amusing ones—merely by misplacing modifiers. For instance, this sentence appeared in the want ads of a newspaper.

> For sale: Piano by owner with large curved legs.

In an earlier edition of this book, I (D. H.) perpetrated this sentence:

> Look at the examples elsewhere in this book of carelessly constructed sentences. . . .

Students who dangle modifiers, or have other problems with agreement (see what follows) should look at the review chapter, especially pages 375 through 384. There is some help on punctuation on pages 386 to 400.

Errors in Agreement. These errors are common when we use indefinite pronouns. *One* and *none* and distributives like *each, every, everybody, nobody,* and *everyone* all take singular verbs. Here are typical errors.

> Everyone says they had a good weekend.
> Everybody had their tennis racket with them.

Common speech accepts most of these errors in agreement; but formal writing rejects them. We should write:

> Everyone says he had a good weekend.
> Everybody had his tennis racket with him.

We should write *he* and *his* to be correct in grammar. Grammar in this standard use of *he* and *his* may, however, conceal sexism. No one has yet found a satisfying alternative that does not seem at times confusing or awkward. We can use *she* or *her* when context and audience allow; we can use the bulky *he and/or she* and *him and/or her,* but the reader quickly grows impatient. We can rephrase the sentence to omit pronouns; we can use the plural.

> Everyone should remember to take her personal belongings from the bus.
>
> Everyone should remember to take his or her personal belongings from the bus.
>
> Take all personal belongings from the bus.
>
> People should remember to take their personal belongings from the bus.

Frequently our writing becomes awkward, not because we use a singular pronoun together with a plural one, but because we use singular nouns with plural pronouns or other mixtures of singular and plural.

> Although a person may not be hungry, a piece of pastry can stimu-
> late their appetite.

Maybe *his appetite*, maybe *her appetite*, but not *their appetite*. We
could say *their appetite*, correctly, if we used a plural in the first part of
the sentence:

> Although people may not be hungry, a piece of pastry can stimulate
> their appetites.

Vagueness of Pronoun Reference. This error is more insidious
than disagreement, because it is harder to detect in a draft. We misuse
this and *that* by using them without having a clear connection to
an earlier reference. Thus, we destroy unity, clarity, and coherence.
We say:

> When I went home at Christmas, the tree wasn't up yet and my dog
> was sick, my mother had to have an operation, and my father was
> worried about money. This bothered me.

What bothered you? *This* properly refers to one thing, and the reader is
forced to choose at random among the items listed. The author might
have talked about *These things*, for instance. Or we say:

> When the Panama Canal opened for shipping, the elapsed time for
> sending merchandise coast to coast in the United States diminished
> by 80 percent, and the cost accordingly. That pleased manufacturers
> especially.

Was *that* the time? The cost? Both? The last sentence, lacking clarity,
fades into vagueness and disconnection.

Often we misuse reference by confusing parts of speech and ignoring antecedents.

> My father is a doctor and that is the profession I want to enter.

> Because we put wire fencing around the chicken yard, they cannot
> escape.

Each of these sentences is understandable, but each is sloppy and im-
properly connected. *That is the profession* fails to connect: a *doctor* is a
person; *medicine* is a profession. In the second example, chickens are
not mentioned; *they* can refer to chickens only by association with the
phrase *chicken yard*. We reach an audience with these sentences in the
sense that people can understand what we are getting at, but there is a
price to pay. Part of any reader's response will be annoyance at our
sloppiness. This annoyance is an impediment to connection; it gives us
a social problem.

The sentences could be revised as follows.

Because my father is a doctor, I want to enter the profession of medicine.

Because my father is a doctor, I want to be a doctor.

Because we put wire fencing around the chicken yard, the chickens cannot escape.

Because we put wire fencing around their yard, the chickens cannot escape.

Consistency of Tenses. The tense, or time, is the form by which a verb signals past, present, or future. We should stick to one verb tense in describing one action. An account of something that happened to us usually sounds best in the past tense, but occasionally fits the present. Summarizing a book, we use either tense, often the present. But choosing past or present (a decision determined by context) matters less than sticking to the tense we start with. In careless writing, we drift back and forth without noticing it.

> The maple turned red in September, a bright range of reds from near-gold to near-Chinese. The sky is blue, and the maples show fiercely against it, making the colors more deep. In October the first frost came, and . . .

The second sentence should take the past tense to agree with its neighbors. On rare occasions, and usually at a paragraph break, we can change tenses. A leisurely description moves into sudden action, and a break from past to present is a good way to signal this change. Be careful if you try this device; and know that you are doing it.

Consistency of Point of View. Shifts in tense violate unity, and so too do other sudden shifts. Pronoun disagreement, already discussed, makes a shift in number. We must not shift the person of the sentence, unless there is compelling reason to. We might carelessly write:

> First you put on your skis, one at a time for most people, and then we take a quick look at the slopes.

The *you* and the *we* are inconsistent. Either pronoun will do.

Equally, we do not move from active to passive in the same sentence, unless there is a compelling reason. We need not say:

> We looked forward to the party and it was greatly enjoyed.

The reader is whirled through time and grows dizzy. Instead, say:

> We looked forward to the party and enjoyed it.

Do not shift from one mood of the verb to another; for instance, from an imperative command to an indicative statement of fact. Do not say:

Keep your eye on the teacher and you should take full notes.

The sentence gains unity if it is one or the other.

Keep your eye on the teacher and take full notes.

You should keep your eye on the teacher and you should take full notes.

When it is half each, it is a minor monster, a mermaid with a human face and scaly fins.

All these instructions ask the writer, for the reader's sake, to keep his voice coming from the same place, in the same tone, with the same number and gender and mood. It is disconcerting—finally impossible to follow—when a voice comes from high and from low in the landscape, from past and from present in time, from singular and from plural in number. As ever, we write well to make connections. Inconsistency and incoherence curse the work of most beginning writers. Here is a paragraph from an essay in which the author lost clarity and coherence by neglecting grammatical unity. He (or she) had no single point of view. The inconsistencies in this passage occur from sentence to sentence in the paragraph, as well as within individual sentences.

The mountain from a distance is long and low, about eight miles in fact, and when you climb it you find that it is covered with tiny bushes. The climbing itself went easily, and it was fun for everybody. I was there by 6 A.M., and all through our climb by three in the afternoon.

In revision, the writer found unity, clarity, and coherence:

From a distance the mountain shows itself long and low, eight miles long and only three thousand feet in elevation at its highest. As we drove close to it, and began our climb, we discovered that its sides were dense with small bushes. All of us enjoyed the easy climb, which took us from six in the morning until three in the afternoon, when we drove west again, into the setting sun, and back home.

––––– **EXERCISES** ––

1. Rewrite the following phrases, to give them emphatic unity or to remove errors or ambiguities.

a. Without knowing which one was best, the chocolate-covered one appealed to me most.

b. Having arrived at the airport fifteen minutes ahead of schedule, my friends were nowhere to be seen.

c. A genius at seven, his parents were worried about his relationships with second-grade classmates.

d. Hopefully, some of these exercises are simple.

e. Everyone wore Levi jackets with their names printed on them.

f. While the sunset was beautiful, the aroma of the garden was more beautiful still.

g. In Zambia, Russia, Poland, and in Venezuela . . .

h. When the game was over, when the stands emptied, when the popcorn was swept up, and the lights were extinguished, a vast silence overtook the stadium.

i. Intelligent, pretty, sympathetic, a good friend, Jane was *FRIENDLY* known to everyone in the dormitory.

j. She danced to prove she didn't care, and implying she did.

k. He answered that he didn't care what she did, that he was furious with her, and he would never to speak to her again.

l. Either you come inside, or get a spanking.

2. Rewrite these sentences so that each is consistent and coherent.

a. Everyone went to the picnic and a good time was had by all.

b. He takes off his coat, loosens his tie, and came to the table.

c. Nowadays, everyone buys their own car.

d. Chester's shoes, mud-caked and which were old, was tied together with string.

e. When old, jogging won't seem so easy for me.

f. On entering when the gates are closed, the dogs must remain inside.

g. Driving out past the red house, a fire was discovered.

h. A man with steel-rimmed spectacles comes to the door and said he will buy Rash deodorant soap.

[The following examples have been cited in *Verbatim*, a magazine about language.]

i. The women included their husbands and children in their pot-luck suppers.

j. Even more astonishing was our saving the lives of little babies who formerly died from sheer ignorance.

k. I can't blame you for wanting to go outside and sit on your ten-minute break.

l. In some countries a person cannot slaughter any animal unless rendered unconscious first.

Structural Unity

Many attributes that give stylistic finish and polish come from the organization of the sentence, rather than from the words the writer uses. Ranging from the definable *parallelism* to the more intangible *rhythm*, these structural attributes are harder to define than grammatical unity. Though their absence does not *prevent* connection with the reader, their skillful use brings pleasure—and pleasure is the very stuff of connection.

Parallelism. Parallelism is essential in formal prose; sometimes we use it in informal prose as well. Parallel constructions are phrases or clauses within the sentence that repeat the same word forms (nouns, verbs, adjectives, and the like) in the same order to perform the same function.

> He quit the job because the boss was cruel, the pay was meager, and the work was dangerous.

> the boss was cruel/the pay was meager/the work was dangerous

After the conjunction *because,* each subordinate clause follows the pattern of article/noun/past tense verb/predicate adjective. Parallelism is not a grammatical necessity, like agreement. But it helps us to manage sentences and to *clarify* our intent.

We use parallelism most obviously when we introduce the parallels with pairs of words: *both/and, either/or, neither/nor, not/but, not only/but also, first/second.* The sentence beginning with one member of these pairs should pivot on the other; and the parallel clauses should use the same form. Do not write:

> Not only did he run into the fire, but also carrying a can of gasoline.

This nonparallel construction is comprehensible but ugly. What's more, it feels stylistically uncontrolled. These clauses are not parallel because the second uses a participle instead of an active verb, like the first clause. We could rewrite it:

> Not only did he run into the fire, but also he carried a can of gasoline.

If we are stringing many clauses together, any departure from the parallelism destroys unity.

> His reasons amounted to these: first, the overwhelming size of the debt; second, that the company was ill managed; third, having so little leisure in such a job.

The sentence can be rewritten in numerous ways; for instance,

> His reasons were first, that the debt had grown huge; second, that the firm was ill managed; third, that the job afforded little leisure.

The parallelism would remain the same—and we would still want parallelism—if we dropped the enumerations.

> His reasons were that the debt had grown huge, that the firm was ill
> managed, and that the job afforded little leisure.

The briefest way to write the sentence would be to make parallels in the
predicate subordinate to one *that*, by using the verb *to be* once and then
implying it elsewhere.

> His reasons were that the debt was big, the firm ill managed, and the
> job time consuming.

Context is also important. The writer would naturally wish to sound
more relaxed and talkative writing a letter to a friend, more concise and
clipped composing an official memorandum. The more concise the
sentence becomes, the more formal the prose.

With *either/or*, *not only/but also*, and similar correlative expressions, be sure to place the words to correlate the same parts of speech in
each clause. We frequently misplace our *either*s and *only*s. Too often
we say:

> Either she ironed all morning, or she watched television.

Because the verbs are being related, the sentence should read:

> She either ironed all morning or watched television.

Here are other ambiguous uses followed by clear ones.

> Either the professor was asleep or drunk. *The professor was either*
> *asleep or drunk.*

> They not only ran to the grocer, but also to the florist. *They ran not*
> *only to the grocer, but also to the florist.*

In making a list, either use an article or a preposition once, at the
beginning of the list, or use it throughout. Either

> The soup, spaghetti, lamb, and salad . . .

or

> The soup, the spaghetti, the lamb, and the salad . . .

but not a mixture:

> The soup, spaghetti, the lamb, and salad . . .

At any rate, do not attempt such mixtures in formal prose. For rhythm
and emphasis, in informal prose or in a poem, one might depart from
parallelism and profit by the departure. The rule of thumb remains—
know what you are doing and why you are doing it.

When one or more prepositional phrases contain several words,
parallelism always repeats the preposition. Say:

> Through wind, through sleet that stung his cheeks, and through snow . . .

Do not say:

> Through wind, sleet that stung his cheeks, and snow . . .

When you use long clauses, introduced by parallel conjunctions, repeat the conjunction. With long clauses, we need the repetition for clarity.

> Although the sun had gone down more than twenty minutes ago, and although shadows thickened in the field, he kept on ploughing.

When we use short clauses, we need only the first conjunction.

> Although day was done, and night approaching, he kept on ploughing.

Also, use parallel parts of speech. Verbs go with verbs in a parallel, nouns with nouns, and adjectives with adjectives. We often violate this rule in making lists:

> From a distance, he looked tall, gray, well-dressed, and a foreigner.

Instead of *a foreigner*, which is a noun, the sentence should fulfill its unity with the adjective *foreign*. A common departure from parallelism pairs an infinitive and a participle.

> He talked to prove he was intelligent and showing off his cultural background.

This writing is stylistically inconsistent, jarring the ear like an untuned piano. We should say:

> He talked to prove he was intelligent and to show off his cultural background.

Two participles would be stylistically acceptable, but the infinitives make a more vigorous sentence.

Another frequent lapse in parallelism is to omit a *to* when infinitives follow each other. In formal prose, we preserve the *to* for all infinitives in a series even when simple verbs follow each other. We do not say:

> To see, want, and buy is the essence of the American consumer.

We say:

> To see, to want, and to buy is the essence of the American consumer.

The longer the clause, the more upsetting it is when we omit a *to*.

> His desires were few: to live on the ocean, to spend at least a portion of each day sketching the seabirds, to sleep alone, and cook for himself only.

Unity departs when the *to* is omitted before *cook*. Yet in informal prose and speech, we occasionally do something that resembles our practice with articles and prepositions; the *to* remains with the first infinitive and is understood with the rest.

> He wanted to move back, get a job, buy a convertible, and drive through town in style.

As with the rule on prepositions and articles, the word *to*, once omitted after the first use, may not slip back in again.

Constructions on two sides of coordinates should agree. If we find ourselves writing,

> Either he was rotten or a badly misunderstood young man.

we should improve it by keeping the parts of speech parallel:

> He was either rotten or badly misunderstood.

The same rule applies even when pairs like *either/or* aren't used. Sometimes we make sentences like this one:

> He hoped that she would come and she would wear the blue dress.

The first clause uses *that* and the second violates unity by omitting it. The sentence should read:

> He hoped that she would come and that she would wear the blue dress.

The word *that* can safely be omitted when no parallel clause is used. *He hoped she would come* by itself is fine, but when "he hoped" more than one clause, we need parallel *that*s. In the single clause, follow your ear.

Emphasis. Because emphasis works to construct a sentence firmly, emphasis promotes unity. When we use emphasis well, we make a unity between sentence structure and meaning and between sentence structure and appropriate emotional tone. Repetition, order, and contrast are three means of achieving emphasis.

Parallelism is emphatic, and parallelism is a form of *repetition*. Where the politician's speech as a whole gathers speed by repeating a phrase—like "and what is your answer to *this*, Mr. President?"—the sentence gathers firmness by repeating parts and structures. The repetition creates dramatic heightening, like quickening drumbeats on a movie sound track.

> We must agree that *the present administration is* bankrupt, *that it has* no cash reserves of the spirit, *that its morale* is a total liability.

Careful development in the sentence can contribute emphasis. This is emphasis by *order*. For emphasis, we put the most important words in the sentence at the beginning or at the end—and they're often best at the end. (See Concluding the Sentence, pages 185–186.) These sentences emphasize beginnings:

> Slowly, as though the engine were harnessed to elderly coolies, we crept out of Granada.
>> Truman Capote, "A Ride through Spain"

> Tears, blinding tears, were running down her face.
>> Thomas Hardy, *Tess of the D'Urbervilles*

These sentences save emphasis for the end:

> I keep wondering if there is an afterlife, and if there is will they be able to break a twenty?
>> Woody Allen, "Selections from the Allen Notebooks"

> One day, perhaps, the earth will have turned into one vast feather-bed, with man's body dozing on top of it and his mind underneath, like Desdemona smothered.
>> Aldous Huxley, "Comfort"

> His form had filled out, his wrinkles were gone, the dull eyes had regained their fire, and there, sitting by the fire, and grinning at my surprise, was none other than Sherlock Holmes.
>> Sir Arthur Conan Doyle, "The Man with the Twisted Lip"

When a sentence like Conan Doyle's is long and delays its most crucial or dramatic part for last, we call it a *periodic* sentence. We postpone the most important part of a sentence—often the simple predicate—by using clauses or phrases or parenthetical remarks, in order to build suspense and gain attention. Periodic sentences promise that something is coming, but hold it back, teasing us, so that the tension holds our interest and the resolution achieves greater power.

> That the spring was late this year, that the dogwood never bloomed, and that the flowers struggled wanly out of the garden, all of these failures must have contributed to the moment when Frederick, suddenly and without warning, shot his wife.

When we have several details or ideas to present in a sentence, the emphatic order is the *crescendo*. If one of the details is a surprise—something that may seem out of place, but really belongs there—it should come last. Otherwise the order is simply that of intensity.

I would appreciate consideration for any opening on your staff, and believe that I could bring to your firm unusual combinations of energy and caution, originality and reliability, youth and experience.

The president has tricked the workers, ignored the military, soaked the rich, and plundered the poor.

It is always the last word or phrase that rings in the reader's mind. Even if it is not the most important, it naturally comes to seem so.

Departures from an emphatic order destroy unity by appearing accidental. A periodic sentence feels constructed and planned, sturdier than a loose sentence, which trails off into "many other instances of this kind." An emphatic order makes us feel control, not randomness. It is one more device contributing to the click of the box.

Varying sentence types can also become emphatic (and thus variety can lend its power to unity) when we shift suddenly from one sort of sentence to another. This is *contrast*. Most commonly, we see a short sentence provide emphasis after several long sentences.

We were told to avoid the kids who played at the far end of the park, for they had a reputation for making trouble. We were also warned more than once to watch out for the older girls who gathered near the high school. There was no end to the instructions and warnings we were given. We ignored all of them.

By contrasting sentence types, we build emphasis into the developing of the paragraph. We need to be sure, however, that we are highlighting the right point.

Balance. Balance and parallelism are related; both have to do with repetition. Both create emphasis. But parallel construction is a matter of maintaining equal grammatical structure, and balance has to do with getting the sentence parts, each with its own weight, into proportion. Balance is style, it is not grammar, nor can it be described grammatically. (Parallelism is style, too, but it can be described grammatically.) A balanced sentence is one in which the main parts of the sentence have approximately the same rhythm and importance. A balanced sentence need not have two parts in balance; it may have three or four or more. Balance is similarity and *sense*; parallelism is similarity and *structure*. A balanced sentence is not precisely parallel in detail, in its two or more parts, but its parts must be similar in structure. Here are examples of balance and parallelism, with the parts printed on separate lines.

Balance

In his day, Frank built model airplanes of balsa wood and went to the movies on Saturday;

now, at the same age, Jim cruises around in his own car and flies to
New York for the weekend.

Freda said it was dangerous,
but Jill insisted on going.

Balance and parallelism

The Grogs wanted only to share and be reconciled;
the Kogs wanted only to kill or be killed.

Parallelism without balance

People possess four things
that are no good at sea:
anchor, rudder, oars,
and the fear of going down.

Antonio Machado

The foxes have their holes and the birds have their nests;
but the Son of Man has no place to lay his head and to rest.

New Testament

The old pine-tree speaks divine wisdom;
the secret bird manifests eternal truth.

Zen proverb

Rhythm. Rhythm and resolution, which we name together because they seem related, are more difficult to define or exemplify than
any other words used in this book. By rhythm we mean sounds and
pauses pleasingly arranged, an emphatic arrangement we might want to
tap our feet to. The Hemingway passage quoted on page 14 succeeds by
its rhythm. Here is another example of superb rhythm, quite different
from Hemingway's, more lush and energetic.

Witches, werewolves, imps, demons and hobgoblins plummetted
from the sky, some on brooms, others on hoops, still others on
spiders. Osnath, the daughter of Machlath, her fiery hair loosened in
the wind, her breasts bare and thighs exposed, leaped from chimney
to chimney, and skated along the eaves. Namah, Hurmizah the
daughter of Aff, and many other she-devils did all sorts of somer-
saults. Satan himself gave away the bride, while four evil spirits
held the poles of the canopy, which had turned into writhing py-
thons. Four dogs escorted the groom.
Isaac Bashevis Singer, "The Gentleman from Cracow"

We find pleasure in the rhythmic combination of words, just as we find pleasure in the rhythms of music or in repetition of line or color in painting. In this example there is a lively pace, an alternation of short and long word clusters that gives us a body sense of wild confusion—which is just what the passage is about. In general, rhythms satisfy our elementary need for order, like the cycling of seasons and tides. But if rhythmic pleasure is essential to the satisfaction of good style, we must remember that the rhythms of words cannot be separated from the meanings of words. Sound and sense go together.

Look at the examples of carelessly constructed sentences elsewhere in this book, as on pages 10 and 204. In these examples we can feel the difference between prose that is strong in rhythm and resolution and prose that is weak in rhythm and resolution. Here are two sentences from Jim Beck's first draft, rewritten for rhythm and sense together.

> Therefore I decided when I was young that I would go to college and applied myself to studies in high school so that I would be admitted.

> I've wanted to go to college since I was young, I studied hard in high school, and I was admitted last winter.

> Coming here has been a disappointment so far because people are not very friendly to freshmen and everyone has their own clique and the whole place is too big.

> I've been disappointed in college so far; the campus is too big, too unfriendly, too cliquish.

I suspect that writers' ears are their most delicate, and possibly their most valuable, piece of equipment. We acquire a good ear by reading and rereading the great masters until their cadences become part of our minds. The stored memory of a hundred thousand sentences becomes the standard of the writer's own ear, just as all the sentences we have ever heard pattern all the sentences we will speak. Craftsmanship comes from studying the accomplishment of the past and then practicing to equal it. To become potters, beginners must learn about clay, about glazes, about wheels and kilns. But they may also look at pots, even feel them—early Greek vases, American Indian coiled clay cooking pots, Babylonian wine jugs, bowls and basins made by their teachers. They will discover the uses, the shapes, the colors, and the techniques that determine good pots. Then they must make their own. Developing sensitivity to good writing tunes the ears of apprentice writers until they learn to make their own.

Resolution. Resolution (sometimes also called "closure") is the art of ending a thing so that the reader feels satisfied. Resolution partakes of sound, sense, feeling, and emphasis. The periodic sentence, holding back its emphasis until the end, is an obvious method of achieving resolution. Here is another periodic sentence.

> Without schooling, without friends, without money, without the accent that is necessary for success in Britain, he arrived in London.

This device of delayed delivery is so pointed that we cannot do it often, and must usually rely on more subtle resolutions. No rules can govern resolution or rhythm because each click of the box is original. But reading and paying attention to examples can help us achieve mastery. The more we know the materials that make style, the more extensive our ability to improvise. Look at the passage by F. Scott Fitzgerald on page 204 and see the slow, rising beginning, the calm plateau at the center, and the slow, peaceful descent at the end. Then contrast it with the more formal and complicated prose of Isaiah Berlin on page 205. Each sentence is its own little dance, in which variety arrives at unity by way of improvisation; and each sentence relates to each other sentence as part relates to part, so that the paragraph is a round of dances that become one dance.

In talking about rhythm and resolution, we are not so much covering new material as looking at old material from another point of view. Asking you to practice rhythm and resolution is asking you to write well.

Concluding the Sentence. I have been speaking—in the sections on emphasis and on resolution—about ending the sentence well. No sentence can have resolution if it trails off in flatness or emptiness. Let us look at some common failures. In conversation and in unedited writing, we frequently start a sentence with high energy and then collapse when we try to conclude it: we have a subject, but we haven't the faintest notion for a predicate. We say,

> The high level of heroin consumption in this country

because we are worried. But we don't know exactly what to say about it, so we reach around for a predicate filler, to end our sentence:

> is a matter of the utmost importance.

> requires our immediate attention.

> is an aspect of contemporary life that must concern us all.

Sometimes a writer will string such sentences together—all strong subjects with weak predicates.

> The high level of heroin consumption in this country is of paramount concern to us all. The solution will require the utmost in international cooperation. Firm international controls are of the utmost necessity. The identity of heroin-producing nations is a

matter of public knowledge. The destruction of crops at their source is one way of dealing with the problem.

Each sentence achieves the art of falling. These dancers trip on their skirts. The writer has a partial idea—like a sentence fragment—but makes it into pseudocomplete sentences with trite predicates. The mind that writes such sentences seems to be disorganized or lazy about organizing. The unresolved, trailing-off sentences communicate a vacuum. Yet, with a little attention, the writer could have talked plainly, with decent whole ideas and an accompanying fullness.

> The high level of heroin consumption in this country requires international controls to destroy the crops at their source in the heroin-producing countries.

We used only a third of the words in this version, and the sentence is unified.

There are no ready formulas for ending sentences, but there is at least one big *don't*. The filler predicate is certain to destroy any possibility of an ending that satisfies us by its rhythm and resolution. Avoid it.

REVISING SENTENCES II

One instructor, for a weekly assignment, asked students to hand in a theme on the subject of television watching. Reading the papers over, the instructor saw an opportunity to follow up recent class discussion of sentences. He asked one student if he could use a paragraph from her paper as an example.

At the next class meeting, the teacher wrote the following on the blackboard:

> The remote-control button has had an untold impact on the way we watch TV and on our minds. We push the button and the image on the screen changes: there is a car chase, a dog food commercial, a news special. The person watching starts to lose track of what he's seeing and its meaning. Everything will come to seem equal in some way. How can you go from a sit-com with a laugh track to a special on starving people in Africa? You can't, inside. Or you shouldn't be able to. But the more you change the screen, the more you have started to forget that there's a difference. And after a while the pictures of the starving person mean less.

The teacher asked his class to take a few minutes to reflect on the passage, both on the statement it was making and on the way that the statement was being made. He suggested to the students that they consider some of the fine points of grammar—agreement, consistency of tense, and point of view—as well as structural matters like parallelism, balance, and resolution. Heads turned to the blackboard as class members started to read.

Twenty minutes later, the instructor saw so many hands waving that he set up a procedure. "First," he said, "let's look at grammar and construction; then we can worry about elegance." A number of students kept their hands up, and soon they were pointing out certain basic inconsistencies. "The pronouns are flipping as fast as the channels," said someone. "It's true," the writer said. "We, he, you. . .Maybe I should avoid the tube myself." The teacher asked the group which pronoun would be most effective. There was a long pause. Then one girl suggested using *you*. "That would make it more direct," she said, "the author talking right to the reader." Another student immediately objected: *you* would make the piece sound condescending, like a lecture. "She should include herself; she should say *we*."

The teacher turned around and studied the board. "It's a hard one to call," he admitted, finally. "But I think I lean toward the plural *we*. It's more inclusive, and it also combines—better than you—with a more neutral subject like 'the watcher' or 'the viewer'; it would be hard to use *we* or *you* in every sentence." He then asked for other observations.

"Tense agreement," said a girl in the front. She pointed out the switch to *will* in the fourth sentence and the use of the past tense "have started" in the eighth. "Both should stay in the present."

The teacher then brought up the matter of sentence structure. After a lull, several students raised their hands. One student thought that the first sentence needed work, that the prepositional phrase *on our minds* sounded weak. He looked down and read from a note on his paper: *a tremendous impact not only on the way we watch TV but also on our minds*. He said that he wanted to add another sentence to emphasize the connection, to make it clear that watching TV can alter the way we think about things. "Something like: *We don't often realize the extent to which our contact with the medium can influence us*." The teacher signaled a pause while he wrote the sentence on the board. "Good idea," he said. "What else?"

This time a student from the back spoke up. He said that he saw a place to use parallelism. The second sentence could make a stronger assertion. He read out his version: *When we push the button, the image on the screen changes: there is a car chase, there is a news special on starving people, there is a happy soft-drink commercial*. Asked why he made the changes he did, the student explained. First, he said, by repeating *there* the writer could isolate and emphasize the changes on the screen. He had made the new order and put in new examples to highlight the absurdity. "Going from images of starving people to images of Fizzy-pop makes more of a statement; it gets the idea across more powerfully." He indicated that he would change the order later, too, in the sentence about the sit-com.

The teacher glanced at the clock on the wall. "I want to point out a nice example of a parallel construction in 'The more you change the screen, the more you start to forget that there's a difference'. Let's make that there *is*, which is stronger. Now I'm going to take the last five minutes to write out a version that uses your suggestions."

> The remote-control button has had a tremendous impact not only on the way we watch TV but also on our minds. We don't often realize the extent to which our contact with the medium can influence us. When we push the button, the image on the screen changes: there is a car chase, there is a news special on starving people, there is a happy soft-drink commercial. The viewer starts to lose track of what he's seeing; he mixes up the levels of significance. Everything comes to seem equal in some way. How can a person jump from a special on starvation in the Sudan to a sit-com with a laugh track? He can't, deep down. Or he *shouldn't* be able to. But the more we change the screen, the more we begin to forget that there is a difference. And after a while the image of the starving person just might come to mean less.

——— EXERCISES ———

1. Decide whether each of these sentences shows parallelism, balance, both, or neither.

   a. Inspiration is the beginning of a poem and it is also its final goal.

      Stephen Spender, *The Making of a Poem*

   b. I saw a new heaven and a new earth, for the old heaven and the old earth had passed away.

      Revelations

   c. The superior man understands what is right; the inferior man understands what will sell.

      Confucius

   d. There are two ways of avoiding fear: one is by persuading ourselves that we are immune from disaster, and the other is by the practice of sheer courage.

      Bertrand Russell, *Unpopular Essays*

   e. The camera can be lenient; it is also expert at being cruel.

      Susan Sontag, *On Photography*

f. Wherever new lines of communication have opened up, wherever ideas new to a people have taken hold of their imagination, people have been able to change.

Margaret Mead, Aspects of the Present

g. A man may take to drink because he feels himself to be a failure, and then fail all the more completely because he drinks.

George Orwell, "Politics and the English Language"

2. Choose five of the sentences in Exercise 1 and using them as models, write five sentences of your own. For example, taking sentence (a) as a model: "Understanding is the first step in education and it is also its desired result."

3. Rewrite these sentences from student essays, using parallelism and balance to improve them.

    a. Mary Pickford was America's sweetheart in her early films and wore long blonde curls and little girl dresses and a sweet, innocent smile and she was thirty-five years old.

    b. The development of nuclear power promises an undreamed of future, and we must be aware of the potential hazards of nuclear waste.

    c. Some estimates of adult illiteracy in the United States put it at twenty million, but twenty-five million is the figure favored by others.

    d. Television commercials urge children to consume sugar cereals, candy and sweet drinks and the principles of good nutrition are ignored.

    e. My little sister stopped being cute at twelve; she borrows my clothes; she whines at my mother; my father buys her anything she wants.

    f. Sometimes it is exhilarating to swim in the ocean; I am usually frightened when the waves are dark and choppy.

    g. The lead guitarist got his fingers tangled in his guitar strap and then he tripped on his microphone and then broke a string and the crowd went wild.

4. Rewrite these sentences to improve emphasis. For instance, the first sentence might read: "Worst for me among all childhood diseases was measles." Compare your versions with those of your classmates. Discuss how different constructions allow for different shades of meaning.

    a. I had all the usual childhood diseases, but measles I remember as the worst.

    b. Because of the availability of handguns, violent crime in the United States is increasing.

    c. I needed glasses and couldn't even see what was written on the blackboard or read the posters behind the lectern.

d. They served exotic fruits for dessert, pomegranates, persimmons, pineapples and mangoes, and I didn't know how to eat them.

5. Revise the following passage so that it has a more satisfying rhythm; for example, the first sentences might become:

> The old man lived in the gloomiest part of the forest in a house made of crude bricks.

> The old man lived in a house made of crude bricks in the gloomiest part of the forest.

> In the gloomiest part of the forest, in a house made of crude bricks, lived the old man.

The old man lived in the gloomiest part of the forest. He had a house there. It was made of crude bricks. All kinds of trees grew around the house. There were oaks, fir trees, and kinds that had no name. They shut out the sun. Only scattered patches and changing shapes of sunlight showed on the ground. The old man didn't mind. He had lived in the city for many long years. He had grown to hate the neurotic scurrying about. And the hypocritic smiles and cement-block faces.

6. Revise these sentences so that they are resolved more concretely.

a. The Boer War was a conflict which was a matter of the utmost importance.

b. *Moby-Dick*, a masterpiece of the nineteenth century, is a great piece of writing.

c. The dark-haired girl that he had only glimpsed before was very attractive.

d. If David and Susan don't manage to compromise somewhat, they'll have trouble.

e. The dog was strangely reserved, almost sinister; Dan didn't like it much.

f. The two of them were excited and pleased with their new car; it performed well.

g. The murder of the senator was a senseless and tragic act.

h. In the face of the increasing violence in our city, drastic measures must be taken.

i. We must try to write better.

j. Racial hatred in this country affects all of us.

7. Look through your newspaper—especially the op-ed pages—and find three examples of periodic sentences. What effect does the writer hope to make by holding back?

Unity of Tone

Earlier, we called some words *fancy,* and we have alluded to formal and informal styles. Now, in a chapter on the sentence, it will be wise to consider the levels of diction, the tones of voice our prose can aim for. By choice of words and syntax, our writing can vary in tone as much as we vary our voices in speech by loudness and pitch. (Think of how "hello" can be said: neutral, questioning, sarcastic, loving, exclamatory—all by the tone with which we pronounce two syllables.) Among other tones, we can in our prose sound calm, precise, strident, humorous, angry, intimate, distant, or reasonable. We think of tone now, as we consider unity in sentences, because consistency of tone is another means of holding our writing together, another means to unity. Logically, tone could be part of other chapters, but this place seems most convenient, because unity of tone begins inside the sentence. Tone is the way we fix on our audience, or the way our audience understands and responds to the feelings with which we write.

In the chapter on words, we mentioned formality and informality, fanciness and colloquialism, which pertain to the tone of diction. In this chapter, we mean the tone of syntax and the tone of sentence structure.

Formality and Informality. Choosing a tone requires *tact.* You do not use the same vocabulary, sentence structure, or organization of thought on contrasting occasions. Audience determines tone; tone is the writer's choice of a connection with the reader. The doctor delivering a paper to his colleagues writes a formal and scientifically exact prose; the same person, contributing to an alumni newsletter, writes a relaxed and conversational prose. If one style wandered for a moment into the opposite, we would have disunity.

> The amino acids were observed to disappear from the patient's urine which was a helluva note.

> "Pa" Barker writes that he and his child bride have settled into suburbia where they are expecting obstetric surgery.

The alumni note could be an attempt at humor, much of which depends on disunity. More examples will follow presently.

Of course *formal* and *informal* are relative, and many points fall between the extremes. We must think about three things; first, what distinguishes formal from informal; second, the occasions requiring or suggesting different tones; third, how much unity of tone is appropriate to an essay or a story and how much variety it will tolerate, accept, or enjoy.

It will be good to start with formal and informal prose writings as touchstones or concrete reference points for our abstractions. For formal prose, look at this passage from Ecclesiastes (9:11) in the King

James translation of the Bible, which always combines vigor and formality.

> I returned and saw under the sun, that the race is not to the swift, nor the battle to the strong, neither yet bread to the wise, nor yet riches to men of understanding, nor yet favour to men of skill, but time and chance happeneth to them all.

Now look at this passage from a contemporary literary essay, in which the writer has used repetition, parallelism, and appropriate diction to convey controlled feeling and conviction:

> The greatest American industry—why has no one ever said so?—is the industry of using words. We pay tens of millions of people to spend their lives lying to us, or telling us the truth, or supplying us with a nourishing medicinal compound of the two. All of us are living in the middle of a dark wood—a bright Technicolored forest—of words, words, words. It is a forest in which the wind is never still: there isn't a tree in the forest that is not, for every moment of its life and our lives, persuading or ordering or seducing or overawing us into buying this, believing that, voting for the other.
>
> Randall Jarrell, Kipling, Auden & Co.

For informal prose, here is a passage from James Thurber's *The Years with Ross.*

> Ross began as a dice shooter in the AEF, and ended up with a gambling compulsion. Nobody knows how many thousands of dollars he lost in his time at poker, backgammon, and gin rummy, but it ran way up into five figures. He finally gave up sky's-the-limit poker, but would often play all night in Reno or Colorado, on his trips West, in games where the stakes were only a dollar or so. He must have won at poker sometimes, but I don't think he ever really got the hang of the game; certainly he didn't bring to it the intuitive sense he brought to proofs and manuscripts. He once told me about what he called the two goddamdest poker hands he had ever seen laid down on a table. "One guy held a royal flush, and the other had four aces," he said. When I asked, "Who got shot?" he looked puzzled for a moment and then said, "All right, all right, then it was a straight flush, king high, but I've been telling it the other way for ten years." His greatest gambling loss occurred in New York, in 1926, when he plunged into a poker game with a tableful of wealthy men. He got off to a lucky start, and was two thousand dollars ahead and going to drop out when one of the players said, "Winners quitters, eh?" Ross, who was drinking in those days, stayed in the game, kept on drinking, and lost thirty thousand dollars.

In diction, formal prose avoids the slangy, the colloquial, or the eccentric. A writer attempting a formal style sometimes falls into temporary informality because he cannot think of the appropriate word, because his vocabulary is inadequate, or because he is too lazy to look for the word. Writing a research paper on exports from a small nation, we want to imply that the minister of the treasury lacked financial integrity; but "lacked financial integrity" is a pompous formula. What do we say of him? If we call him "a crook," we will intrude an alien vocabulary into this paper. The slang is like tactlessness. The best solution is to say something particular, and avoid the generality. Perhaps we can say that he was convicted of taking bribes.

In a more informal context, *crook* might be just the right word, bringing in a slangy touch of roughness. Tact is all. And it is like social tact, which is often called hypocrisy. When you see an old friend for the first time in six months, you may call him all sorts of names that you would not use in front of your priest. When you are introduced to the Romanian ambassador between the acts of the ballet, you do not use the same gruff slang you would use with your old friend; you are more apt to say something original, like "How do you do, Mr. Ceascu?" If you called him "you old son of a bitch" (which is no more original, of course), you would have a social problem. Writing a résumé, or a letter applying for a job, if we turn slangy or idiosyncratic—writing *thru* for *through;* saying *guy* or *gal*—we make a noise like someone who does not know how to act, perhaps someone difficult to put up with in the office. Awareness of audience indicates the writer's sensitivity to the world outside the self: to other people.

Formality Gone Bad. We can help to define our terms by looking at what they are not. The virtue of informality can slide into the vice of slackness, excess, or vagueness. The virtue of formality can wiggle in a hundred directions into the vices of pomposity, fanciness, pretense, jargon, and meaningless abstraction. George Orwell turned a good formality into a horrid one by rewriting the passage from Ecclesiastes that we quoted earlier. His modern version is the High Abstraction of academic sociology. Orwell takes

> I returned and saw under the sun, that the race is not to the swift, nor the battle to the strong, neither yet bread to the wise, nor yet riches to men of understanding, nor yet favour to men of skill; but time and chance happeneth to them all.

and turns it into

> Objective consideration of contemporary phenomena compels the conclusion that success or failure in competitive activities exhibits no tendency to be commensurate with innate capacity, but that a considerable element of the unpredictable must invariably be taken into account.

Orwell's parody, which would pass for good prose with many people, sounds untouched by human hands, like a monstrous frozen dinner fabricated from sawdust and boiled crayons. The Orwell parody cannot be called formal. Because of its imprecision, it could be called sloppy, but not informal; imprecision is a quality in most bad prose, whether it is formal or informal in its intent. This parody ridicules a stiff prose style that *passes for* formality among many writers.

Pompous Language. We use pompous language to paint over a reality we wish to avoid seeing. In Chapter 4, we mentioned euphemisms; sometimes, whole sentences are euphemistic. The airline has the flight attendant say, "Would you care to purchase a cocktail?" instead of "Do you want to buy a drink?" because the second sentence sounds crass, plain, and blunt. For the same reasons, *beverage* is often substituted for *drink*. These words are fancy substitutes for plain talk, and we use them (or they are used on us by commerce) for deceit. They are a vice that formality sometimes supports. But they are not genuinely *more formal*. *Wealthy* is not more formal than *rich*, it is just fancier. *Rich* is not slang; it belongs in the most formal discourse. It is plain, and formality can include plainness without disunity. It cannot, however, include slang without upsetting its wholeness of tone. Think of the difference between *crook* and *rich*. And think of the difference between *tool* and *implement*. Like *rich*, *tool* is plain and perfectly suited to formal discourse; *implement* is polysyllabic and general, and often a pompous alternative to *tool*.

Writing a letter to a potential employer, it is easy to fall into pomposity in the effort to avoid slanginess or familiarity. It is best to avoid "so I worked for this gal doing sales pitches for a tiny bit." But don't go overboard in the other direction with "Therefore I worked with a female individual in the marketing division for a period of time." Say instead that you worked for the manager of the sales department for two weeks.

Formal and Informal Sentence Structure. The question "Do you want to buy a drink?" is neither formal nor informal in itself. "Would you care to purchase a cocktail?" is pompous. "Want to get sloshed?" is slangy, which is not the same as informal. We could use "Do you want to buy a drink?" in a context that was either formal or informal, because its words are plain. Informally:

> The woman came down the aisle looking tidy and cheerful. In back of the makeup and the hair, which looked as if it would break off in chunks if you touched it, perhaps there was a living woman, somebody with a name like Eileen or Carol. She wanted to say, "Do you want to buy a drink?" But the airline had enameled her talk along with her hair. "Would you care to purchase a cocktail?"

More formally:

> When you arrive at the age of fifty, your ability to choose has narrowed, and you find yourself on a narrow road, lacking the old opportunity to expand or wander, facing instead the one bleak point at journey's end. When you were young, you questioned: Do you want to be an actor, or a poet? Will you live in London, New York, or Paris? Now you are no longer young: Will you eat lobster for dinner? Do you want to buy a drink?

The difference here is less a matter of vocabulary than it is of sentence (and paragraph) structure. The difference includes words also, but the difference in vocabulary is relative. *Tidy* and *cheerful* could go in either passage. The idiomatic gesture of *along with* in the first passage is relatively informal; perhaps *as well as* would be the formal equivalent. *Chunks* has an informal sound. But the sentence structure in the second passage—complex, pointed, controlled—mainly accounts for its greater formality.

Informality Gone Bad. The fault typical of informal prose, when it goes bad, is incoherence. It does not hang together. (Pompous formal prose, or jargon, at least *seems* to hang together.) Here is a journalist's parody of what the Gettysburg Address would have sounded like if President Eisenhower, who was famous for his meandering style, had delivered it.

> I haven't checked these figures but 87 years ago, I think it was, a number of individuals organized a governmental set-up here in this country, I believe it covered certain Eastern areas, with this idea they were following up based on a sort of national independence arrangement and the program that every individual is just as good as every other individual. Well, now, of course, we are dealing with this big difference of opinion, civil disturbance you might say, although I don't like to appear to take sides or name any individuals, and the point is naturally to check up, by actual experience in the field, to see whether any governmental set-up with a basis like the one I was mentioning has any validity and find out whether that dedication by those early individuals will pay off in lasting values and things of that kind.
>
> Well, here we are, at the scene where one of these disturbances between different sides got going. We want to pay our tribute to those loved ones, those departed individuals who made the supreme sacrifice here on the basis of their opinions about how this thing ought to be handled. And I would say this. It is absolutely in order to do this.
>
> But if you look at the over-all picture of this, we can't pay any tribute—we can't sanctify this area, you might say—we can't hallow according to whatever individual creeds or faiths or sort of religious outlooks are involved like I said about this particular area.

It was those individuals themselves, including the enlisted men, very brave individuals, who have given this religious character to the area. The way I see it, the rest of the world will not remember any statements issued here but it will never forget how these men put their shoulders to the wheel and carried this idea down the fairway.

Now frankly, our job, the living individual's job here, is to pick up the burden and sink the putt they made these big efforts here for. It is our job to get on with the assignment—and from these deceased fine individuals to take extra inspiration, you could call it, for the same theories about the set-up for which they made such a big contribution. We have to make up our minds right here and now, as I see it, that they didn't put out all that blood, perspiration and—well—that they didn't just make a dry run here, and that all of us here, under God, that is, the God of our choice, shall beef up this idea about freedom and liberty and those kind of arrangements, and that the government of all individuals, by all individuals and for all individuals, shall not pass out of the world-picture.

Oliver Jensen, "The Gettysburg Address in Eisenhowese"

And here, in case you do not remember it, is Lincoln's formal original.

Fourscore and seven years ago our fathers brought forth on this continent a new nation, conceived in liberty, and dedicated to the proposition that all men are created equal.

Now we are engaged in a great civil war, testing whether that nation, or any nation so conceived and so dedicated, can long endure. We are met on a great battlefield of that war. We have come to dedicate a portion of that field as a final resting-place for those who here gave their lives that that nation might live. It is altogether fitting and proper that we should do this.

But in a larger sense, we cannot dedicate—we cannot consecrate—we cannot hallow—this ground. The brave men, living and dead, who struggled here, have consecrated it far above our poor power to add or detract. The world will little note nor long remember what we say here, but it can never forget what they did here. It is for us, the living, rather, to be dedicated here to the unfinished work which they who fought here have thus far so nobly advanced. It is rather for us to be here dedicated to the great task remaining before us—that from these honored dead we take increased devotion to that cause for which they gave the last full measure of devotion; that we here highly resolve that these dead shall not have died in vain; that this nation, under God, shall have a new birth of freedom; and that government of the people, by the people, for the people, shall not perish from the earth.

The parody is twice the length of the original, yet doesn't convey any more information. In fact, it is much less specific—substituting nebulous phrases like "this big difference of opinion, civil disturbance you might say" for clear and simple ones like "a great civil war." The sentences wander and repeat themselves ("It was those individuals themselves, including the enlisted men, very brave individuals . . . ").

It would be easy to continue listing the faults, because they were planted deliberately. But it is more important here to notice how they change the effect the statement makes. The writing is so diluted and directionless that we don't feel the speaker cares for the subject; we don't believe that he is genuinely moved. One fault that helps to create this impression—a fault common to many writers—is repeating pointless qualifications like *I think, I believe,* and *I would say.* Many people mistakenly think that such qualifications make writing more informal and natural. But these personalisms are understood without being said, and they make one feel that if the speaker (or writer) is so tentative about speaking his mind, then he is probably not certain of it.

Be wary of becoming careless in trying to be informal. Carelessness is partly a matter of vague words: *individual,* which is jargon for *person,* is vaguer than *person* or *people.* But carelessness is also incoherent sentence and paragraph structure, sentences that wander without resolution and emphasis. Series of simple and compound sentences are often sloppy and boring. The parts do not mesh; there is no consistency. Whether your purpose is formal or informal, if you write with some respect for variety and unity—with a sense of shape and finish—you will likely avoid such failings.

Subject and Audience. We choose a level of diction to fit subject and audience. We know, before we think it over, that a recollection of a family reunion will be more informal than an essay advocating that the U.S. Postal Service be abolished. Content and circumstance determine permissible areas on the line from formal to informal and will determine whether we choose *crook* or *criminal* before we come to it. If a student remembering junior high school writes,

> After a month of missing wallets and empty purses, we decided that
> somebody in the classroom was a crook.

we read along easily, and the slangy word is vigorous at the end of the sentence. If the student had written,

> After a month of missing wallets and empty purses, we came to the
> conclusion that someone in the classroom was a criminal.

we would find the style ponderous—*came to the conclusion that*—and serious to the point of comedy. *Criminal* is a heavy word for petty thievery in the junior high.

On the other hand, if the student, in an essay on the traffic in heroin, wrote,

In 1975, an investigation organized by Interpol showed that high officials in three Mediterranean countries, in which opium grew, in which opium was refined into heroin, and from which illegal shipments started for the United States, were crooks making vast profits by virtue of their public positions.

the word *crooks* would be inappropriately informal in a sentence so formal in diction and structure. *Criminals* would be the better word.

We must learn to look for errors in tact when we revise; we must look for the low word in the high place and for the high word in the low place. When we have used the wrong word or construction, we can revise it out. If we have written *crook* because we could not think of *criminal*, we can consult the dictionary or thesaurus. If we have fallen into repeated compound sentences in a formal context, we can make some of them complex. If, in a modest piece of prose, we have slipped unintentionally into polysyllables and long, complex sentences, we can simplify. But in order to learn to revise we must learn what to look for.

Mixing Formal and Informal Diction. We would write more easily if prose were either informal or formal, if nothing lived between the poles. But most good prose lives in the temperate regions on either side of the equator. The informal essay enjoys an occasional periodic sentence or unusual word. The formally deft argument uses a sudden colloquialism with charm and wit.

A sentence by E. B. White exemplifies the mixture a witty writer can make. White has been talking with appropriate disdain about a pamphlet on writing that, among other things, admonishes us, "Whenever possible, personalize your writing by directing it to the reader." *Personalize* is a slimy word. As White says, "A man who likes the word 'personalize' is entitled to his choice, but we wonder whether he should be in the business of giving advice to writers." The word is used commercially to mean an imprinted name—*personalized stationery*, for instance—and does not mean *to make personal* or *to direct toward* another person. White's comment, after he quotes the advice, is the sentence

As for us, we would as lief Simonize our grandmother as personalize our writing.

The mini-analogy expresses White's feeling: it would be monstrous to *personalize our writing*. He compares the offensive diction to an unnatural act. At the same time, he uses a cunning and *personal* oddity of diction. The plain way to say the sentence is "we would as soon Simonize our grandmother," but White uses the old-fashioned *as lief*. And *lief* butts against *Simonize,* the old-fashioned word against the trademark. The bizarre mixture of dictions—the *dis*unity—makes its point.

And so the mixture of dictions can be expressive as well as comic. Often it is chiefly comic. W. C. Fields's polysyllables are comic because he uses high words in low matters—or for low purposes, like conning people.

Revising for Unity. Achieving unity in our writing usually requires revision. Go over your prose, thinking of it as something that ought to be as whole and as shapely as a clay pot or a well-designed sports car.

Read your sentences aloud to yourself or to a friend. Look for rhythm and resolution, paying special attention to the ends of your sentences. Look for parallelism, emphasis, and balance. Repair any grammatical disunity that may have crept in. Look for places in which your tone shifts for no good reason, and make appropriate repairs.

____ EXERCISES ____

1. Rewrite these sentences as simply as possible. Cut out all the pretentiousness.

   a. He couldn't comprehend how the thermostat mechanism was to be operated.
   b. Surplus will be maximized when these goals are implemented.
   c. Your utilization of the word *sensuality* is improper.
   d. That wedge is merely a portion of the circle's entirety.
   e. We subscribe to the belief that negligence on your part was responsible for the damage incurred by our apartment's furnishings.
   f. My lower appendage does not have a great deal of mobility, confined as it is by the plaster cast.
   g. Indicate the vicinity of my abode.
   h. His investment in the emotional complex of their relationship, which has been ongoing for somewhat over five years, was minuscule.
   i. Due to private considerations the precise nature of which I cannot reveal, I will not be adopting the course of action you proposed as a substitute for my own.
   j. The culinary offerings of this establishment are not of a very high quality.
   k. The thronged multitudes emitted thunderous vibrations from their collective vocal cords at the point in time when the composer emerged into view.

2. Looking into textbooks, magazines, newspapers, college catalogues, find five sentences in which the writer uses a pompous or fancy construction in place of a plainer one. Rewrite for plainness,

and speculate on the reasons behind the pomposity. Bring both the original sentences and your rewrites to class; be prepared to discuss your findings in small groups.

3. Write ten sentences, five formal and five informal, in which one word stands out as inappropriate to the diction in the sentence. For instance, "The senator, having risen to the platform with difficulty, stated that he believed the measures the Senate had taken in the recent crisis, despite their intentions, were crummy."

4. Take this passage from Ecclesiastes (2:18–19) and make a parody like George Orwell's (see page 194).

> And I hated all my labour wherein I laboured under the sun, seeing that I must leave it unto the man that shall be after me. And who knoweth whether he will be a wise man or a fool? Yet will he have rule over all my labour wherein I have laboured, and wherein I have shown myself wise under the sun. This is also vanity.

5. Use the clause or sentence "he never wanted to write again" in two paragraphs, one formal and the other informal.

6. Write a short account of a real or imagined accident in three tones of voice: for (a) a letter to a relative, (b) an accident report for an insurance company, and (c) a story in the school newspaper.

7. In these passages, analyze diction and structure for formality and informality. Be prepared to find some mixture.

> a. Before we had children I worked in a library. It was a boring job, but I tend to like doing boring things. I would sit on a stool alphabetizing Russian catalogue cards and listening to the other librarians talking around me. It made me think of my adolescence, which was spent listening to the tobacco stringers while I handed tobacco. At night I'd go home from the library and write. I never wrote what the librarians said, exactly, but having those voices in my ears all day helped me summon up my own characters' voices. Then our first baby came along—an insomniac. I quit work and stayed home all day with her and walked her all night. Even if I had found the time to write, I wouldn't have had the insides. I felt drained; too much care and feeling were being drawn out of me.
>
> *Anne Tyler*, "Still Just Writing"

> b. "Omit needless words!" cries the author on page 17, and into that imperative Will Strunk really put his heart and soul. In the days when I was sitting in his class, he omitted so many needless words, and omitted them so forcibly and with such eagerness and obvious relish, that he often seemed in the position of having short-changed himself, a man left with nothing more to say yet with time to fill, a radio prophet who had outdistanced the clock. Will Strunk got out of this predicament by a simple trick: he uttered every sentence three times. When he delivered his oration on brevity to the class, he leaned forward over his

desk, grasped his coat lapels in his hands, and in a husky, conspiratorial voice said, "Rule Thirteen. Omit needless words! Omit needless words! Omit needless words!"

E. B. White, The Elements of Style

c. This is a society which has little use for anything except gain. All is hacked down in its service, whether people, ideas, or ideals. The writer, say, who achieves some entrance into the mainstream of American letters is almost immediately in jeopardy of being stripped of his insight by the ruffians of "success." A man who writes plays and poems, for instance, is asked to be a civil rights reporter, or write a dopey musical —if he is talked about widely enough—if not, there is no mention of him, and perhaps he is left to rot in some pitiful mistake of a college out in Idaho. A man who writes or makes beautiful music will be asked to immortalize a soap, or make sounds behind the hero while that blond worthy seduces the virgins of our nation's guilt. Even a man who is a great center fielder will still be asked to kick up his heels at Las Vegas.

Leroi Jones, Home

VARIETY AND UNITY

We write varied sentences according to the demands of thought and expression. Subordinate clauses often make needed qualifications in longer sentences that in their progress imitate the process of thinking. The simple, succinct sentence embodies the rhythm of a single idea. If our prose has unity, clarity, and coherence, it is usually varied in its sentence structure as well.

But not always. We get in a rut. We lack experience of the long, periodic sentence, or even of the complex sentence, and we tend to fall into a monotony of construction. It helps us, in revision, to look for variety of sentence structure, and if we lack this variety to see if we can appropriately impose it.

Unity and variety need each other. They are the two poles, and the world spins between them. Without variety, there is nothing to be unified. Identically constructed sentences strung together in a row have the unity of glass beads on a string. When we learn how to read, "See Spot run" sentences have this unity, which is perhaps why we want to leave first grade for the second. Paragraphs of successive compound sentences are similarly boring. In this passage from a student essay, the writer, lacking confidence in his ability to use complex sentences, writes beads-and-string prose.

Student government at the high school level is pointless. Principals never allow students any power. School boards are the same. Every year people get elected and nothing happens.

We could revise this passage, for variety, into these sentences—which also supply greater unity and clarity:

> Student government in high school is pointless because no high school principal is prepared to grant real power to students, and no school board would support a principal who experimented with student power. Although elections take place every year, office without responsibility makes nothing happen.

By using different sentence types, we can vary the speed and style in our prose, and at the same time make it more precise. If for no other reason, we must vary our sentences to keep the reader interested and involved. Monotony destroys attentiveness; if the reader sleeps, our clarity is wasted. But variation also allows us to be subtle; it increases the range and conciseness of our expression. The means are not separate from the ends. *A change in style, however slight, is a change in meaning, however slight.* You will find meanings that you cannot express, cannot convey, unless you can find in your box of varied sentence structures the shape you require.

Long Sentences

Short sentences are easy. They are also useful when they are mixed with longer sentences of different types. Longer sentences give student writers more trouble; the more parts a machine has, the more things can go wrong. But to become skillful writers, we must be able to handle varieties of the long sentence.

In the most controlled prose, in the long sentences made by writers being formal, clause follows clause, the sentence is compound as well as complex, and absolutes, participles, and appositives combine with prepositional phrases—a combination of combinations that includes, balances, and ultimately unifies.

If we took the sentence above and separated it into one independent clause for each idea, we might end with something like this:

> Some prose is highly controlled and each sentence is long. This happens when the writer is being formal. There are many clauses. The sentence can be compound and it can also be complex. The sentence can also include absolutes, participles, appositives, and prepositional phrases. This combination makes the sentence inclusive. It gives it balance, and it gives it unity.

This version uses seven sentences and fifty-nine words. The earlier version was one sentence and forty-four words. The gain in brevity is trivial, but the shorter version is more accurate. Subordination adds accuracy, not only by bringing form and content into agreement, but by making direct syntactic connections instead of continually stopping the flow of sense and picking it up again with a pronoun.

But we don't need to make such sentences up; we can find them in the work of many writers. W. H. Auden uses long, formal sentences to define the sea as a symbol in religion and in literature.

> The sea, in fact, is that state of barbaric vagueness and disorder out of which civilization has emerged and into which, unless saved by the effort of gods and men, it is always liable to relapse.
>
> W. H. Auden, *The Enchafèd Flood*

This sentence starts slowly, with *in fact* and *state of,* but ends with a flourish. Auden carries us up the hill, as far as the phrase *and into which,* and then holds us at the summit for a while with "unless saved by the efforts of gods and men" before he takes us downhill to resolve the main thought. The parallelism between the prepositions and relatives *out of which* and *into which* finds its action in the exact verbs *emerged* and *relapse.* It is interrupted, with precise syntactic sense, by the *unless* clause that separates the relative and the verb in the final clause. We might try a version of the sentence as someone else might have written it.

> The sea literally depicts a state of being that is barbaric. Also, it is vague, and it does not have any order in it. Civilization is what has come out of the sea. Civilization is always liable to go back into the sea. But civilization is saved by the efforts of gods and men. Or it has been so far, anyway.

Let us find more long sentences, graceful and agile.

> In the early morning the distant image of Cannes, the pink and cream of old fortifications, the purple Alps that bounded Italy, were cast across the water and lay quavering in the ripples and rings sent up by sea-plants through the clear shadows.
>
> F. Scott Fitzgerald, *Tender Is the Night*

The passage begins and ends with prepositional phrases (*In the early morning . . . through the clear shadows*) and in between are more of them, and adjectives, and a varied use of verbs: *bounded, cast, lay quavering.* The sentence follows the logic of looking, it is a sequence of carefully organized perceptions. The verbs, which follow each other in time, have as subject the three phrases and clauses before—an elaborated subject, which includes the verb *bounded* as well as nouns and adjectives. Then we move into more prepositions and nouns, another verb, preposition and noun, preposition, adjective, and noun. The verbs at the center carry the sentence: they direct the movement of the inner eye.

Fitzgerald's prose is ornate and well ordered, but not so formal as the prose of certain essayists and historians. Here is part of a paragraph by one of the masters of the essay form.

> The concept of the perfect society is one of the oldest and most deeply pervasive elements in western thought, wherever, indeed, the classical or Judaeo-Christian traditions are dominant. It has taken many forms—a Golden Age, a Garden of Eden in which men were innocent, happy, virtuous, peaceful, free, where everything was harmonious, and neither vice nor error nor violence nor misery was so much as thought of; where nature was bounteous and nothing was lacking, there was no conflict, and not even the passage of time affected the full, permanent and complete satisfaction of all the needs, physical, mental and spiritual, of the blessed dwellers in these regions. Then a catastrophe occurred that put an end to this condition; there are many variants of this—the flood, man's first disobedience, original sin, the crime of Prometheus, the discovery of agriculture and metallurgy, primitive accumulation, and the like.
> Isaiah Berlin, "Vico and the Ideal of the Enlightenment"

Most of us are unlikely to compose sentences as long and complicated as the second in the paragraph, but we might study Berlin's technique for a moment just to see what a skilled stylist can do with this fundamental unit of prose. Let us look at the whole in terms of its clusters of sense. "It," writes Berlin, referring to the idea of the perfect society, "has taken many forms," at which point he begins to itemize. But he only reaches the second in his list, "A Garden of Eden," before he begins listing *its* virtues. The dwellers, he claims, were "innocent, happy, virtuous," and so on; he then switches to the negative in order to underscore a set of conditions which did *not* prevail. Positive and negative lists are roughly in balance: the positive list has more terms, the negative list uses more words. Then, as if we have not had enough heaped on our plate, Berlin inserts a semicolon and pushes on. Another list, this one again comprised of negatives, begins the second half of the sentence. Then, cleverly ("Not even the passage of time affected the full, permanent and complete satisfaction . . . "), the writer turns the negatives back into a list of positive virtues. By the time we finish the whole sentence, we have been carried through a logical system that makes either side of the semicolon a reverse image of the other. Thus: Positive Negative; Negative Positive.

The long, complex sentence lends itself especially well to organizing things that are related to each other, like events in history, plots of stories, or arguments with several parts. The art is to distribute the parts of the sentence so that the underlying logic shines forth clearly.

Mixing the Types

We can manipulate the types of sentence we use for variety and to create an expressive effect, to establish a mood, or to emphasize a point. Here are some examples. Keep in mind that the passages get their effect not by the sentence structure alone, but also by the word associations and ideas. Sometimes, for the sake of sense or mood, we manipulate phrases to achieve more regularity than variety.

> In a little house on the mountain slopes above Delphi lived an old woman with her witless son. The house consisted of a single room; one wall was the mountainside itself, and always dripped with moisture. It was really not a house at all, but a ramshackle hut which herdsmen had built for themselves. It stood quite alone away up in the wild mountain, high above the buildings of the city and above the sacred precincts of the temple.
>
> Pär Lagerkvist, The Sybil

The sentence structure here is simple and stable. The construction is uncomplicated and regular. All the sentences except the first are regular in word order, beginning subject-verb and continuing evenly, without parenthetical expressions, or phrases set off by commas, or any other complications in the syntax. The syntax is as undisturbed as the scene. The sentences are medium in length, and similar in length, establishing a rhythm that reinforces the stability and simplicity in the scene described. We participate in the rhythm of untroubled isolation. That rhythm is established, even more, by the uniform length of the main phrases within the sentences. If we listen to ourselves reading the passage, we will find that natural pauses divide the phrases in this way:

> In a little house on the mountain slopes above Delphi/
> lived an old woman with her witless son./
> The house consisted of a single room;/
> one wall was the mountainside itself,/
> and always dripped with moisture./
> It was really not a house at all,/
> but a ramshackle hut which herdsmen had built for themselves./
> It stood quite alone away up in the wild mountain,/
> high above the buildings of the city/
> and above the sacred precincts of the temple./

It has just enough variation to avoid monotony. The even length contributes not only stillness to the scene, but our sense of the narrator's calm, unemotional objectivity.

The following passage from Annie Dillard's *Pilgrim at Tinker Creek* exhibits different sentence constructions, with different effects:

When I slide under a barbed-wire fence, cross a field, and run over a sycamore trunk felled across the water, I'm on a little island shaped like a tear in the middle of Tinker Creek. On one side of the creek is a steep forested bank; the water is swift and deep on that side of the island. On the other side is the level field I walked through next to the steers' pasture; the water between the field and the island is shallow and sluggish. In summer's low water, flags and bulrushes grow along a series of shallow pools cooled by the lazy current. Water striders patrol the surface film, crayfish hump along the silt bottom eating filth, frogs shout and glare, and shiners and small bream hide among roots from the sulky green heron's eye. I come to this island every month of the year. I walk around it, stopping and staring, or I straddle the sycamore log over the creek, curling my legs out of the water in winter, trying to read. Today I sit on dry grass at the end of the island by the slower side of the creek. I'm drawn to this spot. I come to it as to an oracle; I return to it as a man years later will seek out the battlefield where he lost a leg or an arm.

As with the Lagerkvist passage, we can put the Dillard paragraph into long lines to see its structure more clearly and to understand how her complicated sentences work.

When I slide under a barbed wire fence,
    cross a field,
        and run over a sycamore trunk felled across the water,
I'm on a little island shaped like a tear in the middle of
                                    Tinker Creek.

On one side of the creek is a steep forested bank;
the water is swift and deep on that side of the island.
On the other side is the level field
I walked through next to the steers' pasture;
the water between the field and the island is shallow and
    sluggish.

In summer's low water,
flags and bulrushes grow along a series of shallow pools cooled
                                    by the lazy current.

Water striders patrol the surface film,
crayfish hump along the silt bottom eating filth,
frogs shout and glare,
and shiners and small bream hide among roots from the sulky
                                    green heron's eye.

I come to this island every month of the year.

I walk around it, stopping and staring,
or I straddle the sycamore log over the creek, curling my legs out of
                                    the water in winter, trying to read.

Today I sit on dry grass at the end of the island by the slower
side of the creek.

I'm drawn to this spot.

I come to it as to an oracle;
I return to it as a man years later will seek out the battlefield
where he lost a leg or an arm.

Dillard starts with a long complex sentence of description, with three lively verbs in a subordinate clause, and then an elaborated predicate in the main clause. She follows this sophisticated sentence with two simple clauses, a compound joined by a semicolon. The next sentence elaborates the pattern of the second one. The fifth is long and rich, its mass of description tending to obscure the fact that its construction is simple, direct—and compound. Following it is the shortest sentence, and the simplest one so far, in the paragraph. Two sentences later, we find a sentence even shorter and simpler, followed by a compound-complex sentence of great sophistication, and a final image that is startling, almost shattering. Dillard plays the octaves of syntax like a skilled musician improvising at the piano.

Though our focus in this chapter has been on sentences, their use and construction, we should not forget those fundamental components—words. Though Dillard achieves much of her effectiveness here through her grasp of sentence variety, she is also an expert at finding the right word to evoke the sensation she wants. The fourth sentence is a good example. Dillard's water striders *patrol*, her crayfish *hump*, and her frogs *shout* and *glare*. Try substituting *walk*, *crawl*, and *croak* and *stare*. The sentence feels diminished. Writing that touches a reader depends, finally, on everything working together: words and sentences, rhythms and meanings.

Revising for Variety and Conciseness

Look over your own writing for the construction of sentences. Ask yourself if you vary enough to avoid monotony, if your variations are as expressive as they might be, and if your informal sentences are appropriate and sufficiently precise.

Also, see if you can be more concise. To revise for conciseness often requires compound and complex sentences or conjunction and subordination. Concision and precision go together. We ramble on, in our first drafts or in our daily writing, assuming connections and causes but not stating them. If we try to make our prose more concise, by writing complex sentences with precise conjunctions, we often discover that what we wanted to imply does not really derive from what we said. And so this device of revision—by adding the conjunction—

becomes another way of testing the identity of expression and meaning. Precision of time and cause is a responsibility that the loose or compound sentence may evade. In an earlier example, a tiny revision illustrated a small gain in brevity and responsibility:

> I saw her and she was carrying a kitten. It had a crooked tail . . .

became

> When I saw her she was carrying a kitten with a crooked tail.

Maybe the greatest change here is in the tone; the writer seems to be controlling something, not merely rattling on.

Here is a passage from a student essay in which the writer dumps things together without showing relationships. He wastes words by repetition, and he wastes the power in those words by poor organization.

> The building was still burning and firemen couldn't put it out. An hour or so went by. The National Guard looked nervous and young. They drove around in their Jeeps with their guns. They tried to look tough. We didn't know if their guns were loaded or not. They were scary just because they had guns but they looked scared themselves. They were about the same age as the students. Yet they were guarding them.

Because the relationship between remarks is often vague in this passage, we could not rewrite it with certainty unless we knew more facts or knew the feelings the author tried to express. Reading the passage, we may doubt that the student had arranged the facts in his mind with clarity, or had understood his feelings. Later, he revised the passage, and his sentence structure accounted for much of the improvement—though as always with writing, the *whole* shapes everything that it contains; the whole is better, partly because of sentence structure.

> As we watched the building burn for hours, the firemen standing by helpless, we became aware of the patrolling Jeeps of the National Guard, young men the same age as the students they were guarding, young men who tried to act tough but looked as frightened of their guns as we were.

He gained economy and vividness, and also clarity of thought and feeling.

―――― **EXERCISES** ――――――――――――――――――――――――――――――――

1. Revise this passage to introduce varied sentence structure. Use variation not just for its own sake, but to make the writing more

COMBINE (SENTENCES)

REWRITE (SENTENCES)

precise. Remember that commas, semicolons, colons, and periods are aids to rhythm and therefore to meaning, to expressiveness, and to clarity.

Every man who worked on the docks had to wear a hard hat. He also had to wear heavy canvas gloves. The hats protected the men from falling objects. Sometimes crates fell into the hole. Sometimes steel beams were swung down to the dock on cables. There was danger of metal splinters and serious abrasions. These dangers were increased because the longshoremen might work for twelve hours straight. They might work from 6 P.M. to 6 A.M. Some of the men also had jobs during the day. And many of the men drank heavily. This was because they got depressed. Sometimes there would be a shipment of whiskey. The men might pretend to have an accident. They would let a crate fall. It would break open. They would stash the unbroken bottles. And they would hide them. They would drink some when the officials were not around. The officials were paid by the shipping companies. They didn't want to be blamed for missing goods.

2. Find and identify, in the passage you made from exercise 1, a subordinate clause, a main clause, an appositive, a participle, and an adjective with a preposition. If you cannot find one of each, revise the passage to include them.

3. Examine the following passages to discover how sentence structure and variation express content and tone. Try modifying the sentences and see whether the meaning of the passage changes. If so, how?

a. For purposes of pedagogy, I have sometimes illustrated these tendencies by reference to a technically uncomplicated product, which, unaccountably, neither General Electric nor Westinghouse has yet placed on the market. It is a toaster of standard performance, the pop-up kind, except that it etches on the surface of the toast, in darker carbon, one of a selection of standard messages or designs. For the elegant, an attractive monogram would be available or a coat of arms; for the devout, at breakfast there would be an appropriate devotional message from the Reverend Billy Graham; for the patriotic or worried, there would be an aphorism urging vigilance from Mr. J. Edgar Hoover; for modern painters and economists, there would be a purely abstract design. A restaurant version would sell advertising.

John Kenneth Galbraith, "The Technostructure"

b. There they were, those who had wangled their way into war, at the wrong place, doing, in excesses of patriotism or curiosity or self-proof, work that was the wrong work, at the wrong time. They were valuable in some terms I had not run into as an aircraft woman. There were fine editors, good writers, movie actors, poets, in the halls of the OWI at Carlos Place, and I realize now that I was as glamorous to them as they were to me. Somehow I had touched the war they had come to. I knew things I couldn't tell. Gaunt and nervous, aesthetically pleasing in the fashion that pleases at a given time, an object of interest, I had had the experience they had come to share. What I had learned to take for granted, service in the forces was, to them, a fascination. It made them seem somehow younger than I was. I had a sense of knowing things—oh, not events—civilians seem always to expect those—but gray expanses and hours, days, months, of damp indifference.

Mary Lee Settle, "London—1944"

c. Familiarity has perhaps bred contempt in us Americans: until you have had a washing machine, you cannot imagine how little difference it will make to you. Europeans still believe that money brings happiness, witness the bought journalist, the bought politician, the bought general, the whole venality of European literary life, inconceivable in this country of the dollar. It is true that America produces and consumes more cars, soap, and bathtubs than any other nation, but we live among these objects rather than by them. Americans build skyscrapers; Le Corbusier worships them. Ehrenburg, our Soviet critic, fell in love with the Check-O-Mat in American railway stations, writing home paragraphs of song to this gadget—while deploring American materialism. When an American heiress wants to buy a man, she at once crosses the Atlantic. The only really materialistic people I have ever met have been Europeans.

Mary McCarthy, "America the Beautiful" in On the Contrary

6

Paragraphs

USES OF PARAGRAPHS

The paragraph is a small box of sentences, making a whole shape that is at the same time part of another whole. It is a miniature essay itself, with its own variable structure. The paragraph within the essay makes a sign for the reader; it alerts the reader to the part-structure of our essay. Paragraphs give signals and directions and help to connect writers with audiences. Paragraphs are partly arbitrary, and will vary in length and purpose according to the essay's occasion. Frequently a writer arrives at the best paragraphing only in late revision.

In that bible for stylists, *Modern English Usage,* H. W. Fowler writes, "The purpose of paragraphing is to give the reader a rest." I called the paragraph a mini-essay; it is also a maxi-sentence: the blank space at the end of the paragraph, before we indent and begin a new one, is like the period ending the sentence, only longer. Paragraphs punctuate by visual arrangement on the page. Like a sentence, a paragraph tells us that something completes itself and that we have come to the end of a group of statements composing a larger statement. Like a sentence, too, a paragraph should close with the sensation of a click. Now the reader must pause a moment and see what the paragraph was doing.

Look at the preceding paragraph. Its organization is only one of many possible, but it is a common one. It begins with a quotation from Fowler, which announces its purpose. Then it compares paragraph and sentence. Fowler does not make such a comparison; my strategy takes its cue from Fowler's word *rest.* The last sentence suggests the function—pausing—that rest fills. The paragraph elaborates and supports the first sentence, and the pause at the end should grant us a sense of wholeness.

Paragraphs rest the eye as well as the brain. Unbroken print leaves no landmarks for the eye that wanders and returns; we sometimes find ourselves using a finger to keep to the correct line. Though context gives us other reasons for longer or shorter paragraphs, we should not forget that paragraphs are useful as visual aids to comfort in reading. Those little indentations are hand- and footholds in the cliff-face of the essay.

PARAGRAPHS AS SIGNS FOR READERS

As readers we identify the paragraph by the visual sign of its indented white space. Our eyes register PARAGRAPH before our minds have a chance to consider the writer's reasons for pause, or the content of the new paragraph. But the visual sign is itself information; it begins the new content by alerting us that something changes.

The paragraph holds and shapes; it manipulates the reader's attention. When as writers revising we consider our paragraphing, we must as always imagine ourselves readers. Because the paragraph gives the reader a break, writers can gather their materials into units small enough for separate comprehension, and by separating them can allow each collection its own space as part of the whole essay.

The paragraph, by embodying a sequence or development of thought, is more thoroughly directed to audience than the sentence is. Maybe our attention to paragraphing improves our thought, if we consider fullness of development a problem not of the essay but of the paragraph. For beginning writers it may be helpful, learning development to concentrate on the smaller unit; or we may think of the essay's structure as an assemblage of paragraphs in an appropriate order. But paragraphing always includes an element of the arbitrary. Finally it is not so much an aid to the writer's thought as a means by which the writer shapes his material, however generated, toward an imagined audience.

Paragraphing therefore tends to find its form in late revision when we realize that one sentence—say, "These views, so diametrically opposed, may be reconciled if we look at diplomatic history"—might perfectly well come at the end of a paragraph that details the opposition or at the beginning of the next paragraph that does the reconciling. No rule of paragraphing will decide whether this sentence ends one paragraph or begins another; writers must decide, on the basis of a chosen approach to the reader.

The paragraph is a writerly device for leading the reader by the nose.

The reader, we must remember, has certain expectations: the reader does *not* expect, in the formality of a textbook, paragraphs as short as my last one. When we do such a thing we surprise the reader and therefore we had better have a purpose. Did we?

Nor, on the other hand, does the reader expect to find page after page without any paragraph breaks at all. In some old scholarly treatises, and occasionally in essays by modern writers like John McPhee, readers will find such unexpected solid pages of print—and they may find themselves turning blue from lack of breath. But John McPhee is so skillful at leading readers by the nose with firm but gentle transitions, beguiling them by variety of sentence structure and fresh detail, that he manages the stunt. He performs like the child on the bicycle: "Look, Ma! No paragraphs!"

The tone of discourse makes for different expectations. When we read philosophy, or the history of the Peloponnesian War in the fifth century B.C., where detailed elaboration is essential, we expect longer paragraphs; when we read a news story in an afternoon daily we expect shorter ones.

Always, we expect a paragraph to be a unit; if a brief newspaper story gives one paragraph to each sentence, this very repetitiousness is a unity. (And if it continues for too long, this unity becomes totally boring.) More likely the paragraph assembles itself as a unit in a familiar way—like an assertion with details following to support the assertion. (We will list and explore familiar paragraph patterns later in this chapter.) Sometimes a paragraph forms part of something ongoing, like a narrative; the break should happen where, if we had to pause for a glass of water, we would pause. (We would *not* pause, say, in the middle of a sentence.) We expect the beginnings and endings of paragraphs, most of the time, to make small signals of starting and stopping. We expect paragraphs to hold together, without loose flapping parts. All of these expectations belong to us as readers; when we become writers, these expectations become devices for our use.

PURPOSE AND THE PARAGRAPH

Paragraphs advance the writer's purpose, and their shape must reflect that purpose in the development of the essay. As always, purpose adjusts itself to audience, as the writer improvises a structure. Development that follows rhetorical patterns, which we return to later in this chapter, often gives paragraphs an appropriate shape—but they are not the only common structures. A frequent paragraph pattern begins with a generalization, makes a necessary qualification, and then reaffirms the generalization by example. "The personal computer, used in conjunction with telephone lines, will revolutionize the habits of American consumers." This topic sentence makes an assertion which could be questioned; it acquires more authority if it is accompanied by a modest restriction: "We do not mean that Americans will no longer pick up a quart of milk at a convenience store, or that shopping plazas will become ghost towns." After this qualification, the paragraph might illustrate computer shopping at home with two or three examples.

Another common form of paragraph is the question and answer: "Will consumers find enough choice, if they shop by electronic catalogue? That will, of course, depend . . ." Questions need not be literally posed; the same paragraph could begin, in a more formal prose style, "Some commentators believe that electronic shopping will overly restrict consumer choice." In either paragraph, the sentences offering question or objection may be answered or rebutted by sentences that develop the paragraph.

Some essays profit by several paragraphs in a row constructed on similar principles: query or objection followed by reply or rebuttal. Two or three such paragraphs should suffice; when a whole essay is so constructed, the effect is too mechanical, or perhaps too defensive. It is wise to vary the construction of the paragraphs, and to vary the position of the generalization that the paragraph validates or illustrates. Often a topic sentence can conclude a paragraph. The writer could begin an essay by describing a consumer sitting in a den at the keyboard, shopping for a lawn mower; this opening paragraph could end, after its narrative example: "The personal computer, connected to telephone lines, will revolutionize the habits of the American consumer."

UNITY IN THE PARAGRAPH

In pursuing unity of thought and of feeling, the paragraph must contain nothing extraneous. The writer must omit the odd fact which happens to be true, but which is irrelevant to the topic. The odd fact violates unity and distracts the reader.

> We never had enough time to eat lunch in high school: half of the time I'd get a stomachache from hurriedly wolfing down the food. The food was lousy, anyway, and the kitchen help resented the minimum wage. We complained to the administration, but it didn't do any good. We were often held up in getting into the cafeteria because the lunchroom helpers were slow in getting the tables and the food ready. Then, if you were one of the people who got in toward the end, you would have to wait a long time in line. Sometimes the jocks, who acted as lunchroom police, would hold you up, too, trying to bully you into buying a football schedule.

The sentence about lousy food and dissatisfied kitchen help doesn't fit here; it is a digression from the topic "We never had enough time to eat lunch in high school."

We must remain alert to maintain unity of subject matter in our paragraphs, because the associations in our thought, which can lead us to new ideas and perceptions, can also lead us into irrelevance. When we begin to write about a subject, our mind drifts from one thought to another, by personal association. As we have seen in Chapter 3, this random, uncensored thinking can be useful for gathering material. But we must take care that it not lead to rambling disorganization. Because the reader does not share our private memories and feelings, he cannot see the connections we make—and we fail to make contact. Here is an example from a student paper.

> All the recent concern over the slaughter of whales whose species are nearly extinct has reminded me of my childhood interest in whales and other wild animals, especially animals who prey. I was particularly fascinated by the killer whales, which travel in packs like wolves often attacking larger whales. They will tear off the lips and tongue first, their favorite parts. But man has been almost solely responsible for the dangerous depletion of some of the whale populations, such as the blue whale. Still, I can remember the fear that animals like puff adders, tarantulas, and sharks could inspire in me as a child. So I wonder if, in certain cases, we aren't being hypocritical for blaming the people who actually live in lands inhabited by animals like tigers and wolves for killing them. We might be just as frightened and irrational as they are. But that still doesn't make it right.

The thoughts in this paragraph make connections for the writer, but not for the reader. The writer jumps from the threat to whale populations to his childhood interests, then to the habits of killer whales, then to questions of man's rational and irrational fears of predatory animals. To write a unified paragraph, he would have to decide what the topic of his paragraph ought to be and then stick to that topic. We cannot expect readers to be patient with a rambling, disorganized paragraph, nor can we expect them to read our minds and recognize an order that is personal to us.

Two kinds of writing need especially careful paragraphing. Exposition (which sets forth or explains) and argument (which attempts to convince or persuade) should lead the reader's mind by careful steps to understanding or agreement. Paragraphs in argument or exposition are mini-essays. They deal with one topic, or with closely related data, or with an integral segment of a topic. The paragraph is homogeneous. It is orderly—and we must remember that there are many varieties of order. (See Some Ways of Developing Paragraphs, pages 234–239.)

Unity and Topic Sentences

Probably the most common paragraph construction begins with a topic sentence, which brings to the paragraph not only order but also unity. The topic sentence announces the topic and an attitude toward it. The other sentences of the paragraph use a consistent order—often moving from the general to the specific—to explain, elaborate, or enumerate examples or analogies supporting the topic sentence. Then a final sentence draws the elaboration to a conclusion in a way that leads to the next paragraph. Here is a paragraph that begins with a topic sentence and moves from a general statement to particular examples.

> Boston is not a small New York, as they say a child is not a small adult but is, rather, a specially organized small creature with its small-creature's temperature, balance, and distribution of fat. In Boston there is an utter absence of that wild electric beauty of New York, of the marvelous, excited rush of people in taxicabs at twilight, of the great Avenues and Streets, the restaurants, theatres, bars, hotels, delicatessens, shops. In Boston the night comes down with an incredibly heavy, small-town finality. The cows come home; the chickens go to roost; the meadow is dark. Nearly every Bostonian is in his own house or in someone else's house, dining at the home board, enjoying domestic and social privacy. The "nice little dinner party"—for this the Bostonian would sell his soul. In the evenings, the old "accomodators" dart about the city, carrying their black uniforms and white aprons in a paper bag. They are on call to go, anywhere, to cook and serve dinners. Many of these women are former cooks and maids, now living on Social Security retirement pensions, supplemented by the fees for these evening "accomodations" to the community. Their style and the bland respectability of their cuisine keep up the social tone of the town. They are like those old slaves who stuck to their places and, even in the greatest deprivation, graciously went on toting things to the Massa.
>
> Elizabeth Hardwick, "Boston: The Lost Ideal"

Many variations upon this order are possible and are desirable, because a long essay composed of paragraphs equal in length and identical in construction would be boring.

Sometimes we find a topic sentence in the middle of a paragraph, where it provides summary or generalization tying together the particulars that come before and after.

> We hesitated before we stepped into the garden, so heavy was the odor of flowering quince. The garden was orderly, comfortable, and gorgeous, with little benches artfully placed for the weary guest. *Our host, as generous as he was clever, introduced us to his hobby.* We toured among hardy perennials, and walked past annual borders.

> We strolled among fig trees, past palms, to a density of shrubs. We
> floated in joy on the tropical air.
>
> Hermann von Kreicke, *The Migrant Swan*

At other times we find a topic sentence ending the paragraph, as a
summary. We can create drama or tension by starting with description
and detail and building to a conclusion.

> Now and then there is a house of brick. But what brick! When it is
> new it is the color of a fried egg. When it has taken on the patina of
> the mills it is the color of an egg long past all hope or caring. Was it
> necessary to adopt that shocking color? No more than it was neces-
> sary to set all of the houses on end. Red brick, even in a steel town,
> ages with some dignity. Let it become downright black, and it is still
> sightly, especially if its trimmings are of white stone, with soot in
> the depths and the high spots washed by the rain. *But in West-
> moreland they prefer that uremic yellow, and so they have the
> most loathsome towns and villages ever seen by mortal eye.*
>
> H. L. Mencken, "A Libido for the Ugly"

Notice how this structure involves us. We are pulled into the movement by the piling up of details, not knowing exactly where the argument will lead us. The author carries us with him, and the conclusion
arises from the material presented. The principle is the same as that of
the periodic sentence; the most important information is used as the
clincher.

For the opposite effect, look back at the paragraph by Elizabeth
Hardwick. Paragraphs that begin with topic sentences differ greatly in
rhythm and in tone from paragraphs that end with them. The Hardwick
and Mencken paragraphs have different purposes, which make their
different structures appropriate. Hardwick wants to inform and explain.
She tells us our destination as we start; she begins with her primary idea
and then fleshes it out. Mencken wants to persuade us to share not only
his ideas but also his point of view. He wants us to share with him the
stages of the perceptual process. He keeps us off balance at first and
involves us in the accumulating fabric of thought and feeling.

Sometimes we even find a paragraph's topic sentence at the end of
the previous paragraph. The paragraph break serves almost as a colon.

> In general, chronology is the most satisfactory organization.
> *However, we must not rely on it alone.*
>
> We would reduce our psychological world to the order of the clock.
> We would become slaves of "then" and "afterward." . . .

The first two sentences in the second paragraph elaborate the negative
topic sentence which ends the first paragraph, but which could have
introduced the second paragraph just as well.

Sometimes we have no topic sentence, or it is understood or implied as a transition can be understood. A writer may mention that he spent a day in the town of Omaha, then follow with a paragraph:

> The visitor can enjoy the aroma of the stockyards. He can watch the rich sit at their clubs, drinking gin next to pools of chlorine, beside flat golf courses. The visitor can walk up the sides of ugly buildings on dry Sundays. He can watch grass grow, at least in early spring and early fall. He can listen to the medley of rock-station radios in several parks. He can try sleeping for a week or so, until he is able to leave.

He needs no topic sentence; we already know what the topic is. The topic is the place, and the paragraph has unity because we can see that every sentence describes an activity possible in this place.

In argument or exposition, topic sentences often have the flavor of philosophical propositions. For instance:

> When a man needs help, he must know where to turn.

> In the 1960s, the rock guitarist was seen as a kind of god.

> The paragraph is a unit of sense, a discrete idea or topic.

In narrative and descriptive writing, topic sentences often change the scene or introduce signposts in complicated country. Here are some sentences that could be lead-ins to new paragraphs.

> Finally, he thought it was time to return.

> The weather turned fine.

> When they turned the corner, the street changed abruptly.

> Election night began with a bad omen.

> When he heard footsteps outside in the darkness, he turned off the oil lamps and reached for his gun.

> The final chapters seem pointless.

When we revise our prose, it is useful to look into our paragraphs for topic sentences. We do not demand that every paragraph have one—but the *idea* of a topic sentence is a means of focusing and unifying and is therefore essential to clear and forceful prose. We look for the topic sentence of a paragraph—overt or implicit, at beginning, middle, or end—to see if the paragraph is sufficiently unified and whether it has a reason for being.

COHERENCE IN THE PARAGRAPH

Frequently, in unfinished writing, a sentence seems extraneous or irrelevant; the writer has a use for the information, but he has been unable to build the sentence smoothly into his thought. If a fact does not belong in a paragraph, it causes disunity. If it only *seems* not to belong, it causes incoherence.

The writer must learn how to blend his information so that it coheres in a meaningful whole: the relationship between the sentences must be clear. Here is an incoherent paragraph from some daily writing.

> I had been having severe headaches and frequent dizzy spells. I was terrified of doctors. I went to the health clinic. I waited three days. It was the time of finals and I was very busy. I saw a doctor. He prescribed some pills. The problems continued.

It is impossible to tell what the relationships are between the bits of information related here. Did the speaker wait three days before or after going to the health clinic? Did she wait because of her fear of doctors or because she was busy? Was she busy studying for finals, or doing something else? Not only is the sense confused, but the rhythm is irritatingly choppy. Here is a revised and more coherent version of the passage.

> I had been having severe headaches and frequent dizzy spells, but I hesitated to go to the health clinic because I was terrified of doctors. It was the time of finals and I was busy studying for them, so I made the excuse to myself that I didn't have time and that there was nothing the matter with me, just fatigue. Finally, I went, although I waited three days before making an appointment. I saw a doctor, and after he examined me he prescribed some pills. But despite the medication, the problems continued, even after I'd been taking the pills for two weeks.

Notice that much of the coherence comes from the use of conjunctions and subordinate clauses. Although most facts remain the same, the writer has given the reader a good deal more information, because she has connected the facts in a coherent paragraph, using complex sentences and logical transitions. The revision illustrates how a writer can take a mere list of facts and, by keeping her audience in mind, build them into a statement that leaves no question unanswered. In revising, the writer found it necessary to add a few new facts—that she was busy studying for exams, that she took the pills for two weeks. In striving for clarity she realized that her audience would need to know them.

We achieve coherence in our writing when our paragraphs answer the questions that they raise in the reader's mind. If we merely write,

> I was terrified of doctors. I went to the health clinic.

the reader is going to ask, "If you're so afraid of doctors, what compelled you to go?" If we don't answer the invisible question, the paragraph will lack coherence, and the reader will be frustrated or confused.

Similarly, when we make a general assertion, we create the expectation that we will defend it. The reader expects us to justify or explain a statement like "The public was responsible for the war's continuation" or "Statistics show us that the VHS tapes will eventually drive out Betas." The reader does not, presumably, know as much as we know about our chosen subject; we must give the detail, background, statistics, reasons, or explanations that our audience requires and expects of us. We write exposition to deliver information or ideas to other people.

We establish another type of expectation when we use an extended metaphor to enliven and organize a paragraph. Here is a passage from a student paper.

> The beast of civil war lay outside the sheepfold, and its roaring could be heard within the gates. At first its voice, as it had begun to slink out of the foothills, had been low and faint. Then, as it drew nearer to the town, the explosions of large artillery shells had been its approaching steps, and the different pitches of the voice—the snarling of machine guns, the howls of mortar shells—had grown distinct. Now the beast clawed at the walls and breathed heavily on the gates with its mouth aflame. The sheep within huddled together, knowing their throats would soon feel the enemy's teeth, knowing the shepherd had fallen asleep.

The extended—perhaps *too* extended—metaphor compares the enemy to a predatory beast, the city to a sheepfold, and its citizens to helpless sheep. The parts of the metaphor make a coherent sequence, which we would violate if we shifted to another comparison in the middle of the paragraph.

> . . . At first its voice, as it had begun to slink out of the foothills, had been low and faint. Then, as it drew nearer, the infernal machine could be heard stomping out death on the plain with the press of bombs, and the different sounds—the grinding of machine gun fire, the chunking of mortars—had grown distinct. Now the beast clawed. . . .

Coherence and Consistency

We should know a few more mechanical ways to maintain coherence in the paragraph. Just as we need agreement within a sentence, we need agreement within a paragraph. We should avoid changes in verb tense. It is easy, if we let our minds wander, to begin writing a passage or paragraph in one tense and then switch to another. The shift can work, if done consciously and for the right reasons. We may begin in the present tense to be dramatic and then slip into the past tense because the events described actually occurred in the past.

> He sits on the dock, his feet bare on the warm wood, his eyes half-closed in the hot sun, daydreaming about women in black silk

dresses. Suddenly he felt a violent tugging on the pole, and a long shape thrashed in the water ten feet away.

Or we may begin in the past tense and abruptly shift to the present tense, without realizing it, because we want greater immediacy.

> He sat on the dock, his feet bare on the warm wood, his eyes half-closed in the hot sun, and daydreamed about women in black silk dresses. Suddenly he feels a violent tugging on the pole, and sees a long shape thrash in the water only ten feet away.

But usually such shifts are careless mistakes that proofreading should correct.

Another common violation of coherence is to shift pronouns within a paragraph. If we start with *we,* we should not switch to *you.* We must be careful, if we have chosen to use the formal *one,* that we do not fall back into *I* or *you.*

> But if *one* has experienced the mystical conversion described by adepts in almost every culture in the world, *one* may still fall back into the old dualities and pettinesses. But once *we* have felt that stronger intensity of being, *you* can never again remain satisfied with less. The ghost of that experience haunts *us* like a dead loved one.

Coherence and consistency of paragraphs are goals essential to the final shape and value of the essay. We may not achieve these goals until we have written several drafts. After we have sketched our rough ideas, after we have begun to find phrases and sentences to express the ideas, we must edit and revise, refine and shape, to make a point and to reach an audience by means of coherence and consistency.

Coherence and the Paragraph: Transitions

Transitions in our writing are devices for moving from one place to another. They range from single words like *but* to phrases like *on the other hand,* and to subtler devices like repetition or parallelism. Transitions are essential to the coherence of paragraph and paper. You might expect to find this topic with the last chapter, on sentences, or further on, in connection with whole essays, but we put it here because transitions happen *within* the paragraph as a way to move from one sentence to another or *between* paragraphs as a way of moving from topic to topic while keeping the essay whole. *Transitions are thus essential to coherence in paragraph and paper.* A prose insufficient in transitions is like a road map with certain key routes erased. It leaps from subject to subject—place to place—without stated or implied connection. The connection remains in the writer's mind. The reader, like the traveler, gets hopelessly lost.

Overt Transitions. Often a transition needs to be obvious to carry the reader along our passage of thought, to make sure we don't lose him. Perhaps we are making an overt contrast. To draw attention to the contrast, we say, "on the one hand . . . on the other"—which is trite but hard to avoid. Or we use the context of our discussion: "Although most transitions are best left implicit, some are properly overt."

Often we need overt transitions when ideas or actions conflict, when the essay's meaning depends upon keeping the terms of opposition clear. Or if we are piling detail upon detail, we might want to use a transition that calls attention to our multiplicity: "not only . . . but also." Prose that explains, reasons, or argues frequently uses overt transitions.

> Viewed from a suitable height, the aggregating clusters of medical scientists in the bright sunlight of the boardwalk at Atlantic City, swarmed there from everywhere for the annual meetings, have the look of assemblages of social insects. There is the same vibrating, ionic movement, interrupted by the darting back and forth of jerky individuals to touch antennae and exchange small bits of information; periodically, the mass casts out, like a trout-line, a long single file unerringly toward Childs's. If the boards were not fastened down, it would not be a surprise to see them put together a nest of sorts.
>
> It is permissible to say this sort of thing about humans. . . .
> Lewis Thomas, "On Societies as Organisms"

Here Lewis Thomas uses "this sort of thing," at the beginning of a new paragraph, as an overt transitional phrase referring to the comparison made in the preceding paragraph.

Repeated Words or Phrases. One way to achieve continuity within a paragraph (or between paragraphs), to make transitions between sentences and between statements, is to repeat words or phrases. One of the simplest of these devices, so simple that we might not think of it as one, is repeating pronouns. We use it for both economy and continuity.

> Not too long ago *a male friend of mine* appeared on the scene fresh from a recent divorce. *He* had one child, who is, of course, with *his* ex-wife. *He* is looking for another wife. As I thought about *him* while I was ironing one evening, it suddenly occurred to me that I, too, would like to have a wife. Why do I want a wife? (Italics added)
> Judy Syfers, "I Want a Wife"

But you should be careful when using a repeated pronoun, because if it is repeated too often, the prose can become monotonous and confusing.

You can get variety and clarity by occasionally using the name the pronoun refers to. A writer also has to make sure that the reader knows what each pronoun refers to. If we say, "Mr. Cortazar saw that the man was following him closely; he stared at him," it is not clear who is doing the staring. Here we may need to be more explicit: "Mr. Cortazar saw that the man was following him closely; Mr. Cortazar stared at him."

If we want to avoid monotonous repetition, we can use variations (near-synonyms) for the key words in some places.

> His *sculptures* seem like men and women stripped naked. They are *works of art* that seem to lack all artifice, *plastic creations* which, in their emotional if not in their physical presence, have the feeling of natural, organic creations.

These methods are commonly used for transition *between* paragraphs as well.

> . . . and the importance of spatial form in *modern* literature.
> *Modern* thought, as well, has used the metaphor of dimensionality. . . .

Parallel Constructions. We can repeat structures as well as words. Parallel constructions (see Parallelism, pages 177–178) can fulfill a need for transition that is not only structural and logical, but emotional; passages with parallel sentences can work like sentences with parallel phrases, to produce a dramatic effect or to maintain emotional tension.

> Today, now that he is no longer among us, *who can replace* my old friend at the gates of this kingdom? *Who will look after* the garden until we can get back to it? . . . (Italics added)
> Albert Camus, "Encounters with André Gide"

> *We describe* how the poor are plundered *by the rich. We live among the rich. Live on the plunder and pander ideas to the rich. We have described* the *torture* and we have put our names under appeals against *torture,* but we did not stop it. (And we ourselves became *torturers* when the higher interests demanded *torture* and we became the ideologists of *torture.*) Now *we once more can analyze* the world situation and *describe* the wars and explain why the many are poor and hungry. But we do no more.
> *We are not the bearers of consciousness. We are the whores of reason.* (Italics added)
> Jan Myrdal, *Confessions of a Disloyal European*

Parallel constructions that repeat part of a phrase are common and useful transitions, especially in exposition and in argument.

> . . . and they never decided whether they were *Bulgarians or Americans, rich or poor, artists or dilettantes.*

> And we, on our part, could not decide whether they were *heroes*
> *or frauds.* . . .

On our part, in the last sentence, is an overt transition, referring us to
the *they* of the previous sentence.

Transitional Words and Phrases. We use many transitional
phrases to establish the relationship between sentences and between
paragraphs and to prepare the reader for shifts in subject or meaning.
The most common are words like *and, but, or* and *for.* Some are words
of sequence and time—*meanwhile, afterward, before;* of qualification—*again, also, nonetheless;* and of reasoning—*for example, because, therefore.* Although we often try to avoid phrases like these in
fiction or narrative, they are often essential to clarify a sequence of
thought in exposition or argument. These paragraph openings use common phrases to accomplish transitions; they are taken from *The Naked
Ape* by Desmond Morris:

> *Up to this point* I have been concentrating on the social aspects of
> comfort behaviour in our species. . . .

> *In addition* to problems of keeping clean, the general category of
> comfort behaviour also includes . . .

> *Because* of his exploratory and opportunist nature, the naked
> ape's list of prey species is immense. . . .

> *For the next major category*, that of parasites . . .

> *In order* to find the answer to this question we must first assem-
> ble some facts. . . .

We commonly use comparison and contrast for transitions, especially in criticism and analysis. The means of transition are relatively
simple. We describe one of the objects for examination in one paragraph
and then, in a following paragraph, compare and contrast traits of the
other. When we turn to the second object, we often begin with one of
the transitional phrases that make for comparison or contrast, like
similarly, in the same vein, or *however, on the other hand, in contrast,*
or *contrary to.*

> Freud gave a picture of the unconscious mind as containing pri-
> marily memories and the remnants of suppressed desires. He saw
> the sexual drives as being the foundation of the unconscious.
> Jung, *on the other hand*, claimed that Freud's depth psychology
> wasn't deep enough, that there was another aspect of the uncon-
> scious which contained spiritual drives as important as the sexual
> drives. . . .

Remember that even in expository prose it is better to leave out well-
worn phrases *if the sense is just as clear without them.* Many times, we

can cut out the obvious direction signals and rely on implicit transition. Such cutting is often the work of later drafts.

Some of the most obvious clues to transition—within the paragraph or between paragraphs—are words of sequence, like *therefore, later, so, then,* and *next.* They are so obvious that it is pleasant to do without them, if we can.

Implicit Transitions. The order within the paragraph can itself be a means of transition. It gives the paragraph motion; it gives a reason for one sentence following another: left to right, down to up, smaller to larger; or other sorts of order: color to shape, spring to summer to fall to winter; or orders of ideas: from more obvious to less obvious, from less complex to more complex. These motions are clear enough in themselves to allow the movement from subject to subject without explicit directions. We need not say, "after spring came summer," within a paragraph; we can presume that people are aware of the order the seasons follow. We would be more likely to move from rain and early flowers to the longest day of the year, to hot sun and to swimming and to no school.

Sometimes the rest between paragraphs acts as transition. We take a breath, and we pivot on the pause. It shows that we are moving from one grouping to another. We don't always have to be reminded that we are moving. Sometimes we do, and sometimes we do not. Develop *tact* for transitions. Develop a sense also for the multiple means of transition. A good writer uses implicit, overt, parallel, repetitive, and many other forms of transition, and uses them in rapid sequence as he moves through his paragraphs and from paragraph to paragraph. Transitions in complex expository writing are constant and multiple, overt and implicit. Much that is implied depends on orderly thinking and a clear sense of what the reader needs to know.

Suppose we catalogue everything in a boy's pockets. The next paragraph could begin: "Therefore, his pockets bulged as he walked, and he bumped into tables when he passed them. In fact, he bumped into almost everything. . . . " The paragraph could go on about his *clumsiness.* But the *therefore* at the beginning is unnecessary. It is obvious, if we have catalogued twenty items, that these items bulge out his pockets. Transition can be found in image. No reader need be led by the hand so carefully. The paragraph break could read like this:

> . . . He had on his person two rubber bands, a golf tee, two notes from a teacher, a bottle cap, and a gray-brown handkerchief.
>
> His pockets bulged as he walked, he bumped into tables when he passed them. In fact, he bumped into almost everything. . . .

The word *his,* referring to an antecedent in the previous paragraph, holds the two paragraphs together.

Transitions are a glue that holds parts together. You need enough, or the parts will fall apart. But if you have too much, you will see the glue instead of the parts. The space between the catalogue and the bulging pockets is a sort of invisible glue—but it holds because we have sense enough to know that the objects listed cause the bulging. The next transition, from pockets to clumsiness, is less obvious and more necessary. It takes more doing. The only thing that bulging pockets share with clumsiness is that the little boy possesses both of them. Of course we could use a generality for a transition.

> . . . a bottle cap, and a gray-brown handkerchief.
> In fact, he was generally rather gross and clumsy. He bumped into everything. . . .

This transition would work, but it is not elegant. It is obvious and general. Suppose in the next paragraph we want to talk about his table manners, do we say again that he was "gross and clumsy"? No, we have used these words up. The stylish transition happens without drawing attention to itself. We move from pockets to bumping into things by picturing the boy bumping into tables with his fat pockets, and then we do a turn on the word *bumping* and we are off into a new subject before the reader knows it. We want to move the reader from one subject to another gently, by the elbow, and if we have done the job well, the reader does not feel the guiding fingers touch his arm.

———— EXERCISES ————————————————————————————

1. These sentences have been extracted from an orderly paragraph and rearranged. Restore them to a sequence that makes sense. You are the reader, making the writer's text over for yourself.

> a. But within the economics of energy and nature, it is a catastrophe.
>
> b. It is the mainstay of the economy of money.
>
> c. With its array of gadgets and machines, all powered by energies that are destructive of land or air or water, and connected to work, market, school, recreation, etc., by gasoline engines, the modern home is a veritable factory of waste and destruction.
>
> d. It takes in the world's goods and converts them into garbage, sewage, and noxious fumes—for none of which we have found a use.
>
> *Wendell Berry, The Unsettling of America*

2. Decide which sentence functions as a topic sentence in each paragraph. Could it be moved to another place in the paragraph? What would be the effect?

a. Skill is the connection between life and tools, or life and machines. Once, skill was defined ultimately in qualitative terms: How *well* did a person work; how good, durable, and pleasing were his products? But as machines have grown larger and more complex, and as our awe of them and our desire for labor-saving have grown, we have tended more and more to define skill quantitatively: How speedily and cheaply can a person work? We have increasingly wanted a measurable skill. And the more quantifiable skills became, the easier they were to replace with machines. As machines replace skill, they disconnect themselves from life; they come between us and life. They begin to enact our ignorance of value—of essential sources, dependences, and relationships.

Wendell Berry, The Unsettling of America

b. Writing has always been a means of expression for me and for other black Americans who are just like me, who feel, too, the need for freedom in this "home of the brave, and land of the free." From the first, writing meant learning the craft and developing the art. Going to school had one major goal, to learn to be a writer. As early as my eighth year I had the desire, at ten I was trying, at eleven and twelve I was learning, and at fourteen and fifteen I was seeing my first things printed in local school and community papers. I have a copy of a poem published in 1930 and an article with the caption, "What Is to Become of Us?" which appeared in 1931 or 1932. All of this happened before I went to Northwestern.

Margaret Walker, "On Being Female, Black, and Free"

3. Analyze these paragraphs for their unity. (a) Do any of these paragraphs have extraneous material? (b) Does each paragraph contain a topic sentence? Underline topic sentences, and discuss in class. (c) What does the position of each topic sentence accomplish, if anything?

a. The sea, autumn mildness, islands bathed in light, fine rain spreading a diaphanous veil over the immortal nakedness of Greece. Happy is the man, I thought, who, before dying, has the good fortune to sail the Aegean Sea.

Many are the joys of this world—women, fruit, ideas. But to cleave that sea in the gentle, autumnal season, murmuring the name of each islet, is to my mind the joy most apt to transport the heart of man into paradise. Nowhere else can one pass so easily and serenely from reality to dream. The frontiers dwindle, and from the masts of the most ancient ships spring branches and fruits. It is as if here in Greece necessity is the mother of miracles.

Towards noon the rain stopped. The sun parted the clouds and appeared gentle, tender, washed and fresh, and it caressed with its rays the beloved waters and lands. I stood at the prow and let myself be intoxicated with the miracle which was revealed as far as the eye could see.

Nikos Kazantzakis, Zorba the Greek

b. A philosopher—is a human being who constantly experiences, sees, hears, suspects, hopes, and dreams extraordinary things; who is struck by his own thoughts as from outside, as from above and below, and by *his* type of experiences and lightning bolts; who is perhaps himself a storm pregnant with new lightnings; a fatal human being around whom there are constant rumblings and growlings, crevices, and uncanny doings. A philosopher—alas, a being that often runs away from itself, often is afraid of itself—but too inquisitive not to "come to" again—always back to himself.

Friedrich Nietzsche, Beyond Good and Evil

4. Here are some incoherent paragraphs. (a) Consider the different sorts of incoherence in each paragraph. Which paragraphs can profit by reorganization? In class, reorganize them. (b) Which paragraphs need further development in order to achieve coherence? In class, speculate on the directions development might take. (c) What reasonable readers' expectations do these paragraphs violate?

a. The heavy wooden door was painted red, but the wood showed through in many places where the paint was flaking off. Dandelions covered the lawn, but there were few weeds in the dark grass. A white and black cat lay curled by the door. Three huge oaks threw their shadows across the wide lawn. Far off, a deer was watching from the edge of the woods. There was no knob on the door.

b. The days were unusually hot and humid, even for that part of the state. Joe didn't want to go to the beach. His girlfriend, Linda, did. She wasn't a good swimmer. She loved to swim. Joe was working on his car. He was a fanatical sports enthusiast.

c. He had found that the wolves subsisted mainly on a diet of mice. Farley had been dropped in the middle of the Canadian tundra. He discovered that the hunters were lying, and that they themselves were the insane murderers. Hunters had been complaining that the wolves were slaughtering thousands of caribou for the sheer pleasure of killing. He had made an astonishing discovery. He had been assigned to investigate the killing of caribou by timber wolves.

d. Robert and Daniel crouched in the cave, listening for the sound of approaching footsteps. He thought the troops must have left the area by now. For the moment he was reassured by the silence, but he worried about the sharp pain in his knee, and he wondered if he would be able to walk on it if he had to. He was glad to have his old friend with him. He looked at him. Their gazes meeting, he felt tears come to his eyes from straining to see in the half-darkness, and from thinking where he and his friend had been just yesterday.

e. When the gate opens at last, four thousand music lovers push, crush, and shove each other forward in an immense mass. The sun glares down, the musicians struggle to tune their sweaty instruments, and the ice cream salesman exhausts his stores in twenty minutes. Finally the music started at 1:30.

5. Here are two coherent paragraphs, from the essay in which E. B. White speaks of Simonizing his grandmother. Look at these para-

graphs for their unity and their coherence. (a) How does White achieve consistency within these paragraphs? (b) How does he accomplish transitions?

> Communication by the written word is a subtler (and more beautiful) thing than Dr. Flesch and General Motors imagine. They contend that the "average reader" is capable of reading only what tests Easy, and that the writer should write at or below this level. This is a presumptuous and degrading idea. There is no average reader, and to reach down toward this mythical character is to deny that each of us is on the way up, is ascending. ("Ascending," by the way, is a word Dr. Flesch advises writers to stay away from. Too unusual.)
>
> It is my belief that no writer can improve his work until he discards the dulcet notion that the reader is feebleminded, for writing is an act of faith, not a trick of grammar. Ascent is at the heart of the matter. A country whose writers are following a calculating machine downstairs is not ascending—if you will pardon the expression—and a writer who questions the capacity of the person at the other end of the line is not a writer at all, merely a schemer. The movies long ago decided that a wider communication could be achieved by a deliberate descent to a lower level, and they walked proudly down until they reached the cellar. Now they are groping for the light switch, hoping to find the way out.
>
> *E. B. White,* "Calculating Machine"

6. A student writing an essay about a teacher's strike wanted to make these points in one paragraph:

1. Teachers have no legal right to strike.
2. The teachers' union claims the strike is their constitutional right.
3. Some school boards try to fire striking teachers and hire new ones.
4. Striking teachers sometimes find judges who will issue injunctions against this firing and hiring.
5. Picketing disrupts the classes with new teachers.

Here is a first draft of the paragraph.

> Of course it's against the law for teachers to strike anyway. Some teachers say that the law against striking is unconstitutional. So the school board fires the teachers who are striking and hires new teachers who are looking for work. The striking teachers get a judge to make an injunction against the school board. The picketing disrupts classes with the new teachers.

This first attempt was incoherent. Does the paragraph have a topic sentence? Does it have *a topic?* Does one sentence follow from another? Does the last sentence appear to belong in the paragraph? Rewrite this paragraph, paying special attention to coherence. Or write a paragraph of your own using the student's five points as rough notes.

7. Analyze these paragraphs for their transitions, both within paragraphs and between them.

When Saint-Exupéry begins his second paragraph, which word especially links it to the end of the first paragraph? What binds the third paragraph to the second? When the fourth paragraph follows the third, an idea rather than a word makes the transition; underline the words that are intellectually related to each other.

Once again I had found myself in the presence of a truth and had failed to recognize it. Consider what had happened to me: I had thought myself lost, had touched the very bottom of despair; and then, when the spirit of renunciation had filled me, I had known peace. I know now what I was not conscious of at the time—that in such an hour a man feels that he has finally found himself and has become his own friend. An essential inner need has been satisfied, and against that satisfaction, that self-fulfillment, no external power can prevail. Bonnafous, I imagine, he who spent his life racing before the wind, was acquainted with this serenity of spirit. Guillaumet, too, in his snows. Never shall I forget that, lying buried to the chin in sand, strangled slowly to death by thirst, my heart was infinitely warm beneath the desert stars.

What can men do to make known to themselves this sense of deliverance? Everything about mankind is paradox. He who strives and conquers grows soft. The magnanimous man grown rich becomes mean. The creative artist for whom everything is made easy nods. Every doctrine swears that it can breed men, but none can tell us in advance what sort of men it will breed. Men are not cattle to be fattened for market. On the scales of life an indigent Newton weighs more than a parcel of prosperous nonentities. All of us have had the experience of a sudden joy that came when nothing in the world had forewarned us of its coming—a joy so thrilling that if it was born of misery we remembered even the misery with tenderness. All of us, on seeing old friends again, have remembered with happiness the trials we lived through with those friends. Of what can we be certain except this—that we are fertilized by mysterious circumstances? Where is man's truth to be found?

Truth is not that which can be demonstrated by the aid of logic. If orange-trees are hardy and rich in fruit in this bit of soil and not that, then this bit of soil is what is truth for orange-trees. If a particular religion, or culture, or scale of values, if one form of activity rather than another, brings self-fulfillment to a man, releases the prince asleep within him unknown to himself, then that scale of values, that culture, that form of activity, constitute his truth. Logic, you say? Let logic wangle its own explanation of life.

Because it is man and not flying that concerns me most, I shall close this book with the story of a man's gropings towards self-fulfillment as I witnessed them in the early months of the civil war in Spain. One year after crashing in the desert I made a tour of the Catalan front in order to learn what happens to man when the scaffolding of his traditions suddenly collapses. To Madrid I went for an answer to another question: How does it happen that men are sometimes willing to die?

Antoine de Saint-Exupéry, Wind, Sand and Stars

8. In this passage by Mark Crispin Miller, underline the topic sentence of the first paragraph. (a) How does the paragraph grow from this sentence? (b) Is every other sentence in this paragraph related to the topic sentence? (c) How do the sentences proceed? Underline transitions. (d) Do you find implicit transitions in this paragraph, and later between paragraphs? Find the basis for each implicit transition.

We may have a lot to learn from watching movies, but we're very good at seeing through them. People know how to jeer at the old-fashioned propaganda turned out by Hollywood for nearly half a century, from D. W. Griffith's (racist) *Birth of a Nation* in 1915 to Doris Day's (sexist) comedies of the early 1960s. "It is, generally, a bad time for illusions," writes Mickey Rooney, brooding over the disappearance of "nice clean movies" and "the illusion of the great star." Most would agree, but not mournfully. Having had our consciousness raised over the past fifteen years, we are proud enough of our awakening to shrug off all our naive dreams.

For example, it is now doubted that a lot of wishing and a little struggling invariably pay off. (The success of *Rocky* is only a fluke.) According to the old movies, success always comes to the peppy and the resolute. Those kids in the chorus get that bilious entrepreneur to lighten up and tap his feet, and so it's on to Broadway! That earnest lawyer-fella touches the hearts of decent folks all over, and so it's on to the White House! While artists usually succumb to the agonies of Genius, inventors, athletes, scientists, and businessmen, people with a Great Gift or a Great Idea, end up quickly vindicated and beloved, looking benevolent in powdered hair.

At the same time, many movies dramatized the sorrows of the wealthy, as if to assure us that we were better off as we were—with the sun in the morning and the moon at night and a diet of Spam. Throughout the Depression, the movies implied that money was poison, that only regular folks knew how to have fun, that the rich and their lackeys seemed faintly European, or worse. And in later films like *Caught, Humoresque, Young Man with a Horn*, and *A Place in the Sun*, among others, a humble person's romance with someone wealthier leads straight to disaster. Although the travails of the rich continue to provide Americans with a vindictive thrill, class conflict is no longer part of the story. When we see a bunch of stuffed shirts vexed by some happy-go-lucky man of the people, we sense that the moment is old-fashioned, as in *Heaven Can Wait* (based on *Here Comes Mr. Jordan*, 1941) or *Hair* (which alludes heavily to *Hallelujah I'm a Bum*, 1933). (The success of these recent films is probably a fluke.)

From the 1940s through the early 1960s, the movies taught that women who worked in office buildings were always sad. Whether boss or secretary, the working woman continually fought the melancholy of life without a man. The secretary was a little better off, since she at least could serve the guy of her dreams, concealing her adoration under brisk efficiency. The female executive was far more wretched. She had to strain to seem commanding, like an adolescent knowing that his voice might crack at any moment. Her employees were always handsome men, strolling into her office, leaning on her desk, every suave phrase really meaning: "How about it?" After fighting these assaults for a while with clipped retorts and starchy looks, she would finally give in, loosen her collar, let down her hair, and murmur "Darling!" in the arms of her rightful master.

Mark Crispin Miller, Boxed In: The Culture of TV

DEVELOPMENT IN THE PARAGRAPH

Once we pass beyond the single sentence, we become involved in development and its problems. As we must develop paragraphs to substantiate generalizations, so too we must develop paragraphs to make our associations clear to the reader. Frequently, we lack fullness of development because we do not take the reader into account. We put forward a generalization, perhaps, and a conclusion that we have arrived at, but we do not lead the reader through the thinking that proceeds from introduction to conclusion. Perhaps in our own thinking we have leapt from generalization to conclusion by intuition—but the reader will not necessarily leap along with us.

Eventually, as we go over development, we will need to investigate length and order. But first, we must look at methods for developing paragraphs.

Some Ways of Developing Paragraphs

We can develop a paragraph in countless ways. No list can be comprehensive. But looking at some methods of paragraph development can help us to see the range of possibilities. The type of development we choose—the *how* in the paragraph—depends on the material we are using—the *what* in the paragraph—and the purpose we have in mind—the *why* of the paragraph. If we are listing Paraguay's annual imports, we develop by listing, and not by comparison and contrast. *The container takes its shape from what it contains.* One of our tasks in organizing a paper is to find the means of development that is *most appropriate to our material.*

Earlier we spoke of improvised shape, like generalization followed by qualification followed by example, or question and answer (objection and rebuttal). We have also mentioned chronology and spatial sequence as useful ways of organizing paragraphs (see also pages 243–246). We need to consider a few more. On occasion the reader must learn *what* something is; the writer must develop a paragraph by means of *definition.* Sometimes a reader needs to know what something is *like* or *not like;* the writer must develop a paragraph of *comparison* or *comparison and contrast.* Sometimes the reader needs to know the *parts* of a thing, what makes it up; the writer must supply *analysis.* Or the writer must use *classification,* he must tell us the species of something, perhaps; is it animal or vegetable? Sometimes we must develop our notion of a thing by discussing its *cause* and its *effect.*

These different ways of approaching and organizing a subject are called rhetorical patterns (we will discuss the varieties more fully in Chapter 7). They can serve as models for whole essays, but more commonly they provide us with shapes for whole paragraphs; they are like blueprints for the basic ways in which thought moves. They suggest various means of development. When we find an unsupported generalization, we discover an opportunity for development, making use of the rhetorical pattern of example. But all processes of writing can help paragraph development. When we revise we should be alert for the journalist's six questions (see page 59), and for opportunities to reach our audience by explaining—which is after all the function of exposition.

We may organize a paragraph to *define* or *elucidate:*

> An addict does not merely pursue a pleasurable experience and need to experience it in order to function normally. He needs to *repeat* it again and again. Something about that particular experience makes life without it less than complete. Other potentially pleasurable experiences are no longer possible, for under the spell of the addictive experience, his life is peculiarly distorted. The addict craves an experience and yet he is never really satisfied. The organism may be temporarily sated, but soon it begins to crave again.
>
> Marie Winn, "Television Addiction"

The paragraph begins in the negative, dispelling a common assumption, and defines by isolating distinctive features.

Or we can develop paragraphs to *compare* and *contrast:*

> In other respects, the film follows Hearst's career with mixed fidelity. The plot adjustments are significant. Both Hearst and Kane were only children, born in 1863, and both were expelled from Harvard. Hearst's father and mother were not, like Kane's, poverty-stricken boardinghouse keepers. George Hearst was a well-to-do farmer's son, whose silver strike at the Comstock lode made him a millionaire, and whose later interest in the Homestake Mine still further increased his massive fortune; he became a senator and earned a respected place in the *American Dictionary of Biography.* In the film these parents are left a deed to the Colorado Lode by a defaulting boarder, Fred Grange, and the Kane fortune is thus founded not by the acumen and push of a paternal figure but by blind chance.
>
> Charles Higham, *The Films of Orson Welles*

Comparison and contrast works when we talk about a relationship or conflict, and are not merely separating facts about two or more subjects. Here, the first sentence states the mixture that is the paragraph's topic, and the rest of the paragraph gives examples of each ingredient in the mixture. Notice that the paragraph, when it compares and contrasts Hearst's life with Kane's, carefully maintains the order in which it first mentions them: Hearst-Kane. This order helps to avoid confusion, and makes for coherence.

Or, to *analyze:*

> The "me decade" did not result from a sudden effusion of selfishness or decadence; it is the logical consequence of a public surface tolerance combined with a loss of individual historical depth. In a sense, people become more like one another (wear the same clothes, go to the same schools, read the same books, are informed by the same media, go to the same parties, are "liberated" into the same mores). In another sense, they lose the social inheritances that, while differentiating them from one another, also instilled in them profound common values. Inwardly, each is animated by nothing more profound than personal preference and idiosyncrasy. Homogenized yet fragmented, the society of the supreme "me" (find yourself, be true to yourself) is the logical expression of a materialistic humanism.
>
> Michael Novak, "On God and Man"

We analyze when we need to explain or to demonstrate the mechanism of a process or an act. We tell how it works rather than what it is. Novak points out possible reasons for the modern cult of the self, and then argues step by step to show the larger causes that underlie the reasons.

We can also develop paragraphs to *classify:*

> We can thus say that while the average human being is a mixture, some people are mainly "digestion-minded," some "muscle-minded," and some "brain-minded," and correspondingly digestion-bodied, muscle-bodied, or brain-bodied. The digestion-bodied people look thick; the muscle-bodied people look wide; and the brain-bodied people look long. This does not mean the taller a man is the brainier he will be. It means that if a man, even a short man, looks long rather than wide or thick, he will often be more concerned about what goes on in his mind than about what he does or what he eats; but the key factor is slenderness and not height. On the other hand, a man who gives the impression of being thick rather than long or wide will usually be more interested in a good steak than in a good idea or a good long walk.
>
> Eric Berne, "Can People Be Judged by Their Appearance?" in *A Layman's Guide to Psychiatry and Psychoanalysis*

Berne separates people into groups according to their bodily appearance, relating psychological classifications to physical ones.

This paragraph, from an essay about television advertising, is developed to show *cause and effect:*

There is good reason to suspect that this manic obsession with cleanliness, fostered, quite naturally, by the giant soap and detergent interests, may bear some responsibility for the cultivated sloppiness of so many of the young in their clothing as well as in their chosen hideouts. The compulsive housewife who spends more time washing and vacuuming and polishing her possessions than communicating to, or stimulating her children creates a kind of sterility that the young would instinctively reject. The impeccably tidy home, the impeccably tidy lawn are—in a very real sense— unnatural and confining. Yet the commercials confront us with broods of happy children, some of whom—believe it or not—notice the new fresh smell their clean, white sweatshirts exhale thanks to Mom's new "softener."

Marya Mannes, "Television Advertising: The Splitting Image"

In her argument, the writer observes negative results of advertising, where an image of cleanliness leads to a slovenly reality. The process resembles that of *analysis,* which also seeks after causes.

We may organize a paragraph to *make an assertion and give reasons:*

The country is vastly indebted to him (Louis Brandeis) for his creative work in the field of labor relations, in dispelling misunderstanding between management and labor, and in making collective bargaining an effective instrument for industrial peace. He successfully arbitrated or conciliated many labor disputes. In 1910 he was arbiter of a serious strike in the New York City garment trade. Not content with settling the immediate dispute, he devised the famous "protocol" for the permanent government of labor relations in the industry, with provision for the preferential union shop, for a Joint Board of Sanitary Control, and for a continuing Board of Arbitration composed of representatives of the public as well as of the employers and the union. The procedures thus developed and successfully tested served as a model in other industries. For several years he served as impartial chairman of this board of arbitration.

Irwin H. Pollock, *The Brandeis Reader*

The writer begins with a contention and then substantiates it by reciting information upon which he bases it.

Or to *make a statement and then give relevant facts:*

Gandhi recognized that the whites in South Africa thought they needed protection against a majority consisting of Negroes and Indians. The province of Natal, in 1896, had 400,000 Negro inhabitants, 51,000 Indians, and 50,000 whites. The Cape of Good Hope Colony had 900,000 Negroes, 10,000 Indians, and 400,000 Europeans; the Transvaal Republic 650,000 Negroes, 5,000 Indians, and 120,000 whites. In 1944, the five million Negroes hopelessly outnumbered the million and a quarter whites.

Louis Fischer, *Gandhi: His Life and Message for the World*

This last category resembles the one before it, except that *facts* (or statistics) take the place of *reasons*, which are arguments based on a value put on events.

Or to *list:*

> Now the leadership elements of the Democratic Party began to filter through the suite of the nominee in a parade that was to last the rest of the day, to assist him in making up their mind. First of the big-city leaders to arrive was David Lawrence of Pennsylvania. Following him came the New York crowd—Wagner, Harriman, DeSapio and Prendergast; then William Green of Philadelphia; then DiSalle of Ohio; then Bailey and Ribicoff of Connecticut; then all the others.
>
> Theodore H. White, *The Making of the President 1960*

First, White tells us what sort of men they are whose names will follow, and then the occasion that brought the men together, and then the names.

Even in the examples chosen, these methods are not exclusive. One paragraph may use more than one method, or one method may involve another. "Relevant facts" usually come in "lists." In the next paragraph, the author develops the idea primarily by an assertion followed by reasons, and his final sentence is a list.

> If conventions epitomize the mythology and legendry of American national politics, then Chicago epitomizes the convention city. For one hundred years, ever since the nomination of Abraham Lincoln at the Wigwam, it has been the favorite city of political convention-goers. Counting notches for fourteen Republican and nine Democratic national conventions in the last twenty-five quadrennials, Chicago can boast that here were first named all the following Presidents of the United States: Lincoln, Grant, Garfield, Cleveland, Harrison, Theodore Roosevelt, Harding, Coolidge, Franklin D. Roosevelt, Truman and Eisenhower.
>
> Theodore H. White, *The Making of the President 1960*

Or to make clear by *elaboration or rephrasing:*

> The "duende," then, is a power and not a construct, is a struggle and not a concept. I have heard an old guitarist, a true virtuoso, remark, "The 'duende' is not in the throat, the 'duende' comes from inside up, up from the very soles of the feet." That is to say, it is not a question of aptitude, but of a true and viable style—of blood, in other words; of what is oldest in culture; of creation made act.
>
> Federico García Lorca,
> "The Duende: Theory and Divertissement"

Here, because the word names something more spiritual than intellectual—something harder to define than a concept—the author does not try so much to define and to elucidate as to name and rename, to offer description and metaphor, until we begin to comprehend the intangible.

Notice that the progress within these quoted paragraphs is the motion of thought. The exact detail, the example that locates the general in the particular, the comparison, the logical steps—these motions develop the thought and unify the paragraph at the same time. Paragraph development makes coherence.

Development: Length and Completeness

Our paragraphs will vary in length, following no set rule. The length must be *adequate;* we must take the time and space to flesh out our arguments, to justify our contentions, to explain our theories, or to describe our characters. We discussed this need for completeness in Coherence in the Paragraph, but we must repeat it here. We must never forget that the reader is another person, who must be given reasons if he is to be persuaded of our opinions and must be given details if he is going to see what we see. We must not simply assert, "President Smith is the worst, most dishonest president we've had," and then propose to limit his power. We must tell *why* he is so bad. We must supply reasons, facts, arguments, details *adequate* to the assertion. We must develop the paragraph to make our assertion coherent.

Undeveloped paragraphs bedevil beginning writers. Many times paragraphs remain undeveloped because the writer does not adequately imagine the reader. Here is a paragraph from a student paper.

> When you study dance, you learn either modern or classical ballet. Some people prefer one kind of dance and some another. I learned modern dance and I prefer it.

The writer continued the paper by describing the pleasures of modern dance. But her opening paragraph is undeveloped and lacks a sense of audience, because it begs either for definition or for comparison and contrast. One or two sentences of development, giving the reader an insight into the difference between forms of dance, would establish the necessary background for the discussion of modern dance.

Less frequently, writers are afflicted with too much disorganized detail, so that the writing loses force. As another student wrote in a paper:

> I bought my first car with money I earned working for a summer in a tuna canning factory. I was anxious to keep it running in top condition. It was a 1973 VW bug, with a good engine (from a 1975

VW van) and a pretty good body, with just a little rust below the doors. My friend repainted it for me, bright red, and we rebuilt the engine and almost set the garage on fire. The upholstery is in terrible shape. I change the oil and the oil filter every 1500 miles and the car gets about 25 miles per gallon, but the windshield wipers don't always work, and the insurance costs a lot.

We must keep in mind what is important and what is not. We must give reasons, but only so many as we need to make our point. With too many reasons the reader will be confused, bored, or feel bullied.

To decide whether our detail is adequate—neither too little nor too much—we must develop judgment and tact; we must look at what we've written not only as a writer, but from the point of view of a reader.

Because adequacy always depends on context, it's useless to lay down rules for paragraph length. Different kinds of writing, however, usually need paragraphs of different lengths. Generally the more formal the writing, the more lengthy the paragraphing. In narrative and fiction, we use paragraphs with more varied lengths, and in informal writing our paragraphs shorten. Newspaper writing breaks up the solid column of print by making a paragraph out of every sentence or two.

In exposition, or in writing up research, we may move from topic to topic by long paragraphs that introduce a subject, elaborate it, enumerate it, explain it, or conclude it. We may frequently write paragraphs as long as a typewritten page. But if the paragraphs get much longer, we should cut them down. We can always find a place where we can make a break that is not wholly arbitrary and give the reader a rest. One argument could make a six-page paragraph, but it would be tiring to read. If we look back at it, we can find the steps in the argument. We can break between one step and another, even though the pause in reasoning is small. In a long description, we can break between one part of the subject and another. Talking of a barn, we can break between remarks about the colors things have, about the shapes they take, and about the uses they are put to. Suppose we want to write equally about ten houses in a block we grew up on. Ten tiny paragraphs would be too choppy; one paragraph would be two pages of solid print. Here, we can subdivide our houses by talking about one side of the block and then the other or by making a division for three architectural styles, or different shades of paint, or lengths of time houses were occupied by the same tenants.

Some paragraphs must be short. When we write dialogue, we show a change of speaker by indenting a new paragraph.

"Did you go downtown after lunch?" He was tapping the arm of his chair with his index finger. Behind his glasses his eyes wandered.

"Yes," she said. "I suppose I did."
"Why?"

But such paragraphing is mechanical. In descriptive or expository or narrative writing—usual ingredients in essay or autobiography and frequently in story—short paragraphs feel choppy, a rash of blurts, like someone who talks in the manner of a machine gun. When we move from dialogue to description or narration, we should provide a change of pace by keeping the paragraphs relatively long. The long paragraph is a rest, a relief after several short ones: here is a bed big enough to lie down on. We do not want

> The room was large, the chairs comfortable. He sat down on the overstuffed sofa.
> All around him the ticking of clocks wove a mesh of sound. There was dust on the windowpane, and the rugs were shabby.
> Dark pictures hung on the walls, and the woodwork was dark.

It is too much like standing up and sitting down all the time. We want to relax and read the description straight.

> The room was large, the chairs comfortable. He sat down on the overstuffed sofa. All around him the ticking of clocks wove a mesh of sound. There was dust on the windowpane, and the rugs were shabby. Dark pictures hung on the walls, and the woodwork was dark.

Such a paragraph might continue for another five or six lines.

Sometimes when we chop our prose into too-short paragraphs we may be deceiving ourselves with handwriting, which can make a few words into full-sized paragraphs, and think that we are writing a long paper when we are not. Or perhaps we find it difficult to move from one thing to another within the paragraph, and so we break the paragraph to indicate a switch to another topic. And at times, short paragraphs reveal our laziness. We fail to collect and to develop our thoughts and so write paragraphs that are little more than a sentence announcing a topic, paragraphs lacking detail, elaboration, and support. We need to think of further ideas to support arguments or details to make description carry feeling.

In narrative, the paragraph break is even more arbitrary than it is in exposition. We could justify one after every sentence, we could justify none at all; but neither of these solutions would be tolerable. Therefore we break for a rest when it is most nearly logical, as when the character turns a corner, or sees something new, or understands what is happening. Thought does not flow without pause; think of a paragraph as a unit of thought.

It is tempting to be dogmatic: "Outside of dialogue, keep your paragraphs between 200 and 250 words." Life would be more comfortable, and writing easier, if simple prescriptions solved our problems. Although a highly formal essay might follow some such rule, most good modern writing has much more variety to it. As it is hard to type the best contemporary stylists as formal or informal, so it is hard to put limits on paragraph size. Although formal writing leads toward a more uniform length of paragraph, it can use something as short as a one-line paragraph. A skillful writer may make a long statement in periodic sentences, a 350-word paragraph that concludes with a flourish, and follow it by a paragraph that reads, in its entirety,

> On the other hand, maybe this reasoning is haphazard.

Then he may write another long paragraph. The one-liner has been a change of pace—at the same time restful, offhand, and refreshing: it keeps us on our toes. We don't know what might come next, we are perpetually a little off balance. Look at this example from a student paper:

> When you approach the city from the east, you enter a down-trodden world with shabby filling stations, electric signs with letters missing, potholes, boarded-over houses, and bars which never close—dark holes of degradation and hopelessness. Next to them often you see old men asleep in gutters. No one looks young or happy or as if there is any future. The only thing you see which is bright and shiny and new is a police car.
>
> But that is only a part of the city.
>
> To the west and to the north, the lakes attract fine houses. To the south, past the new buildings of prosperous businesses, the farmlands spread in abundance. . . .

Here, the one-line paragraph—which makes a transition between the two longer paragraphs—could easily become a first sentence for the second paragraph, but the student has chosen this rhythmically shocking brevity to underline, to make even more emphatic, the totally changed scene that his prose begins to describe. Because its effect is so dramatic, use the one-line paragraph sparingly.

On the other hand, look at these paragraphs of description, more nearly equal in length:

> The river widens; islands appear; but there is no solitude in this heart of Africa. Always there are the little brown settlements in scraped brown yards, the little plantings of maize or banana or sugar cane about huts, the trading dugouts arriving beside the steamer to shouts. In the heat mist the sun, an hour before sunset, can appear round and orange, reflected in an orange band in the water muddy with laterite, the orange reflection broken only by the ripples from

the bows of the steamer and the barges. Sometimes at sunset the water will turn violet below a violet sky.

But it is a peopled wilderness. The land of this river basin is land used in the African way. It is burned, cultivated, abandoned. It looks desolate, but its riches and fruits are known; it is a wilderness, but one of monkeys. Bush and blasted trees disappear only toward Kinshasa. It is only after nine hundred miles that earth and laterite give way to igneous rocks, and the land, becoming hilly, with sharp indentations, grows smooth and bare, dark with vegetation only in its hollows.

Plant today, reap tomorrow: this is what they say in Kisangani. But this vast green land, which can feed the continent, barely feeds itself. In Kinshasa the meat and even the vegetables have to be imported from other countries. Eggs and orange juice come from South Africa, in spite of hot official words; and powdered milk and bottled milk come from Europe. The bush is a way of life; and where the bush is so overwhelming, organized agriculture is an illogicality.

V. S. Naipaul, *The Return of Eva Perón*

These even, full, adequate paragraphs march in rank and in good order, helping to convince us—even by their shape itself—that they are calm, logical steps in a progressive statement of thought or opinion. At the same time, the writer creates tension within the paragraphs by setting up contrasts—river and shore, vegetation and cultivation, native agriculture and imported culture.

The variety and unity of the paragraph resemble the variety and unity of the sentence. The effective contrast, when the one-line paragraph follows the complex one, resembles the pleasure we take in a short, simple sentence after a long, complex sentence. A writer can mix a pleasing variety of sentences and paragraphs without violating the unity that holds the essay together.

Development: Order and Clarity

If we do not want to irritate or confuse the reader, our information or argument must be orderly. Things must follow each other with a sense of purpose. Purpose makes clarity. We cannot say, "Oh, I forgot to say . . . ," or leave out steps in our progress. We must move in an orderly way, from earlier to later, or from less to more important, or from periphery to center, or from smaller to larger, or from larger to smaller. Sometimes we will want to move from center to periphery, from present to past. But we must not scatter our sequence—from larger to smaller to larger to larger to smaller to largest to larger to smallest to large. We may want A B C D E F. On occasion we may want Z Y X W V, but never A Q I X L D.

The order in the following paragraph is fine; we move from generality in the topic sentence to particulars that describe and substantiate it.

> Winter is a catastrophe. Life on skid row is lived out of doors, and the cold and the snow bring with them intense suffering. The men often get drunk enough to lie in the streets in the midst of a storm. The first time one sees a body covered with a light blanket of snow, stretched out on the sidewalk, the sight comes as a shock and a dilemma. Is the man dead or just drunk? Or worse, the habitués are so obsessed and driven that stealing goes on in the dead of winter, and a man who needs a drink will take the shoes of a fellow alcoholic in the middle of January.
>
> Michael Harrington,
> *The Other America: Poverty in the United States*

The following paragraph, organized in a different way, moving from pieces of information to a general conclusion, is also well constructed.

> Last January as he was about to leave office, Lyndon Johnson sent his last report on the economic prospect to the Congress. It was assumed that, in one way or another, the Vietnam War, by which he and his Administration had been destroyed, would come gradually to an end. The question considered by his economists was whether this would bring an increase or a decrease in military spending. The military budget for fiscal 1969 was 78.4 billions; for the year following, including pay increases, it was scheduled to be about three billions higher. Thereafter, assuming peace and a general withdrawal from Asia, there would be a reduction of some six or seven billions. But this was only on the assumption that the Pentagon did not get any major new weapons—that it was content with what had already been authorized. No one really thought this possible. The President's economists noted that plans already existed for "a package" consisting of new aircraft, modern naval vessels, defense installations, and "advanced strategic and general purpose weapons systems" which would cost many billions. This would wipe out any savings from getting out of Vietnam. Peace would now be far more expensive than war.
>
> John Kenneth Galbraith, *How to Control the Military*

The organization in this paragraph, however, is not satisfactory:

> The birds often flock in huge numbers on trees, sometimes breaking limbs off. They may bury a car parked below them in white dung. Starlings can be a terrible nuisance. The dark purplish-black pests may tear up a whole lawn in the process of searching for worms and insects, particularly as winter approaches and live food gets scarce. Their antics can drive a homeowner out of *his* tree. In large enough numbers, they can create a din of voices that blocks

out all other sounds in the area. Their cries are strident and irritating.

Here the order is unclear. In this paragraph we move from specific to specific to general to specific to general to specific to specific, without meaningful progression. It would make much better organizational sense to begin, "Starlings can be a terrible nuisance," and to end, "Their antics can drive a homeowner out of *his* tree."

In writing a paragraph we usually have to settle on some controlling principle of order or sequence and then keep to it. Earlier we showed some methods of developing paragraphs for exposition. Two of the simplest and clearest means of ordering, appropriate for all sorts of writing, are simple chronology and spatial proximity, discussed briefly when we looked into transitions. Here we see the order of time and space used to create coherent exposition.

> Anchorage has a thin history. Something of a precursor of the modern pipeline camps, it began in 1914 as a collection of tents pitched to shelter workers building the Alaska Railroad. For decades, it was a wooden-sidewalked, gravel-streeted town. Then, remarkably early, as cities go, it developed an urban slum, and both homes and commerce began to abandon its core. The exodus was so rapid that the central business district never wholly consolidated, and downtown Anchorage is even more miscellaneous than outlying parts of the city. There is, for example, a huge J. C. Penney department store filling several blocks in the heart of town, with an interior mall of boutiques and restaurants and a certain degree of chic. A couple of weedy vacant lots separate this complex from five log cabins. Downtown Anchorage from a distance displays an upreaching skyline that implies great pressure for land. Down below, among the high buildings, are houses, huts, vegetable gardens, and bungalows with tidy front lawns. Anchorage burst out of itself and left these incongruities in the center, and for me they are the most appealing sights in Anchorage. Up against a downtown office building I have seen cordwood stacked for winter.
>
> John McPhee, *Coming into the Country*

Chronology is probably the easiest method for ordering the material in a paragraph and perhaps the most common. At times, in narration and exposition, we want to leap ahead and then catch up. We must use this violation of chronological sequence, however, only when we are fully aware of what we are doing. Careful use of spatial proximity helps the reader create a clear mental picture.

> In December 1941, Congress declared war on Japan, Germany, and Italy. The declaration was an immediate result of the Japanese attack on Pearl Harbor, but earlier events had made such a move inevitable. Perhaps the Treaty of Versailles. . . .

Here, the opening sentence states the ultimate topic, an event to be reached by way of a series of causes, and the paragraph develops by reverse chronology. Presumably, the writer will later turn around and advance through the twenties and thirties in a conventional forward direction. If this essay began by referring to the earliest event mentioned—that is, if it had followed regular chronology—the reader might have expected, for a moment, that the Treaty of Versailles would be the subject.

Development: Order and Forcefulness

Clarity is not our only consideration when we organize paragraphs; we must also organize for appropriateness and forceful effect. Look again at the paragraphs by Hardwick (p. 218) and Mencken (p. 219), keeping in mind the discussion of topic sentences. Look at the order in the paragraphs compared with the effects achieved. By their positions the topic sentences give *force* to these paragraphs.

Or take the method that lets us order according to spatial proximity. It can be more than a means to clarity; it can direct the reader's attention significantly and achieve dramatic effect. Here is a passage from *Gandhi* by Louis Fischer.

> At Rajghat, a few hundred feet from the river, a fresh pyre had been built of stone, brick, and earth. It was eight feet square and about two feet high. Long, thin, sandalwood logs sprinkled with incense were stacked on it. Mahatma Gandhi's body lay on the pyre with his head to the north. In that position Buddha met his end.

Notice how the paragraph moves gradually closer to its subject, like a camera that dollies in for a close-up in a film. We start from far back and gradually zoom in. If the author had described the body of Gandhi first, and then its surroundings, the passage would be less forceful. Again, it is the principle of the periodic sentence applied to the paragraph.

When we consider how we organize our paragraphs, we must always consider our *purpose* in writing. In expository writing, we want to be sure that the reader knows what we are doing at all times. We therefore want to avoid listing statistics before telling what they demonstrate. Imagine the other paragraph I quoted about Gandhi with the first sentence placed at the end.

> The province of Natal, in 1896, had 400,000 Negro inhabitants, 51,000 Indians, and 50,000 whites. The Cape of Good Hope Colony had 900,000 Negroes, 10,000 Indians, and 400,000 Europeans; the Transvaal Republic 650,000 Negroes, 5,000 Indians, and 120,000 whites. In 1914, the five million Negroes hopelessly outnumbered the million and a quarter whites. Gandhi recognized that the whites

in South Africa thought they needed protection against a majority consisting of Negroes and Indians.

Revised as above, the order makes the paragraph confusing and pointless. The reader does not know what is going on until he finishes reading the paragraph. He will be confused, bored, and inattentive.

And yet if our purpose in writing is to create an ominous or tense atmosphere—in narrative, perhaps, either fictional or autobiographical—we might want to list unexplained details first, waiting for the end of the paragraph to offer an interpretation. This suspenseful order would give our paragraph *force*.

> The forest, all at once, had grown silent. The monkeys had stopped their chattering, and the birds darted their heads apprehensively. The wind in the trees became audible, and then, faintly, the sound of drumming rose from the village enclosure. It could only mean that Godzilla had awakened once more.

Imagine how anticlimactic it would be in a film to show the monster suddenly appearing and then to pan around the trees. It wouldn't make emotional or dramatic sense.

THE ORDER OF PARAGRAPHS

The developed paragraph is a unit of thought and feeling. The content makes the paragraph, and paragraphs become ways of organizing the subject's complexity (for ourselves and for others) into units we can comprehend. One breakthrough in writing an essay comes when we see which part belongs with which part. We take tiny pieces and assemble them into larger units, and assemble the larger units into the focused paper. The middle unit is the paragraph. It associates detail into order; it concentrates; it begins to narrow our focus. We might start with these notes for an autobiographical essay:

> summer I was eight
> going hunting with my uncle
> gun laws and the NRA
> the bounty on coyotes
> my .22
> killing the coyote pup
> how I felt afterward
> my uncle and the VFW
> Fourth of July parade

Before we can order the whole essay, we must associate these small units with each other in an informal outline. If these notes are on file cards, we can simply make piles of them. Each pile would be a potential paragraph. If the notes are listed on a piece of paper or in a notebook, we can associate one with the other by lettering and numbering each item, linking like to like with the same number. The most obvious order might start with the remembered summer, and hunting with an uncle and a new .22, then switch moods to tell an anecdote of killing a coyote pup, then consider gun laws and the National Rifle Association; then it might mention a parade of VFW members, including the uncle, carrying rifles. A different order might begin with the recent parade, and return to the memory. Any order is arbitrary, but some orders are better than others. We wish to show here not so much a *best* ordering of the whole, as a useful, preliminary sorting of material into units, small collections of notes, which may turn out to be paragraphs. For instance:

B_1	summer I was eight
B_3	going hunting with my uncle
D	gun laws and the NRA
C_1	the bounty on coyotes
B_2	my .22
C_2	killing the coyote pup
C_3	how I felt afterward
A_2	my uncle and the VFW
A_1	Fourth of July parade

This way is only one of many. It is the second ordering suggested above, from parade to memory. The units represented by the capital letters are not necessarily single paragraphs. Maybe A would be two paragraphs— first a description of the VFW parading, the uncle puffing along in step, and then a close-up of the uncle, leading to a memory. The items grouped under C—the anecdote about killing a coyote pup and the writer's feelings—might take several paragraphs. But regardless of how many paragraphs each subject takes, the *order* would be

Fourth of July parade
my uncle and the VFW

summer I was eight
my .22
going hunting with my uncle

the bounty on coyotes
killing the coyote pup
how I felt afterward

gun laws and the NRA

Many a beginning writer, or a writer who has not learned to paragraph, might write the essay following the order in which the notes originally appeared. The result would be chaos, moving back and forth in time by random association. That is the way we talk, thinking of points afterward and crying, "Oh, I forgot to say . . . !" But writing is harder and requires organization. The paragraph is our middle unit of organization between sentences that incorporate raw data and the finished, shapely essay. In developing explanation or narration, the pause lets the reader know that a limited subject has been dealt with, and that we now move to another topic—perhaps arising from the last one, perhaps in contrast to it, certainly different. The paragraph becomes a unit of meaning. The look of it on the page makes a statement; it tells us that a topic, or a detachable unit of an argument, or that an event, or a detachable unit of an event, is complete here. Like commas and sentence structure, paragraphs create meaning in our prose.

In order to make statements with paragraphs, we must be able to construct good ones. The paragraph must have *unity*, and for unity we often require a *topic sentence*. The paragraph must have *coherence* within itself, and a series of paragraphs must cohere to form the essay; coherence requires *transitions*. Finally, we must learn to *develop* the paragraph until it is adequate in its fullness and in its *length*, and until it presents its material in the best possible *order*.

Make sure that your paragraphing is useful, to the mind that understands and to the eye that reads. Consider your paragraphs for their unity and variety, their coherence and adequacy of development, and their clarity and effective ordering. Consider their internal organization and their transitions, both internal and between paragraphs, both overt and implicit.

In late drafts of a paper, think of what your paragraphing communicates to a reader. Do your paragraphs give the right signal? Read as if you were someone else, and decide if your paragraph can be improved for clarity's sake—in shape, in wholeness, in development, in transition, in order.

REVISING PARAGRAPHS

When his teacher assigned an informal topical essay, Mark Matson decided to write about his recent visit to the town where he had grown up. This is his first version.

> I got the shock of my life when I went back to visit my old home town. I had heard about the new factory and how it had made a big impact, but I didn't realize what that could mean. Riding in on the train gave me my first clues about what to expect. But it was when I

strolled around looking at familiar places that I found some of my worst fears about life coming true.

I read a lot of newspapers. I know about the destruction of the ozone layer and the effects of acid rain and problems with crowding in the cities, but mostly I think of these as affecting other people. When I get depressed by the news, I find myself thinking about Garwood, the perfect small town. At least I used to.

I had so many memories of the place. I remembered big trees, nice houses and lawns, friendly people, and a quiet, relaxed feel in the air.

But riding in on the train made me think about those newspaper stories about crowding, smog, and so on. I looked out the window and saw new subdivisions and malls where there used to be open fields. And there were cars everywhere. I remember when it was so quiet that you could play ball in the street.

As I walked away from the station I started to get depressed. I realized that nothing stands still. Here was a place that I had kept frozen in my heart. I really expected that it would look the same. Now I had to face the truth.

The streets were crowded. There were new stores everywhere; everything was glass and metal. The traffic downtown was terrible, with horns honking. The smell of car exhaust was overpowering. The worst thing was the river. I walked over the bridge, and when I looked down I saw that the water was brown and covered with a kind of foam. I remembered when it was blue and clean. We used to swim there.

Whose fault was it? Well, there is never any easy way to point the finger. But in this case we ought to take a good hard look at the price of progress. Building the Aerodyne factory in Garwood is progress. It has brought new people and a great deal of money to the area. The price is the loss of a way of life and the arrival of all sorts of modern ills, like pollution and crowding. I am sorry I visited. It would have been nicer to keep certain images the way they were. When I think of Garwood now I have the feeling that something has been stolen from me.

Mark's teacher was not happy with this first version. He noted in his comment that the subject was promising, as was Mark's way of weaving observations and reactions together with the narrative of his arrival. "But," he wrote, "you are not getting the best use from your arrangement." After cautioning Mark about a number of problems and rough spots—tired expressions like "shock of my life," and too many abrupt short sentences in paragraphs five and six—he addressed himself to the core weakness: structure and paragraphing.

"Take this apart," the teacher suggested, "and look at the different pieces. Try to decide which perceptions are the most important. Is there some way that you can strengthen both the continuity and the sense of contrast between memory and reality? Why not mention Aerodyne earlier—by name—and let the reader get some idea of the culprit? Think about our class discussions on paragraphing. *Comparison and contrast* will obviously be useful. How about *analysis* or *cause and effect?* Maybe you can clarify the link between the new plant and the changes you saw in the town. Some more use of *assertion* might organize your final paragraph better. Overall, stay with a logical sequence (for example: expectation, arrival, shock, and reaction) and try to keep your own movements consecutive (on the train, at the station, walking into town, crossing the river) so that we can follow."

Mark broke his essay into small chunks. He underlined the parts that he thought were more important and looked to see if they were connected in some logical way. He circled every sentence that was about a memory and thought about ways to bring the recollections together. Then Mark wrote out the different kinds of paragraph organization on a separate sheet. He looked from the sheet to his essay, back and forth, and considered how to tighten individual paragraphs. He also paid close attention to beginnings and endings of paragraphs; he penciled in ideas for stronger connections. After making many such notes, and after two frustrating false starts, Mark came up with what he felt was a much more unified essay.

> I read the newspaper every day, not because I want to, but because I think that we have to be informed about what is happening in the world. The news is never good. A typical front page will have reports on pollution, corrupt officials, drugs and murders, and on-going wars in the Middle East.
>
> When I put the paper aside, I usually feel depressed. I try to think about these different problems and about what can be done to make the world better. But usually I start thinking about escape. And when I do, I picture Garwood, the perfect small town. I grew up there, and I dream about going back.
>
> That is, I *used* to dream about going back. Recently I took the trip: I found out that certain dreams are better left untouched.
>
> Riding in on the train, I sorted through my memories and fantasized about what I would find. I pictured the quiet, tree-lined streets, the neat houses and lawns, the small shops with friendly owners, kids with dogs, you name it. I must have been thinking of one of those old barbershop calendars.
>
> Before the train even reached the station, I knew that I was going to have to readjust my ideas. We were rolling through the outskirts—there never used to be outskirts—and I felt my heart sink. Where were the farms and open fields? All I could see through the window were shopping malls and subdivisions. I almost looked at the train schedule to make sure that this was the right stop.
>
> Then I remembered. Before my family moved away there was a

lot of talk and argument about the new Aerodyne plant. Some people said that if the company built in Garwood it would be opening the door to big city problems. The newspaper called it a "Pandora's box." Other people argued about the benefits: new business, expansion, and revenue.

There's no question about those benefits, but they look suspiciously like the evils that came out of the box Pandora opened.

The plant was built on top of Sear's Hill. Hundreds of workers and their families were brought in. Smart developers bought up the farmland on the west side of town and put up tract housing. Shop owners thought about ways to expand. People started to see dollar signs.

Walking up toward town from the station, I felt like a visitor from another galaxy. Everything was changed. Somebody had waved a wand and covered the old town with glass and steel. The streets were wider; parking meters were growing where the trees used to be. I actually saw a traffic jam at the intersection of Main and Wilder.

These changes shocked me, naturally, but the real shock came when I crossed the far end of Wilder and started over the bridge. I looked down at the river below and nearly got sick to my stomach. The blue water I remembered, where we swam and fished, was dirty brown. Dead brown. Some awful kind of foam was gathered behind the rocks and logs. I didn't have to look up the hill to know where the mess was coming from.

For so many years I had kept Garwood frozen in my mind as an ideal place to live. It was my mental retreat. Whenever I got depressed by the ways of modern life, I dreamed of going back. No more. They say you can't go home again, and they're right. When I think of Garwood now I feel as if something has been stolen from me.

____ EXERCISES _____

1. Rewrite the paragraphs from student papers on pages 216–217. Expand or delete, and organize details as necessary.

2. Develop one of these topic sentences in a short paragraph, using one of the methods discussed in the chapter.

   a. We live in a highly competitive society.
   b. Green is a cool color.
   c. Sitting by the fire on a cold winter night is a pleasure I miss at school.
   d. It is not difficult to make bread.
   e. The man was dressed in a most peculiar fashion.

3. Read these paragraphs and comment on their methods of development. (See pages 234–239.)

a. It's sometimes argued that there's no real progress; that a civilization that kills multitudes in mass warfare, that pollutes the land and oceans with ever larger quantities of debris, that destroys the dignity of individuals by subjecting them to a forced mechanized existence can hardly be called an advance over the simpler hunting and gathering and agricultural existence of prehistoric times. But this argument, though romantically appealing, doesn't hold up. The primitive tribes permitted far less individual freedom than does modern society. Ancient wars were committed with far less moral justification than modern ones. A technology that produces debris can find, and is finding, ways of disposing of it without ecological upset. And the schoolbook pictures of primitive man sometimes omit some of the detractions of his primitive life—the pain, the disease, famine, the hard labor needed just to stay alive. From that agony of bare existence to modern life can be soberly described only as upward progress, and the sole agent for this progress is quite clearly reason itself.

> *Robert M. Pirsig, Zen and the Art of Motorcycle Maintenance*

b. When I think about the qualities that characterize the best friendships I've known, I can identify five: rapport, affection, need, habit, and forgiveness. Rapport and affection can only take you so far; they may leave you at the formal, outer gate of goodwill, which is still not friendship. A persistent need for the other's company, for their interest, approval, opinion, will get you inside the gates, especially when it is reciprocated. In the end, however, there are no substitutes for habit and forgiveness. A friendship may travel for years on cozy habit. But it is a melancholy fact that unless you are a saint you are bound to offend every friend deeply at least once in the course of time. The friends I have kept the longest are those who forgave me for wronging them, unintentionally, intentionally, or by the plain catastrophe of my personality, time and again. There can be no friendship without forgiveness.

> *Philip Lopate, "Modern Friendships"*

c. We are a practical, inventive people on whom the weight of tradition rests but lightly. In many lands of the world, people confronted with an unpleasant situation will quietly adjust themselves; in the United States, a man's first impulse is to change things for the better. This willingness to experiment came naturally to the pioneers, who had no precedents on which to build. It has remained a trait of the industrial pioneers whose ability to adapt and change has laid the basis for America's supremacy as a manufacturing nation.

> *Ray Allen Billington, "The Frontier Disappears"*

d. Each boxing match is a story, a highly condensed, highly dramatic story—even when nothing much happens: then failure is the story. There are two principal characters in the story, overseen by a shadowy third. When the bell rings no one knows what will happen. Much is speculated, nothing known. The boxers bring to the fight everything that is themselves, and everything will be exposed: including secrets about themselves they never knew. There are boxers possessed of such remarkable intuition, such prescience, one would think they had fought this particular fight before. There are boxers who perform brilliantly, but mechanically, who cannot improvise in midfight; there are boxers performing at the height of their skill who cannot quite comprehend that it won't be enough; to my knowledge there was only one boxer who possessed an extraordinary and disquieting awareness, not only of his opponent's every move or anticipated move, but of the audience's keenest shifts in mood as well—Muhammad Ali, of course.

Joyce Carol Oates, "On Boxing"

4. Take this excerpt from the *Detroit Free Press*, tiny newspaper paragraphs, and copy it out into longer paragraphs, as you would organize paragraphs in an essay. Break the paragraphs logically and usefully.

Here's what the historic arms limitation agreements signed here Friday night in the Kremlin mean.

What they do, essentially, is to freeze a "balance of terror" between the world's two nuclear superpowers.

Each side, in these agreements, retains the ability to kill millions of defenseless civilians on the other side.

Washington and Moscow will be defended from nuclear attack with anti-ballistic missile systems (ABMs).

But Detroit and every other major city in the U.S. will remain undefended. So will Leningrad and Kiev, and other major cities in the Soviet Union.

Thus each side, in a sense, will hold the civilian population of the other side hostage—as a means of discouraging the other side from launching nuclear war.

The fact is, as Henry Kissinger, White House national security adviser, has put it: "Both sides are now vulnerable to each other . . . this has been a fact now for five or six years."

The new SALT agreements seek to freeze the 25-year-old nuclear arms race at that point—on the theory that a "balance of terror" is the best guarantee either side has, in this terrifying age, of preventing war.

But what of other major questions?

How important are the agreements? Can they work? Can they be monitored? Don't the agreements give the Soviets a numerical advantage? What will they mean to the average citizen?

James McCartney

5. Look at the length of paragraphs in these examples. Do the authors provide variety in length and type of paragraph? Do any paragraphs seem choppy? Are transitions adequate? Make notes in the margin for class discussion.

a. What, in our human world, is this power to live? It is the ancient, lost reverence and passion for human personality, joined with the ancient, lost reverence and passion for the earth and its web of life.

This indivisible reverence and passion is what the American Indians almost universally had; and representative groups of them have it still.

They had and have this power for living which our modern world has lost—as world-view and self-view, as tradition and institution, as practical philosophy dominating their societies and as an art supreme among all the arts.

By virtue of this power, the densely populated Inca state, by universal agreement among its people, made the conservation and increase of the earth's resources its foundational national policy. Never before, never since has a nation done what the Inca state did.

By virtue of this same power, the little pueblo of Tesuque, in New Mexico, when threatened by the implacable destroying action of government some twenty-five years ago, starved and let no white friend know it was starving. It asked no help, determined only to defend its spiritual values and institutions and its remnant of land which was holy land.

If our modern world should be able to recapture this power, the earth's natural resources and web of life would not be irrevocably wasted within the twentieth century, which is the prospect now. True democracy, founded in neighborhoods and reaching over the world, would become the realized heaven on earth. And living peace—not just an interlude between wars—would be born and would last through ages.

John Collier, Indians of the Americas

b. Pop stands for mutability and glitter. Its mode is the 45 single and the pinup, and its value is measured by record sales and the charts. Pop is about dreams and escapism and ecstatic moments; it believes in clichés and its philosophy is "give the people what they want." It is egalitarian by nature—anyone can make it—and capitalist.

Rock is about the search for permanence within the free-floating values of the marketplace. It is about tradition (blues, country, and folk roots), and it is hierarchical in that it believes in geniuses and heroes. Its mode is the long-playing album and the in-depth interview. Rock wants deep emotion and catharsis and truth; it has a religious element that pop does not. Rock believes in originality and self-expression in defiance of crass commercialism.

If this seems to suggest that pop means shallow and rock means depth, consider which is the more profound experience —Smoky Robinson's "The Tracks of My Tears" or Led Zeppelin's "Stairway to Heaven"? And yet the one is a pop, the other a rock classic. And far from being rigid categories, pop and rock often intertwine—where would you put "River Deep Mountain High"? Where would you put Prince? How do you classify punk?

Mary Harron, "Pop As a Commodity"

6. These phrases might be informal notes for an essay. Arrange them into several groups, each capable of becoming a paragraph. Then write a brief paragraph starting with topic sentence (a) or (b).

    a. Pets should be allowed in the dormitory.
    b. Pets should not be allowed in the dormitory.
        dogs vs. other animals
        sanitation and health laws
        noise, barking during the night
        exercise and traffic
        responsibility for feeding and care
        roommates and allergies
        community considerations
        student life and its demands
        safety
        school vacations and care
        abuse of pets and negligence
        companionship and loneliness

7. Here is a short essay on baseball. I have mixed up the paragraph order and numbered the paragraphs in the mixed-up order. See if you can restore them to their original sequence.

1. At any one point, there's anticipation, deliberation, preparation: "Now" is a building-up. "Now" is never only for itself. It's cumulative "progressing," in strife, to form the game's unfolding. Nor are any two games alike, any more than two art works that push themselves into being through the resistance of time, incident by incident, in head-on conflict by two complicated machines designed to win through accidents and opportunity. "What's happening" is contingent. There's a whole game to be gotten through.

2. This is to see baseball as an artwork-in-the-making affair, totally unrehearsed, improvised by more than eighteen men, who thrust in their various skills while the moving parts pass through innings, highlighted by crucial plays, to the conclusion being thereby created.

3. The game in progress is a structure-in-the-becoming; if you see it, through time, as a whole, all the separate episodes can come flashing together, and interlock, to shower aesthetic illumination on a drama of its own devising.

4. Like literature, music, opera, theater, and the dance, baseball takes place in time. (Architecture, sculpture, and painting don't—they're purely spatial.) The performer and the observer, while a game is in progress, look back and look ahead: the present action is laid out in a shifting, dramatic time field. A rhythm, of sorts, weaves its way through the "accidents" on the playing field. A current play, involving positioning and decisions, is affected by what was previous in the game, and is having its effect on what's to come later; the game may be seen as an organic unit. Every pitch has its place in there, somewhere.

Marvin Cohen, Baseball the Beautiful

7

Forms for the Essay: Rhetorical Patterns in Exposition

EXPOSITION

Before we take up argument and research, we must look into the principal form of prose we need to write, not only at the university but elsewhere. Most writing assigned in college is exposition. Exposition is explanation, exposing a subject for an audience, making it clear. The word *exposition* comes from a Latin verb meaning "to set out," and it becomes an English noun meaning "something displayed for public inspection." We write exposition not only in college; most writing required in professional life is expository—in business, in teaching, in technology and science, in law and medicine. When social workers deliver papers, when geologists make reports, when hospital officials release information on new diagnostic equipment, when marketing managers report on the activities of their competition, they write expository prose.

In itself, exposition is not argument, although it usually forms part of an argument. Argument lacking explanation moves toward bombast or harangue because it presents unsubstantiated opinion. Exposition does not tell a story, though it may include narrative to explain something essential. Even pure description may be a necessary part of exposition.

We might think of exposition as the foundation upon which most essays are built. By itself it can make a whole essay. If you were spending an exchange year in England, you might feel called upon to write an expository essay explaining baseball or percolator coffee to your teacher and your classmates. If you wrote about Einstein's discoveries in physics, you would need exposition to arrange your information in order to make contact with your audience.

> But there was another consequence which Einstein now brought forward for the first time. If light is produced in a star or in the sun, an area of strong gravity, and then streams down on the earth, an area of weak gravity, its energy will not be dissipated by a reduction of speed, since this is impossible, light always having the same constant speed. What would happen, Einstein postulated, was something very different: the wavelength of the light would be shortened. This "Einstein shift," the assumption that "the spectral lines of sunlight, as compared with the corresponding spectral lines of terrestrial sources of light, must be somewhat displaced toward the red," was spelled out in some detail. However, he was careful to add the qualification that "as other influences [pressure, temperature] affect the position of the centers of the spectral lines, it is difficult to discover whether the enforced influence of the gravitational potential really exists." In fact the Döppler shift, produced by the motion of the stars relative to the solar system, was to provide an additional and even more important complication.
>
> Ronald W. Clark, *Einstein*

Pausing in his biography to explain a scientific discovery, the author analyzes a natural process. He is making use of *process analysis,* a common rhetorical pattern that answers the question "How does it happen?" or "How does it work?" Other rhetorical patterns have other uses. We touched briefly on these patterns in Chapter 3 and Chapter 6—now we must examine their advantages more closely.

RHETORICAL PATTERNS

Patterns of rhetoric are ways of thinking. Writers and thinkers in ancient times discovered that the mind structures sense in a limited number of ways, and that these could be classified and studied. The science of *Rhetoric* was born; and these basic forms still determine the way we think and communicate. Frank Rodriguez in Chapter 3 used the rhetorical pattern of *comparison and contrast* for a way of thinking, observing differences between two situation comedies about war. Other patterns of rhetoric offer other models of thought. We use these models to reach our readers or listeners, to make contact with other people. Because these patterns are universal, ideas can be transmitted from speaker to listener, from writer to reader. Consideration of audience may suggest purpose. Making things clear to an audience, exposing, we need to define terms—and *definition* itself is a prominent rhetorical pattern.

Each of the most common rhetorical patterns answers a question, and these resemble the journalist's six questions. *Example* answers "For instance?" *Classification* answers "What kind is it?" *Division* answers "What are its parts?" *Cause and effect* answers "Why did it happen?" *Process analysis* answers "How does it happen?" *Comparison and contrast* answers "What is it like? What is it unlike?" *Definition* answers "What is it?"

Because these rhetorical patterns also reproduce the questions we ask ourselves about a subject, they are doubly useful. In Chapter 3 we introduced them briefly because they can help us in the process of writing—to invent and to get ideas, as well as to organize, to construct, and to develop an essay. Because these patterns provide ways to develop writing that is thin, we discussed them briefly when we spoke in Chapter 6 of developments in the paragraph. Now we must look more closely at how these rhetorical patterns can structure our writing.

Suppose we start with a general topic and wish to generate material. Suppose the topic is community colleges. We could ask ourselves to list *examples* of community colleges, with concrete detail. Or we could jot down various ways to *classify* community colleges, according to size, location, sources of funding, or curricula. We could *divide* one community college into its components—faculty, administration, staff, and student body. We could ask ourselves what social needs *cause* the establishment of community colleges; now that they are established, we could ask what *effects* they have. We could *compare and contrast* community colleges with four-year colleges, with residential colleges, or with technical institutes, and examine the differences. We could investigate the *process* of founding a community college or look at the specific attributes that *define* such an institution. By this time, we would have acquired much material for our essay. Then we would need to investigate the material generated to look for a purpose for our essay, and our purpose would depend on our sense of an audience. Whom do we write for, and why? Probably, a paper on community colleges would use more than one of these rhetorical patterns; but it would most likely not use all of them.

Rhetorical patterns are enormously flexible; we can adjust them to our needs. Each of these devices can structure an entire paper or support one segment of a paper, even as short as a sentence of *example.* Good essays blend rhetorical patterns in a sequence demanded by the essay's purpose. These patterns often work in combination. If we write a *process analysis* about planting an apple orchard, and we use a term or a concept likely to be unfamiliar to our audience, we will need *definition* within process analysis; when we define a term, one method of definition uses *example:* the definition of a cooking apple may be clearer if we give the example of a Gravenstein. Frank Rodriguez used comparison for his rhetorical pattern, yet he ended his essay by suggesting historical or social *cause and effect* as the source of the contrast he found.

Although some assignments require us to use a specific pattern, so that like Frank Rodriguez we look for things to compare and contrast, other assignments set before us a general topic; it is our job to find a focus and a mode of construction. The same opportunities or necessities will appear when we join the working world, although they will not announce themselves in rhetorical terms. Sometimes a report for the manager will call for comparison and contrast of two options. The manager making the assignment does not consider the pattern of rhetoric; but if we understand what we are asked to do, we can do it better by making use of rhetorical patterns.

At other times, our investigation of a business option, or a book, or a past event may best use process analysis, or classification, or example. The rhetorical patterns are, as we indicated, modes of construction that are also modes of thought; by their shapes they can help us narrow the topic and show us a way to think about it. If Frank's teacher had assigned a topic rather than a pattern—television, for instance—Frank could have used the rhetorical mode of comparison and contrast to narrow his subject to two contrasting situation comedies. Or he could have used classification to separate types of television programs. Or he could have used division to analyze the repeated structures of one type.

Although we seldom find an essay in a book or magazine that is purely an example of one pattern, it is useful as we study writing to practice using these patterns one at a time. Practice fixes the uses in our minds and keeps the patterns available for future use. Familiarity will bring confidence: eventually we will combine uses with the skill of a juggler rotating clubs.

For one more example: suppose we find ourselves charged, in later life, with writing a report on the market for liability insurance in shopping centers. Do we need to use definition? To answer such a question we must consider our audience. If we work for Metropolitan Life Insurance Company, we probably do not need to define "liability insurance." But the term "shopping plaza" may require some limitation for an audience of insurance company executives; maybe we need to use definition at the beginning of our report. We may well need classification, differentiating shopping plazas according to the numbers of units; or we may need division, if sections of plazas require different types of insurance. When we put forward options we may well use example, either historical or hypothetical. Connection between insurance and plaza may require an example that indicates cause and effect. Considering audience and purpose, we may use comparison and contrast.

By mentioning hypothetical topics—community colleges, apple

orchards, and insurance for shopping centers—as examples, we enter the subject of rhetorical patterns.

Example: "For example?"

Example or illustration is fundamental to discourse that explains. We say something general, and then we make it clear by locating it in one or more examples. "Students today are more practical than they were fifteen years ago." Such a generalization cries out for an instance. The word *practical* needs to be pinned down more precisely. "They major in subjects that will lead to jobs." This example of practicality suggests examples more particular still; frequently we progress from a broad generalization to an example which remains fairly general to a further example which becomes more specific. "History majors have declined by 40 percent in fifteen years; economics majors have increased by a third, and the new major in computer science has grown by 16 percent a year."

We use example as the first of the rhetorical patterns because it forms part of so many others. When we compare and contrast we often compare and contrast examples; analyzing process, we clarify a generalization of process by example; one of the chief modes of definition is definition by example.

The scale of example is infinite. It can range from one word— "Perennial plants such as geraniums . . . "—to the long historical work that begins with a generalization about the repeated shapes of revolutions in history and spends its length showing the pattern by narrating many examples of revolution. Of course the author would probably use other rhetorical patterns as well. Within each example of a revolution, he might analyze historical process; terms would need definition: "An oligarchy is. . . . "

Examples allow the writer to clarify and explain generalizations to a reader, making connection with the audience. When the student used the word *practical*, the word could mean different things to different people. (Art history may be a diversion for the future science major, but highly useful for the person intending to teach art.) Concrete illustrations specify the sense in which *practical* is used. We choose our examples depending on our audience. If we are addressing the garden club, probably we need not explain "such as geraniums"; our audience can supply its own list of perennial plants.

When teachers complain that an essay lacks detail—a frequent complaint—they usually lament the lack of examples. Someone may write that animal fat contains more calories than a comparable amount of vegetable fat. But we gain clarity and interest if we hear that three ounces of hamburger adds up to two hundred fifty calories, and that three ounces of baked potato amount only to sixty. As always, balance is essential. Without generality we lack statement or idea; but without example we lack salt to make the baked potato idea palatable.

Misuses of example are common, especially when we support a generalization with a single example or insufficient detail. (In Chapter 8 we will speak of the argumentative error of generalizing from a particular.) In the expository use of example, we need to consider whether the example fairly represents what we claim. Three ounces of baked potato, if we add butter and sour cream, may grossly exceed the hamburger patty's calories. We must take care, for the sake of honest communication, that the example truly supports the generality. Sometimes the brief example, like *geraniums*, will speak for itself, but often, when we consider audience, we must explain why the example applies. In a generalization about a well-made automobile, we may need to define *fuel injection* or *independent suspension*. We should avoid the obvious or trite examples as we avoid the cliché in language. When we use a general word like *fruit*, it is unnecessary to give an example "like apples or oranges"; we offend our audience when we condescend to it.

Thinking by Example

When we generalize in conversation with a friend, saying, "Studying for an exam in psych takes a special kind of brain," we may hear the response, "For example?" To think by using examples, we should keep a questioner inside our heads. Example is so fundamental to exposition, we do well to ask ourselves, "For example?" and "For instance?" throughout the process of writing—when we generate notes toward a paper, when we look critically at a draft, and when we give an essay its final polishing revision. Thinking by example will clarify and develop our language and thought. Specificity carries our ideas across the page to our reader.

Suppose Frank Rodriguez had been assigned an essay, not in comparison and contrast, but in example. He would have searched for a generalization to support, and he might still have found his subject on the small screen. Suppose he generalized: "Television helps keep families together because people stay home to watch programs," or "Television impedes mental growth because it does everything for the viewer." The inner critic, responding to either generalization, must ask, "For example? For instance?" Frank could have begun to build an essay by a line of examples supporting either generalization.

An Example of Example

In a northeastern school a few years back, a teacher in advanced composition assigned her class John McPhee's *Oranges* as a model of good prose for reading and class discussion. Originally a *New Yorker* series of articles, *Oranges* tells everything about the fruit—its history, its botany, its geography, its economics. In the book the author uses various rhetorical patterns many times over. When the teacher spent two weeks of class time on exercises in the rhetorical patterns, she used McPhee as a model and assigned her students exercises and essays using the seven major patterns to discuss the general subject of apples. Because the college sat amid many orchards, she encouraged her students to base their papers on interviews. When she repeated the experiment in the following year, the class became known on campus as "Apples and Oranges." Here is a brief example theme from that class:

The Growth of Orchards

In the narrow valleys of New England, intensive fruit growing has replaced the general subsistence farm on which a family kept cows, sheep, chickens, and pigs while growing a large vegetable garden. Some farmers now plant a few intensively fertilized acres of strawberries or blueberries, often marketed to customers willing to do their own picking. But such enterprises require nearby cities for their customers. On the sloping hills of northern New England and western Massachusetts, unable to accommodate the farm machinery that makes large herds of milk cattle economical, the family-sized apple orchard provides a common crop.

At Bone's Orchard outside Montague, Massachusetts, the family of Richard Bone tends eight hundred trees including twenty-five varieties from the old McIntosh to the new Empire. The family of five runs its thirty acres as a vertical conglomerate, setting out new trees and cutting down old ones that have slowed down their production, trimming and fertilizing, picking the crop with the assistance of neighbors. Then they sell bushels and pecks of apples, and gallons of apple cider, in front of their house from a roadside stand.

Classification and Division: "What kind is it? What are its parts?"

We classify to organize the welter of our world. We ask "What kind is it?" or "What are its parts?" If we do not thus classify our personal possessions, we can never find anything. Moving into a new house or apartment, we put the bedroom things into the bedroom, the kitchen things in the kitchen. We will never discover our eggbeater if we have mistakenly classified it among the pajamas. Before we study, most of us will put our books and notes about economics in one place, our chemistry things in another. Similarly, when we must organize our thoughts—to begin a paper about the presidential election of 1984, or to study for an exam about the causes of the 1914–1918 war—we need to classify or divide the information to set it in order, before we can understand or remember it.

Classification is a form of thought. Our minds constantly fit things into categories: apples, towns, automobiles, left-handed people, musical instruments. When we consider friends we have known, towns we have lived in, apples we have eaten, or cars we have driven, our minds tend to classify these things. We all know the common speech-opener: "There are two kinds of people . . . " We group according to similarities, and then we discriminate differences. If we classify voters, we separate people into Republicans, Democrats, Socialists, Prohibitionists, and this discrimination depends on one characteristic: their voting habits. Thinking of cars we have driven, we classify according to mileage, price, country of origin, size, or any other discernible quality; they are all automobiles. Of course classification leads to comparison and often contrast, because the large class depends on similarities— what all seashells or automobiles have in common—and the subdivisions depend on contrasts of striping or handling, size, or horsepower.

Classification keeps our thinking orderly. Essential to good order in classification is parallelism, which keeps categories uniform. If we classify forms of literature, we may speak of fiction, drama, and poetry, and the classification remains parallel. If we were tempted to classify literature into novel, drama, short story, poem, and sonnet, our thinking would become muddled: drama is a general category but novel and short story are subcategories of the general notion fiction; poetry is a general category and sonnet a particular form within the category poetry. Parallelism keeps the borders of our thinking clearly defined.

When we outline a subject, we keep categories parallel by using parallel numbers or letters—roman numeral, capital letter, arabic numeral, lowercase letter:

I.
   A.
      1.
         a.

Beneath each topic of equal worth, we indent and subclassify or divide. Under the general subject of wartime economics, we might classify

I. Industry

with further classification into

   A. Production for the military

and

   B. Production for civilians

It might be necessary, under A and B, to divide the subject into geographic areas:

      1. Eastern area
      2. Southern area
      3. Midwestern area
      4. Mountain area
      5. West Coast area

We might go on to
    II. Transportation
and then subdivide into Sea and Land, subdividing Land further into
Rail and Highway. Classification and division are modes of thought
that supply borders, frames, and containers.

    Division is also characteristic of human thought. While classifi-
cation sets many things in order—apples classified as McIntosh, Delicious, Baldwin, Northern Spy—division separates single things into
their parts. Division gives us the anatomy of an object; understanding a
thing by means of its components is *analysis,* or cutting up. An apple,
for instance, is composed of skin, stem, flesh, and seeds. To analyze the
federal government, we divide it into three parts: executive, legislative,
and judicial. To analyze our Buick, we divide it into chassis, engine, and
body.

    When we analyze by division, we analyze a static thing: the fin-
ished automobile, the ripe apple. It is important to distinguish between
the analysis of a single, static object—for which we use the rhetorical
pattern of division—and the narrative analysis of action or process, a
pattern we will take up later.

    In writing, when we follow the rhetorical pattern of classification
or of division, we should be careful not to confuse the two. Sometimes a
good writer will begin an essay by classification and end it with division—with thoughtful logic and excellent results. We could classify
plays as tragic, comic, historical, and pastoral—and then analyze the
anatomy of the tragedy, dividing the one dramatic form into components; Aristotle in his *Poetics,* for instance, distinguished plot, character, diction, thought, spectacle, and song.

    But the two patterns are different. Often in careless writing we
may start using one pattern and end using the other, not knowing what
we do, with monstrous results—as if the Creator's attention had wandered, and He set a robin's head on a daffodil's stem. If we began a paper
with an analytic division of the federal government into its components, we would wander into incoherence if we took off from the
legislative third of the division and started classifying the different
legislatures of the world. Do not wander, like a careless talker, from one
pattern to the other without noticing it. The result makes disunity,
much as mixed constructions do in individual sentences.

Thinking by Classification and Division

    We cannot think by classification and division until we have
ideas, topics, or facts to classify and divide—just as it is difficult to sort
our possessions into a house until the moving van has arrived. Therefore we think by classifying after we have first taken notes or brain-
stormed or written an early draft, after we have generated material to

classify. One useful trick is to set outline numbers and letters next to the words and concepts that are parallel, in the margins of notes or drafts. If our economics notes list "new freighters 1943," we should recognize a submember of B, Ocean, which is a submember of II, Transportation; when we see a note on "air freight beginning 1944," we should recognize a new category, C, Air, which we had not earlier considered.

Here, classification not only organizes material generated, but also points out a step in thinking; it helps us to generate ideas by creating a third division under "Transportation" that we had not planned on. The writer not wary of classification might include her remarks on the beginnings of air freight as a hasty addendum to remarks on sea or land transport, and confuse the audience by disorder.

An Example of Classification and Division

As an exercise in classification and division, one student began:

Slicing Apples

We classify apples by the names we give them, by calling them McIntosh, Baldwin, Cortland, and Gravenstein. The names taste good, but only if you can attach a memory to them. Each of these fruits, if we dissect it, is composed after all of the same components—pith or meat, skin, core, and seeds. We tell them apart, for pleasure and nutrition, by taste, smell, and characteristics that suggest their use. But there is more than one way to slice an apple: A McIntosh is smaller than many other apples, sweeter, and does not keep so well; it is best to consume it within thirty-six hours of picking. On the other hand the Cortland. . . .

Cause and Effect: "Why did it happen?"

The rhetorical pattern of cause and effect answers the question "Why did or does or will it happen?" In exposition our explanatory purpose often requires us to assemble causes or to speculate on them. Scientific writing often examines phenomena for causes and effects: "Bubonic plague was transmitted by fleas from infected rats." When we explain cause and effect by reciting statistics and scientific facts, we maintain objectivity or at least its appearance. Historical speculation is a different matter: causes tend to be multiple, and often involve the vagaries of human motivation. Do we really know the origins of Napoleon's mania for conquest? Still, like the scientist, the historian tries to marshal evidence, usually by means of multiple examples, to suggest causes that led to war, or to defeat for one party and victory for another.

Here the rhetorical pattern of cause and effect approaches persuasion, and indeed this pattern forms a major device in argument and persuasion. When editorial writers tell us, "The death penalty will not serve as a deterrent to murder," they usually argue by cause and effect, citing statistics. We listen for reasonableness in such assertions. If writers wish to convince an audience, they must make their steps in causation logical and support them by detail. Unsupported statements which ignore causal relationship—as if an editorial writer stopped after the one-sentence assertion—will convince no one. (In Chapter 8 we discuss the use of cause and effect in argument.)

Cause and effect is common to most explanation, however, not only to persuasion. A comparison and contrast essay on the utility of bicycles and automobiles, even if the writer does not decide for one or the other, will use cause and effect to locate differences. In comparing and contrasting two television comedies, Frank Rodriguez ended by using cause and effect to suggest a reason for the differences he had discovered. He showed how changed historical circumstances—namely the disastrous defeat in Vietnam—led to changed public attitudes toward war.

Columnists on the business pages of daily newspapers frequently explain by cause and effect. Why have Japanese cars made inroads on the American market? The exposition may lead us to encounters with the problem of multiple causation. If we discover four or five possible causes, we must decide the relative importance of each. What accounts for the popularity of Japanese cars? Is it primarily marketing, design, size, convenience, or price? (Notice that possible causes form a classification.) If you show, by statistics and examples, that price is the primary factor, you may wish, considering your audience, to take the investigation one step further, to inquire into the cause of the cause. Claiming that lower price is the immediate cause for the consumer's choice, one writer argued that it was neither the higher salaries of American workers nor the Japanese use of robotics that accounted for the price differentiation. Instead, he said it was the huge range of models offered by each American manufacturer—more than twenty thousand possible options for one model. He contrasted this with the few options offered by Japanese firms; the variety of options, he concluded, causes the difference in price range.

It was the purpose of this writer, addressing a business audience, to take his cause and effect analysis from one cause (lower price) to a cause further back (simplicity of model range). Audience determines purpose, which determines strategy. Another writer might wish to go further still, to try to determine the causes in national character for the different strategies of the manufacturers.

In exposition we must always remember the needs of an audience. If we seek to explain an increase in arrests of teenagers for drunken driving, perhaps our audience will not be satisfied to learn that statistics show an increase in teenage drinking. We will need to push further, to seek causes for the increase in drinking. If an airplane crashes because of a mechanical malfunction, perhaps we will need to investigate reasons for the malfunction, and not simply demonstrate the cause of the crash by naming it. Was the cause poor maintenance? Original design? Misuse or abuse?

But when we use the pattern of cause and effect, we must know when to stop. Talking about the causes behind company failure, or war, we could recede historically to the Declaration of Independence, or the Pilgrim Fathers, or the visit to Japan by Admiral Perry—and never arrive at the end of our linked chain. Considering what an audience may reasonably require, we must narrow the focus or the scope of cause and effect accordingly; we must recede so far and no further. Otherwise, we will discover that the seeds of the present wars of the Middle East extend backward in history from Mahomet II to Timur, the Crusades, Mahomet I, Constantine, Augustus, Alexander, Moses, and the Pharaohs.

We use the pattern of cause and effect, not only when we talk about what has happened, but when we predict the consequences of actions not yet undertaken. We explain that because our candidate will control health-care costs, the nation's budget deficit will decrease. In business writing, we propose actions based on cause and effect predictions. If we market product X by campaign Y, we will reach market Z. The writer, targeting his audience as the company targets its market, uses examples and statistics to support causal predictions.

Thinking by Cause and Effect

Explaining by cause and effect is basic to thinking. We assume that every phenomenon, from the sun rising in the morning to a shipwreck to a great painting, results from a cause or, more probable, multiple causes. When we undertake any topic, we should consider the appropriate use of cause and effect. Reading notes or plans or drafts toward an essay, we should encourage the inner critic to ask *why*. Why does this happen or that? And is it relevant to tell our audience why? Does it suit our purpose to carry investigation of sources backward in time, for the sake of the audience we address? Does the audience need explanation of cause for comprehension or clarity?

To think well by cause and effect, be sure that you avoid assertion without evidence or example. Never be satisfied to have found one cause, but consider the possibilities of multiple causation. Making a chain of causes, be careful not to omit a link. Never confuse sequence with cause; forgetting your umbrella did *not* make it rain.

An Example of Cause and Effect

Ruinous Health

When an apple tree has been neglected for some years, disease and undirected growth combine to spoil its fruit. Only worms eat the small, sour apples; people will never touch them. Spraying one spring will keep the insects away, but we will need more than spray to bring the old tree back: the pruning saw must restructure the tree's growth before it will be healthy again.

A tree's natural, healthy growth works against its future health. Vigorous new limbs, growing without our careful attention, keep sunlight and air from reaching the mature limbs. Untended branches rub against each other, breaking the bark, leaving an open sore by which disease may enter the tree's trunk. New shoots start up at the base of the old tree, draining energy from the soil. Eventually, as the new shoots grow into small trees, they extend leaves that rob the old tree of sunlight. Sun makes sugar. When untrimmed branches keep sun from blossom and apple, the result is small apples that never sweeten.

Burgeoning growth is its own undoing. The remedy is the saw, for amputation makes the remaining limbs stronger—open to necessary sunlight, taking necessary energy from soil.

Comparison and Contrast: "What is it like? What is it unlike?"

We use comparison and contrast to shape our papers—as we saw Frank Rodriguez do in Chapter 3—or we use it as part of the paper. It is a habit of our thought, even at its most almost, to divide or classify and then to compare and contrast. "There are two kinds of people in the world," we say, or three, or four—and then we use this unlikely generalization as a way to consider and explore human characteristics. Our minds operate by contraries: oasis calls for desert, and nothing brings winter into mind like a summer day.

We use comparison and contrast for clarification within sentences and paragraphs. In an earlier paragraph, I used the caloric count of a hamburger as an example of an example. Perhaps that detail by itself would mean little to most readers; in order to let that detail speak to an audience, I could supply meaning for "two hundred fifty calories" by comparison and contrast.

Meats are fattening; a hamburger patty two and a half inches across contains about two hundred fifty calories. On the other hand, a medium-sized potato, a member of the starch family often accused of fattening us, contains only sixty calories. On a scale the potato outweighs the hamburger patty two to one; in my metabolism the hamburger alone—without bun, without ketchup, without fried onions—is four times more fattening than the potato.

Here the writer uses comparison and contrast with the clear objective of persuading his audience; purpose is clear, and clear also is the writer's general notion of audience.

Comparison and contrast can be a tool for judgment and decision. We compare sweaters or used cars before we buy one; we compare colleges before we choose where to apply. But we also compare and contrast simply to define or to explain. When we say that a hamburger is fattening, what does the statement mean? Is it fattening compared to a mushroom? Is it fattening compared to a gallon of ice cream? To make the word *fattening* mean anything, we require comparisons; comparison and contrast define one word.

In a paper for a government course, we might compare another country's representative government with America's, to illuminate the differences or to understand our own system better, by seeing its familiar shape against the unfamiliar background of a different system. It is not necessary, in comparison and contrast, to take sides. Although comparison and contrast often contribute to argument, we can use this pattern for exposition alone. So often, in our real lives, it is not clear which alternative is preferable: if we are accepted at three good colleges, it may seem to make no difference which one we attend. Still, we can list differences and characteristics, like locale: rural, urban, small-town. We can find distinctions to compare and contrast, to set matters out for understanding—in the hope that clarity may facilitate choice.

Using comparison and contrast does not imply that we must make a choice among matters compared. Many reports required in the professional world do not require a decision from the reporter. Maybe we are asked to explain the differences among office systems supplied by Wang, IBM, Apple, and Xerox. Studying, classifying, we set out the differences; our bosses will do the choosing. On some occasions comparison and contrast results in a hung jury. On others, the essayist plays the role of researcher and then of decider: we can reach an audience by comparing and contrasting with apparent impartiality, and then explain that we have demonstrated superiority by juxtaposition.

We compare and contrast things which have something in common, and which have some differences as well. *M*A*S*H* and *Hogan's Heroes* are both television shows set during a war, but they also differ. *War and Peace* and *Anna Karenina* are both novels, both by Leo Tolstoy—and they differ considerably. Things compared must have enough in common and enough in contrast, and a purpose must be served in making the comparison. What is this comparison *for?* To compare *War and Peace* and *Love's Wicked Surrender*, it may not be enough that both are novels. What purpose do we serve by comparing them? Maybe if we address an audience that does not know the difference, our essay serves a purpose.

Whenever we compare and contrast, we face a structural problem. How long do we go on talking about A's qualities before we move to the contrasting qualities of B? If we balance each sentence with a look at both A and B, the alternation will be too swift; our heads snap back and forth as if we were watching Ping-Pong again, and our necks get stiff. A student wrote:

> Green olives are an acquired taste, which I've thought ever since my sister's wedding reception when I got sick after eating twenty of them. Now I like black olives better. Green olives come in three sizes, Large, Extra Large, and Gigantic. Black olives have four, Huge, Colossal, Supercolossal, and Absolutely Enormous. You can buy green olives with pits, or stuffed with those awful little red things, or maybe onions. Black olives are sold with or without pits (so you don't have to hide them under your plate, or in your mother's African violets). Green olives are packed in squatty green jars. Black olives are piled into tall jars or in cans with wild labels.

These sentences give us whiplash. On the other hand, if we talk about A for ten pages before we get to B, we create another problem. When the reader starts seeing, on page eleven, the qualities of B that correspond to the earlier qualities of A, he has forgotten the details ten pages back. Always keep the audience in mind, and beware the confusion of too-swift alternation or of too-distant comparison.

In comparison and contrast the order of the points is essential; we must keep them parallel. If we are comparing and contrasting educational institutions according to admission policy, class size, and tuition, we must be sure that the points proceed in the same order in our speaking of each institution. If we use one order for one institution and a different order for the other, we lose the reader in a jumble of incoherence:

> Alice is taller than her sister Josephine, but Josephine has naturally curly hair like her father, and stands on the short side. Alice's hair is blond and straight like Uncle George's, and she likes to play tennis. Josephine plays the violin, but prefers jazz and disco music.

Because these comparisons jump back and forth, we have difficulty following them.

Analogy is sometimes described as a form of comparison. Analogy looks for similarity in things that may appear very different to make a point. According to Oswald Spengler, civilizations like organisms go through a life span, are born, live, and die. But civilizations, literally speaking, are *not* organisms like mosquitoes and sequoias. Spengler's analogy compares political and social forms with living, growing, breeding, dying organisms, in order to attribute a life span to institutions. Analogy is different enough from ordinary comparison and contrast so that we took it up on pages 137–138, after we discussed simile and metaphor.

Thinking by Comparison and Contrast

We think by contrasted examples; we define by difference. The caloric value of hamburgers is clarified by a contrast with potatoes. Probably every essay we write can use comparison and contrast as we develop paragraphs. As a larger tool of thought, comparison and contrast forms a system of perception by opposition that requires us to classify parallel items and juxtapose similarities and differences. The trick in writing, as we present compared and contrasted material to an audience, is to tread a line between too-rapid oscillation and too-separate characterization of each. When we plan an essay of comparison and contrast, and when we look for a structure after generating the material, we may find it especially useful to sketch an informal outline.

Examples of Comparison and Contrast

Eating Apples and Cooking Apples

Apples generally fall into one of two categories—those good for eating and those good for cooking. What makes a good eating apple? For one thing the skin should be pleasant to taste—not too thick or waxy and never bitter. The pulp should be pleasantly sweet without added sugar, and the texture should be crisp and moist, not dry or mealy. A perfectly fresh McIntosh is the best eating apple there is—soon after picking. After a couple of days the skin loses its tender crispness and the pulp becomes mushy. The McIntosh is a poor keeper, as the best eating apples tend to be; they are an ephemeral delight.

Because the skin of a cooking apple is usually removed in making apple pastries and sauces, a tough skin is no impediment. The thick and waxy skin of the Rome Beauty covers firm flesh, perhaps a little drier than the McIntosh, so that a Rome Beauty will never turn to mush when it's cooked. In general the drier, firmer-fleshed apples are good keepers that hold their shape in pies and pastries.

Finally, the qualities that make a good eating or cooking apple are a subjective matter. I hate the Delicious apple in all its incarnations, and yet to go to the supermarket in January you would think that it is the only apple that has come down to us from the Garden of Eden. Because she was not making pies that day, Eve was probably reaching for a McIntosh, a Granny Smith, or possibly an Empire—a cross between a McIntosh and a Delicious that has the succulent sweetness of the Mac and the firmness of the Delicious.

A Choice for the Home Gardener

Old-fashioned apple trees grow twenty-five feet high and nearly as wide. One tree can displace a large portion of a suburban or city garden. But botanists have solved the space problem by grafting standard-variety branches onto the roots of dwarf trees that grow from nine to fifteen feet high.

Saving space is not the only convenience of the smaller trees. Gardeners can put away their ladders; they can prune, spray, and harvest dwarfs and semidwarf apple trees while standing on the ground. Also, these trees are quicker to mature, yielding fruit several years before their standard-sized progenitors.

On the other hand, if you're looking for lots of apples, the standard varieties might be best. Remember that you need good storage facilities, or equipment for making cider, or a market for your produce. But if you simply wish to provide your family with home-grown apples in modest quantities, the smaller trees may serve your purposes better, both for health and for beauty, for pink and white blossoms in the spring, for fresh fruit in the fall.

Process Analysis: "How did it happen? How does it work?"

In Chapter 3, when we looked into methods of essay writing, from assignment through note-taking and brainstorming and sprinting, through drafts and revisions, we used the rhetorical pattern of process analysis. *Analysis* separates things into components; with *process analysis* we investigate the components (or steps) in a sequence. When we observed the history of Frank Rodriguez writing an essay, we analyzed a process.

Process analysis is the rhetorical tool by which we explain the steps and sequences in an operation. We can separate two common categories of process analysis according to their purposes. We give directions by process analysis: how to run a political campaign; how to bake an apple pie. Or we give information by process analysis: how Nixon was elected in 1972; how Julia Child learned to make knishes. For each, we narrate the steps in a process. Strategy differs according to purpose, according to our relationship to an audience: either we instruct our audience in the art of winning public elections or we tell them how it was done.

Exposition or explanation commonly needs process analysis, which answers the question "How?" *How* is a car manufactured? *How* does the internal combustion engine work? *How* do you change a tire?

The answers to these questions differ from one another in tone: the answer to the first might make a scientific article; the answer to the second would be a feature story in a newspaper; the answer to the third would be a set of practical directions. But the three are alike in *pattern:* in each answer, exposition analyzes a process, a continuing sequence of events. Process analysis describes sequence or chronology. This pattern demands that we follow chronological order, advancing from a beginning by steps to an end.

When our analysis of process explains how something is made— automobile, perfume, skyscraper—we have something like an encyclopedia article. The writer's task is narrative and often descriptive; the writer must struggle to clarify scenes and actions for the reader. Where process analysis gives directions—how to change a tire, how to make waffles, how to find an apartment in Manhattan—the writer must take special care to consider the audience's level of knowledge. When we give directions we assume that we know something that our audience does not know. Therefore, in a process analysis essay giving directions, we have to remain aware of audience, especially by defining terms. If we write scientific or mechanical process analysis, we usually require much definition. How do you change a tire? We must define *lug* for a reader who does not know a lug from a roofing nail.

Thinking with Process Analysis

We must be wary of confusing process analysis with cause and effect. If we write an essay on *why* yeast makes flour and water rise in a bread pan, we write a scientific explanation, in which necessary effect follows particular cause. But if we write an essay on *how* to bake bread, with a recipe and steps of action, we analyze a process. If we bring the chemistry lab into the kitchen, mixing up *how* and *why*, the essay may become incoherent through internal disorder. Keep *why* distinct from *how*, cause and effect from process analysis. Or if the shape of your essay requires that you use both patterns one after the other, be certain that you retain control.

Encyclopedia articles often show how exposition works as process analysis—by addressing the *how* of a process, explaining how crude oil becomes gasoline and how gasoline makes the internal combustion engine work. At the same time, the scientific entries in the encyclopedia tell us why gasoline is flammable and why parts of the world are richer in petroleum deposits than others. Cause and effect analysis is analogous to the science of the laboratory; process analysis is more like engineering and applied science.

Process analysis, like the other rhetorical patterns, can make a whole essay or a small part of one. Suppose you had a general interest in forms of energy. You might begin a paper by classifying energy according to its sources: oil, fission, wind, coal, water, sun. You might compare and contrast the sources. Focusing on petroleum you might narrate the journey of crude oil from discovery to extraction to refining to transportation to retail sales to vehicle. This narration would be a sequential, chronological analysis of process. This analysis could occupy most of an essay, with much detail; or, cut down with skill, it could become a paragraph or two.

When we revise any paper, we should look through it to recognize the rhetorical pattern of process analysis. Sometimes a writer approaches this pattern without realizing it, and uses it badly by omitting definition or by leaving the analysis incomplete. If we refer to a process we must detail or explain it for an audience that might not be aware of its progress; we must include all the necessary steps. We must look back to see whether we have defined terms with a clear notion of audience.

An Example of Process Analysis

Planting an Apple Tree

The first step is to choose the appropriate site. Apple trees flourish best on rolling land; planting on the sides or tops of hills allows cold air to drain away during potentially damaging frosty spring nights. Hilly terrain also provides good water drainage; apples cannot abide wet feet.

Once the site is chosen, the next step is soil preparation. Where topsoil is shallow the subsoil should be enriched with organic matter, with compost; in sandy soils, we should mix compost with peat.

Plant the young tree no deeper than it grew in the nursery, spreading the roots well in the hole. Put the topsoil back first, and tamp it firmly with your foot. Water well, allowing the water to drain completely into the soil. Then finish filling the hole with the subsoil. If you dug up sod to plant the tree, replace the sod face down, and mulch with three or four inches of hay, straw, or leaf mold. Give the tree another good soak, and don't allow the soil to dry out for at least ten days.

Definition: "What is it?"

To define, we may need to analyze a process, or to present an example, or to use other rhetorical patterns—but definition, however we achieve it, is itself a pattern of rhetoric. We list it last because it combines so much. Definition often groups things that are alike and differentiates them from unlike things; in this mode it uses comparison and contrast, or at least comparison, as when a dictionary defining *portal* resorts to synonyms (see pages 89–91) for comparison: *entrance, door, entryway.*

Classification is often crucial to definition. We begin to define something by naming the class it belongs to.

A car is a vehicle. A sparrow hawk is a bird. Then the definition distinguishes the particular species from other members of its class by means of contrasting examples: a car is mechanical, unlike a horse; it is self-propelled, unlike a bicycle. If we look up *sparrow hawk*, we find first that it is a bird and then, in narrowing details, what sort of a bird it is: its characteristics, its markings, its habits. We go from the broadest classification—*bird*—to the narrowest description of bands of color.

Definition must often move deeply into description. Some portions of definition—like naming the bands that distinguish one bird from another—require exact observation, adjectives of color, details of width in inches or millimeters. An ichthyologist, telling us about a newly discovered Antarctic fish, needs description as much as he needs classification.

Frequently we need definition in exposition to clarify matters for an audience. In analyzing the process of changing a tire, we may realize that the reader needs to know what a lug is. In writing about downhill skiing, perhaps we mention moguls. If we think of our audience, we know that we must define *mogul*, because readers who have not skied may find *mogul* an obscure word.

When writing for a general audience, always define a word that comes from a particular sport or pastime, discipline or profession. Such definition is invaluable, in the service of clarity. We use simple definition in our writing when we recognize: this is the kind of word that would drive me to the dictionary if I wasn't familiar with its use in this context.

The types of definition illustrated above are simple: we define by near-synonym, by description, and by class. We need simple definitions in order to reach an audience quickly, to clarify with economy, but the brief elucidation of terms is incidental to the larger purposes of an essay. On another level, definition may fill the largest purposes of all. One might call Plato's *Republic* a huge definition of *mind.* Although we would not write a whole essay to define *lug*, as thinking human beings we may write at length to define an abstraction like *courtesy.* Thought about such an abstraction follows the rhetorical pattern of definition. The meaning of *sparrow hawk*, like the meaning of *vacuum cleaner* or *Abraham Lincoln*, is agreed upon. But suppose we define a subjective or philosophical word: *conservatism* or *imagination* or *romanticism* or *democracy.* We can write an entire essay to define the ideas required for a deep understanding of such a word; we can write a book—we can write a library of books. Definition is the rhetorical form most common to philosophical writers. Wanting to understand *wisdom,* or *good,* or *literature,* or *social class,* we pursue philosophical definition. These definitions may require us to use other patterns of rhetoric. To define *democracy,* we must compare and contrast it to other forms of government. To define *maturity* we need to classify stages of growth; the movement from one to the next is process analysis. Almost every definition cries out for examples: of *literature,* of *courtesy.* Our thinking's purpose determines our essay's pattern; and purpose as usual requires a sense of audience.

Thinking by Definition

When we revise, it is imperative to check back for undefined terms. Sometimes we fall into using a special vocabulary incomprehensible to our readers. More often, we use vague or general words (*conservative, middle class*) without defining them, without allowing our audience to understand how we use them in the context of our thought. For the first lack we can supply quick definitions perhaps by synonyms or classification; the trick is knowing that they are needed. For the second, probably the best revision would replace a vague word with a more particular phrase. But if we cannot discover the right particular, we can supply a definition for the term. We must take some time to define an abstraction as we use it. Or we can write a whole essay to explore the meaning of the abstraction.

When we write a whole essay of definition, we should reconsider the other rhetorical patterns, to judge which of the modes (possibly two or three of them) will best deliver our understanding to our audience. Defining one word, do not forget to check its etymology in the *Oxford English Dictionary* or in other dictionaries that supply the sources and history of words. (See Chapter 4.) Although essays that open with a reference to the dictionary ("*Webster's* defines *democracy* as . . .") are common to the point of cliché, the writer will sometimes discover that a word's origins provide an image, almost an example, which gives color to definition and helps to make contact with an audience. Thus, the root *demos* in "democracy," meaning *common people,* alerts us to a shade of meaning we may wish to emphasize in an essay on the differences between Democratic and Republican parties.

Examples of Definition

The American Apple Pie

Apple pie, as we know it in this country, consists of slices of this fruit, mixed with sugar and seasoning, baked inside a crust of dough.

Usually cooked and served in a shallow, round dish, this desert is as common as the flag and as American as apple pie.

Apples and Evil

The most useful fruits, apples first discovered their utility in the definition of sin. It was sin, or evil, for man and woman to eat the fruit that God forbade them to eat, the tree that bore the knowledge of good and evil. It seems that the writers of the Old Testament, or at least the authors of Genesis, believed that there is no evil without consciousness of evil. Although it would be illogical therefore to equate consciousness with evil, we can at least acknowledge that after we have eaten the fruit of the knowledge of good and evil, true innocence is no longer possible. Once that consciousness exists, we are moral beings, prone to the evil or sin that we are born to, and subject to the moral universe. Evil is disobedience, and it is also a result of disobedience, but if there were no evil there could be no possibility of good. From early in the history of the Christian church, thinkers have recognized this paradox. If Adam and Eve had not disobeyed God, if man had not fallen, Jesus would have had nothing and no one to redeem. This is the paradox of the fortunate fall, the happy sin, by which traditional Christians find themselves praising the wicked eating of an apple in paradise.

Narration: "What happened?"

With narrative we tell a story; we recount events in succession and tell what happened. Much of our everyday conversation tells stories.

By itself narrative is a form of writing parallel to exposition, description, and argument or persuasion. But narrative is also used in the service of other forms. With process analysis we narrate as we explain how something works in a sequence. When we use example, sometimes our example is a story. Narrative (the history of innovative baking, the campaign of Cyrus against the Greeks) may support argument. Much newspaper reporting is narrative, of murders and baseball games. Telling a joke is narrative.

When we tell a story, we must find our way between two extremes. The narrative must have enough detail so that the reader knows what is happening. But it must not have so much detail that the reader gets bogged down. The detail must be appropriate; it must have the right quality, as well as the right quantity, and the audience must be able to follow and appreciate the motion of sequence. Here is a fragment from a paper.

When I heard the doorbell, I stood immediately, my heart pounding. I knew it was her. I didn't answer it quickly, and heard the door opening toward me. I must have forgotten to lock it! I looked around for a second. Then I picked up my suitcase and climbed through the open window.

This was the first version:

> When I heard the doorbell, I placed my hands against the arms of the chair and pushed myself upright immediately. My heart pounded in my chest. I knew it was her. For some reason, I didn't move toward the door right away. I just stood there and stared, my heart pounding, my legs shaking. Then I heard a sound like the doorknob turning, and a creaky noise as she must have started to push the door open. I realized that I had forgotten to lock it when I came in from the drug store. I looked all around to see if there was any way to escape. I saw the window open beside me. Without thinking of what I was doing, I picked up my suitcase, checked the fasteners on it, set it on the windowsill and lowered it to the ground, which was only about 2½ feet down. Then I sat down on the sill myself, swinging my legs through, and pulled the rest of my body after me.

This student was commendably rich in detail. But by the end, we feel as if we have watched someone sleep eight hours. We have stopped paying attention, for total recall is totally boring. We want the essential narrative and nothing more. The revision does it. If the writer had gone further in cutting and had written

> When I heard the doorbell, I climbed out the widow.

we would have missed some crucial information. We must always be sensitive to audience—how much is needed? How much is too much when we tell a story?

The time we take to tell a story need have little to do with the elapsed time of the event itself. Writing about a football game, we may spend two pages on one play that took only twenty seconds of the game. When we finish narrating this crucial play, we might summarize the other fifty-nine minutes and forty seconds in a brief paragraph. Purpose, and clarity for audience, determine narrative—not fidelity to the original duration of things.

The structure or order of narrative is often uncomplicated, a straightforward sequence of events as they happen: first this occurred, then that. But on some occasions we begin our story with its ending, then flash back and tell in chronological order the events that led up to the conclusion. Reading a sports story, no one wishes to wait until the end of the story to find out who won. The journalist's lead paragraph tells us the outcome; then usually the reporter will narrate the progress of the game with detailed attention to crucial moments.

In narrative we need to be aware of the point of view from which we tell the story. If we tell about three people, it is confusing when we skip from one point of view to another. If it is not actually obscure it is incoherent and displeasing. Here is an anecdote with a confused point of view:

> Indignant, the dwarf climbed to the ceiling and perched in the candelabrum, hissing and spitting like a frightened cat. Griselda watched in fascination but with growing terror. Rumpelstiltskin made up his mind to act.

We should stay inside the mind of one of the three characters. If we must switch from one side to another—if we narrate the siege of Troy, in an epic, we might need to move from Greek intentions to Trojan beliefs—we must strive to make clear transitions. When we switch point of view, we must be open about it.

Transitions can be a problem. Telling a story out loud, we may fall into a pattern: ". . . and then . . . and then . . . and then. . . ." Writing it down we should be more careful. We may need *later*; we may need *meanwhile*; a strong narrative makes these words obvious and very often unnecessary.

Here is a passage from a book by a doctor who spent a year in Vietnam. It begins with exposition and ends with narrative.

> The western perimeter of the camp bordered on a "free-fire zone." Anyone or anything that moves in that area is free game and can be shot, mortared, or bombed. All of the military maps had it marked as such and supposedly all civilians in the area had been informed.
>
> The camp dump was in this "free-fire zone." Each morning at the same time a truck drove out to the dump and all of the tin cans, cardboard containers, wrappers, and garbage from the camp was dumped about fifty meters inside the zone. Within minutes, the dump was filled with Vietnamese from nearby villes (hamlets) gathering cans and garbage. The marines in the watchtower would fire close to them to frighten them away. A few days earlier, an eight-year-old Vietnamese boy had been wounded by these warning shots and was brought to the aid station where he was kept until his wounds were healed. One day he stole an orange soda from a marine who shot and killed him as he tried to run away.
>
> John A. Parrish, M.D., *12, 20 & 5*

This is a good example of narrative used in exposition and ultimately, as you can see, in an argument about war's brutality that does not need stating.

An Example of Narration

Trouble in the Orchard

When Richard Bone woke on an October night two years ago, he felt that something was wrong without knowing why he felt as he did. He pulled on a coat over his nightshirt; he pulled long boots lined with felt over his bare feet. Then he set out the back door into his orchard where he had spent a long day with his neighbors picking trees of their ripe apples. At first he saw nothing out of order. Then he made a series of observations in quick succession. First, there was a large bird's nest in an old tree where there had been no bird's nest earlier that afternoon. Second, there was a dog underneath the tree, which made Bone remember that it was a howling sound which had waked him.

But third, he knew that the bird's nest was not a bird's nest, and that the dog was not a dog.

What looked like a bird's nest was a hedgehog come to banquet on his McIntoshes. What looked like a dog was an Eastern coyote or coydog. When Bone returned with his shotgun, the coyote had departed. The hedgehog had not—but it was soon among the departed.

Description

Description often becomes necessary for clear exposition, and we use it sometimes within rhetorical patterns: in classification, in definition, in comparison and contrast, and elsewhere. Description serves the essayist's purpose, and reaches the reader, when it contrasts the coloring of apples; for this contrast, each apple must be described. Description by itself amasses details to *evoke* place, scene, or time of day; we feel that we are there. Evocative description, of course, frequently forms a part of fiction and autobiography. Here is how James Agee begins to describe the remembered summer evenings of childhood:

> Supper was at six and was over by half past. There was still daylight, shining softly and with a tarnish, like the lining of a shell; and the carbon lamps lifted at the corners were on in the light, and the locusts were started, and the fire flies were out, and a few frogs were flopping in the dewy grass, by the time the fathers and the children came out.
>
> James Agee, "Knoxville: Summer 1915"

The order we give to details, in description, is usually *spatial*. But words follow each other—they are not simultaneous in the way a picture seems to be—and we necessarily move in words from point to point in a sequence that has to be chronological. So in description we talk about space by taking steps in time. In describing a scene, we can begin from the periphery and move to the center or move from the center to the periphery. The order is not always crucial: it is crucial that there *be* an order, that we do not move from center to periphery to center to periphery to periphery.

Description can move from precise objective measurement (6.5 inches long) to subjective exaggeration (as big as an aircraft carrier). In much writing, we mix these extremes according to purpose and audience. If we write scientifically, we remain objective and exclude the subjective. On the other hand, when we write to make the reader feel with us, we often use figures of speech and subjectively exaggerated images to embody emotions and to touch the reader.

Some writers seem to think of description as filler or padding—not only beginning writers, but also so-called professionals who write the less skillful stories in adventure or confession magazines, and are paid by the word. In these stories, we may see description used to delay information, to tantalize.

> Rhonda turned from the window, her eyes wet. "Belinda," she said to me, "I could forgive you for Ron. I could forgive you for Bruce. I could even forgive you for Althea. But there is one thing I could never forgive you for!"
>
> She turned back to the window, her eyes flooded with tears. My cheeks suffused with shame. Over her shoulders, I could see the sweet meadows of home, adeck with lilacs and daisies, their sleepy heads waving in the soft breezes of June, while above, storm clouds gathered to chase away the white puff-ball clouds of early morning.
>
> "They Had a Name for Me," *Real Romance*

Description's main function here seems to be to create suspense, as a delaying tactic to keep the reader on edge. To be sure, such writing also shows a heavy-handed attempt to use description as a good writer does, *for the meaning and the feeling that images carry*. This anonymous writer has the protagonist look at the fields in an attempt to symbolize her past innocence, contrasted to the torment ("storm clouds") of the sinful present.

Description must be believable if it is to reach the reader. Evocations that appear to be pure symbolism lessen the reader's involvement. But there is room for invention, especially when we use comparisons (simile, metaphor, analogy; see pages 134–138) that carry feeling.

In *Ulysses*, James Joyce has Stephen Dedalus look at the sea when he is feeling depressed. "The ring of bog and skyline held a dull green mass of liquid." Though the description is literal enough, it expresses Stephen's emotions. Here is a passage from the book about Vietnam from which I quoted earlier. The author describes finding some bodies washed up on a riverbank.

> Four nude, markedly swollen, water-logged bodies lay side by side on their backs. Each had a massively swollen face. Eyes seemed to try to bulge out of sockets whose contents were as big as apples. Their lips were three times normal size and each mouth was open and round like that of a fish, with a massive splitting tongue protruding skyward. A thin, bloody fluid trickled from their nostrils.
>
> Massive edema and rigor mortis held their arms up and out in front of them with fat fingers reaching toward the clouds. Their

scrota were the size of softballs, and their swollen penises stood as if erect. Their knees were bent in identical frog-leg positions. The smell was overwhelming and hundreds of flies circled around those which were already busy inspecting the mouths and nostrils. There was not a mark on the front of their bodies.

John A. Parrish, M.D., 12, 20 & 5

The accurate description has modifiers that come from fresh observation, not from the worn tracks: *fat* fingers, *frog-leg* positions, *massively swollen*; it has statements of fact and measurement, like "massive edema" and "three times normal size"; it has comparisons that embody feeling, like "mouth . . . open and round like that of a fish," " . . . as big as apples," and "scrota . . . the size of softballs." Parrish's purpose is to move (repel) his audience; he succeeds by the manner of his description. The reader is forced to visualize the scene.

Statistical accuracy in description must never be confused with emotional accuracy. Again, sometimes we must lie to tell the truth. A contemporary poem ends with a sudden vision: a hundred cows in a field. Reviewing this poem, a hostile critic (carried away by his anger into absurdity) asked *how* the poet could tell that exactly one hundred cows were in the field. He received a postcard from the poet: "I counted the teats and divided by four." The poetic approximation has a long tradition. It does not lie, because we know that it is not intended to be statistically accurate. When Wordsworth says of daffodils, "Ten thousand saw I at a glance," we do not suspect him of counting. If we write, "The sandwich was as thick as the toe of Italy," we are saying that it was very thick—so thick that it astounded and delighted us. If we say, "The sandwich was two and five-eighths inches thick," we are being pedantic, and expressing little astonishment. Mere accuracy is all right, but the exaggeration is a lie that is truer to the feeling than accuracy is. Sometimes in writing you can be accurate in both ways at once; maybe a list of ingredients could be literally true and so carry an astonished reaction to abundance: "salami, bologna, ham, roast beef, corned beef, Swiss cheese, provolone, onions, lettuce, red peppers, olive oil, vinegar, and, I believe, oregano."

Although we use description for many purposes, we also use it purely, and many instructors assign brief descriptive papers or paragraphs for practice in description, much as they assign exercises in the rhetorical patterns. Here is a description of an apple orchard:

An Example of Description

Bone's Orchard

The orchard faced north on a gentle slope above the farmhouse and the barn. The trees were evenly spaced, and from the hills across the valley the orchard looked like the squares of a quilt. In spring the massive blossoms turned the slope a uniform white. All summer the green leaves of the mature trees blended into the grass of the hill, and the orchard seemed to retreat into a greened shade. In autumn, as one approached the orchard, one became aware of a rich harvest of redness weighing down the old boughs. For a few weeks ladders and apple-pickers poked among the trees, until the fruit was picked clean, packed into crates for shipment to stores, or squeezed into gallons of fresh, tangy cider. In winter the black leafless branches looked starved and skinny against the snow.

Notice that this writer has started close up, moved farther back, and then moved close again—while following the chronological order of the seasons.

Rhetorical patterns, then, along with narration and description, are the structuring devices essential to anyone who writes. It does not matter what purpose the prose is to serve, or what audience it is directed to, for these modes are closely linked to the structure of all human thought. They describe the possible movements of that thought much as the laws of physics describe the basic behavior of bodies in space. The best thing we can do for our writing is to study and practice these patterns until their use becomes second nature.

_____ **EXERCISES** _____

1. Prepare for in-class discussion one paragraph on a topic of your choice. The paragraph should make use of two rhetorical patterns. Class members will be asked to identify the patterns and to comment on their usefulness.

2. Here are ten topics. For each topic, make notes employing one of the rhetorical patterns; among your sets of notes, include all seven rhetorical patterns. For instance, if the topic were thunderstorms, you could *classify* them, discerning sorts of storms; you could tell how they occur, by *process analysis*; or you could *define* a thunderstorm. Discuss in class the purposes served by suggested patterns.

pollution	snowmobiles
baseball	zoos
cousins	freshmen
state parks	graveyards
supermarkets	shoes

3. In class discussion, discover ways of using all seven rhetorical patterns, in addition to narrative and description, in writing about one subject. (See the series of apple essays in this chapter.) Try automobiles, houses, books, or fast-food franchises. Discuss the

purposes each pattern can serve. Notice how the patterns engender ideas.

This exercise can lead to a written assignment.

4. Divide the class into seven groups, one for each rhetorical pattern. Let each member of each group find in a current newspaper or magazine an example of the assigned pattern.

5. Find rhetorical patterns and forms of exposition in textbooks for other courses. Notice the modes of thought appropriate to different disciplines—history, psychology, business—and the characteristic patterns or forms that these disciplines require. Is history narrative above all? What else is it?

6. Here are four passages from essays. Determine which rhetorical pattern or patterns are employed in each. Determine the purposes for each pattern.

a. To test properly the mechanic removes the plug and lays it against the engine so that the base around the plug is electrically grounded, kicks the starter lever and watches the spark-plug gap for a blue spark. If there isn't any he can conclude one of two things: (a) there is an electrical failure or (b) his experiment is sloppy. If he is experienced he will try a few more times, checking connections, trying every way he can think of to get that plug to fire. Then, if he can't get it to fire, he finally concludes that *a* is correct, there's an electrical failure, and the experiment is over. He has proved that his hypothesis is correct.

Robert M. Pirsig, *Zen and the Art of Motorcycle Maintenance*

b. Paradox surfaces at dinner. That my boys are radically unlike each other is no news, but it takes a new shape. Tim's in favor of capital punishment, admires the word *conservative*, thinks "as long as we were in Vietnam we should have gone all out to win." I would think these views natural to the age of fourteen if he had not always been conservative, preferred the most disciplined of his teachers, shown extreme modesty from the age of six. Alex at eleven is radical-liberal in all his views, political, sexual, social. At five he defended his right to play house by announcing he was a feminist. Confessed to me last year with real and obvious guilt that the idea of homosexuality "put him off, so far." Yet Tim is personally a peacemaker and Alex an authoritarian. I also, I notice, am a liberal and a troublemaker. And Freen, who has never been known to make an issue where there is none, is the paradigm of the Willing To Let Live, often surprises me by the firmness of his discipline, sometimes makes me uneasy with the brutality of his wit, now amazes me by defending Tim. He has no patience with disruptive activists, will not espouse feminism as a Cause but only, perpetually, in practice.

—Janet Burroway, "Opening Nights: The Opening Days"
from *The Writer on Her Work*

c. The first baseline in defining Presidential types is *activity-passivity*. How much energy does the man invest in his Presidency? Lyndon Johnson went at his day like a human cyclone, coming to rest long after the sun went down. Calvin Coolidge often slept eleven hours a night and still needed a nap in the middle of the day. In between the Presidents array themselves on the high or low side of the activity line.

The second baseline is *positive-negative affect* toward one's activity—that is, how he feels about what he does. Relatively speaking, does he seem to experience his political life as happy or sad, enjoyable or discouraging, positive or negative in its main effect? The feeling I am after here is not grim satisfaction in a job well done, not some philosophical conclusion. The idea is this: is he someone who, on the surfaces we can see, gives forth the feeling that he has *fun* in political life? Franklin Roosevelt's Secretary of War, Henry L. Stimson, wrote that the Roosevelts "not only understood the *use* of power, they knew the *enjoyment* of power, too. . . . Whether a man is burdened by power or enjoys power; whether he is trapped by responsibility or made free by it; whether he is moved by other people and outer forces or moves them—that is the essence of leadership."

James David Barber, The Presidential Character

d. What is pornography to one man is the laughter of genius to another.

The word itself, we are told, means "pertaining to harlots—the graph of the harlot. But nowadays, what is a harlot? If she was a woman who took money from a man in return for going to bed with him—really, most wives sold themselves, in the past, and plenty of harlots gave themselves, when they felt like it, for nothing. If a woman hasn't got a tiny streak of harlot in her, she's a dry stick as a rule. And probably most harlots had somewhere a streak of womanly generosity. Why be so cut and dried? The law is a dreary thing, and its judgments have nothing to do with life. . . .

One essay on pornography, I remember, comes to the conclusion that pornography in art is that which is calculated to arouse sexual desire, or sexual excitement. And stress is laid on the fact, whether the author or artist *intended to* arouse sexual feelings. It is the old vexed question of intention, become so dull today, when we know how strong and influential our unconscious intentions are. And why a man should be held guilty of his conscious intentions, and innocence of his unconscious intentions, I don't know, since every man is more made up of unconscious intentions than of conscious ones. I am what I am, not merely what I think I am.

D. H. Lawrence, "Pornography,"
in Pornography and Obscenity

8

Argument and Persuasion

In Chapter 7 we covered exposition and rhetorical patterns, then took a look at the uses of narrative and description. Now we turn our attention to argument and persuasion, a large category of writing useful far beyond the classroom. Like the other modes we have studied, argument and persuasion make use of certain patterns and habits of thought. Many of these are second nature to us; we resort to them without thinking as soon as we want to convince someone to do something or to agree with us. We argue and attempt to persuade when we give our friends reasons for taking a particular weekend trip. We do the same when we try to sell ourselves on the merits of one course over another. The basic procedure is simple: we line up the best reasons we can think of, and we try to anticipate objections so that we can counter them with convincing assertions. Writing to argue and persuade, we use the same tactics, only in a more formal manner.

The terms "argument" and "persuasion" are similar, but they are not synonyms. Persuasion has a more general application: when we persuade someone we move them; we bring them over to our way of doing or seeing things. Argument is a means of persuasion, the setting out of a logical structure by which we move the other person to accept our view. The steps of an argument are like the rungs of a ladder; by climbing them the person arrives at a new position. Our position.

In the first paragraph we used the phrase "to sell ourselves" to characterize the process of persuasion. The verb *sell* gives us another way to look at the matter. Argument and persuasion are, in effect, the selling of a point of view. We approach the undecided or doubtful party—sometimes it is ourselves we are trying to convince—like a car salesman moving in on a prospective customer. "Look," we say, "you won't find a better value than this." We go on to itemize: it has this and this and this and this . . . (We describe). You may think the Flame-thrower gets better mileage or has a longer warranty, but in fact . . . (We compare and contrast). Our engineers and researchers have been testing this model over a specially designed course . . . (We use process analysis). Their tests have shown that the specially designed suspension system, because it uses a new alloy . . . (We use cause and effect).

The point should be clear: while persuasion and argumentation have goals different from exposition, they make use at every turn of expository tactics. Indeed, without an expository foundation, most argumentative writing would collapse into bombast. Exposition provides the underpinnings for the built-up structure of persuasion.

In writing expository prose, we assemble details—facts, anecdotes, descriptions—to understand or to explain, not to take a position and support it. On occasion, we might seem to argue that something is superior to something else—say, the Cubist painters to the Impressionists—when we are really only giving our personal preference. If we explain our own likes and dislikes, we write exposition; we do not argue that anyone else should feel as we do. Exposing a preference is valid exposition. When we read someone else's praise of duck hunting, we can enjoy and understand it, without feeling any pressure to bag a bird for ourselves.

The honest writer avoids some forms of persuasion or attempted persuasion. "The rhetorician would deceive his neighbors, / The sentimentalist himself "—as we quoted before from W. B. Yeats—and in much dishonest writing the writer fails on one or both counts. To indulge in rhetoric is to inflate or otherwise distort expression. Politicians on the campaign trail are commonly guilty of this abuse of language. Audiences may be impressed and swayed in the short run; in the long run they often discover that they have been cheated; and they are unforgiving. The same holds true for writer and reader.

The honest writer, then, argues on behalf of genuine beliefs; he does not claim to hold positions just to score a point. He avoids the favorite devices of the rhetorician and sentimentalist. The loaded word —when the dictator's police shoot "unarmed civilians" or "a traitorous rabble"—or loaded syntax—when the beer company's advertisement asks, "As a lawyer, what do you think of Fitz's?"—can combine to make a whole essay into a loaded argument, or propaganda. Words and phrases seem to say one thing and really say another. In good writing, we must avoid such subterfuge.

Persuasion, perceptible and imperceptible, is an element we live in; we breathe it in with our oxygen. We live in a country that promotes a marketplace of goods and ideas, and persuasion is one of our national industries. Although political speeches and newspaper editorials are obvious exercises in argument and persuasion, we are influenced to a far greater degree by the ubiquitous claims of advertising. We are subject to it daily on television and radio, in newspapers and magazines, over public address systems, and on billboards. Thousands—hundreds of thousands—of people spend their working lives trying to persuade us to buy this new car over that one, this scented cat food, this diet plan. We are the audience addressed by this mammoth industry; we are the readers whose responses they predict—and bank upon predicting. As we study argument and persuasion in English composition, we can start to identify and understand how those arts are practiced upon us in daily life.

Argument is not only external but internal. In our everyday lives, we argue with ourselves as we approach decisions: Look for a summer job or enroll in a computer course? Major in marketing or Chinese? Buy new running shoes or wear out our old ones and save the money? Every time we use the word "should" to ourselves we lurk in the vicinity of an argument. Argument does not have to be a matter of loud voices and thumping fists; argument can simply test alternatives. We ask ourselves: *this* or *that?* And as we do so we inevitably ask *why?* If we tune in closely to our normal thinking process, we will find that much of it includes this internal debate. We are arguing our way forward through the day, making choices, giving reasons; every move we make is an argument won.

USES FOR ARGUMENT

Knowing how to argue is a useful skill. We use it on ourselves in order to arrive at decisions; we use it with others as we discuss business strategies or policy changes on committees, as members of the local PTA, a law office, an environmental action group; we use it as fundraisers for a cause, like saving whales; we use it in applying for foundation grants and in drafting a letter to the editor of our hometown paper; we use it when we discuss child abuse, toxic waste, tax cuts, pothole repair, working mothers, and university investment policies. Our ability to express opinions persuasively—to present our views systematically as arguments—will allow us to make some difference in public life. If we lack the necessary skills, we are condemned to sit at the sidelines. Instead of doing the moving, we will be among the moved; more persuasive voices will convince us of what we must do.

Most of the time, in writing argument, we work with debatable material. We cannot prove our thesis as a mathematician or philosophical logician can, by manipulating his own terms. We cannot measure results in a cyclotron like a physicist. We end with probability and persuasion, not with certainty or proof. If we had verifiable certainty then argumentation would not be necessary: the verification would speak for itself. The *proof* we arrive at might be called "the agreement of reasonable people," which just happens to be one of the old-fashioned senses of the word.

Matters of fact are rarely arguable. When we disagree about the running time of the Boston Marathon, how many films Clark Gable made, or the population of Minneapolis, we can look it up. Disagreement about facts is pointless. And it is likewise pointless to argue about personal preference or taste. We either do or don't like gulf shrimp, punk rock, jogging, or polyester suits. There is little hope, and usually little purpose, in trying to persuade others to feel as we do.

But opinions—about value or worth, about meaning or interpretation, about solutions to problems—are arguable. People *differ* in their views about two-career marriages, bilingual education, book censorship, burning the flag, and a thousand other things. We have our own ideas about what is right, and we usually have reasons for thinking as we do. Through persuasion and argument we try to convince our parents, our friends, our employers, our neighbors, or our legislators.

AUDIENCE IN ARGUMENT AND PERSUASION

Argument is a process by which we persuade ourselves or others. Most argument in writing is, of course, directed outward, though we may have had to go through some inner debate in order to clarify our position to ourselves. Once we know what we believe, we face the next stage of the process: we must determine how to bring others around to our view. And while the steps of argumentation tend to follow a pattern of logic, the specific application of that pattern depends entirely upon whom we are trying to reach. A presentation on the perils of toxic waste disposal will be slanted one way to a group of environmentalists, another way altogether to lawyers representing the chemical industry. Before we can shoot, we have to find the target.

Market research identifies audiences for manufacturers; writers must make the decision on their own. The job is simpler when we stand to speak in front of an audience, and the comparison of the speaker's task to the writer's can illustrate the writer's difficulties. When we address a group of listeners, we can tell much about our audience by glancing around the room: age, economic status, sex, often degree of education, often social class. As we speak, we can test the success or failure of our efforts by observing the expressions on people's faces, by noting attention or inattention, by laughter, coughing, or applause.

But when we write an essay we address an unseen audience, and we cannot profit from response—unless we try out paragraphs on friends or roommates. When we write to persuade, we must work to keep the unseen audience in mind; we must try to visualize them, making a mental comparison between writing and public speaking, so that we can organize information, ideas, and reasons to elicit response from our real readers.

The first requirement is that we establish a believable, trustworthy presence. Our tone must meet our audience as equals, as if we were face to face. We must not speak down, as if to young children, nor should we appear to be hiding anything. Our tone must show our argument as fair, as open to modification or to further discussion. Argument needs to imply the process of dialogue, in which the other side has a voice. When we present the opposition view, as we often do in the course of making our points, we must treat it with respect, just as if we were hearing out the objections of an audience member. We gain nothing by being curt, shrill, or dismissive.

Tone of address to audience is fundamental. To find it we have to feel respect for the opposition. Often it helps to imagine a single person whose views and opinions differ from your own, but whom you value as an adversary. Think of a skeptical teacher or a friend with good debater's instincts. Write to convince, not to alienate. We lose our chance for a hearing unless we establish rapport and maintain it. Rapport depends first on identifying audience and then on using common sense in addressing it. When we give examples of the occasions for persuasion, we categorize by audience. An argument for breast feeding over formula feeding addressed to suburban American mothers would be very different from one addressed to Third World mothers. A plea for more police foot patrols would take a different form if we proposed it to residents of an urban neighborhood with high crime statistics than if we made the suggestion to a suburban neighborhood worried about taxes.

One important reason for locating the audience for the argument, aside from establishing an appropriate tone, is to help us to set out the context for the information. An argument moves forward from point to point, in sequence, giving facts and reasons. To know what to say and what to omit, or how precise to get, we have to know whom we are trying to convince. Recall the example of toxic waste disposal cited earlier. Not only is it essential that we know the disposition of the audience—whether members are environmentalists or corporation lawyers—but we must also know its level of competence. If we put together a mass of technical statistics for newly joined members of the Sierra Club, we risk losing their attention. We would risk the very same—or worse—if we presented the corporation lawyers with a beginner's lecture on the inadvisability of putting poisons in the earth.

The best way to assess an audience is to become it. Imagine for a few moments that you *are* the person you would like to reach. What kind of background information would you need? What would be the tone and approach most likely to make you prick up your ears and listen? What are some objections you might raise as you listened or read? Can you, as the writer, defuse objections in some way—by putting them into your essay and addressing them? Maneuvers like this are not only practically useful, but they also help develop the elasticity of mind that is an asset in all argumentative writing.

REASONABLENESS IN ARGUMENT

Most of the time, we persuade by being reasonable—and also by *seeming* so. The *being* comes from clear thinking and argumentative structure; the seeming is a matter of tone. We will *be* reasonable if we write with clarity and avoid typical errors of thinking (these will be taken up later). We will *seem* reasonable by refusing to be dogmatic or overly assertive, by allowing time to opposing points of view, and by writing with the modesty that distinguishes between fact and opinion. This does not mean that we should continually qualify our remarks by tagging them with phrases like *in my opinion;* it is more a matter of attitude. If we are writing about the Indiana Pacers and we assert that they ended the season badly, with a 44-58 win/loss record, we are not being dogmatic. If we come out and say "The Indiana Pacers are a terrible team and their disastrous season shows it," then we are airing out our own feelings; there is no necessity or logic in the utterance.

Of course it is natural to mix fact and opinion when we write. We are obligated for the sake of honest writing only to know which is which. A fact is information that can be documented from historical and scientific sources. ("Truth" is illusive; the scientific "facts" of one century may look like errors to another; a "fact" is what we can reasonably accept as true.) A fact is also a statement of personal experience that can be accepted as reasonable. "It rained all day, May 31, 1921" can be a fact; a check with the weather service of the place in question can bring confirmation. To say "Hester looked intelligent" is opinion, or surmise, and not fact. When we refer to someone else's documented opinion—"Her minister thought that Hester looked intelligent"—we are on the border between fact and opinion.

When we quote the minister, we have quoted an outside source, and this makes us appear objective; the source itself, however, is subjective, offering only opinion. We can use such a reference to help persuade, provided we do not lean on it too heavily. On the other hand, if we try to make the minister's opinion the fulcrum for our essay ("But contrary to her doctor's statement, we know from her minister that Hester looked intelligent. Therefore . . . "), the opinion will not move the rock of legitimate doubt and the essay will collapse. We have let ourselves seem unreasonable.

For persuasive argument, we must discover a tone that uses fact when it is relevant, inserts opinion modestly and reasonably, allows time for doubts and objections, and builds a sequential argument by paragraph steps that the reader can follow. Conviction is one thing, belligerence or insistence another. It is the difference between "Let me show you how I think and maybe you will begin to think as I do" and "Agree with me or else you're a fool!"

In the debate about cutbacks in federal funding for social programs, together with increases in defense spending, it is common for partisans of one side or the other to pretend that their opponents are warmongers who despise the poor or else bleeding hearts who think we need no army to protect ourselves. Telling arguments acknowledge that the opposition has its points. Here are sentences from two essays with different emphases:

> Although a strong defense is necessary for a country like the United States, which has worldwide interests and influence, we will jeopardize our future security if we neglect the real needs of the poor and education for the next generation of Americans.

> Of course there is a degree of poverty and suffering that any government must guarantee to alleviate, but without a believable force for defense, the United States will find itself lacking the prosperity that can supply the alleviation.

In each passage the writer attempts to acknowledge the opponent, and to indicate that the writer's mind is not closed to other kinds of reasoning. As readers we nod and think "Yes, that sounds reasonable."

For a purer and more sustained example of argument, we might go to the op-ed page of a newspaper. This particular column ran side-by-side with another column, which was entitled "Missing: The influence of black women . . . " This column's title read " . . . and men, too". The author is identified as William Raspberry, "a syndicated columnist."

> If I could offer a single prescription for the survival of America, and particularly black America, it would be: Restore the family.
>   And if you asked me how to do it, my answer—doubtlessly oversimplified—would be: Save the boys.
>   So much of what has gone wrong in America, including the frightening growth of the poverty-stricken, crime-ridden and despairing black underclass, can be traced to the disintegration of the family structure.
>   Everybody knows it, but too many of us have been reluctant to talk straight about it. We know that children need intact families that include fathers. But we fear to say it lest we appear to be blaming hard-pressed single mothers for the very problems they are struggling to overcome.

The point, however, is not to assign blame but to encourage analysis that can lead the way to solutions.

Nathan and Julia Hare put it this way in their book "The Endangered Black Family":

"There is nothing wrong with being a black-female single parent—and one rightfully makes the most of any situation in which she finds herself. But there is something wrong with why a black woman is so much more likely to experience the single-parent situation, why one race can freely imprison, send off to military duty, unemploy and otherwise destroy the oppressed black woman's eligible male supply.

"Also, there is something wrong with glorifying this problem instead of rising up to change it. People will speak here of 'options,' but forced or unintended options must be called by some other name."

That's from a pair of radical black social scientists. Now hear this from white ethologist Phon Hudkins:

"The family is the only social institution that is present in every single village, tribe or nation we know through history. It has a genetic base and is the rearing device for our species."

And from conservative Richard John Neuhaus, editor of the *Religion & Society Report:* "Millions of children do not know and will never know, what it means to have a father. More poignantly, they do not know anyone who has a father or who is a father . . . It takes little imagination to begin to understand the intergenerational consequences of this situation."

It strikes me as it strikes these writers—as it struck Daniel Patrick Moynihan a quarter century ago—that children unlucky to be born into single-parent households are, if not doomed, at least at serious disadvantage.

Hudkins believes the disadvantages include not just poverty and crime and hopelessness, but also poor health produced by the stress of family-lessness.

The question is what to do about the children of deteriorating and never-formed families. The first thing to do is to provide as much help as we can for these feckless children in their present circumstances: education, mentoring, role-modeling, job training, help toward self-sufficiency. The second is to devise policies to restore families. Hudkins, who has been ridiculed for his contention that female dominance is eroding America's strength, has it right in the prescription he offered in a recent open letter to the president:

"If families are to be formed and survive, young males must be prepared for skilled jobs to support these families. In order to do this, we must target our government aid and our compensatory education and training programs for disadvantaged young males."

We can't rescue America's families unless we make up our minds to save the boys.

The Boston Globe, July 18, 1989

In this essay, Raspberry is not so much arguing systematically as attempting to persuade the reader that his point is sound. Still, we can note a few things about his procedure that will be useful when we set out to practice argumentation. The first consideration is tone. Raspberry is open and direct; he addresses the general reader of the newspaper. The diction is simple, neither pompous nor condescending. With his second sentence he uses the second-person pronoun "you," thus making a connection through direct address. And in his fourth paragraph he once again reaches out. "Everybody knows it," writes Raspberry, thereby including us in the upcoming debate.

But Raspberry is not just being friendly. It is the purpose of his column to capture the attention of a constituency. Raspberry wants to reach those reasonable, well-meaning people who without reflection hold a particular view about the plight of single mothers with families. His point is that to remedy that plight we must bring it into the open, into the public eye; too many of us, however, fear to discuss the situation as it needs to be discussed because we fear to look as if we blame "hard-pressed single mothers for the very problems they are struggling to overcome."

Once he has identified and addressed his audience, Raspberry sets out to change minds. He does this not through a logical sequence of arguments, but rather through a powerful appeal to common sense. Raspberry quotes from three different sources; with each quotation comes an identification. First we hear from "a pair of radical black social scientists," then from a "white ethologist," and finally from a "conservative" editor. Raspberry is, in essence, giving us views from all parts of the spectrum: the left, the scientifically neutral, and the right. The sources are all presented as respectible public figures—and as thinkers who have all come to the same conclusion. Raspberry has thus saved himself the work of arguing. He says, in effect, "If reasonable, thoughtful people from all parts of the political spectrum come to the same conclusion in this matter, it must be the right conclusion." He finishes by spelling that conclusion out unambiguously.

Later in this chapter we will discuss the use of sources in building arguments. For the present, as we look back upon Raspberry's presentation, let us focus most closely upon his use of tone and address to build consensus.

TIME FOR THE OPPOSITION

When we hope to persuade, we need to pay court to the opposition—and the opposition is a portion of our audience. We need to imagine possible rebuttals of our position, so that in our argument we can anticipate them. This is the first principle of debating: the good debater is one who has planned out counter-arguments for every attack on his position.

Sometimes we can take on the objections directly. Suppose we are arguing that television news is an abomination. Suppose we argue that television newscasters have become celebrities, that they are hired for looks and personality rather than for their competence as journalists. We might say, "Networks claim that because television is a visual medium, on-camera appearance is basic to a reporter's ability to communicate with the public. But . . . " Then we could contradict by means of anecdote, example, or appeal to a hypothesis. To acknowledge possible objections in this way weakens their effectiveness even as it makes the position advanced sound reasonable and open-minded.

Thinking of opposing arguments is also a natural system for generating and gathering ideas. We must put ourselves on the other side, and consider the evidence that argues against our thesis. To find out the probable objections to our argument about newscasters, we have to make an effort to think like an executive at a television network: what would such a person say to defend the network's hiring policies? If we argue that possession of handguns should be illegal, we must consider the argument that Americans have a constitutional right to bear arms. If we contend that impounded dogs and cats should not be used for laboratory experiments, we must answer the argument that by sacrificing unwanted animals we may save human lives. By considering the counter-notions, we can develop our argumentative material and discover the form that our argument must follow to convince the audience. The internal antagonist—the voice that keeps saying "Yes, but what about . . . ?"—is essential to good argument.

As we consult this internal antagonist, we may find ourselves succumbing to the Ping-Pong effect: for every assertion we formulate a counter-assertion. While such a to-and-fro is an excellent way to explore all sides of an issue and locate the argumentative possibilities, it should not provide the form for our essay. The reader would quickly get a crick in the neck from looking this way and that. Don't say:

> It has been argued that smokers have a right to smoke in public places because they are members of the public. But what about the nonsmoking public whose rights to breathe clean air are infringed upon?

Such a volley may work once, to introduce a conflict of views, but if it were sustained for more than a paragraph, the reader would quickly grow restless. Often it is best, in avoiding the Ping-Pong tactic, to lump all opposition ideas together, perhaps in one paragraph, and then answer them in another. Or we might acknowledge and counter an argument in the flow of one sentence:

> Although smokers claim the right to smoke in public places, they
> forget that nonsmokers have a right to breathe uncontaminated air.

Consulting the inner antagonist, we will find new positive ideas
by forcing ourselves to reply to objections, and usually a frontal attack
is more forceful than a defense. Suppose we want to contest the high
salaries paid to professional football players. Trying to gather examples,
we imagine the antagonist answering, "Professional athletes are worth
what they are paid because they attract thousands of fans to the games."
We can acknowledge and counter this idea by saying, "By creating a cult
of overpaid superstars, we are gradually turning a sport into a celebrity
show."

Our most persuasive argument, in the long run, derives from
praise for our point of view, rather than blame for the opposition. If
we record too many opposing arguments—more than we need to over-
turn the objections—our own position may start to blur out of focus; we
lose unity, and we may lose the sound of conviction. Usually we deal
with opposing views obliquely, raising them in dependent clauses
while allowing the main clauses to carry our argument: "Although
smokers claim the right to smoke in public places, they forget that
nonsmokers have a right to breathe uncontaminated air." This device
raises the issues that belong to the opposition but keeps our direction
clear.

Giving time to the opposition allows us to sound open-minded.
No one wins an argument by asserting that the other point of view is
wholly invalid, and that anybody who disagrees with us is ignorant or
stupid. We must admit the facts and give credit to valid lines of reasoning; if we don't, we undercut our own validity and lose our audience,
especially the one we most want to reach—the misguided fool who
disagrees with us.

One thing we should remember as we generate ideas and strategies
by giving time to the opposition is the usefulness of sources. We can
usually make a good deal of headway on our own, by putting ourselves
in the position of the adversary. But sometimes it helps to confront the
position as it has been worked through, or argued, by another writer.
Fortunately there is no shortage of material: almost any topic we can
think of has its *pro* and *con* partisans. A library search will generally
yield books and articles in newspapers and journals representing any
point of view we desire. But we must be aware of certain dangers. If we
consult the views of others before we have formulated our own clearly,
we risk losing the tone of independent conviction that marks good
argumentative writing. It is all too easy to start parroting the arguments
and sequences of another thinker. We need to be aware of the hazards of
plagiarism: not only is it wrong—and punishable—to use another

writer's words without attribution, it is also wrong to take the structure of another's argument as one's own. We are far less likely to face this risk if we work out our pattern of arguments and counter-arguments *before* we look elsewhere.

Once we do have our basic thoughts in order, however, a check of the documented positions of others can help us a great deal. We may discover lines of argument or objection that we had not considered and that may have a place alongside ours. Or we may, like William Raspberry, find that certain positions have been summed up by others with eloquence and conviction. Our essay may profit from direct incorporation. We might want to write, "The position against gun-control has been summed up most persuasively by Max Bulet in his book, *Our Right to Murder . . .* " and then go on to quote the passage. This tactic is most effective when we use it to highlight counter-argument. We might follow the quotation giving Bulet's position with a sentence signaling our rebuttal: "Bulet's argument depends upon several fallacies . . ." or "What Bulet neglects to tell his reader . . . " When we argue against a clearly stated position, one that can be attributed to a spokesman, our own points stand out in greater relief. At the same time we show the reader that we have made time for the opposition.

Using the clearly stated arguments of another writer on our own behalf, as part of *our* argument, is less advisable. Though the points may be good, we surrender authority. The reader is likely to think, "This other person says it better than the writer; why don't I just read *her* article?" We must at all costs avoid undermining the reader's faith: when we argue we must not only take control, we must keep it.

THE ORDER OF ARGUMENT

Once we have gathered valid support for our argument—first by debating with ourselves, *then* perhaps by checking the stated views of others—we face the task of organization. I already cautioned against using the structure of the Ping-Pong game. There are other kinds of order to consider.

Audience and purpose interact to determine the shape of argument. In any list of argumentative details and evidence, some will make a stronger case than others; some will be more interesting or appealing to our audience. Generally, we want to save the best, the strongest, for last. One good way to order argument, therefore, is by increasing intensity. After we introduce the issue—"The administration claims that the need to raise teachers' salaries and improve facilities will require an increase in students' fees next semester"—we counter it with facts or statistics in order of increasing importance, as we see these, or as we understand our audience to see them. Thus we might write: "But our faculty salaries are already higher than those at other colleges in the state, and the computer center houses equipment that pays its own way with time-sharing. Many students depend on government loans, which become less available, and they will leave school if tuition increases. The administration's well-paid faculty will teach to classrooms full of machines and empty of students." The persuasive effect derives from the crescendo.

Another shape of argument states its main thesis at the beginning, at center stage under spotlights: "Next year's planned increase in tuition and board will contribute to the downfall of this institution." After introducing our argument with a thesis statement, we continue by acknowledging points that argue against our view and by countering them. We then conclude with a summary that rises to our most persuasive point: "Tuition hikes will deny many students, who have already taken on extensive loans and extra jobs, the opportunity to finish their education. The tuition increase will discriminate against the people whom this university was intended to serve." The conclusion echoes the thesis statement in its force.

Most arguments are structured as variations of one of these two patterns. The important thing is to set out the terms of the debate early on: one can begin with a statement of the opposition view and then proceed to take apart its premises, or one can assert one's own position and rebut possible objections. Either way, the writer must lead the reader from point to point in such a way that the conclusion will come with a sense of finality. Ancient rhetoricians used to close their arguments with the initials Q.E.D. (*quot erat demonstrandum*), meaning "as has been demonstrated." We want to leave our reader with the same confident click.

To write argument we frequently use the rhetorical patterns discussed at length in Chapter 7. It will be useful to run through the patterns again, in the new context of argument and persuasion.

Example is the backbone of argument, the support it requires to become convincing. If we try to persuade people to contribute to the public library system, we may list examples to show what money can achieve.

We argue by *example:*

> to acquire new library materials, from books to computers; to increase hours providing more services; to expand children's programs by adding new staff; to improve facilities allowing community groups to use the library for film festivals and lectures; to preserve old books and manuscripts; and with climate control to prevent further deterioration of the library collection.

We argue by *classification and division:*

> In seeking candidates for membership in the Sierra Club, we look for people who have demonstrated an interest in the outdoors or in

protecting the environment. We send you this invitation in the hope that you are such a person. . . . Whether you particularly enjoy hiking, backpacking, camping, canoeing, whitewater rafting, or simply appreciation of nature. . . .

From a letter of solicitation,
the Sierra Club

To persuade people to become members of a special group (*classification*) this letter goes on to identify the characteristics and interests of that group (*division*).

We argue by *cause and effect:*

Despite a thirtyfold increase in outlays on social programs for the poor, the condition of impoverished blacks in the United States has been steadily deteriorating since the launching of the War on Poverty and the Great Society in the 1960s. These redistributionist schemes, by destroying incentives for work, thrift, and family support, have created in our inner cities a tragic wreckage of demoralization, rage, unemployment, and crime, raised the illegitimacy rate to fifty-five percent of all black births, and driven fathers altogether out of the ghetto family and national economy.

George Gilder, "But What About Welfare's Grim Side?"
The New York Times

We argue by *comparison and contrast:*

Unlike the Bulldog I, an expensive proposition for the home computer because it requires a large initial investment, the Mastiff III plugs into the family television set. It is compatible with many Mastiff programs and can grow with your family, whereas the Bulldog I lacks flexibility.

We argue by *process analysis:*

Put into practice, computer-aided robotics could mean startling changes in farming before the end of the century. The dairy barn of the future, for example, might look like this:

Cows wearing identification tags walk through the door and are "recognized" by an electronic sensor. They amble to their permanent feeding stations and eat a ration tailored to their individual needs, weather conditions, and milk production. Sensors implanted in their bodies weigh and check the animals for nutrient levels and early detection of disease.

G. V. Perkins, Jr., "What's New in Agriculture"
The New York Times

And we argue by *definition*, which includes other rhetorical patterns:

Either America is an open society or it isn't. If it is, the country has nothing to fear from such political and literary luminaries as Nobel

Prizewinner Gabriel García Márquez, playwright Dario Fo, Salvadoran insurgent leader Guillermo Ungo and Chile's widowed First Lady Hortensia Allende. But the Reagan Administration has refused to grant all of the above—and dozens more—the entry privileges customarily accorded other figures of their stature. The country seems more of a closed company with ever-slamming door. The exclusion of famous people deters thousands of others from the arduous and humiliating application process, where detailed probes are made into political and affectional ties. No particular threat to national security need be divined: radical thinking, organizational affiliation or sexual preference is enough to keep the Administration's critics out.

Editorial, The Nation

The writer defines open and closed societies by listing controversial visitors to whom our country is a closed door. A society that excludes possible critical visitors is not an open one.

LOGIC AND EMOTIONALISM

If we wish to persuade, we must be reasonable: we must appear logical. Argument may be fueled by feeling, but in persuasion the appeal to emotions is dangerous. If our appeal appears to violate reason the reader loses confidence. The photograph of a weeping child does not provide a *reason* for doing whatever the caption asks. After all, a caption-writer could use the same melancholy photograph to illustrate the hardships faced by refugees on either side in any war.

Whether we think to ourselves or on paper in a public forum, we must avoid illogic in order to think well. All of us know some logic, perhaps without giving it the name; often we use the name of common sense for thought we accept as reasonable. For example, common sense tells us not to generalize from particulars. Suppose I read in the paper about a drunk teenager who killed a pedestrian in a hit-and-run accident. Suppose I told you about it and added, "Therefore, we should raise the drinking age to protect society from drunk teenagers." You would be right to ridicule my logic: I would be guilty of violating common sense by arguing from insufficient evidence. One teenager cannot be made to stand for all.

The use of an anecdote or example is not necessarily generalizing from a particular; it depends on how we do it. If I had been modest in my declaration, I could have said, "I know that we cannot generalize from one case, but this sort of news item seems characteristic. There have been a great many fatalities involving drunk teenagers. A careful look at the statistics might cause us to re-examine the laws." Here the anecdote is used to introduce an issue that may be debated in less subjective terms.

When we caution against emotionalism, we are not blaming feelings but their misuse, as when emotionalism appeals to feeling in order to disguise a defect in thinking. If we say,

> The United States needs a strong defense. Anyone who is against the draft is a traitor to those who have sacrificed their lives to preserve freedom.

we give no reasons to support our claim. With words like *traitor* and *sacrifice* we name-call and breast-beat. Charged words persuade only the already persuaded; they alienate those we wish to reach. This writer's counterpart on the other side of the fence might write,

> Anyone who advocates the peacetime draft wants America to rule the world for the sake of the military-industrial complex.

A writer can defend either position without resorting to loaded language:

> With our commitment to free enterprise or capitalism, in a world that contains many opponents of free enterprise, we would be naive to reduce our armed forces unless we can be certain that our opponents will do the same. Although all sensible people dread the possibility of war, it can be argued that we can prevent war only by preparing for it.

In this fragment of argument, the writer carefully avoids the unfairness of loaded words, and gives the antagonist at least the benefit of a dependent clause.

Loaded words, begging the question, and unsupportable claims for cause and effect all contribute to errors in thinking; we may lump them under one general label—*emotionalism pretending to argue.* Soon we will look at the related subject of logical fallacies, which we are more apt to fall into if we are arguing from feeling. We must watch ourselves carefully for bad thinking and bad writing whenever we take on a heavily charged issue: abortion, capital punishment, school prayer, disarmament, pornography, or freedom of speech.

STYLE IN ARGUMENT

Loaded words make bad prose. To avoid fooling ourselves and trying to fool others, to appear reasonable, we have to apply to argument the stylistic standards of clarity and forcefulness discussed in the chapters on words and sentences. When we use a passive verb instead of an active one, we may detach our subject from responsibility and distort our argument. At very least we weaken the tone of conviction essential to making a strong case. If we write in the passive mood,

Mistakes were made . . .

or

Toxic wastes were dumped at the site over twelve years . . .

we avoid placing responsibility. *Who* made the mistakes, and *who* did
the dumping? The active mood supplies a subject and attributes responsibility:

The Boxtex Company dumped toxic wastes at the site over twelve
years . . .

Abstract nouns and euphemisms can also combine with the passive to diminish the force of concrete and direct expression:

A process of repatriation was employed . . .

To argue with clarity, we must use conjunctions with care; we
should never imply cause or sequence that evidence cannot support:

While the Congress delays additional military aid to Central
America, the Soviet Union supplies arms and troops to the rebel
forces . . .

The reader of this sentence might mistakenly conclude that the two
parts of the sentence are causally linked: either that Congress is delaying the supplies *because* the Soviets are supplying arms, or else that
the Soviets are acting as they do *because* Congress is delaying. Neither
inference is necessarily supported by the facts.

It is difficult, in working on a paper in argument, to discover our
own errors, especially when we feel strongly about the subject. Often
we misuse verb forms and abstract nouns in early drafts of an argument
without knowing it. It helps to find a clear-headed friend to read the
draft for us. It likewise helps to set the paper aside for a time, then to
return to it with the eye of the inner critic. Many argumentative errors
are not merely mechanical; they are learned errors—fallacies—by
which we fool ourselves. Here is some would-be argument from an
impromptu essay:

The governor wants to raise the state drinking age to twenty-one.
Adults drink as much as they want and get bombed on cocktails
when they get home from the office, but they want to stop kids from
having a casual beer. It is true that teenagers are picked up for
driving under the influence and getting involved in car accidents.
Everybody should be more careful and drunk driving is to be
avoided. But there is no reason why teenagers should not relax on
weekends with a few beers.

There is no argument in this passage; assertion and innuendo reek of special pleading. The writer avoids the connections implicit in his sentences; he ought to confront weekend relaxation with the argument about highway deaths, but he does not want to make the confrontation. If he wishes to work on his thinking, he can find much to say that is reasonable, even persuasive, on behalf of his point of view. If the author revises these sentences for their prose style, the argument will improve. Bad style allows the illogic of emotionalism to wander into common fallacies of thinking.

COMMON FALLACIES IN THINKING

When we discussed rhetorical patterns earlier, we described them as mapping the sequences that thought naturally follows. We can make use of the same analogy to explain logical fallacies. Briefly: they are misreadings of the map, wrong turns taken. The path of a fallacy often looks like the other, desired path, but it leads us away from clarity and common sense. If we recognize some of these fallacies, or false paths, we stand a better chance of avoiding them in our argumentation.

Many common fallacies in thinking are misuses of *induction* or *deduction*. We meet them every day in newspapers and advertisements and in the rhetoric of political campaigns. *Inductive reasoning*, or *induction*, draws general conclusions from particular examples or evidence—Sherlock Holmes's speciality.

> Because the plums were in the refrigerator when I left, and because George was the only person remaining in the house, and because the plums have disappeared, and because there are plum pits in the sink, I conclude that George ate the plums.

Deductive reasoning, or *deduction*, on the other hand, applies a general truth to a specific instance. We deduce by three-step thinking called the syllogism. The most famous syllogism is probably "All men are mortal. Socrates is a man. Therefore, Socrates is mortal." No beginning philosophy course is complete without a nod to this sample of deductive reasoning.

We use both induction and deduction in our thinking and our writing. From time to time we misuse or misapply the logical form and fall into error. A common slip, as in the example of the drunk teen driver, is that we arrive at a general statement from a sole supporting fact, or from too narrow a range of particulars. These are errors, or fallacies, of induction. When we generalize too rashly from a particular we sound silly. We claim that New York City is a rotten apple because one taxi driver was rude to us. We claim that motel chains are dishonest because an aunt was shortchanged in San Diego. We generalize poorly when we do not collect sufficient evidence; we assume that because X happens once or twice, X will always happen.

This caution should not be construed as advice to avoid the particular. Often an argument takes on persuasive power because we present a specific bit of evidence—carefully—as typical of the generalization. The argument's effectiveness, however, depends upon the general validity of the assertion; a generalization is never demonstrated by one particular. If we began an essay on public television by describing one offensive commercial, and said, "Therefore we must have at least one national network without advertising," we would be illogical. But if, after mentioning the particular commercial, we listed other offensive advertisments, noting a trend, and gave statistics on the programming time devoted to commercials, perhaps we could make a generalization that would appear to follow.

Deduction, too, can lead to fallacy when we misuse it. The most common problem is the overinclusive premise or conclusion. "Everybody who goes to medical school is out for money." "Lawyers are all corrupt." "All people who drive BMWs are yuppies." The next link in the argument would likely be "X goes to medical school . . ." But these assertions do not resemble "All men are mortal." This latter is true beyond dispute; none of the others stands on similarly solid ground. The writer must be wary of bold assertions; a logical cross-checking is essential.

Another false step commonly taken begins with wrongful or arbitrary associations. Politicians thrive on guilt by association. Because socialists believe in free medical care, a wily campaigner may insinuate that *anyone* who believes in free medical care is a socialist. If we attach a negative emotional association to the word *socialist*, then our thinking may be affected. If the rival candidate is not a socialist, or inclined to socialist views, then we have been misled.

A linked fallacy, which also depends upon association, attacks the person instead of the issue. The name given to such bad argument is *ad hominem*, which is Latin for "to the man." We often resort to this tactic in argument when we lose our tempers or when our logic deserts us. When someone defends cutting down trees to make a parking lot, we attack *him* instead of questioning the need for additional parking spaces. We say, "You're in favor of this plan because you like carbon monoxide more than maple trees." Name-calling may satisfy something in the name-caller, but it avoids thought. A friend says, "I believe in a socialist form of government, because the profit motive, which is basic to a capitalistic system, robs us of our humanity and corrupts our intelligence to serve materialism." We rebut, "You always were nuts."

Argument *ad hominem*—so long as we're using Latin terms coined by ancient scholars of rhetoric—can be construed as a species of *non sequitur,* which means "it does not follow." It does not follow that X wants to cut down trees because he loves carbon monoxide. Common sense tells us that nobody loves, likes, or even tolerates this poison. When we commit a non sequitur we give a statement or idea which *appears* to grow out of an earlier one (by causation, by chronology, by logic), but which upon examination fails to make the trip:

> He was a doctor and therefore an all-around man.

> She left an hour ago, although her car wouldn't move.

Comedians sometimes use the non sequitur to humorous effect. Woody Allen is a master:

> I believe my consumption has grown worse. Also my asthma. The wheezing comes and goes, and I get dizzy more and more frequently. I have taken to violent choking and fainting. My room is damp and I have perpetual chills and palpitations of the heart. I noticed, too, that I am out of napkins.

Non sequiturs sometimes result when we try to make complex sentences in pursuit of conciseness: "My uncle was born in 1902 in Miami where he sells lawnmowers and garden tools."

When we use the rhetorical pattern of cause and effect, we sometimes unintentionally create the non sequitur or the related fallacy of *post hoc ergo propter hoc.* We needn't be scared away by the Latin. The literal meaning is "after this, therefore because of this. " When we fall into this fallacy, we mistake sequence for cause. We assume that if B follows A, A must cause B, but our assumption is not logical and often leads to confusion. If we say, "Cousin Eveline visits and I get a headache," we are suggesting a cause and effect relationship. In fact, Cousin Eveline may be a delightful person, and the headache may be from a cold contracted the same day. We need to monitor sequential links to make sure that we are not suggesting cause where none exists.

Another instance of misapplied causation is *begging the question.* In this error the arguer assumes the truth of a premise that readers may question. The arguer could try to prove the assumption, but does not. Instead, he merely repeats it—it is so because it is so. Someone might say, "The rising incidence of lymphatic cancer proves that early advocates of the test-ban treaty were correct." This writer neither demonstrates that lymphatic cancer *is* rising, nor shows that nuclear testing causes the disease. Causation asserted but unsupported indicates sloppy thinking. Sometimes misused conjunctions beg the question: "Although middle-aged, he wore Levis." Again, an untenable connection is advanced through a careless expression.

We don't want to instigate a witch-hunt for fallacies, but several more need to be mentioned before we turn to look at the process of argumentation. One of these might be called the either/or fallacy, and for a good example we can turn back to the quotation from *The Nation* we used (pages 300–301) for an example of argument by definition. Although the passage defines what it means by a closed society, it begins with an example of the either/or fallacy: "Either America is an open society or it isn't." There is an attractive, no-nonsense tone in this introductory sentence; but in fact it *is* nonsense, for it implies that there are no degrees between one extreme and another. If the United States and the Soviet Union are both closed societies, as the 1984 editorial seemed to assert, does the writer really wish to imply that there is no difference in degrees of openness? We should be alert whenever we make a statement using strongly polarized terms; not every instance of this fallacy uses either/or. "Because Herbert Perkins is not a superb human being he is a rotten person."

Finally, we should beware of using analogies as if they were facts. Analogies themselves can be most useful in argument; they can illustrate the sense in which we mean a statement that might otherwise seem tenuous or elusive. But we must be sure to use them as clarifications or elucidations and not as statements of fact. Suppose we want to write about different civilizations that seem to have features in common—like beginning, development, fulfillment, and decay. To carry this idea to a reader, we invent an analogy: each civilization is like an organism—it is born, it grows up, it matures, it becomes old, and it dies. So far so good. We embody the abstract thought, associating it with concrete organisms. But many writers become so accustomed to a dominant analogy that they begin to take it literally. Arguing later that our own civilization must end, we say, "Like all organisms, our society must come to death." The argument is invalid because a civilization is not literally an organism, and therefore we have not proved that what is true of an organism will be true of civilization. Remember: the analogy is not the thing itself.

THE GENERAL FALLACY: IMPRECISION

Many writers undermine their own arguments by misusing statistics. Some would-be persuaders ignore the differences in mean, median, and average. Others use out-of-date figures; we mislead in 1990 if we speak of northeastern American cities according to the 1970 census. Some quote statements out of context, distorting their intended meanings. We have all seen movie advertisements or book blurbs that edit reviews to advantage. The critic writes: "It is an attempt at making a work of art in which the flaws far outnumber the felicities; there are no moments of greatness." The ad reads " . . . work of art . . . felicities . . . moments of greatness."

Ambiguity accounts for various imprecisions—misplaced modifiers, pronouns with uncertain antecedents, and words used without definition. A common flaw in argument is the use of one word in several senses. We fool ourselves into thinking we have said something profound when we have only played with a word. Abstractions lend themselves more readily to ambiguity than concrete words. Some writers use these terms so loosely that they can mean anything and therefore mean nothing; "free society" and "democracy" are useless without definition and context. Watch out for prose like this, from a theme about campus politics:

> Jerry was a liberal, but not so liberal as Mary Hunter, who was out in left field. Some of the professors, even the most liberal, were conservative compared to Mary Hunter, who claimed that they didn't deserve to be called liberals at all.

We have no idea what meanings the writer attaches to *liberal* and *conservative*; there is no attempt at definition.

As we have said before, writing to reach an audience, we must place ourselves in the position of the audience. Read over your own prose with a cool eye and a common sense attitude. Can you, as reader, get clear sense from what you, as writer, have put on the page? The work is not finished until the answer is an unambiguous yes.

LOOKING FOR AN ARGUMENT: PROCESS

In Chapter 3 we watched Frank Rodriguez as he worked up a theme comparing and contrasting two television shows. Now we will follow another student through some of the stages of writing a paper in argument.

When his teacher assigned an essay in argument, Jerome Williams did not go through his usual period of indecision. For once he knew exactly what he wanted to write about. A week earlier his father and his older brother had argued (his brother called it an argument; his father kept calling it a "friendly discussion") at the dinner table. The subject was drugs and gang violence. The whole family had watched a television special the night before. Afterward, Jerome's father and brother had expressed different views about what should be done to remedy the situation. Jerome's father said that criminals and offenders only understood one thing—force—and that the government had to take action. More police protection, stiffer penalties, more prisons—nothing else would work. If that meant raising taxes, he said, then so be it. Jerome's brother was against such a solution. He argued that the only answer was to legalize drugs and make them available as liquor is. The profit motive would disappear, the gangs would disband, and the streets would be safe. "You're a dreamer," his father said.

Jerome had listened as his father and brother went back and forth, arguing and trying to convince each other of the rightness of his position. He had a hard time making up his mind. He was surprised to find that some of his brother's arguments made sense, and his father was not able to rebut them. Jerome felt that this was an issue that concerned many people in his city; he wanted to think his way through to a clear position of his own. What better way than by writing an argument paper?

When Jerome first sat down with pencil and paper to work out his ideas, he did not know which side he wanted to argue. His first step was to make a list. On the left side of the page he wrote *arguments for legalization*, on the right side *arguments against*. He then tried to replay the discussion as he remembered it, listing his brother's points on one side, his father's on the other.

arguments for legalization:

1. eliminate profit motive
2. reduce gang presence
3. free up funds and resources used in war on drugs
4. control sales and distribution
5. ease strain on prison system
6. safer neighborhoods

arguments against:

1. drugs addictive and dangerous to users
2. legalizing sends message that it's OK to use drugs
3. more people would use drugs
4. strain on hospitals, families; problems at the workplace

When he had written out his lists, Jerome sat and stared at his paper. He wasn't sure what to do next. The listing hadn't given him his answer; he found himself as divided as before. When he was writing down his brother's reasons, he had sided with that position. When he wrote the counter-arguments, *those* seemed most convincing. He knew one thing, though. Sitting and staring all night was not going to get his paper written. Jerome therefore decided that he would argue his brother's case: he would take a stand *for* the legalization of drugs. The points he had listed seemed strong, and besides, there were more of them; he could appear to be overpowering the opposition.

The question was how to get started. He knew that it was not enough just to write out the arguments for one view, then the arguments for the other. He also knew that he should avoid the quick back-and-forth, where each argument immediately matches up with a counter-argument, like a high school debate. His teacher had said that this argument should read like an essay. "The shape itself should be persuasive," he had said.

Jerome used some time walking around the house, ending up in the kitchen with a glass of milk and a piece of cold chicken. He was tempted to find his brother and ask him for advice, but then he stopped himself. This was *his* argument, *his* essay, and he had to work things out for himself. But the thought of his brother was enough to suggest something: as Jerome was rinsing out his glass, the word "Prohibition" popped into his head. He suddenly remembered one of the points his brother had been making. During Prohibition, he had said, it was against the law to make, sell, or consume alcohol. But what were the results? Those who wanted to drink drank. The illegality of alcohol made it attractive; bootleggers organized into criminal gangs in order to control sales; gang warfare was rampant. . . .

Jerome felt he had what he needed. A comparison would allow him to give his argument some shape. He could end by saying something along the lines of "It didn't work then, and it won't work now." He was ready to go back to his room and get to work. He knew from experience with writing papers that his best strategy now would be to sprint a short rough draft. If he got that right, then he could come back to fill in details and look for ways to polish. Jerome sat down and got to work:

> There are many good arguments for keeping drugs illegal and for imprisoning users and dealers. Drugs are addictive and dangerous; some people feel they are immoral. Widespread use of drugs like cocaine and its derivative crack puts a strain on hospitals; it causes untold damage within families. Not least, it affects productivity at the workplace. Some people believe that to legalize the drugs or to lessen the penalties would send a message out that it's OK to use drugs. The drugs would be cheaper and more people would try them. More people would get addicted and the problems would worsen.
>
> But then, people said similar things back in the 1920s when Prohibition outlawed the manufacture, sale and consumption of alcohol. If alcohol were available, people would become drunks. Families would be destroyed, and so on. What happened? The illegality just made the product more attractive. Those who wanted to drink were going to find a way; they were going to pay more. Selling bootleg alcohol became very profitable. So profitable, in fact, that the criminal types got interested. Gangs formed; gang-wars were fought over control of territory. Thugs like Al Capone became millionaires. Why? All because people were willing to pay money to take a drink.
>
> Sound familiar? The situation is in many ways similar to the one we face today. Urban areas have become war zones as rival gangs shoot it out to decide who is going to control the crack and cocaine

sales in a certain area. Innocent people are shot daily. The government responds by bringing in more and more police. But what is the
effect? Our prison system can't begin to cope; offenders cop plea
bargains and are back on the street immediately. Taxpayers foot
larger and larger bills. Prohibition was a disaster, and so is the
present situation.

There is only one logical solution: To treat these drugs as we treat
alcohol, to control quality, price and distribution. With the profit
motive removed, gangs will stop terrorizing our neighborhoods.
The streets will belong to peace-loving citizens again. Sure, some
people will get addicted and will pay the price. But isn't this true of
alcohol as well? The money now spent on massive police enforce-
ment and on the legal costs can be spent on the creation of treatment centers. After all, there is no stopping people from doing what
they want to do. We are responsible for our own decisions. Everyone
knows that these drugs are addicting and that they can lead to
death. Everyone knows that cigarettes cause cancer. The only answer is to give people a choice. And to launch an ambitious program
of education. When the facts are known, most sensible people will
say no.

Jerome stopped writing. He had the feeling that something was
wrong with his approach. When he read his words over, they seemed to
make sense until the last paragraph. He didn't like what he was saying;
he didn't know if he believed the conclusions he was reaching. The
analogy with Prohibition was effective, a good organizing tool, but the
more he looked over what he had written, the more he felt bothered.
Then he realized what it was: in his heart of hearts he did not believe
that alcohol and cigarettes could be equated with crack and cocaine.
Alcohol and cigarettes were bad, sure, and when abused over a period of
years could cause grave health problems. But were they really in the
same class as drugs? From what he had heard and read, Jerome knew
that the drugs, especially crack, brought on intense and disorienting
reactions. Great pleasure, but then, very soon after, horrible pangs.
Crack was extremely addictive. He read that the deprived user would do
anything to get more. He had never heard of anyone killing for a cigarette or a drink.

As he thought about this, Jerome became convinced that the
analogy was not workable. The risks of having a drug like crack available to anyone over a certain age (how else could they legislate it?) were
too great. Obviously, too, minors would get hold of it, just as they now
get hold of alcohol. How would he feel about living in a society where a
great many people were walking around under the influence of a powerfully addictive and potentially deranging substance? *Scared.*

Jerome found himself in a dilemma. His argument essay was due
in two days, and he had just realized that he did not believe in the
position he planned to present. It was easy enough, he supposed, to

come up with more arguments to strengthen the anti-legalization case, but then he would have to find another way to give his paper shape. He hated to throw out the Prohibition comparison; did he *have* to? Maybe not. Jerome stopped and picked up what he had written. He had an idea. Maybe he could keep the analogy and simply turn it around, saying something like: *those people who propose legalization like to point to the failure of Prohibition, but what they don't understand is that alcohol and narcotics are very different.* Jerome sat down and took out a fresh sheet of paper. He liked the twist; in some ways it was better than the original line of argument. It also reproduced the progress of his own thinking. He had started by believing the analogy; the fact that it didn't hold up had convinced him that the position was wrong. Maybe he could do the same kind of thing in his paper.

Jerome tried sprinting again. This time he began by presenting the pro-legalization view as clearly as he could, first summing it up, then bringing in the comparison with Prohibition. Reading over what he had written, Jerome was satisfied that he had given fair time to the opposition. In fact, he thought, the case sounded quite convincing. Now it was time to change the reader's mind. He wrote:

> The comparison between the current drug crisis and the situation during Prohibition is a good one. In both cases we find people undeterred by laws, risking imprisonment to buy their alcohol or their drugs. In both cases we also find a substantial increase in crime as gangs form and attempt to control lucrative illegal sales. Our history books tell us that Prohibition was a great failure. What does that say about current drug laws?
>
> This kind of reasoning is fine—up to a point. There is just one hitch: alcohol and crack are not the same thing. Liquor, though damaging when abused, is familiar. We know what it does and we have ways of dealing with that. Millions of people drink in social situations and never become alcoholics. Crack and cocaine are different. They are highly addictive and they cause violent changes in personality. We have not even begun to understand the kinds of damage they do to the body and mind. If we legalize these drugs, arguing that adults can make free and responsible choices, we are making a great mistake. Maybe normal adults can make such choices, but is a person with a desperate craving for a high a "normal" adult?

Jerome wrote quickly. He knew that some of his sentences were rough, and that certain links would have to be tightened. But he felt confident. In the several paragraphs that followed, he set out some problems with current drug policy: ineffective policing of neighborhoods, crowded prisons, plea-bargaining loopholes in the legal system . . . Then he reiterated his major point: that a society had a moral and legal obligation to promote the safety and well-being of its citizens; that while there were serious problems with meeting the legal part of that obligation, this was no reason to give up on the moral consideration. The only answer was to work harder, to ask for the leadership that would find ways to confront and solve the drug crisis.

Jerome was tired but satisfied. He knew that he hadn't said everything there was to say, and that there was probably a better order for his arguments. But he also knew that the argument was now his, not his brother's or his father's. He had learned from their exchange of views, but he had worked his points through for himself. More important, he now believed what he had written; it was not just argument for the sake of writing a paper.

The next day, Jerome went to the school library. Now that he was sure about his views and his process of argument, he wanted to read what others had written on the same issue. The library, as always, was intimidating, with three floors of stacks and an enormous room for periodicals. Jerome suspected that the material he wanted was in journals and newspapers: this was a recent controversy. He also knew from past experience that the best policy was to stop at the reference librarian's desk.

The librarian noted a few listings on a slip of paper and directed Jerome to the *Readers' Guide to Periodical Literature.* He paged through several of the volumes, beginning with the most recent. He checked under both "drugs" and "narcotics" and found a great many entries; subheadings in bold type helped narrow his search. He jotted down the titles of several promising articles, noting their date and place of publication. Twenty minutes later Jerome seated himself in a window seat with a small stack of journals.

Not all of the articles turned out to be relevant to his subject, but those that were had all sorts of usable material. Jerome began making notes; from time to time he copied out a quotation, making sure to write the name of the author, the article, and the publication under each citation. He had worked too hard for his ideas and he was not going to risk any appearance of "borrowing." Still, Jerome often had to wonder. He came across ideas and arguments that were very similar to the ones he had come up with on his own. Who owned these ideas? Did anyone? He could only conclude that common sense was universal; a certain overlap was inevitable. He had to make extra sure that someone else's words didn't stray into his paper without acknowledgment.

Jerome read through four articles. Two were general feature stories on the nation's drug crisis, one was a ranting call for universal legalization of everything (useful to attack? he wondered); the best of the group was a piece from *The New Republic* entitled "Crackdown." Indeed, the authors, James Q. Wilson and John J. DiIulio, Jr., argued at great length a position quite similar to his own. Jerome found himself writing a number of quotations in his notebook. At a certain point he started to worry: not that he was reproducing Wilson's and DiIulio's argument—there were significant differences—but that he was finding more and more documentation that he would have to attribute. He didn't want to spend half of his paper quoting others. But their arguments were good ones that he had not thought of; not to include them would weaken his case.

Jerome finally decided to use two of the points from the article in his own argument. He would give proper credit, but he would keep the discussion to a minimum. He knew that competing voices could undermine the force of an argument. His teacher had urged independent thought in this assignment.

When Jerome had copied out the quotations he wanted, he returned the journals to the desk and started for home. It was time to get to work on the final draft. Here is what Jerome handed in the next morning:

The Case Against the Legalization of Drugs

Our American cities have become war zones. You can't pick up a newspaper or turn on the television without hearing about murders and drive-by shootings. Night after night on the screen you see young people being hauled away in handcuffs or on stretchers covered by sheets. And behind every story, it seems, is another story—drugs. Cocaine and its derivative "crack" are brought into inner city areas and sold for tremendous profits. This is what the gang warfare and the violence are all about: money. For whoever controls the turf also controls the profits. And innocent people are paying with their lives.

Some people have made the argument that the only way to put a stop to this violence is to legalize these drugs. Once crack and cocaine are controlled and distributed by responsible agencies, they say, the profit motive will disappear, and the gangs will disappear with it. Parts of this position are hard to dismiss. Proponents of legalization point to the disastrous condition of our legal system: prisons are overcrowded, dealers and users go free on easy plea-bargains; smart dealers are willing to take the risk of dealing for a chance at the profits. Pro-legalization advocates ask: wouldn't it be better to spend the money on treatment centers? Others say that this is a free country and that adults ought to make their own choices about what they do with their bodies and lives.

Some of the arguments of the pro-legalization advocates compare the present-day situation to Prohibition in the 1920s. There are certain similarities. The fact that the production, sale and consumption of liquor was against the law did not stop the activities of people who wanted to drink. It only made liquor harder to get and, therefore, more expensive. This played an important part in the emergence of syndicated crime. Whoever controlled the distribution and sales of bootleg liquor stood to make a great deal of money. Gangs formed and went to war to secure territory. Powerful gangsters like Al Capone terrorized the cities. Isn't this what is happening with drugs like crack and cocaine? Shouldn't the failure of Prohibition convince us that legalization is the best policy?

The comparison between the current drug crisis and Prohibition looks good on the surface. In both cases we find people undeterred by laws, risking imprisonment to buy their alcohol or their drugs. In both cases we also find a substantial increase in crime and gang warfare. If you don't pay close attention, you're apt to think the two situations are identical. They're not.

Alcohol and a drug like crack are not the same, and if these two substances cannot be seen as similar, the whole analogy fails. Alcohol, though it causes damage when it is abused, is a familiar thing. We know what it does and we have ways of dealing with the problems it causes. What's more, millions of people drink in social situations and never become alcoholics; most people use liquor in safe ways. Crack and cocaine are different: they are highly addicting and they cause violent changes in personality. We have not even begun to understand what kinds of damage they do to the body and mind. If we legalize these drugs, arguing that adults can make responsible choices, we are making a grave mistake. Maybe normal adults can make such choices, but is a person with a desperate craving for a high a "normal" adult?

Nor would adults be the only users. In the same way that alcohol is readily available to minors who want it, these drugs would be there for the taking. More than ever, in fact. They would be cheaper and young people would know just where to find them. It would be all but impossible for adults to educate them against use. Their legality would send the message that doing cocaine and crack was OK. We might get rid of the drug gangs, but we would have gangs of new drug takers. The trade-off is not worth it.

There are other arguments to consider. In their article entitled "Crackdown" (*The New Republic*, July 10, 1989), James Q. Wilson and John J. DiIulio Jr. make the point that legalization would be an experiment the results of which we simply cannot predict. We don't know enough about the drugs or their users. Are we ready to rewrite the laws? Wilson and DiIulio also bring up the crucial issue of addicted mothers. What are a baby's rights? Shouldn't babies have the right to begin life without a life-threatening drug addiction?

Of course, arguing against legalization does not make our present problems go away. We have ineffective policing of neighborhoods, over-crowded prisons, plea-bargaining loopholes in our legal system. The crisis intensifies daily. What are we to do?

Wilson and DiIulio make a statement that needs to be heard. They write: "We believe that the moral and welfare costs of heavy drug use are so large that society should continue to enforce the laws against its use for the sake of keeping the number of users as small as possible. But we recognize that by adopting this position, we are placing a heavy burden on those poor communities where drug use is endemic. We are allowing these neighborhoods to be more violent than they would be if the drug were legal."

There are costs that must be understood. But the final fact is this: that a society has a moral and legal obligation to secure the safety and well-being of its citizens. We are having trouble right now in meeting the legal part of the obligation, but this is no reason for turning our backs on the moral considerations. The only answer is to keep working at every level—blocking the production, fighting the smugglers, locating the dealers, monitoring gang activities, increasing street protection, building necessary prisons, expanding the legal facilities, educating the young . . . We should be doing everything we can to eradicate this tremendous problem.

──── EXERCISES ────────────────────

1. In an example given earlier in the chapter, two sentences expressing opposing views about smokers' rights were combined into one: "Although smokers claim the right to smoke in public places, they forget that nonsmokers have a right to breathe uncontaminated air." Look at the groups of sentences below. Can you combine the shorter sentences into a single sentence? Try putting one side of the argument in a dependent clause, as in the example given.

    a. The Olympic committee's rules governing drug use must be obeyed. Steroids have been shown to enhance stamina and improve athletic performance.

    b. Deep-fried foods taste delicious and are popular with restaurant goers. Medical tests have proved that diets high in cholesterol and saturated fats can lead to the onset of heart disease. Deep-fried foods are high in cholesterol and saturated fats.

    c. The livelihood of millions of Brazilians depends upon the clearing of rain forests to make room for farmland. The earth's ozone layer is being depleted at an alarming rate. Trees are valuable because they convert carbon dioxide into oxygen and help to regulate atmospheric balance.

2. Working individually or in small groups, collect and analyze five opinion pieces from the op-ed pages of a newspaper. Find the writer's thesis. Make an outline that shows the structure of the argument. Does the writer attempt to convince? Can you identify any tactics of persuasion? Be prepared to present one op-ed piece to the rest of the class for discussion.

3. Pick a topic of controversy—gun control, sexism in the workplace, the rights of unwed mothers—and write two different open-

ings for an op-ed piece. The paragraphs should reflect diametrically opposed positions.

4. Using the same issue you chose for exercise 3, write two more paragraphs, both reflecting the view that you are most partial to. One paragraph should begin with a statement of the opposition's position and end with a statement rejecting that position; the other should begin with a statement of your thesis and then make time for the opposition. Look over Jerome Williams's different approaches to his topic.

5. Describe the flaws in these arguments.

    a. You're stupid! That's why I'm right.

    b. In 1989, Rupert Hudmill announced that he was no longer associated with the Virgin Vampires. When he decided to destroy the punk rock group, Hudmill gave no reasons.

    c. When Luke hit the first pitch into the left-field stands, it was obvious that Mitchell could no longer pitch.

    d. When we consider the question of aid to underdeveloped nations, we should always consider first that we, too, are an underdeveloped nation.

    e. Since democracy died in Rome with the elevation of Caesar, one can no longer go to the Romans for lessons in the democratic process.

    f. No one who dresses like that could possibly know Mozart from Mantovani.

    g. Warmongers who masquerade as friends of Egypt or Israel attempt to deceive the gullible.

    h. Everybody who votes for Cynthia is a racist.

    i. You can't change human nature.

    j. There will always be conventional warfare.

6. Study the advertising in a selection of magazines: *Time, Mechanix Illustrated, New York Times Magazine, The New Yorker, Penthouse, National Enquirer, Harper's, Ace Comics, The Atlantic, Sport, Fortune, Ms., Family Circle.* Discuss the audience for the ads in each magazine. Write a brief paper explaining how the advertisements attempt to persuade different audiences.

7. Write an application to a computer dating service for a friend. Present your friend's qualities (appearance, personality, special talents). Try writing different versions to appeal first to one imagined audience and then another. For instance, direct yourself to a service addressing populations in Boston, Salt Lake City, Atlanta, or any city or area that you know.

8. Pick one of these situations in which to practice the art of persuasion.

    a. The city announces plans to route a new highway directly through your residential neighborhood, which will require the demolition of well-maintained single-family houses and a park. You head a community action group trying to stop this proposal. Address the city's planning board.

b. Applying for your first job after college, write a cover letter for your resume to convince your prospective employer. Apply for the best job you can imagine getting.

9. Break up into groups of three or four for debating. Meet with one of the other groups to determine what issue you will debate and which side your group will take. Use 30 minutes to prepare for a 10-minute debate. Your teacher will set the rules and will moderate.

10. Here are two passages that argue a point of view. Examine them with these questions in mind: (a) Is the line of argument clear? (b) Is it reasonable? (c) Does it seem balanced, acknowledging the opposite point of view? (d) How is it organized? (e) Does the argument display any logical fallacies? If so, how do they affect the argument?

a. Women's roles have always been more tightly bound than men's to parenthood, more limited by conceptions of reproduction as mysterious, ritually impure, restricting the development of either mind or soul. As a result, women's rebellion against the simple maintenance role that has been their lot is more vivid than men's. Since the beginning of social life, the performance of men's activities, however tedious, dangerous, or humdrum, has been associated with ideas of achievement that both men and women have often mistaken for innate superiority. If men are conscripted and sent to war without ever being consulted by the distant old men who control the corridors of power, they, too, have no more choice over their lives than women without contraceptives have for preventing an unwanted pregnancy.

In this moment of vision, people caught in one kind of life that they have never questioned are getting a glimpse of the way other peoples live; the current questioning of the status of women is part of the whole process of questioning a social order that no longer meets the newly aroused hopes of the people who live within it. The voices of women are combining with voices all over the world against a new worldwide system of political and economic exploitation of the land, the sea, and the air, and the endangered populations that depend upon them.

But there is a difference between women's voices and the voices of all the others who live meaningless lives within a world where they have no part in decisions made too far away. The revolts of the oppressed—slaves, serfs, peons, peasants, manual workers, white-collar workers—are part of the periodic attempts to correct social systems that are seen as exploitative and unfair. But this is the first time in history when the progress made in the control of disease and reproduction has offered to the female half of the population escape from a lifelong role that was defined for every one of them simply by gender. Having one or two children and rearing them together as parents who have chosen parenthood means for men and women—but most of all for women—permission to participate at every level in our highly complex society.

And it is not only women who gain—society gains. Where one half of the best minds were consumed in the performance of small domestic tasks, society can now draw on them. Where women's experiences—inevitably different from men's because women all had mothers with whom they could identify—have been fenced off from contributing to the high-level planning of the world, they can now be used in the attack on such problems as chaotic abuse of food, resources, human settlements, and the total environment. When women are once more able to participate in decisions and are free to be persons as well as parents, they should be able to contribute basic understandings that are presently lacking in the world. These basic new understandings include the fact that food is meant to be used to feed human beings, not to serve as a weapon or commodity; that towns were meant for generations to live in together, not only as barracks or bedrooms; that education can be used to make life meaningful; that we do live in a world community that is here but is unrecognized, in all its interdependence and need for shared responsibility.

Margaret Mead
"Needed: Full Partnership for Women," *Saturday Review*

b. To the editor:

Your editorial of March 3 decries the potential loss of excellence at the *Harvard Law Review* as a result of its plan to specially choose women or members of racial minorities in addition to picking its staff on the basis of class standing and writing competition.

The myth of the law review, and the corresponding system of job placement accompanying it, is pervasive and wasteful. Each year thousands of students are accepted at the nation's law schools, facing not only three grueling years of study and an equally grueling period of preparation for the bar exam but also the prospect of being precluded from the better law jobs or from any law job at all.

Law firms and corporate law departments in every major city screen job applicants on the basis of first-year law school grades and membership in law reviews, avoiding year after year the burden of attempting to evaluate potential employees on the basis of overall experience and ability.

Employers visiting the top law schools each year grant interviews only to the upper 10 to 15 percent of each class. Some law schools have tried using lottery systems to open up interviews to a few non-law-review students, but the fear that employers will stop coming to such campuses inhibits real changes in the system.

The ability to practice law, to utilize intellect and experience in the representation of clients, does not correspond to the ability to attain top grades in first-year law school classes. The antiquated system of fear, uncertainty and intimidation that characterizes the average first-year curriculum serves more to perpetuate a tradition of trial by fire—similar to the hazing of fraternity pledges—than to teach young lawyers how to succeed in the complex world of law, business and government that they must face after graduation.

Upon attainment of top grades, moreover, law review members in many cases experience two years of intellectual isolation, sharply decreased class attendance and much time spent engaged in two key law review activities—editing one another's papers and socializing. As a result, the nation's top law schools and corporations contain many law associates with limited life experience and business or common sense;

it is not unusual for new associates at top New York firms to fail to pass the bar examination on first sitting.

Law review does very little to prepare one for the realities of practice in such industries as banking, energy, transportation, telecommunications and entertainment, to name a few. At the same time, the need is increasingly apparent for training in areas of specialization in order to create lawyers with the necessary skills to do the jobs they must do.

Law reviews do represent a high level of excellence in the intellectual pursuit of legal analysis at America's law schools, and as such constitute a worthy tradition for the bar. Many law reviews serve as well as legal fraternities of value to members throughout their lives. While any employer, as any school, needs some basis for choosing among applicants, the use of law review membership for such a purpose is outmoded and arbitrary, serving as an insult to thousands of bright young graduates frozen out of good jobs by this traditional system.

Rather than bemoan the loss of tradition, we should re-examine the basis for analyzing law school graduates seeking employment to allow for fairer evaluation and fuller utilization of skilled lawyers.

John G. Ives, Letter to the Editor, *The New York Times*

12. Look at Barbara Levine's research paper (on pages 343–366). What is her basic thesis? How does she develop her argument? How could she have organized her information differently? Could she have used different language to change her tone, to argue more persuasively?

9

Writing Research

Research is a way to learn things. The research paper, a particular result of the general method, allows us to gather evidence from library investigations and present it documented in an essay.

Although research often supports an argument, our purpose in writing a research paper is first to gather and present information assembled from reading. A research paper can answer a question ("How did the United States acquire Alaska?") or bring together current thinking about an issue (disposal of radioactive waste, or photocopying and copyright law). Research is a method of study, or investigation, a way of learning independently. Skill in research is indispensable to formal, academic study; it can also be useful: long after we have left college we can research the voting record of a member of Congress, regional recipes for chicken soup, family history, designs for solar houses, local zoning laws, Japanese business practices, the microchip industry, or the social influence of the potato.

Many composition courses specify a research paper as a final task. Not only does such a paper require students to learn methods of research, but it also provides an ambitious project by which students can demonstrate what they have learned about writing.

When you write a research paper, the first thing you must do is choose a subject: the first thing, and probably the most important. Choosing a subject may resemble the process of unpacking Chinese boxes, starting with a large box, moving to the smaller one inside it, then to a smaller one inside *that*, until finally we arrive at something of suitable size. We must, as always, *limit the topic*. Often—maybe *usually*—the hardest part of a research paper is finding a suitable topic and then limiting it.

Broadness, however, is not the only trouble that can afflict a topic. In fact, broadness need not be a grievous problem; one can almost always whittle a broad topic down. "Vegetable Gardening" can become "Raising Organic Tomatoes," and "Voting in a Democracy" can become "Absentee Balloting: Its Effects on the Two Parties."

When a subject is too scientific or too technical, on the other hand, only years of specialized study will prepare a student to write about it; "The Effects of Gamma Rays on *Drosophila*" is as difficult in its particularity as "Genetics" is in generality. Here, we must abandon our desired topic and look for something less technical. Other subjects prove impossible because research material is insufficient. "Vampires in Albania" sounds fascinating enough, but the library is unlikely to provide the necessary sources. Still another kind of problem is the subject about which there is little to say—a subject adequately covered by an encyclopedia entry, like the history of basketball.

In writing a research paper, then, the most important decision is choosing a manageable topic—a topic neither too large nor too small to be handled in the assigned number of pages, and a topic neither too technical for a lay audience nor too specialized for the facilities of a university library. It should be a subject we are interested in: if we have a choice, we should not write about taconite mining when we really want to investigate artificial intelligence or Brazilian deforestation.

Sometimes a topic will narrow as we read about it. We concentrate on one feature of a topic and discover this concentration as we read over our early notes. As we first go about finding sources, we must remain alert to all possibilities of our general subject.

Because the library is the starting point for most research papers, let us look at some ways of using it.

USING THE LIBRARY

Libraries hold our collective past. Large university libraries, with huge collections of books and current periodicals, with microfilm and microfiche, with special archives of rare books and manuscripts, can satisfy the most specialized inquiry. But even the smallest library contains more resources than any of us are likely to need in a lifetime. When we walk into a reference room or into the library book stacks, we enter a universe of possibilities. The first sight of a big academic library can overwhelm us: *All These Books!* How do we find our way? Many students, entering the largest library they have ever seen, at first want to flee to the dormitory in terror, perhaps to settle down in front of the television set with a bag of potato chips.

But the road maps are there, and people to help. In the next few pages we will talk about library catalogues and reference collections, but first, we want to mention the most obvious things—things sometimes overlooked. Many colleges offer library orientation, and you should never ignore such help. Many also provide a small guide to their facilities, printed or mimeographed, which you can keep and consult when you need to. Finally, there are the librarians—at a desk labeled Information, or at the reference desk, or wherever, who sit there in order to help you out, to advise you, and to acquaint you with the resources stockpiled around you. *Never be afraid to ask a librarian a question.* Whatever you ask, the librarian has probably heard it before: Where do I find out about vampires? What do you have on gene splicing? How do you spell *Drosophila?* Who wrote "Mary Had a Little Lamb"?

The librarian will not find the answer for you, but will show you how to find it for yourself.

THE LIBRARY CATALOGUE

The library catalogue is a record of everything in the library—books, periodicals, newspapers, government documents, microfilm, microfiche, records, films, and other special materials. Many libraries still use a traditional three-by-five-inch card file, organized alphabetically. Other libraries, however, have switched to computer printouts, access to computer terminals, or a microform that we can read on a viewer. For all these, the organizing principle is the same.

Most books are represented by at least three entries or cards in the catalogue. One is alphabetized under the author's last name; to find *David C. Edwards*, you look under *E* and not under *D*. Another is alphabetized under the first major word of the title; *General Psychology* is found under G. A third is alphabetized under the subject PSYCHOLOGY. (Look at the sample author, title, and subject cards on page 324.) Naturally enough, many books are listed under more than one subject; three entries are the *minimum* that will represent each book.

Each library card contains all sorts of useful information. In the upper left-hand margin is the *call number*, which is like a coded address, telling us where in the library's stacks we may find the book, grouped on a shelf with others on the same subject. Libraries usually use one of two main systems to classify their collections. The Dewey Decimal System is based on ten number categories: 000s are general topics, 100s philosophy, 200s religion, 300s social sciences, and so on through 900s. The Library of Congress System, a combination of letters and numbers (A for general works; B philosophy, psychology, and religion; C auxiliary sciences of history; D history; and so on through Z), allows more possibilities for subdivision. Many college libraries are

Subject card

PSYCHOLOGY.

Edwards, David C
BF 121   General psychology ₍by₎ David C. Edwards. 2d ed.
.E3   New York, Macmillan ₍c1972₎
1972

Title card

General Psychology.

Edwards, David C
BF 121   General psychology ₍by₎ David C. Edwards. 2d ed.
.E3   New York, Macmillan ₍c1972₎
1972

Edwards, David C
BF 121   General psychology ₍by₎ David C. Edwards. 2d ed.
.E3   New York, Macmillan ₍c1972₎
1972   xiv, 466 p. illus. 24 cm.

                Bibliography : p. 452–462.

                1. Psychology.   I. Title.
                BF121.E3 1972   150   71–156986
                                                             MARC
Author card   Library of Congress   71 ₍4₎

changing from Dewey Decimal to Library of Congress because the latter is more flexible and better suited to extensive collections.

The call number on the sample cards uses the Library of Congress System. The mark BF means that the book is classified under psychology (an offshoot of philosophy); 121 means that it is a general work or an advanced textbook; .E3 is the Cutter number, which is derived from the author's last name and groups the title with others on the same subject in alphabetical order by author; 1972 is the date of this edition and is included so that the book will be shelved after any earlier editions the library may already have. If classified in the Dewey system, the call number for Edwards's book would be $\frac{150}{E3}$ because 150 is the classification for psychology.

The catalogue also records the edition of the book if other than the first, publisher, date of publication, number of pages (lowercase roman numerals for introductory material, arabic numerals for text), whether the book has illustrations or special features (Edwards's book has a bibliography from pages 452 to 462), often the author's birth and death dates, and, toward the bottom of the card, the other subject headings under which the book is represented in the library catalogue. Those who know how to read a catalogue entry know a good deal about a book before they ever look at it: Is it recent or dated? Is it long or short? What subjects does it touch upon? Preliminary evaluation of a title can save us time and footwork.

When we are doing research, subject entries are especially useful because they bring together at our fingertips the library's resources on a specific topic. But author and title entries are also essential. Sometimes in our background reading we find a title but no author, or we read of an author without reference to books published. Title and author entries provide additional access routes to needed information.

Here are a few things to remember about the organization of the library catalogue:

Most library catalogues are arranged in one alphabet like a dictionary, with author, title, and subject cards interfiled. Occasionally, a library separates its card catalogues into three files for author, title, and subject. Make sure that you understand your own library's organization.

Library catalogues are alphabetized word by word, not letter by letter (*New York* comes before *Newark*), and initial articles (*The, A, An*) are ignored (*A Writer's Reader* is filed under *W*, not *A*). Abbreviated words are alphabetized as if they were spelled out (*St.* as *Saint*) and so too are numbers (*5* as *five*). *Mc* and *M'* are alphabetized as *Mac*, and names with prefixes like *de* and *von* are alphabetized by ignoring the prefix (*von Kreicke* comes under *K*).

Remember that subjects may not always be listed under the words that first occur to us. If we look up "Farming," we may be told "See Agriculture." If there is no entry under the name we have thought of, we should look under near-synonyms. *Roget's Thesaurus* may help, or a librarian can show us the list of subject headings the library uses. Sometimes we may find several titles under our subject; if we look up "Agriculture," we may find an entry that says "See also Livestock," indicating that additional information is under another subject heading.

A writer is an author before he is a subject. Books *by* W. H. Auden will appear before books *about* W. H. Auden.

Subject headings for history are arranged chronologically, not alphabetically. Under "United States—History," "War of 1812" comes *before* "Civil War."

REFERENCE WORKS

First let us consider a reference book *about* reference books: the comprehensive *Guide to Reference Books* by Eugene T. Sheehy (10th ed.; Chicago: American Library Association, 1986), including sections on computer-readable data sources. (The Sheehy book is known to many librarians as "Winchell," after an earlier editor named Constance M. Winchell.) Most college libraries have this book or others like it, which are worth looking at because they list and describe the enormous range of materials available in a reference room—encyclopedias, dictionaries, yearbooks, almanacs, atlases, gazetteers, and hundreds of specialized reference works.

Here, we can examine only a sampling of the most essential reference sources.

Encyclopedias contain general articles, often with bibliographies included, on the entire range of human knowledge. The most widely known is the *Encyclopaedia Britannica,* divided in its newest edition into two multivolumed parts. The *Micropaedia* of ten volumes provides—as the root "micro" suggests—short entries and bibliographies for most topics and serves as an index to the detailed, nineteen-volume *Macropaedia,* which includes immense articles on large subjects, some, like the entry on China, as long as a book.

The *Encyclopedia Americana* is another useful general encyclopedia, with a notable emphasis on American topics. Although less scholarly than the *Britannica* or *Americana, Collier's Encyclopedia* remains useful. Each of these encyclopedias publishes a yearbook reviewing the previous year's significant events. *The New Columbia Encyclopedia* is a compendious one-volume work for quick reference.

Dictionaries include the historical *Oxford English Dictionary* (see page 98) and *A Dictionary of American English on Historical Principles,* which trace word origins, etymology, and the evolution of meaning and usage. Unabridged general dictionaries include *Webster's Third New International Dictionary, Funk and Wagnall's New Standard Dictionary,* and the *Random House Dictionary.* In addition, there are any number of special dictionaries of slang, dialects, idioms, clichés, usage, synonyms, etymology, and abbreviations.

Dictionaries of quotations contain pithy, often familiar remarks by well-known authors. *Bartlett's Familiar Quotations* and *The Oxford Dictionary of Quotations* arrange quotations chronologically by author and have extensive subject indexes. H. L. Mencken's *A New Dictionary of Quotations,* like many others, arranges quotations by topic and has an index of authors.

When we need biographical information, we can look in several places. Encyclopedias include biography. Biographical dictionaries often include people we do not find in encyclopedias. *Who's Who* gives brief, basic facts about the living, as do *Current Biography* and *Contemporary Authors. The Dictionary of National Biography* (DNB) covers British subjects and *The Dictionary of American Biography* (DAB) Americans; *Webster's Biographical Dictionary* and *Chambers's Biographical Dictionary* are international. *Biography Index* and *Biography and Genealogy Master Index* guide the researcher to a wide range of other biographical sources. There are also regional and occupational volumes of *Who's Who*, and specialized compilations like *Notable American Women, Contemporary Poets*, and *American Men and Women of Science.*

Invaluable to anyone researching contemporary problems are the indexes to periodical and newspaper articles. (The library catalogue tells only that the library subscribes to a specific periodical, and sometimes where it is shelved; it does not give information about articles.) Periodical indexes are a record of contemporary thinking on hundreds of topics. The most general periodical index, lined up in thick green volumes, is the *Readers' Guide to Periodical Literature*, which indexes popular and a few specialized and scientific magazines. For more scholarly sources, there are the *Humanities Index* and the *Social Sciences Index* (formerly published together as the *International Index* and then as the *Social Sciences and Humanities Index*). *The New York Times Index* gives a daily index to current events. Other indexes include *Poole's Index to Periodical Literature* and the *Nineteenth Century Readers' Guide to Periodical Literature* for the vast number of periodicals that provided popular entertainment and education in the nineteenth century. Specialized indexes guide us to periodicals in science, technology, art, business, education, psychology, public affairs, and so on.

The Monthly Catalogue of U.S. Government Publications indexes titles from the Government Printing Office on an extraordinary variety of topics.

When we want to find a review of a book, we can look in the "Book Review" section at the end of the bound volumes of *Readers' Guide* under the author's last name. Or we can look in two special indexes: *Book Review Digest*, which includes short quotations from reviews as well as full reference information, and *Book Review Index*, which indexes more than three hundred periodicals.

Sometimes it is not a periodical publication we need to find but a book. We should consult a general bibliography like the *United States Catalog* and *Cumulative Book Index*, which together list almost every book printed in the United States for the last eighty years. *Publisher's Trade List Annual, Books in Print*, and *Paperbound Books in Print* record titles that are currently available from publishers. All these sources can help us discover full information on a title in order to request an interlibrary loan.

Yearbooks and almanacs collect statistical material. We mentioned the yearbooks published by the encyclopedias. There are also annual publications like the *World Almanac, Information Please Almanac, Facts on File, Statistical Abstract of the United States*, and the

Guinness Book of World Records, which record population figures, sports results, world leaders, notable events, economic statistics, and other annual facts.

Basic reference sources for maps and geographic information are the *Encyclopaedia Britannica World Atlas,* the *Rand McNally Cosmopolitan World Atlas,* the *Times Atlas of the World,* and the *National Geographic Atlas of the World.* Historical atlases preserve the geographic past—the route of the Lewis and Clark expedition or Sherman's march to the sea during the Civil War.

When we leave these general categories and become specific, we can find reference books *within* all disciplines: scientific and medical *Who's Who's;* encyclopedias of music and of architecture, of archaeology and of anthropology; and indexes to works of art. Many of these special reference books are listed in the card catalogue under the subject name of the discipline itself. And do not forget to consult the kindly librarian.

Under the subject of literature are innumerable reference works, from histories of the literatures of various languages to dictionaries— like the *Oxford* companions to English, American, and world literatures and the *Oxford Classical Dictionary. Twentieth Century Authors* has been useful to thousands of students. Some of these books, like the last mentioned, quote criticism of the authors discussed, and most of them include bibliographies of works by the authors and of works written about them.

In almost all fields of study are reference works that can help us with research. I cannot list everything that might come in handy. (Sheehy alone runs to more than eight hundred pages.) A few titles hint at the range that you can expect: Grove's *Dictionary of Music and Musicians; Contemporary Biography; The Dictionary of the History of Ideas; The Timetables of History; Encyclopedia of American Biography; Congressional Record; New Catholic Encyclopedia; McGraw-Hill Encyclopedia of Russia and the Soviet Union; Bibliography of Comparative Literature; Anthropology Today: An Encyclopedia Inventory; Mental Health Book Review Index; International Bibliography of Political Science; Nuclear Science Abstracts; Chambers's Technical Dictionary; Chemical Abstracts; Mathematical Reviews; Encyclopedic Dictionary of Physics*—and on and on and on.

New technology has introduced nonbook materials useful to researchers: microfilms and microfiche and direct computer-terminal access to databases (such as ERIC, the Educational Resources Information Center).

When we work on a subject with a local connection, or sometimes on larger topics, we should remember a reference work seldom considered: the telephone book. Frank Rodriguez called a UHF station for the starting dates of two situation comedies (see Chapter 3). The Yellow Pages help us most: when we look into zoning laws, or the mortgage policies of banks, we may find real estate agents or bank officers who are willing to talk to us and supply us with statistics and documentation. Large firms, in manufacturing especially, often include departments of public relations, whose job is to answer questions from the public and to supply information. Always remember that if we write on a disputed subject, self-interest may inform what our sources tell us, and the information selected for us. The president of a utility company will doubtless view the issue of nuclear power with opinions unlike an environmental activist's.

On many subjects, the United States government listings in the white pages may give you numbers to call—the Internal Revenue Service, the Postal Service, the Department of Agriculture. Remember that state and local agencies may be as useful as federal ones.

Another resource we sometimes overlook is our academic community itself. Within the college or university, we can find specialists who will help us define a topic by narrowing our focus, and point us toward specific books and articles in the library. From these people we can discover where to look for recent thinking about almost any subject.

Sometimes a personal interview provides fresh information or a perspective too new for print. A tape recording, made with the permission of the informant, may provide fresh and accurate quotations for a paper. We may question not only academic specialists, but anyone with special information—even members of our own families. Interviews, after all, are the basis for most journalism, as well as for oral historians. What better source on old logging methods than a seventy-six year-old neighbor whose father and grandfather were lumbermen? All families have untapped stories to tell. What was it like to work in a munitions factory in World War II? To survive the Great Depression? To patrol Vietnam in 1967? Uncles, aunts, grandparents, and parents are only waiting for us to ask them.

DOCUMENTATION

As you do your research, you <u>must keep track of your sources.</u> When you write your paper, you must record where quotations and information come from, so that a reader can identify the source and locate it.

Books recommend different systems of documentation, and people working in various disciplines use their own preferred styles. Instructors will require a consistent style of documentation, and many will use the recently revised guidelines adopted by the Modern Language Association: *MLA Handbook for Writers of Research Papers* (3rd ed., New York, 1988). The new *MLA Handbook* departs from the method of annotation traditionally used in the humanities, which called for full footnotes or endnotes as well as a bibliography repeating much of the same information. Taking its cue from the style rules of the American Psychological Association (APA), widely used in the social sciences, the *Handbook* substitutes simplified parenthetical notes within the body of the text. These are keyed to a list of works cited, which we add to the end of the research paper and which contains full citations. The *MLA Handbook* has also expanded its coverage of non-print sources to take account of technological innovations in handling and storing information. It describes how to document films and television programs as well as computer software and databases.

LIST OF WORKS CITED, OR BIBLIOGRAPHY

The list of works cited includes all the sources a writer has consulted to write a research paper, primarily those mentioned in the parenthetical in-text notes, organized alphabetically by the authors' last names. When we write a research paper we will use a list of works cited by necessity; but we must remember *always* to use a bibliography, or similar list, in *any* paper for which we have consulted *any* sources—a book in the library, an informant in an interview, *Newsweek*, a television program.

As you begin to gather information for your research paper, you will want to make a preliminary list of works cited. Whenever you consult a book, an article in a reference work, a newspaper report—any source at all, even if you think you might not use it—take a note. Make notes also of potential sources you come across in your reading. Three-by-five-inch index cards are handy for this purpose because they are easy to add, discard, and rearrange. Your information will fall into three main units, each separated from the next by a period: author, title, publication information. For each book that you consult, record on one card the whole library call number (not to be included when you type your list of works cited, but helpful if you wish to return to the book), author, full title and subtitle (underlined), place of publication (only the first if there is more than one), publisher, and date of publication. The *MLA Handbook* lists shortened forms of publishers' names that simplify our task. Most publishers are represented by one word; any university press adds "UP" to the name of the university. Publishers are listed by the first proper noun of their names: Random House becomes Random; Coward, McCann & Geoghegan becomes Coward; and Farrar, Straus & Giroux becomes Farrar. Exception occurs when the first noun

is somebody's first name: William Morrow & Co. becomes Morrow;
Alfred A. Knopf becomes Knopf. Be sure to record special information:
Is it a second or later edition? A reprint? If a translation, who translated
it? Is there more than one volume? For each periodical article, record
the author if one is named, title of article (in quotation marks), title of
periodical (underlined), volume number (if a scholarly journal), date,
and page numbers. Initial accuracy, however tedious, will save work
later. Your bibliography cards will contain all the information necessary for your final list of works cited; you can alphabetize your cards
and make your list of works cited directly from them. On the next page
are some sample working cards for a list.

The *MLA Handbook* includes a thorough discussion of the proper
manners to use in a list of works cited. Here are sample citations.
Notice punctuation.

A book with one author:
Tedlock, Dennis. *The Spoken Word and the Work of*
Interpretation. Philadelphia: Pennsylvania UP, 1983.

A book with two or three authors:
Herman, Edward S., and Noam Chomsky. *Manufacturing Consent: The*
Political Economy of the Mass Media. New York: Pantheon,
1988.

A book with more than three authors:
Leavitt, Emily Stewart, et al., eds. *Animals and Their Legal Rights.*
3rd ed. Washington: Animal Welfare Institute, 1978.

A book with an editor:
Waters, Lindsay, ed. *Paul de Man: Critical Writings*
1953–1978. Minneapolis: Minnesota UP, 1989.

An article from an edited book:
Lish, Gordon. "True Confessions of a Failed Reader." *The Art of*
Literary Publishing. Ed. Bill Henderson. Yonkers: Pushcart, 1980.
230–38.

A translated book:
Schulz, Bruno. *The Street of Crocodiles.* Trans. Celina
Wieniewska. New York: Penguin, 1977.

A book in several volumes:
Johnson, Edgar. *Charles Dickens: His Tragedy and Triumph.* 2
vols. New York: Simon, 1952.

A new edition:
Arensberg, Conrad M., and Solon T. Kimball. *Family and Community*
in Ireland. 2nd ed. Cambridge: Harvard UP, 1968.

A periodical article:
Mumford, Lewis. "The Cult of Anti-Life." *Virginia Quarterly Review*
46 (1970): 198–206.

> *Fox, Michael*
>
> *Agricide: The Hidden Crisis That Affects Us All*
>
> *New York: Schocken, 1986*
>
> *See especially chs. 1 and 7, also bibliography*

> *Singer, Peter*
>
> *"Unkind to Animals"*
>
> *New York Review of Books*
> *Feb. 2, 1989*
> *pp. 36-38*
> *review of recent books on animal rights*

An article in a popular (monthly or weekly) magazine:
Greenwald, John. "The Search for Shelter." *Time* 30 Apr. 1984: 50–51.

A magazine article with no author given:
"Talk of the Town." *New Yorker* 22 Nov. 1982: 35–40.

A newspaper article:
Perkins, G. V. "What's New in Agriculture." *New York Times* 25
   March 1984: F17.

A lecture:
Jensen, Jack E. Lecture. Colby-Sawyer College. New London, NH, 25
   May 1983.

An interview:
Freemont, Helen. Personal interview. 27 June 1983.

A book review:

Pyne, Stephen J. "A War Against the World." Rev. of *The Control of Nature*, by John McPhee. *New York Times Book Review*, 6 August 1989: 1+.

A recording:
Thomas, Dylan. *Dylan Thomas Reading His Complete Recorded Poetry.* Rec. 1949–53. Caedmon, TC 2014, n.d.

A radio or television program:
Prairie Home Companion. PBS. WGBH, Boston. 17 October 1988.

Computer software:
Tobias, Andrew. *Managing Your Money.* Computer software. MECA (Micro Educational Corporation of America), 1984. 128K, one disk drive.

NOTES

We use <u>parenthetical notes in the body of the text to identify the sources of quotations or paraphrases, facts or opinions that we have derived from others</u>. Because in-text notes refer to the full list of works cited at the end of the research paper, usually the parenthetical citation needs only the last name of the author, or editor or translator, or a short title, and the appropriate page numbers: (Tedlock 43), (*Prairie Home*). It depends on how we enter the source in our list. We can still use endnotes to comment on or to qualify a portion of the text, to mention related but less important information, or to list numerous references (more than three) that would make an in-text parenthesis unmanageably long and disruptive to the attention of the audience. But most documentation appears within the text. The revised *MLA Handbook*, in its guidelines on documentation, requires a close relationship between the text and the notes. When we mention the author's name in a sentence, we need not repeat it in the note:

> In Tedlock's discussion of the transcription of oral narrative (31–61), he . . .

Here, page numbers are sufficient. If we refer to a whole work, mentioning the author's name in the sentence eliminates the need for any note:

> Tedlock has continued the discussion of narrative style and structure in storytelling.

A reader can look in the list of works cited, under "Tedlock," to find the work referred to. If we have consulted more than one work by an author, we must add a short title to the note in order to specify the work cited:

> In his latest work (Tedlock, *Spoken Word*), he describes his methods for analyzing and evaluating verbal performance.

These conventions make it easy for readers to locate the source of our ideas, to check the original, or to find the leads for their own research.

The writer need not note material that is general knowledge. When we mention that the horse is a domesticated animal, we need not supply a source; the information is generally available. But if we supply information about the evolution of the horse from the eohippus, we should refer to our source.

If we quote an author directly, or paraphrase someone else's idea in our own words, without crediting the source of our information, we are guilty of *plagiarism*—a word that comes from the Latin for "kidnapped." Plagiarism, which is defined and discussed in Chapter 1 (and cautioned against in Chapter 8), is serious business. When we neglect to credit our sources, even unintentionally by carelessness, we pass off someone else's words and thoughts as our own. Ideas and arguments are a kind of property, and using those of another writer is considered theft. We must always provide notes to acknowledge our indebtedness. Notes certify our honesty and fairness, and record our dependence on ideas other than our own.

For additional advice on notes, consult the *MLA Handbook.* Parenthetical notes should remain simple and concise. Here are some samples of parenthetical notes that correspond with the sample citations on pages 331–333.

> *A book with one author:* (Tedlock 43)
> *A book with two or three authors:* (Cordell and Matson 148)
> *A book with more than three authors:* (Leavitt et al. 15)
> *A book with an editor:* (Henderson 126)
> *An article from an edited book:* (Lish 235)
> *A translated book:* (Schulz 53)
>
> Unless you are specifically discussing a work as a translation and have entered it in your list of works cited under the translator's name, this note is enough.
>
> *One volume in a multivolume book:* (Johnson 2: 929–40)
> *The whole volume:* (Johnson, vol. 2)
> *A periodical article:* (Mumford 198)

Some abbreviations frequently used in notes and lists of works cited include:

cf.	compare (not "see")
ch., chs., chap.	chapter(s)
ed., eds.	edition, edited by, editor(s)
e.g.	for example
et al.	and others
i.e.	that is
illus.	illustrated by

ms., mss.	manuscript(s)
n., nn.	note(s)
n.d.	no date of publication given in book
n.p.	no place of publication or no publisher given
rev.	revised
trans.	translated by, translator(s)
viz.	namely (however, avoid using)
rpt.	reprinted by, reprint
UP	university press, used in documentation

A RESEARCH PROJECT

Barbara Levine walked back to her dorm one evening during the spring term of her freshman year, worrying about her research paper assignment, a ten-to-twelve-page paper due in four weeks. She had no idea what to write about. That afternoon, she had stopped at her instructor's office; she had hoped to get some suggestions for a topic. But her instructor had confined herself to questions. "What are you curious about?" she had asked. "What would you like to spend some time studying?" Barbara had no answers, and as she paused in the entryway she admitted to herself that she felt discouraged.

Later that night, after dinner, Barbara sat at her desk. "Write about something you are *interested* in," her instructor had urged her. She repeated those words to herself as she doodled on a sheet of paper. Well, she thought finally, she liked animals; she had some ideas about studying to be a veterinarian. But veterinary medicine was simply too huge a subject. Where would she start? Then she remembered an article she had been reading recently while waiting at the dentist's office. It had to do with the debate over animal rights: were animals simply property, or were they entitled to protection? This had started her thinking about the treatment of animals grown for food. She had heard all sorts of terrible things about crowding, force-feeding, and light deprivation. She had also seen advertisements protesting the cruel confinement of veal calves—the pictures showed an animal trapped in a pen no bigger than a coffin. Maybe there was a paper to be written either on the general or on the more specific topic. But where would she start to look for information?

During a free period the next day, Barbara ventured to the library. She spent some time walking to and fro through the stacks on the main floor; then she wandered over to the periodicals room and scanned for magazines devoted to farming or to animal rights. "This won't do," she thought. She had looked high and low and had come up with nothing more than a technical bulletin published by the Humane Society. She was about to leave to make a conference appointment with her teacher when she noticed the reference librarian at her desk.

Five minutes later, Barbara was sitting with pencil and paper in front of a row of big green volumes. The librarian had told her that this was the best place to begin any preliminary research: The *Readers' Guide to Periodical Literature*. These volumes, bound by year, listed under general headings the articles published that year in general and specialized periodicals. Barbara opened one volume at random and looked under the heading *Animals*. The listing, she saw, went on for pages. But then she noticed the various sub-headings: a quick scan brought her to *Treatment*, which was just what she was looking for. There she found listings like the following:

ANIMALS—Continued

Treatment

**Scientist helps stir new movement for animal
rights [M. Fox] D. Nevin. bibl. (p. 152) il pors
Smithsonian 11:50–9 Ap'80**

The reference, Barbara correctly assumed, was to the journal *Smithsonian*. She copied out the other information in her notebook. She wrote "11:50–9"—whatever that meant (it meant the eleventh volume, pages 50 to 59; "il pors" meant "illustrated" and "portraits") and "Ap '80". Down the page she noticed several other possible references: *Animal Experimentation, Animals—Protection, Humane Societies*. Suddenly there were many leads to follow; it was exciting—but she would have to keep her search focused. Barbara spent the next hour going through the more recent volumes of the *Readers' Guide*, taking notes on references, trying to confine herself to citations dealing with farm animals.

When she had filled several pages with numerals and abbreviations, Barbara stopped. She decided to take the next step. She set out to track down the very first article she had listed. To do this Barbara had to make another quick stop at the reference librarian's desk. He explained to her what the numbers and abbreviations referred to and pointed her toward the bound-volume stacks. Barbara had no trouble finding the volumes of *Smithsonian*—there was a whole wall of them—and she sat down right in the aisle with volume 11.

Glancing over the article, Barbara saw that it might be useful to her at some later point. She didn't want to waste precious time in reading and taking notes just yet. She wrote a few phrases next to the

```
HV
4708
.517        Salt, Henry S.
          Animals' Rights Considered in
          Relation to Social Progress
          Preface by Peter Singer

          Early classic, originally published.
          1892, preface (1980) by Peter Singer
          gives historical background.
```

numbers in her notebook—reminders in case she wanted to return—and then turned to look at the bibliography at the end of the article (the *Readers' Guide*'s "bibl") listing three books, a magazine article, and a scientific report. All made some reference to animal factories. Barbara sensed that she had found a controversial topic for herself.

The next afternoon after class she returned to the library and started looking in encyclopedias for general information on animal factories and animal rights. She found nothing. Then she went to the card catalogue to look up the titles from the bibliography at the end of the *Smithsonian* article. Her library owned two of the books.

Reading, she began to compile information and started keeping a list of works cited on three-by-five index cards, one card for each book or article she came across. Under the bibliographic information, she added a note to herself about each source. She kept her cards together with a rubber band, two piles that slowly expanded—one for works cited, another for quotations, summaries, facts, and specific details that she would eventually need to document. She was careful to code her notes to her list of works, to indicate exact page numbers for her references, and to distinguish between quotations and her own summaries, paraphrases, and speculations.

Over the week, Barbara went through the library's catalogue looking at subject cards and tracking down books she found references to. Under *Animals—Treatment*, she found seven titles besides the two she already had, and most of these books provided cross-references to other possibilities. One thing led to another; it was like finding her way through the maze at an amusement park—and sometimes just as confusing. But gradually she began to feel familiar with her topic, and the various pieces of information that she had collected began to fall into place. She jotted down ideas for the shape and purpose of her paper. She didn't try to put her notes in any order, only to gather as many as she could, writing down her fragmentary ideas so that she would not forget them: "an ancient issue . . . man given power over animals in Bible . . . " and "legal aspects, laws that should be passed?" and "health concerns—animal diet and human diet."

Gradually she found herself narrowing her topic. As she looked over *Animal Experimentation* and *Animal Rights—Ethics*, she decided that she wanted to keep to the specific issue of animal rights on factory farms, which the author of the *Smithsonian* article had sketched. She concluded from her preliminary research that the issue of the mistreatment of veal calves was too narrow a subject for her; it would, however, fit in well as a special instance within her larger topic. She began to concentrate on cross-references like *Cattle—Confinement Methods* and to pass over references to antivivisectionism and animal rights movements.

Barbara started to feel more comfortable in the library's reference room and stacks. It became easier for her to locate what she needed. When she could not find one important book in her library, she applied with the aid of a librarian for an interlibrary loan from another college. Another title was being used by someone, but the same librarian showed how the library could recall it for her. On one book that sounded important she reached a dead end; the library did not own and could not locate *Animal Machines* by Ruth Harrison. Barbara felt frustrated—but then she found two articles by Ruth Harrison in a collection of essays on the subject.

Barbara learned how to use a microfilm machine to read an article from a back issue of *The New York Review of Books;* she found a useful review of current studies on animal treatment. A librarian then showed her how to look up government publications. She found specialized periodical indexes in the reference room and used the *Social Science Index.* At the beginning of her search, Barbara had worried about finding enough information to write a ten-page paper. Now she worried about finding too much. She photocopied magazine articles and essays so that she could take them home with her. She wrote notes in the margins of the copies, and underlined with red marker specific information she wanted to use. When she used portions of books, she photocopied the title page, which contained the author, title, and publishing information she would need, and the pages that contained quotations she might need for her paper. She used a tiny stapler to keep together the pages photocopied from each book.

Taking notes in earnest, Barbara switched to four-by-six-inch index cards, because they had room to copy longer quotations and summaries. To save time and avoid recopying, she used some of her cards to index her photocopies: she recorded author's last name, page number, and a rough subject heading. *Cows—Hormones* would lead her to a page about Farrah Faucets, a cow cloned because she was a good milker. For her other notes, she wrote the last name of the author in the upper left-hand corner of the card, adding a short form of the title for authors of more than one book consulted and the page number(s) from which her information came. Usually she jotted a general subject heading in the upper right-hand corner of each card to make sorting easier when she was organizing her thoughts. Most of the time, she summarized or paraphrased important ideas or points related to her argument. One government report said, "In the future, animal breeding programs may be augmented by biotechnology to achieve desired changes with unprecedented speed and selectivity." Barbara summarized, on her index card, "Biotechnology will be a determining factor in how animals are bred in the future." Sometimes she quoted key phrases or opinions directly. She was careful to copy the punctuation and the words exactly and to enclose the material in quotation marks so that she wouldn't mistake the words for her own when she was writing.

A week before her paper was due, Barbara began to organize her notes into related groups. She would describe animal factory systems, with examples and evidence, showing them to be unjust and inhumane. She knew that she would have to leave out much that she had learned. The long history of animal mistreatment had fascinated her as she read about it, but she could do no more than allude to a historical background. (It might, however, be a good place to begin her paper, she thought.) And although animal factories in America produced all kinds of meat, she would not have room to talk about most of the factory methods. She decided to concentrate on poultry, because use of factory methods originated in the poultry industry; she would also find space to speak about veal calves.

She tried out a brief thesis statement: "Protein factories exploit animals in an inhumane way for profit." She consulted her general notes and sketched an informal outline by which she would prove her thesis. When she started this informal outline, she left many spaces between items on her list so that she could backtrack and fill in. Some items she listed twice—first to introduce the subject, later to return and *develop* it. *Animal rights*, for instance, needed to be mentioned at the beginning of the paper, in a context that would lend direction to the exposition of her facts; later, ideas about animal rights (and laws to guarantee them) would form some part of the conclusion of her paper.

When she finished the preliminary list of topics, Barbara assigned letters of the alphabet to each of her items so that she could organize her notes into piles listed under a capital letter. As it happened, she found herself with a complete alphabet of items—twenty-six in all.

A human–animal history	N old/new
B intro.—animal factories	O James Beard quote?
C intro.—animal rights	P vs. reality of situation
D ecology	Q crowding
E health	R anemia
F chicken intro.	S other animals
G crowding	T livestock industry
H feeding	U morals/
I light	V money
J "vices"	W present situation
K cruelty	X animal rights—THESIS
L deformity	Y laws
M veal	Z conclusion

Barbara then sat on the floor of her room to sort the note cards by subject headings into rough piles corresponding to large divisions of her outline. She put aside several which didn't fit anywhere—or which might be fitted into several places.

Beginning a draft was like swimming: should she wade in slowly to get used to the water, or should she jump off the high board? She wrote: "Humans and animals have lived on the earth together for thousands of years." It sounded obvious but she decided to leave it for the moment. She wrote another general sentence and then moved to her note cards for specific information. She described how factories process chickens, and let facts and statistics speak for themselves; then she discussed the raising of veal calves. As she wrote, using her index cards, she kept track of her sources in parenthetical notes, copying the author's name and relevant page numbers from her notes and photocopies.

The day after she finished her first draft, Barbara read it aloud to her roommate. By hearing herself read it and by responding to her roommate's questions, she found sections where her thinking was unclear or her paragraphs jolted into each other without smooth transitions. She revised—reworking tangled sentences, clarifying confused modifiers, adding ideas to explain transitions. Some quotations were too long. Barbara looked up information on the use of ellipses in quotations (see pages 397–398) and recast sentences so that they took quotations smoothly inside themselves. All the time she wrote she was consulting the Critic Inside (see Chapter 3)—she wrote comments in the margins of her successive drafts, urging herself to greater originality, completeness, and clarity. She tinkered with the order of ideas in her paper, cutting and pasting, shifting paragraphs until she found the most logical sequence of ideas. Some ideas, and some information, fit nowhere in her paper; with regret she omitted a few favorite items.

Harrison (in Leavitt)   Law-England
p. 71
Brambell Committee, set up in mid-sixties
to examine animal husbandry, reported
in 1965: (legislation, 1968)
   "In principle we disapprove of a degree
of confinement of an animal which
necessarily frustrates most of the
major activities which make up its
natural behavior."

Note card:
quotation

Singer, _Animal Liberation_   Poultry
p. 116

   "Ultimately, the most convincing way
a bird can indicate that its conditions
are inadequate is by dying."

   egg losses run 10-15% per yr. from
crowding and stress

Note card:
quotation and
statistics

Fox, _Agricide_   Animal Rights
xv.   Corporate Impact On
   "Culture and industry have recently
become mutually exclusive, the latter being
developed at the expense of the former."
   Corporate concern with profit has
brought about a restructuring of
American farming, bringing the family
farm — the values it represents — to the
edge of extinction.

Note card:
quotation and
paraphrase

Two days before her paper was due, Barbara went back to her last draft and read it through with as much detachment as she could manage. Before she began to type the final draft, she remembered that formatting requirements varied from instructor to instructor and from discipline to discipline. Her experience had been that many of her instructors were flexible about formatting and that they asked only for consistency; others allowed little or no departure from instructions they had provided. To be sure that she would not be penalized for this kind of slip, Barbara read the notes she had taken in class the day Dr. Jensen outlined the requirements for this paper. Then she typed the text, rechecked notes to make sure they were accurate and referred clearly to her final list; she added a title page, an outline, and her final list of works cited. The title page was easy. Barbara remembered about the outline, however, only after she was finished writing. Although she had not worked the paper into shape from a written outline, she knew that she could easily derive one from her paper. Because she had taken good notes on her index cards, and because she had organized the cards before drafting her paper, she had constructed it clearly. The ordered pile of cards had been her outline.

Here is the paper she handed in. We have added a few notes in the margin to point out transitions and ways of documenting information.

Animal Rights and Animal Wrongs

by
Barbara Levine

English 102, Section M

Dr. Jensen

May 20, 1989

Animal Rights and Animal Wrongs

Thesis: The way we treat food animals
reflects our wasteful view of the earth
and its resources, which must change.

  I. Introduction

      A. Long—term perspective

      B. Animal Factories

          1. Institutionalized
              inhumaneness

          2. Waste and pollution

          3. Health

          4. Agribusiness

 II. Examples of factories

      A. Chickens

          1. Factory Conditions

              a. Crowding

              b. Lighting

          2. Vices

              a. Aggressive behavior

                 (1) Pecking

                 (2) Cannibalism

              b. Poor health

          3. Death and the dollar

      B. Veal

          1. Original source

          2. Factory conditions

               a. Crowding

              b. Anemia

      C. Other animals

III. Supporters of factory systems

    A. Agribusiness

        1. Tax incentives for investment

        2. Animals as ''output''

        3. Technology

    B. Feed, equipment, service companies

    C. Agricultural researchers

IV. Protecting animal rights

    A. British example/Swedish law

    B. U.S. must follow

    C. Direct, indirect benefits of changed production modes

        1. Reduce speciesism

        2. Reduce other costs of factory system

V. Conclusion

    A. Humane approach is practical

    B. Regaining our humanity—view toward the future

Animal Rights and Animal Wrongs

lively title attracts attention and names the paper's subject

Humans and animals have lived on the earth together for thousands of years— ever since humans evolved from the higher apes. One mark of our separation, and supposed superiority, was that we began using and exploiting our fellow creatures. We killed them for food, harnessed them to pull our loads, and took their hides for our coverings. Indeed, using animals in this way has been taken as a sign of being human (Peters 228). We have acted as if animals existed primarily to be of use to us. From the first we have abused them for amusement, sport, and luxury, as well as for the necessities of survival.

note credits an idea

The belief that human beings come first is continuous in our history. In Genesis we read that God gave Adam power over all creatures. But what is meant by power? Does it mean that we can use these creatures as we see fit, with no regard for their rights? There is no easy answer to this question. Philosophers have been debating the status of animal life for centuries, and the issues are live today in the writings of Peter Singer, Tom

first two paragraphs are general, to be followed by a more specific paragraph

Regan, and others. But as important as
their questioning may be, it does not do
much to ease the plight of animals: our
exploitation of living creatures is worse
today than it ever was.

Since the 1950's, modern technology
has created the assembly—line protein
factory in which animals undergo, as
protesters say, ''restrictions and
manipulations that would be regarded as
atrocities if practiced on humans''
(Mason and Singer xiii). The number of
animals raised under these conditions is
staggering: nearly 3.5 billion broiler
chickens, 280 million battery hens, 1
million veal calves, and 50 million pigs
in a year (Fox <u>Agricide</u> 7). This vast,
institutionalized exploitation raises the
question: do animals have the right to
humane treatment? Writers like Singer and
Regan argue that they do. But under the
Uniform Commercial Code, which sets out
consumer guidelines, animals constitute
''goods'' (Zak 71).

There are other issues as well. Animal
factories produce enormous waste and
pollution. They use land and energy
resources carelessly. They manufacture
meat in quantity by compromising quality,

*transition
introduces the
main subject of
animal factories*

*quotation worked
into sentence,
source noted*

*note credits source
of information*

*note credits
magazine article*

which harms human health. Powerful
agribusiness conglomerates expropriate
the small farmer and contribute to the
decline of rural life. They channel to
animals large amounts of grain that, if
distributed as grain, could relieve
hunger throughout the world.

What are these factory systems like? A
look behind the scenes––at a factory
building for poultry, a veal confinement
shed, a cattle feedlot, or a pig ''bacon
bin''––would be a gruesome eye–opener for
anyone. ''The modern chicken,'' say the
authors of Animal Factories, ''is a business
creation'' (Mason and Singer 3). Today we
take eating chicken for granted, but only
the development of factory methods in the
poultry industry after World War II[1] has
made the chicken inexpensive enough for
the American table. The chicken is twice
as unlucky as other animals, for we eat
its eggs as well as its flesh. Poultry
producers have bred two varieties of the
White Leghorn, one designed for meat, the
other for eggs. Both broilers and layers
are kept in animal factories.

From ten to fifty thousand, and in
several large West Coast businesses, as
many as 90,000 day–old chicks are brought
from hatcheries and placed in a long

*question introduces
the main section of
paper, answered in
next 12 paragraphs*

*quotation and
source in text*

*endnote 1 refers
reader to other
sources for
information
outside scope of
discussion*

*transition sentence
leads to detailed
description*

windowless building. Often the chicks
crowd on concrete floors. Sometimes as
many as four or five are stuffed into tiny
cages, 12 by 18 inches, to prevent the
pile—ups that can suffocate them if they
are loose. It is the lesser of two evils,
but just barely. These little cages have
no perches because those would take up
room, and chickens stand on the gridded
bottom as best they can. Standing up is
especially hard for layers because the
bottoms of their cages are often slanted
to allow eggs to roll down to the
collection shelves. Bird droppings fall
through the wire to an area below that
may not be cleaned at all until the crop
of birds is finished. One employee can
supervise mechanized food and water
supplies for thousands of birds. The
factory managers manipulate electric
lights, according to the protein they
wish to manufacture: darkness quiets
broilers so that they gain more weight,
and eighteen hours of simulated daylight
stimulate layers to produce more eggs
(Singer 100—108; Smith and Daniel 267—69;
Nevin 54—55).

     Crowding keeps birds from establishing
their natural social hierarchy and
creates boredom and stress. Stress

*note combines
sources for
information in
paragraph*

*a descriptive
paragraph moves
onward to specific
abuses, from lesser
to greater*

produces the ''vices,'' as the
manufacturers call them, of pecking and
cannibalism, as well as greater
susceptibility to disease. But instead of
cutting down on crowding, and lowering
profits, producers routinely de-beak
chickens with a hot knife. This
mutilation is most certainly painful to
the animal and it makes it difficult or
impossible for some hens to eat. Because
layers live longer, they may have to be
de-beaked a second time. To counter the
increased possibility of disease, poultry
producers feed their birds a high-
additive feed containing antibiotics,
tranquilizers, and appetite stimulators
(Singer 102–104). As consumers of store-
bought broilers, we cannot be sure how
much of what we're tasting is chicken,
and how much is chemical additive.

Observers have called these chicken
and egg factories ''an Inferno as
terrible in its own way as any of the
circles of Dante's hell'' (Smith and
Daniel 287). Ultimately, they frustrate
all the birds' natural instincts to walk,
scratch, take dust baths, nest, stretch
their wings, defend themselves, and claim
a place in the pecking order. Methods for
reviving fallen-off egg production can

*quotation used to
introduce writer's
criticism*

cause death from shock. Manure piled
underneath cages gives off a searing reek
of ammonia. The wire of the cages damages
feet and claws, in some cases causing a
chicken's foot to grow to the wire
(Singer 111, 114–15).

Because the buildings depend on
automated ventilation systems, a
mechanical or electrical failure kills
thousands of birds. But factory chickens
don't live long anyway. Broiler hens are
slaughtered at eight or nine weeks; egg
layers are worn out after fourteen months
and are shipped off to become chicken
pie, soup, fast food and pet food (it is
ironic to think of less valued animals
being used as feed for more valued ones).
By contrast, a free-run chicken lives up
to fifteen or twenty years (Mason and
Singer 5). Peter Singer observes in his
book, Animal Liberation, that ''ultimately, the
most convincing way a bird can indicate
that its conditions are inadequate is by
dying.'' And the birds do indicate this
very thing: the mortality rates on egg
farms run as high as ten to fifteen
percent (116). Even so, these protein
plants remain profitable operations. A
spokesman sums up the industry outlook:
''The object of producing eggs is to make

*notice transition
from detail to
general information*

*author mentioned
in text; therefore,
note includes only
page number*

money. When we forget this objective, we
have forgotten what it is all about''
(Singer 108).

Over the last thirty years the barn–
yard chicken has all but disappeared––what
shoppers imagine they are buying is very
nearly a memory. Replacing it are
industrialized egg machines and additive–
filled monsters with deformed feet, too
heavy to stand on their own bones and
muscles. Only artificial coloring makes
egg yolks and chicken flesh yellow,
allowing the consumer to believe that
nothing has changed.

paragraph sums up the poultry business before turning to veal

Compared to the poultry producer, the
veal farmer operates on a much smaller
scale. Veal farms usually keep fewer than
a hundred animals at a time. Yet Singer
calls raising calves for veal the ''most
morally repugnant'' of all the factory
systems (127). Originally, veal was the
naturally pale and tender meat of male
calves killed before weaning. These
calves never weighed much beyond 90
pounds, and killing them for meat was a
practical way for the dairy farmer to
dispose of animals he could not raise to
milk. But expensive restaurants, many of
them catering to the new cuisines,
want this meat. And now there are

transitional and sentence introduces additional example

European methods of raising veal calves

contrast of new and old

to weigh more than 300 pounds

(Singer 128).

In one of his cookbooks, food writer
James Beard has written:

> Good veal has always been difficult to
> find. But recently a Dutch process has
> come to our shores and is giving us
> limited quantities of much finer veal
> than was generally available before
> . . . The process consists simply of
> taking calves from their mothers' milk
> to small stalls, where they are fed
> with vitamins and powdered milk that
> contains no iron to darken the flesh.
> Also, the calves are kept comparatively
> quiet during their milk regime. Thus,
> they have delicate whitish-pink flesh
> and clear fat and are deliciously
> tender (qtd. in Mason and Singer 126).

quotation (longer than four lines) indented ten spaces, double-spaced

quotation taken from a secondary source, usually it is preferable to quote the original

Maybe gourmet cooks and diners would
like to believe this health-spa
description, but the true picture is
horrible. Newborn calves are taken from
their mothers to a windowless concrete-
block building containing slat-floored
wooden stalls only two feet wide. These
stalls are in fact more like coffins.
Here the calves stay for the sixteen
short weeks of their lives. They eat only

transition by contrast, descriptive paragraph

a high-intensity diet of nonfat milk, vitamins, minerals, antibiotics, and drugs for growth and weight. They do not so much eat as get force-fed. They have no water at all, and in their thirst they gorge themselves on their liquid feed, thus gaining weight faster and making more money for their owners.

These calves remain chained in their stalls, usually in complete darkness for twenty-two out of twenty-four hours; this is to cut down on movement which would toughen their meat. The slatted floors hurt their legs. They cannot extend their feet when they lie down. They cannot groom themselves or turn around. The heart-wrenching photographs in magazine advertisements calling for an end to this inhumane treatment are not exaggerated.

break paragraph to preserve readable length

Stalls housing these animals have no straw for bedding; straw contains iron, and iron would darken the calves' meat. The ideal white, or milk-fed, flesh comes from acute anemia. By the time the calves are three and a half months old, weighing about 330 pounds, they are seriously ill and would die of anemia if they were not slaughtered for restaurant food. Some calves crave iron so much that they lick iron stall bars and their own urine, which contains iron residues.[2]

endnote 2 gathers sources too long for inclusion in text

   The veal industry, finding it profitable to supply a steady demand for pale meat, deliberately induces severe anemia, constrains movement to the point of paralysis, and produces an extremely sick animal, prone to ulcers, watery bowel movements, and pneumonia. The mortality rate of veal calves runs as high as fifty percent (Mason and Singer 25). One large veal producer expresses the industry view: ''Farming is about money production, not food production'' (Singer 130), and the demand for veal is such that producers can absorb high calf losses and still turn a solid profit.

another paragraph of summary, before moving on

   A similar kind of exploitation occurs in cattle feedlots and dairy-cow and pig confinement sheds.[3] Producers encourage rapid gains in weight by adding growth stimulators to grain. Until 1979, these chemicals included DES, since banned by the Food and Drug Administration as a cause of cancer (Mason and Singer 61, 69; Robbins 218–19, 224–25). Cows and pigs are kept immobilized in stalls and must be bred continually to supply the system. The results are obvious and depressing:

endnote 3 refers reader to further information on subject

bored, aggressive animals showing all the symptoms of stress.

How did the livestock industry get like this? The big answer is simple: because there were profits to be made. In the last few years, agribusiness interests have bought their way into the system. These corporations have the capital needed for starting up (Singer 98); they have not hesitated to push the smaller independent farmers and producers out of business. Some factories are then promoted as opportunities for capital investment or as ways to reduce taxes. U.S. tax policies have encouraged large-scale investment by nonagricultural companies like Greyhound, ITT, and John Hancock Mutual. These companies make their decisions based on the so-called ''bottom line,'' on ''input and output costs and values'' (Mason and Singer 18). Businessmen, searching for a uniform, profitable end-product, translate animals into ''raw materials'' and ''conversion units,'' the value-free vocabulary of technology. This way of thinking—by people who never set eyes on a suffering veal calf or chicken—makes it all too easy to pursue inhumane policies. And while we might accept a cost-effective

another question leads to an answer in following paragraphs, helps reader locate place in argument

note credits an idea

note credits a direct quotation

approach in the manufacturing of plastics
or cars, its hard consequences on the
lives of animals make such cost—
effectiveness intolerable in meat
production.

Two other groups have encouraged the
owners of animal factories: commercial
feed, equipment, and services companies
find their best customers in agribusiness;
and agricultural research institutions at
our universities, subsidized by tax
dollars, find projects and grant money for
developing these exploitative systems.
The articles and advertisements in
Successful Farming, the principal trade journal,
discuss output, productivity, and
innovation as if they were referring to
the manufacture of computer chips.
Meanwhile, the small farmers, who lack
the capital for buildings and equipment
to compete with agribusiness interests,
must sell out and leave the land. Some
smaller producers have found a way to
compromise: they have adopted factory
methods with the help of suppliers who
sell them feed and stock and buy back the
finished animals (Robbins 214–16). But
like the barnyard chicken, the
independent small farmer, or producer, is
nearly extinct.

As automation increases, the conditions in which animals are kept only worsen. It is economical to employ fewer human supervisors, but this means less attention to individual animals in distress. Instead of eliminating the methods that cause stress and its problems—aggression, cannibalism, tail-biting, and more disease—farm experts turn to <u>more</u> mechanization, <u>more</u> mutilation, and <u>more</u> genetic manipulation. E.F. Schumacher, economist and advocate of smallness (his book is called <u>Small Is Beautiful</u>), testifies to the craziness of this approach when he says that it is like trying ''to cure a disease by intensifying its causes'' (35). The solution to problems caused by technology always seems to be more technology.

Scientific methods have already given us anemic calves, neurotic chickens, and bored pigs that gnaw on their own tails. Yet researchers continue to try to ''improve'' agricultural practices and increase efficiency. There have recently been attempts to breed animals that eat and digest faster and sleep less so that they can put on more weight. Other researchers have looked for ways to make

transition to conclusion based on research

commercial feeds out of animal wastes,
cement dust, cardboard, and newspaper,
lending new meaning to the old saying
''You are what you eat.'' Still others
have tried to develop chickens without
neck feathers because these feathers clog
decapitating machines (Mason and Singer
47–49).

These practices have not gone
unnoticed or unprotested. Various animal
rights organizations have actively sought
to publicize inhumane treatment and have
lobbied for legal reforms. But small
groups of activists are simply no match
for the vested interests of large
agribusiness corporations. Nor have many
scientists come forth to call for
changes. Indeed, mentioning ''animal
rights'' brings down the wrath of a
scientific community heavily involved in
laboratory experimentation with animals.
People who favor humane treatment for
animals are dismissed as sentimental and
faint–hearted. But Dr. Michael Fox,
director of the Institute for the Study
of Animal Problems, a Washington DC–based
organization, says that animal–rights
activists merely want people ''to see
animals as animals and treat them so''

(Between Animal 58). He claims that depriving
an animal of its natural needs is as
inhumane as inflicting unnecessary pain.

partial title cited for author with two books in "Works Cited"

    In the mid-1960's, Ruth Harrison
alerted the British public to the horrors
of factory systems in England. Her book,
Animal Machines, prompted the government to
investigate the conditions she described.
The Brambell Report of 1965, from a
specially appointed committee of the
British Parliament, acknowledged that
animals are capable of suffering and
outlined a bill of rights for animals. It
held that animals should be able to get
up, lie down, turn around, stretch, and
groom. This may not sound like much to
ask, but in fact it represented a great
step forward. In addition, the committee
asked that agricultural animals be fed on
a diet sufficient for health and receive
adequate light. The committee condemned
slatted floors without bedding, de-
beaking, de-tailing, and similar
mutilations. It condemned any ''degree of
confinement of an animal which necessarily
frustrates most of the major activities
which make up its natural behavior''
(Harrison 71).

    Legislation for animal rights was
enacted in England in 1978, setting up

minimal codes of practice for animal
factories and an advisory council to keep
watch on practices. So far, the United
States has no similar laws. Both Holland
and France, the first countries to
practice veal confinement methods, now
prohibit methods still common in the
United States (Nevin 58). Sweden enacted
stringent laws of protection in 1988.

It is vital that we pass legislation
for animal rights in the United States,
even if we only begin with small matters.
Precedents must be set in the courts; the
process must get underway. If we only
reduce crowding and allow animals room to
move and socialize, we will eliminate
many of the conditions now treated with
tranquilizers. We must take action: by
publicizing inhumane conditions, by
boycotting products if necessary. A
message must be sent to agribusinesses.

*argument, with
supporting facts*

Animal factory systems not only inflict
suffering on animals, but also impose
other hidden costs on all of us (Mason
and Singer 73–93, 127). They are
wasteful: over 140,000 tons of poultry
meat are condemned at processing plants
every year (Mason and Singer 77). Instead
of valuable nitrogen from the manure of
free-ranging animals, factory systems

release potent pollutants, full of antibiotics and chemicals, onto the land and into water supplies. Enormous amounts of fossil–fuel energy power the ventilating, heating, and feeding machines: tons of fertilizer, much of it petrochemical, go to grow the quantities of grain used for animal feed. Some scientists have estimated that if the whole world ate the high–protein meat diet that Americans do, the world's petroleum reserves would give out in a matter of years (Pimental et al., 847).

note for more than three authors

     As uninformed consumers, we are part of a self–perpetuating cycle: we buy and eat the meat that factory systems produce; our purchases make the market profitable, and therefore producers build more factory farms. While the cycle continues, our health may be suffering from the additives given to animals to make them put on weight, prevent disease, and tranquilize them. Industry overuse of antibiotics has produced drug–resistant forms of bacteria like salmonella, gonorrhea, and typhoid (Mason 61; Mason and Singer 83). Research further links the high meat consumption of the American diet to heart disease, diabetes, stroke, and cancer. The animal factory stands at

transition from waste of resources to dangers to health

the center of a web of intricately
related moral and environmental problems.

    If we have learned anything from the
ecological disasters of recent years—
disasters like the Alaskan oil spill, the
discovery of toxins at Love Canal, the
ongoing destruction of our ozone layer—
it is that our future survival will
depend upon the recognition of the
interdependence of all planetary life. We
live in an ecosystem, and maintaining the
necessary balance requires that we treat
all living creatures—and systems—with
respect. We must seek to coexist with
animals; we must stop the inhumane
domination which treats them like so
many tons of raw material. As Peter
Roberts said in a symposium on animal
rights, ''By denying them light,
movement, exercise, occupation and the
social contact of their own kind, we
reverse their evolution and in so doing
we reverse our own'' (132).

    If we can magnify cruelty so
thoughtlessly, and end by harming not
only animals but ourselves, perhaps we
can reinvent humane conscience in
ourselves as well. When we think about
the technology that we invented to serve
us—and which seems instead to ruin us

transition from
negative to positive

and our companions on earth--we should listen to Wendell Berry. As a farmer and a poet, he writes:

> Our great dangerousness is that locked in our selfish and myopic economics, we have been willing to destroy far beyond our power to understand. We are not humble enough or reverent enough (85).

use of strong quotation from authoritative source

If we can find this humility and reverence in ourselves, then we can begin taking the steps to right the massive wrong that we have perpetrated.

summary of argument

Notes

[1] See Smith and Daniel, chs. 12–14.

[2] Summarized from Singer 127–35; Mason and Singer 13–14, 27–29; Mason 62; Hutchings and Caver 97–98.

[3] See Mason 58–63; Singer 118–26, 135–38.

Works Cited

Berry, Wendell. A Continuous Harmony:
Essays Cultural and Agricultural. New
York: Harcourt, 1972.

Fox, Michael W. Agricide. New York:
Schocken, 1986.

———. Between Animal and Man. New York:
Coward, 1976.

Harrison, Ruth. ''Animals in Factory
Farms.'' Animals and Their Legal
Rights: A Survey of American Laws from
1641 to 1978. Ed. Emily Stewart
Leavitt et al. 3rd ed. Washington:
Animal Welfare Institute, 1978.
69–73.

Hutchings, Monica, and Mavis Caver. Man's
Dominion: Our Violation of the Animal
World. London: Hart–Davis, 1970.

Mason, James B. ''Livestock Factory.''
Country Journal. Oct. 1980: 58–63.

Mason, Jim, and Peter Singer. Animal
Factories. New York: Crown, 1980.

Nevin, David. ''Scientist Helps Stir New
Movement for Animal Rights.''
Smithsonian. Apr. 1980: 50–59.

Peters, Michael. ''Nature and
Culture.'' Animals, Men and Morals: An
Enquiry into the Maltreatment of
Non–humans. Ed. Stanley Godlovitch,

Roslind Godlovitch, and John Harris.
London: Gollancz, 1971. 213–31.

Pimental, David, et al. ''The Potential
for Grass–Fed Livestock: Resource
Constraints.'' Science 207 (1980):
843–48.

Robbins, William. The American Food
Scandal. New York: Morrow, 1974.

Roberts, Peter. ''The Experts Say This Is
Not Cruel . . . '' Animals' Rights––A
Symposium. Ed. David Paterson and
Richard D. Ryder. London: Centaur,
1979. 131–34.

Schumacher, E.F. Small Is Beautiful. New
York: Perennial Library, 1989.
rev. ed.

Singer, Peter. Animal Liberation: A New
Ethics for Our Treatment of
Animals. New York: New York Review,
1975.

Smith, Page, and Charles Daniel. The
Chicken Book. Boston: Little, 1975.

Zak, Steven. ''Ethics and Animals.''
Atlantic Monthly. March 1989:
69–74.

10

A Brief Review of Grammar, Punctuation, and Mechanics

This book is mostly about style and structure, about making writing lively, honest, energetic, and clear. As you move through the text, you find grammar when you need it. Here, we want to make a concentrated review of the most common errors in grammar, punctuation, and mechanics, so that the beginning writer who feels confused —What *is* a whole sentence? When *do* I use a colon?—will have a place to come for answers to questions. It may also serve the writer who, after a summer vacation or a year away from the classroom, needs a quick review of grammar and mechanics concentrating on errors frequently made.

If our grammar is loose and shabby, our punctuation random, and our mechanics haphazard, we will lose our audience. We must put sentences together by rules, because rules describe the readers' expectations. If our language ignores these rules—if we substitute commas for periods or neglect to match parts of sentences to each other—readers will be confused and bored; they will not follow where we want to lead them, even if our ideas are profound and our information fascinating.

When things go wrong in mechanics and grammar, for an inexperienced writer, they go wrong usually because of a few mistakes. If you can follow six general rules, you will avoid most of the errors beginners fall into.

1. Make whole, clear sentences.
2. Match the parts of sentences that need matching.
3. Connect modifiers with what they modify.

4. Keep the sentence consistent.
5. Keep punctuation clear.
6. Keep mechanics conventional.

These rules will become useful only if we do some explaining and give examples. Almost everything mentioned here is repeated from earlier chapters; this chapter is repetitious, but it ought to be useful. It differs from the text in the approach to writing. In the text we talk mostly about the choices a writer can make to express meaning with vigor and clarity. Here, you can read about the swamps that you as a writer can sink into, which keep you from reaching your goal.

Many inexperienced writers have trouble with only one or two of the problems we list and not with the rest. People sitting next to each other in class may have opposite troubles in writing. Neighbor A writes sentence fragments, B uses commas for periods, C mixes up pronouns, and D dangles modifiers. None of them has the problem that the other has, and each is thoroughly confused by his own problem. With this chapter, each student can go directly to his particular problem; we hope it can help the whole alphabet of writers.

MAKE WHOLE, CLEAR SENTENCES

Sentence Fragments

Beginning writers commonly make sentences—groups of words beginning with a capital letter and ending with a period—which don't complete an action. In an essay a student wrote

The effects of World War II.

as if the phrase told us something. But the sentence is incomplete, a sentence fragment. What *about* World War II? Did he want to say

Hungary suffered the effects of World War II.

or

World War II brought prosperity.

or what? In his essay, the writer had said

The economy began picking up finally in 1939. The effects of World War II.

He needed to connect the sentence fragment to the sentence, making something like this:

The economy began picking up in 1939 because of World War II.

The best writers sometimes put sentence fragments to good use (see pages 153–156), but when you are inexperienced, you should avoid them entirely. Wait until you have developed a firm and exact feel for the whole sentence's shape. Do not write

> He was a good teacher. Being sympathetic with students and fascinated by his subject.

Instead, write something like

> He was a good teacher, sympathetic with students and fascinated by his subject.

Do not write

> The pumpkins froze. When the blizzard arrived unexpectedly in October.

Instead, write something like

> When the blizzard arrived unexpectedly in October, the pumpkins froze.

Here are some inadvertent sentence fragments, indicated by italics.

> *After the sun finally sank behind the hills.* It was dark and we were ready.

> The principal of my high school was a nice person *Believing that every kid was potentially all right.*

> *Seeing the Buick with all its tires flat and rusted out in the grass, with no license plates on it.*

> The people at the fair stared at the twins and began to talk about them. *Because they looked different, I guess.*

> Teachers in my opinion do not have the right to strike and miss their classes. *When students have already paid their tuition.*

Inadvertent sentence fragments are mainly of two kinds. Many fragments are subordinate clauses treated as if they were whole sentences. In three of the examples, the sentence fragments begin with *because, after,* and *when.* These words—like *although, since,* and *while*—mean that the clauses they introduce depend on, or hang from, a main clause; they are dependent or subordinate clauses. In the preceding examples, the main clauses (not in italics) make whole sentences themselves. The sentence fragments could become subordinate clauses in complex sentences.

> Teachers in my opinion do not have the right to strike and miss their classes, *when students have already paid their tuition.*

The other category, shown in the second and third examples, is the fragment that modifies a main clause and ought to be separated from it by a comma—not by a period and a capital letter.

> The principal of my high school is a nice person, *believing that every kid is potentially all right.*

Watch out for sentence fragments that begin with an *-ing* word, just as you watch for fragments beginning with *when* or *because.*

You can correct sentence fragments in several ways. You can correct *many* sentence fragments simply by using a comma instead of a period. Or you can add a verb to the fragment and make it a whole sentence, equal to the other.

Here are some alternate repairs for sentence fragments used earlier.

> He was a good teacher. He was sympathetic with students and fascinated by his subject.

> He was a good teacher because he was sympathetic with his students and fascinated by his subject.

> The blizzard arrived unexpectedly in October, freezing the pumpkins.

> The blizzard arrived unexpectedly in October, and the pumpkins froze.

> Because the blizzard arrived unexpectedly in October, the pumpkins froze.

> We saw the Buick with all its tires flat, rusted out in the grass, no license plates on it.

> The principal of my high school was a nice person. He believed that every kid was potentially all right.

> The people at the fair stared at the twins and began to talk about them; they looked different, I guess.

> After the sun finally sank behind the hills, it was dark and we were ready.

> The sun finally sank behind the hills. It was dark and we were ready.

Notice that frequently a sentence fragment can become a whole clear sentence when we remove the subordinating word, like *because,* or change the modifying participle into a subject and a verb—like *we saw* for *seeing.*

_____ **EXERCISES** _____

1. Each of these five passages contains one or more sentence fragments. Identify each fragment, and revise it into a whole sentence in two ways.

    a. When the sun rose high in the sky. All of us gathered twigs and fallen branches to make a fire. Then making breakfast for the whole group.

    b. No-fault insurance helps all motorists. The good and the bad. Every state should pass no-fault automobile insurance.

    c. When the Ford Motor Company named a new car the Pinto, they did a lot of research into the power of names. Names on the final list were largely the names of animals. Based on the discovery of a market research firm.

    d. The morning of our trip to school, the car all packed and ready, the rain falling in sheets outside.

    e. Never too late to learn! That is what my high school civics teacher always told us. Which we heard so often that we didn't hear it anymore.

2. Combine the sentence fragments in this paragraph into whole sentences.

> When I rented my first apartment, I learned a lot. How to make spaghetti. By the potful. And to keep dirty shirts and socks from piling up on the floor of my closet. I'll never forget the first time I went to the laundromat. Pouring bleach straight on the clothes. Holes in everything. Even my favorite jeans.

Comma Splices

Comma splices (or comma faults) and run-on sentences are the opposite of sentence fragments. In the comma splice, a comma is forced into the work a period is meant for; in the sentence fragment, a period is pressed into the service a comma is designed for. Here is a typical comma splice, two whole sentences incorrectly joined by a comma:

> The Union stands back from the street about a hundred feet, it was built when land was still cheap.

Substitute a period for the comma, capitalize the next word, and you have two real, whole sentences.

Often the same writer makes sentence fragments and comma splices, because both errors depend on an insecure grasp of what makes a sentence. By reading our prose aloud, pausing according to the punctuation, we can sometimes discover these errors in time to revise them.

The comma splice is confusing to the reader, because two whole ideas are connected (spliced) as if they were not each whole and separate. The writer gives a signal by the comma but the sentence denies the message that the comma carries. The comma gives us the information that we are reading one continuous idea, which conflicts with the wholeness of each of the two spliced sentences. The best writers sometimes use the comma splice to good effect (see pages 166–167), but the beginning writer should avoid the device entirely, until he has developed a firm sense of the sentence.

Writers often make comma splices when they use conjunctive adverbs like *however, moreover, consequently, therefore, besides, then,* and *otherwise*. When these words connect main clauses, we use a semicolon between the clauses, before the adverb, and a comma after the adverb. Do not write

She was intelligent, moreover she had a Ph.D. from Harvard.

but write

She was intelligent; moreover, she had a Ph.D. from Harvard.

Here are comma splices taken from student essays.

The port of New York has minimum safety requirements, some vessels have to dock in Hoboken.

The inevitability of war became obvious to even the most casual observer, maneuvers were constantly being held.

My father grew up on a potato farm in Idaho, he never saw a movie until he was twenty-two years old.

She walked through the door into the dining room, she wore nothing but a bikini.

When they were little, they liked to play in the empty warehouse down the block, it was a spooky and exciting place.

I didn't know where the arboretum was, somebody had to show me.

We were late for the movie, however it started late.

Never eat vegetables from a can which looks puffed up like a balloon, that's something I learned at camp.

Whoever saw the man running away saw the burglar, that's the only possible explanation.

Making a sweater from acrylic gets you into other problems, wool is better when you are beginning.

The canoe started tipping as I approached the falls, I was terrified that I would lose all my gear.

When you correct a comma splice, you have four alternatives. Two of them require only a change in punctuation; two of them require another word.

1. Substituting a semicolon for a comma repairs most comma splices. Making a comma splice often means you want to show a close connection between two whole sentences. You try to move quickly from one to the other, without the long pause implied by a period and a capital letter. The semicolon was invented for just this purpose: to show that two whole sentences follow quickly upon each other and are closely related.

Here are comma splices repaired by semicolons.

The port of New York has minimum safety requirements; some vessels have to dock in Hoboken.

The inevitability of war became obvious to even the most casual observer; maneuvers were constantly being held.

When they were little, they liked to play in the empty warehouse down the block; it was a spooky and exciting place.

2. Or you can use a period and a capital letter; they will always be correct.

My father grew up on a potato farm in Idaho. He never saw a movie until he was twenty-two years old.

Never eat vegetables from a can which looks puffed up like a balloon. That's something I learned at camp.

3. On the other hand, you can make a complex sentence, if you find that one sentence can depend on the other, by using a subordinating conjunction.

When the canoe started tipping as I approached the falls, I was terrified that I would lose all my gear.

4. Or you can connect the two sentences into one compound sentence with *and, but, or, not, yet,* or *so;* the two clauses will be equally strong, or coordinate.

I didn't know where the arboretum was, so somebody had to show me.

The port of New York has minimum safety requirements, and some vessels have to dock in Hoboken.

She walked through the door into the dining room, but she wore nothing but a bikini.

Each of these four solutions makes a slight difference in tone or meaning. In your context, one of the four will be best. Compare these variations of one sentence:

When they were little, they liked to play in the empty warehouse down the block; it was a spooky and exciting place.

When they were little, they liked to play in the empty warehouse down the block. It was a spooky and exciting place.

When they were little, they liked to play in the empty warehouse down the block because it was a spooky and exciting place.

When they were little, they liked to play in the empty warehouse down the block, and it was a spooky and exciting place.

The writer's choice should depend on mood and rhythm appropriate to context. The semicolon makes a slight pause and the period brings the thought to a full stop. The conjunction *because* makes the second part of the sentence depend on the first, implying cause and effect. The conjunction *and* connects two clauses in an equal partnership.

―――― **EXERCISES** ―――――――――――――――――――――――――――――――

1. Here are five passages from student essays. Identify the comma splices, and revise the passages into whole, single sentences. Use any of the four methods listed above. Then revise these passages again, using another of the four methods.

    a. Carbon monoxide filled the foggy air, we could breathe only with difficulty.
    b. Sunset fell rapidly, we had to hurry to set up our tent.
    c. When the waitress removed an empty platter, she was back with a full platter a moment later, I never ate so much in my life, I was so full I thought I would burst.
    d. Riding a bike you must never expect someone driving a car to notice you, you must always watch out for yourself.
    e. The carrots pulled easily from the wet ground, it had rained for a week.

2. In this paragraph, make whole sentences from the comma splices.

> Behind my uncle's barn sat four old cars, they were in various stages of disintegration, most were rusting in the tall weeds. The grille on the '32 Chevy grinned like decayed teeth, I thought when I was little, the doors sagged open. Years of rain had soaked the velour upholstery, the windows were shattered in weblike patterns from kids throwing stones. I would get in on hot summer afternoons, put both hands on the steering wheel, pretend to drive.

MATCH THE PARTS OF SENTENCES THAT NEED MATCHING

Matching Subjects with Verbs

When the subject of a sentence is one thing (singular), the verb must be singular also. When the subject is more than one thing (plural), the verb must be plural also. In standard English, we say, "The newspaper covers the waterfront murders," not "The newspaper cover the waterfront murders"; or we say, "The newspapers, which share a reporter, cover the waterfront murders," not "The newspapers covers the waterfront murders."

Here are some frequent pitfalls and how to avoid them.

Sometimes we get into trouble because a phrase comes between the subject and the verb and confuses us. If we have a single subject followed by a prepositional phrase that ends with a plural, we may make the verb plural, because the plural phrase rings in our ears. "The newspaper of the six northern suburbs" is a singular subject. We should say

> The newspaper of the six northern suburbs covers the waterfront murders

not

> The newspaper of the six northern suburbs cover the waterfront murders.

We should say

> The newspaper with four ace reporters covers the waterfront murders.

not

> The newspaper with four ace reporters cover the waterfront murders.

With words like *anyone, each,* and *everybody* (called indefinite pronouns), we should use a singular verb. It's confusing: *everybody* refers to many people, but it's a single thing, a single "body"—as single as the *one* in *anyone* or *everyone*. We must say, "Everybody hurts this morning''; ''Anyone who goes out alone at night takes a chance of being mugged''; and ''Each member of the orchestra pays annual dues.''

None can be either singular or plural, agreeing with a singular or plural noun elsewhere in the sentence. Context decides.

> Many cows are happy, but none is so happy as a cow in spring.

> Many pigs are intelligent, but none are so intelligent as Wilbur and Angeline.

Do not say

> Everybody in town are going to the circus.

> Each of the forty-seven students howl like wolves.

Always find the subject (*everybody, each*) and make sure that the verb agrees.

When you write a sentence that uses *either . . . or, neither . . . nor,* or *not . . . but,* use a singular verb if both subjects are singular.

> Either the red-haired witch or her broomstick was on fire.

If one subject is plural and the other singular, the rule says that the verb should agree with the subject closest to it. Thus the rule would allow

> Either her two broomsticks or the red-haired witch was on fire.

But such a sentence, technically correct, is stylistically ugly. For style's sake, when one subject is plural and the other is singular, put the plural subject nearer the verb and use a plural verb. Say

> Either the red-haired witch or her two broomsticks were on fire.

Do not say

> Either her two broomsticks or the red-haired witch were on fire.

or

> Either the red-haired witch or her two broomsticks was on fire.

Do not say

> Neither the father nor the son want to follow the witch's track.

It should be *wants,* a singular verb. Do not say

> Not the Prime Minister but the members of his Cabinet believes in amnesty.

It should be *believe,* a plural verb matching the plural *members.*
These sentences are incorrect:

> Neither Hitler nor Genghis Khan were conspicuous for humanitarianism.

Not the first potato but the second and the fourth contains the microfilm.

Either the roof or the shingling over the sheds were giving off a putrescent odor.

When your sentence uses a verb like *is* or *are* (a linking verb, a form of *to be*), make sure that the verb matches the subject of the sentence and not a noun that comes afterward. Say

The best part of the team was its outfielders.

not

The best part of the team were its outfielders.

Say

The outfielders were the best part of the team.

not

The outfielders was the best part of the team.

These sentences are incorrect:

The middle chapters was the section of the book I liked best.

The best section of the book were the middle chapters.

Watch out for agreement of sentences beginning with "There is." Sometimes we begin such a sentence expecting a singular subject, then alter the subject without remembering to alter the verb. It is correct to say

There is one table in the room.

It would be incorrect and disagreeable to say

There is one table and one chair in the room.

_____ **EXERCISES** _____

1. Identify and correct the errors in these sentences.
   a. Each of the colored pencils have a different shade.
   b. The store with its aisles of groceries, hardware, soft goods, and paperbacks, rest back from the road.
   c. The green part of Northern Spy apples always taste best.
   d. Neither the horse nor the cows in the barn hears the siren.
   e. Either Bozo or Emmett Kelly get the prize.

2. In this section on matching parts, on pages 374–376, are many incorrect sentences introduced by "Do not say." Correct the errors in these sentences.

3. Rewrite this paragraph, making subjects and verbs agree.

Fifty workers, dressed in gray canvas coveralls and aluminum helmets, descends into the dark, damp caves. Each carry a pail and a small curved knife. They emerge from the elevator and scatters among the earth-filled frames. Slowly, rhythmically, they fan out in groups of five which moves along the frames. Their helmet lights fall into yellow cones on the mushrooms, pale faces clustering in the blackness. There is no sounds except the dull thud of mushrooms tumbling one by one into pails, like soft rain. No clocks, which would measure off the minutes left in a shift, but a siren to tell them when to break for lunch. None of them hurry.

Matching Pronouns with the Words They Refer To

Pronouns (*he, she, it, this, that, you, we*) take their identity from a noun which comes before them, and which they refer to, called their *antecedent*. The noun can come before them in the same sentence, or it can appear in a sentence close enough to have the reference clear. Pronouns must match their nouns both in number (singular or plural) and in gender (male or female).

Mostly, we match pronouns to their antecedents without trouble. Here are a few troublesome exceptions.

In formal writing, we use a singular pronoun (*he, she, it*) with an indefinite pronoun like *anybody, everybody, each, none,* and so forth. We say

Everybody carried his tennis racket.
None of the actresses received her paycheck.
Each of the seals extended its flipper.

not

Everybody carried their tennis racket.
None of the actresses received their paycheck.
Each of the seals extended their flipper.

This is a rule of formal writing although we often bend it in informal speech. To avoid *his* as sexist, or to avoid *his or her* as awkward, we sometimes use the incorrect *their* (see pages 173–174). If you do it, know that you are doing it. Perhaps it is best, if possible, to avoid gender entirely.

Everyone carried a tennis racket.
None of the actresses received a paycheck.
Each of the seals extended a flipper.

Words like *team, committee, jury, class,* and *orchestra* are collective nouns. They are singular words that refer to plural collections of people. Use a singular pronoun when you describe the whole group; use a plural pronoun when you describe the many members. Say

> The team climbed on its bus.
> The team dispersed to their lockers.

Don't say

> The jury went to its separate rooms.

> The committee voted to disband themselves.

> The team voted to distribute their winnings among twenty-four ballplayers.

> The group destroyed their petition to remove the governor.

When a pronoun matches two or more nouns joined by *and*, it is always plural.

> When the boy and his dog wanted supper, they went to the tavern.

When a pronoun matches nouns joined by *or, nor, either . . . or, or neither . . . nor* and one of the nouns is plural, the pronoun matches the nearer of the two. When you use such a pair of nouns, the sentence sounds better if the second of the two nouns is the plural. Say

> Although neither Margaret nor the Hamiltons are late, they hurry to the concert hall.

Don't say

> Although neither Margaret nor the Hamiltons are late, she hurries . . .

or

> Although neither the Hamiltons nor Margaret are late, they hurry . . .

Never use a pronoun when it could refer to either of two words before it. We must use pronouns so that the reader will always be *certain* which previous noun they refer to. Uncertainty is confusing and intolerable. Don't say

> When Wilhelmina declared herself to Bertha, she was aghast.

> Leaving his father's house and the dry valley, he was happy to see the last of it.

Both of these sentences lack a clear antecedent to the pronoun. They are ambiguous. Which of the women was aghast? Was he happy to see the last of the house, or of the valley, or of both? To be clear, we should say something like

> Wilhelmina declared herself to Bertha, who was aghast.
> He left the dry valley, happy to see the last of his father's house.

Don't use the pronoun *this* or *that* or *it* to refer to general ideas in a previous sentence or to an antecedent that is not there ("This is true . . . "). Watch out for *this* and *that* when you use them as pronouns. Don't say

> The streetcleaners roared down the street, raising clouds of gritty dust, mowing down the lilac bushes on the corner of the lawn, and dumping gravel all over the grass. That made my mother furious.

That lacks a clear antecedent, and the sentence drowns in imprecision.

Here are more examples of pronoun error from student essays. Troublesome pronouns are in italics.

> The state legislature never got around to getting the bill out of committee until October, and *it* was the reason the scholarships were never funded.

> Susan's brother is in his third year at Harvard Medical School, and *this* is the profession she wants to enter.

> The next thing that happened was that the screen door got stuck open and the mosquitoes could get in and the dog would get out whenever he wanted. My mother started crying about *this*.

> Preferential voting is fair because it gives the voter a chance to give a graded opinion of the different candidates, and therefore opens the way to third parties. *That* is the real justification for preferential voting.

> Down the block from me there was a family that had three cats. One of them was a big red tom named Mio, the biggest cat I ever saw— thirty-four inches long not counting his tail, and twenty-eight pounds. The kids in the neighborhood couldn't get over *this*.

We make another common error when we use a pronoun far removed from its antecedent. The result is more ambiguity, vagueness, and imprecision. Here are two examples.

> The partnership of Hudnut and Greenall was breaking up; business had declined, Hudnut's wife was ill, and Greenall's son had run off to Tibet. One Tuesday, *they* suddenly stopped speaking to each other.

> When Sharon looked across the classroom, Bill winked and Larry looked away. Outside the window the clouds gathered for rain, and students were beginning to drive off for lunch, many of them carrying no books at all. Suddenly two girls ran toward a car that had stopped to pick them up. *She* saw that *it* was Matt.

_____ **EXERCISES** _____

1. In these sentences, underline the errors in pronouns and what they refer to.

    a. When the Senate and the House convene, on rare occasions, they do not know how to behave toward each other.

    b. Panthers feed on zebras when they can, and zebras feed on grass. As a result of this, panthers live near the grasslands.

    c. I was late for registration because my father had the flu and then our car broke down outside Tucson. That made me more nervous than ever.

    d. Uncle Bruce is a career man in the navy, stationed in San Diego now, and it makes me think about enlisting myself.

    e. The department decided to hold their annual picnic on Riverside Drive.

    f. The Boosters Club adjourned its meeting and went to its respective houses.

    g. Either Rita or Carole were tardy last Tuesday.

    h. Everybody had their ticket to the rock concert.

    i. When Rosalyn and Alice finished dinner, she decided to provide dessert.

    j. Penelope and Roger had been married seven years. Then Roger met Goneril and fell in love. They did not know what to do.

2. Rewrite the sentences in the first exercise to correct faulty pronouns.

3. Here is a paragraph from a student essay with several examples of pronoun-antecedent and pronoun-verb disagreement. Revise to correct mistakes.

> In their cowboy movies, John Wayne and Gary Cooper each represents the idealized western hero. Walking slowly down the dusty main street of any frontier town, he commands respect. Neither ever flinch in the heavy crossfire of bank robbers or cattle rustlers. The crowd of townsfolk who look on know their sheriff will win the day. None doubt their safety under his leadership. That's why they are examples of courage and social order in a reckless age.

CONNECT MODIFIERS WITH WHAT THEY MODIFY

In most sentences, we write phrases that describe (modify) other things in the sentence. We use prepositional phrases as modifiers (to define, to limit).

the bar *with the lavender paint*
the girl *in the straw hat*
the chapter *about grammar*

For similar purposes, we use clauses beginning with words like *that*, *who*, *since*, and *because*.

the worst storm *since the winter of 1978*
Herbert, *who tipped his homburg*

And we use phrases beginning with *-ing* words (participles), which also modify.

> the chapter *containing the examples*
> *hanging from the skylight,* the plumber

Most of the time we have no trouble controlling these phrases or clauses. We will find no trouble at all if we avoid two common errors.

Make sure that modifiers beginning a sentence really modify what the sentence claims they modify. If we start a sentence "Hanging from the skylight," we tell the reader something; we guarantee that the noun that will begin the main clause is what is hanging.

> Hanging from the skylight, the plumber screamed that he had climbed up there to escape the terrorists.

Too often, we are careless and make a sentence like the next one— which seems to start like the sentence above, and then changes its mind.

> Hanging from the skylight, the plumber looked at the huge spider's web.

Common sense can untangle the mess. The reader will eventually understand that the spider's web is hanging, not the plumber. In the meantime, the reader has been first confused and then annoyed by the misdirection.

Here are more examples of dangling modifiers, which are shown by italics.

> *Being a wreck with no gears at all,* she got the bicycle free.

> *Riding in a new car,* the beagle chased me half a mile.

> *Driven by his desire to succeed,* the test was easy.

> *Before making a reservation,* my roommate recommended a travel agent to me.

> *Humbled by circumstances,* the town looked better to him now than it had looked before.

Make sure that your word order says what you want it to say when you place modifiers in a sentence. This advice applies to adverbs and adjectives, as well as to phrases or clauses that modify. The wrong word order can alter your meaning.

> I told her I would gladly lend her my car.

means one thing.

> I told her gladly I would lend her my car.

means something else.

She heard only the words that hurt.

means one thing.

She only heard the words that hurt.

means something else.

He said only that he loved her.

means one thing.

He only said that he loved her.

means something else. It is the writer's job to know the meaning and to say it. Here are some examples from student papers in which mistakes in word order made sentences that are ambiguous, misleading, or silly.

Hattie is the cousin who gave me the present in a housecoat.

Joseph borrowed an egg from a neighbor that was rotten.

The autobiography tells the exciting life of the man who lived it quickly and modestly.

The lecturer told us about the problem of alcoholism in room A-14.

—— **EXERCISES** ————————————————————————

1. Correct the mistakes in the four sentences that end the preceding section.

2. Discover and correct the errors in the following sentences.

   a. Desperate, clinging to life, our teacher told us about the surrounded tribe.
   b. Igor attempted one last time to climb the hill lacking food and ammunition.
   c. Never certain of which side of the road to drive on, American roads drove the Englishman crazy.
   d. Full of conceit, the application form looked like a cinch to him.
   e. I walked the last five miles to the city tired and full of martinis.
   f. She said that animals only burp the way he did.
   g. Without his fortune, or his youth, or his good health, the old house looked warm and solid to him.
   h. I used the reference section without getting lost because of a librarian's help.
   i. We walked on a neighborhood street without coats.
   j. Without potholes we walked on a neighborhood street.

3. Discover and correct the misplaced modifiers in this paragraph.

> Walking against rush hour traffic, the worn green raincoat gave the old man a sinister air. He was trying only to find Flossie. He shuffled along the pavement carrying the little red dish calling her name. His bony feet were beginning to hurt him encased in broken leather boots, and the corn throbbed on his toe. Frightened and tired, the police station stood on 104th Street just ahead.

KEEP THE SENTENCE CONSISTENT

Once we start a sentence, we commit ourselves to continue it as we started it. In the second and third sections of this Review, we discussed the commitments to match number and gender and to connect a modifier with what it modifies. We also commit ourselves to other consistencies.

When we write parallelisms, or parallel constructions, as in a series of clauses, we must keep the words grammatically parallel for the sake of consistency. Otherwise, we find our sentences beginning to come apart, to veer off the road into incoherence. We list adjectives or we list nouns, but we do not list three adjectives followed by one noun. Don't say

> He was tall, rich, funny, and a bank robber.

Say something like

> He was tall, rich, funny, and fond of robbing banks.

When one phrase is constructed by one grammatical formula, its parallel phrase must be constructed in the same way. Don't say

> The dog had a long nose, a black tail, and barked loudly.

Instead say

> The dog had a long nose, a black tail, and a loud bark.

Don't say

> The cities are deserted, the countryside parched, the government paralyzed, and the economy not in a healthy condition.

Instead, say something like

> The cities are deserted, the countryside parched, the government paralyzed, and the economy ruined.

Here, the sentence must continue with phrases ending in *-ed* words (past participles), or it will be inconsistent.

Consistency is the rule. If you start a sentence—or a linked group of sentences—with one subject or person, be consistent. Don't say

When you get a good grade, one should be proud.

Say either *you* or *one*, and stick to it.

Don't use the active voice in one part of a sentence and shift to the passive in another, when you could perfectly well keep the active and use the same subject.

We could hear raucous sounds from the party as the house was approached.

Be consistent in using the past or present of verbs. Don't say

He went into the room, closed the door, opened the window, and goes to bed.

Remember that we need consistency within related sentences, as well as within the sentence. Here is an inconsistent paragraph.

The median tax on houses in Centerville is $852 a year. You could appeal to the city assessor if you wanted to. But one is advised not to; he can always hit you for more tax, and you are punished for asking.

EXERCISES

1. Revise the paragraph at the end of the preceding section so that its sentences are consistent.

2. Locate, name, and correct the inconsistencies in these sentences.

   a. She walked like a princess, ate like an ape, and her hair was at least five feet long.
   b. If you write a page a day in your notebook, you will discover that one learns from practice.
   c. Harriet opened the window to get some fresh air, and we all breathe deeply.
   d. Geology is boring, chemistry fatiguing, history overwhelming, but English was a useful class.
   e. We lifted the rock, peered into the mud, and a thousand grubs were seen.

3. Rewrite the following paragraph to make the subject singular and the verb tense present.

The banditos waited in the canyon rocks for the evening coach from Sagebrush. They knew it carried bags of gold for the Union army, and they intended to grab the gold and disappear into the hills. At last, a cloud of dust appeared on the horizon. The men tensed, crouched lower against the jagged rocks, and watched intently, guns readied. When they saw the driver cracking his whip over the screaming horses, they opened fire.

KEEP PUNCTUATION CLEAR

Learning to punctuate correctly, we learn the conventions that an experienced reader expects of us. No one can argue that the conventions of English punctuation are ideal. But they are clear, and for the most part they are sensible.

End Punctuation

At the end of a sentence, we use a period, an exclamation point, or a question mark.

Period. Periods end sentences. Periods also indicate abbreviations (*Mr., no., St., etc., i.e., Mass., U.S.A.*). (See pages 400–401.) And periods indicate omissions in quoted material. (See page 397.)

Exclamation point. Use exclamation points only for a proper exclamation:

Oh! Zap!

or for a remark almost shouted:

It's Godzilla!

Avoid using them frequently, or they diminish in effect, like a vague intensifier.

I could not make out the face! Then I saw. It was Algernon!

Question mark. At the end of a sentence asking a direct question, we use a question mark.

Did you ask Fernando?
Have you bought the paper, the pins, and the manila envelopes?

Do not use a question mark to end a sentence that includes a question but does not ask it (an indirect question). These sentences are incorrectly punctuated:

He asked what time it was?
I waited to find out where the carnival was?

They should end with periods.

Commas

The most common mark of punctuation—and the most commonly misused—is the comma. We will not talk here about the comma splice, because we discussed it on pages 371–373. Here are some of the main uses of the comma.

To separate whole clauses. In the compound sentence, where two or more whole clauses are connected by *and, or, nor, for,* or *but,* we use a comma just before the connective.

> The faculty senate debated for three hours, but no one could resolve the issue of the blind pig.

When the main clauses are short, the comma is optional. The pause is shorter, and therefore the rhythm different. We can say either

> The wine was old, and we drank it slowly.

or

> The wine was old and we drank it slowly.

On the other hand, we can also opt to use the semicolon, which creates a longer pause, instead of the comma. Sometimes we want this extra pause when the main clauses are especially long, when they themselves contain commas, or when we make strong contrast between the two parts of the sentence.

> The cliff was red, solid, and perpendicular; and the car disappeared into the face of it.

To separate items in a series. We use commas to separate words in a series:

> The dress was black, green, and purple.

to separate phrases in a series:

> She wore it to parties, in the bathtub, and at work.

to separate subordinate clauses in a series:

> She explained that it was warm, that it needed washing, that it was comfortable, and that it was in good taste.

and to separate whole clauses in a series:

> She shook her head, she stood up, and she left the room.

When we use *and* with each item in a series, we do not use the comma.

> He touched first and second and third.

It is possible to omit the comma before the *and* in a series of words or short phrases:

> He touched first, second and third.

but it can seem ambiguous, as if the baserunner were able to straddle and touch second and third at the same time.

To set off introductory words and groups of words. Adverb clauses, transitional phrases, and phrases introduced by verbals or prepositions, when they come at the beginning of the sentence, usually require a comma to set them off from the main clause. These adverb clauses need a comma:

> *If a dunce applies himself thoroughly,* he can dream of becoming president.

> *When I turned to the left at the end of the lane,* I found the old house intact.

Omitting these commas would leave the sentence hopelessly awkward and confusing. If the order of clauses is reversed, a comma, though possible, is no longer necessary.

> A dunce can dream of becoming president *if he applies himself thoroughly.*

> I found the old house intact *when I turned to the left at the end of the lane.*

An introductory adverb clause, if it is short, need not always carry a comma. A comma is optional in

> *If I lead* he will follow.

Introductory phrases of transition, like *on the other hand,* usually need a comma.

> On the other hand, sometimes they don't.
> In fact they are optional.
> In fact, they are optional.

Retaining the comma is appropriate in formal writing and is acceptable in all writing. Omitting the comma is rhythmically more colloquial. Interjections like *oh* or *shucks,* however, almost always take the comma.

> Gosh, that's not what you said the last time.

We use a comma when the sentence begins with a long phrase governed by a preposition.

> *In the century after the Civil War,* progress in civil rights was almost nil.

When the introductory prepositional or verbal phrase is short, the comma is optional and may be omitted when omission does not cause ambiguity.

At twelve she was full-grown.
Having won they adjourned to a saloon.

To avoid ambiguity. Sometimes we need a comma to indicate a pause which the voice would make, in speech, for clarity, but which is not otherwise necessary.

Outside the fields spread to the river.

is clearer with a pause:

Outside, the fields spread to the river.

To find such potential ambiguities in your prose, sometimes it is help-ful to read it aloud, pronouncing it as it is written—which means pausing where there is a comma, and *not* pausing where there is *not* a comma.

To set off nonrestrictive, or parenthetical, clauses. It is useful to know the difference between a restrictive and a nonrestrictive clause. A restrictive clause describes or limits its subject, providing essential information.

The knight *who was dressed in black* won all the events in the tourney.

Here, "who was dressed in black" defines the knight, as if we were pointing a finger. The absence of commas lets us know that there were other knights besides the one "who was dressed in black."

The building *that overlooked the river* was the most popular of all.

In such restrictive clauses as these, no comma separates the clause from the rest of the sentence.

Nonrestrictive clauses, on the other hand, do not define; they could become separate sentences or coordinate clauses, and unless they are very short, they take commas at both ends. We could also write sentences in which the clauses above become nonrestrictive.

Sir Galahad, *who was dressed in black,* won all the events in the tourney.

This sentence, as opposed to the restrictive example above, could be broken into two sentences, with no violence done to the meaning.

Sir Galahad was dressed in black. He won all the events in the tourney.

Or, using the clause from the other example, we could have the sen-tence

The library building, *which overlooked the river,* was built in 1975.

To enclose words, phrases, or clauses that are like a parenthesis. Quotations are common parenthetical elements. So too are phrases and words like *of course, naturally,* and *heavens to Betsy.* When asides or parenthetical expressions appear at the beginning of sentences, place a comma after them. When they appear at the end of sentences, put a comma just before them.

> God knows, the situation is desperate.
> The situation is desperate, God knows.
> Fellow Americans, I speak to you as a concerned citizen.
> I am a representative of the people, of course.

Omitting commas in these examples would make the sentence ambiguous or hard to read.

> God knows the situation is desperate.

Does He?

At times the commas can be omitted with no awkwardness or confusion, and the omission becomes optional. Short sentences in which word order precludes ambiguity give us this option.

> The situation was of course desperate.

On occasion one can take stylistic advantage of the rhythmic speed offered by this option.

Use a comma before and after parenthetical expressions within a sentence.

> I think you're tired, Fred, and hungry.
> The student worked, in a manner of speaking, for three whole days.
> I heard him calling, "There's my bubble gum," to the audience.

To set off appositives. Appositives are nouns or noun substitutes placed next to another noun to explain or define that noun.

> Peter, *the flying dwarf,* escorted Tarquina, *his good fairy.*

In many of our first drafts, we use too many commas, or put them where they do not belong. Beginning writers often feel that something is going wrong if they haven't used a comma lately, and so they shake commas over their prose like salt. Here are some sentences, taken from student essays, which have some commas they should *not* have.

> But, it was not too late.
> Clarke came by, later.
> When I left she, followed me.
> The dimensions were, approximately three by five.
> I quickly saw Ed, and Sara.

He thought she was sickly, and studious.
The old barn was painted, red.
A runner, who likes to win, has to train, every day.
The agency sold, life, fire, and theft, insurance.

____ **EXERCISES** _____

1. Remove unnecessary commas from the last group of sentences above.

2. The following sentences omit commas necessary to clarity. Add commas where they belong.

a. The indiscreet Martian insensitive to the feelings of Earthlings disintegrated the beagle.
b. "Horrors" I said to the surrounding observers.
c. Of course the narrative begins to become incoherent when Hermione reaches this part of the journey.
d. If there is war in the Middle East within the next decade the winners will be losers.
e. Beyond the river widened.
f. Deciding that cinnamon toast was preferable to fried sardines we looked in the bread box.
g. In a million or two million years the human toenail may disappear.
h. In truth the final dispensation of the profits available to the institution will not be accomplished until the end of the decade.
i. When we take the S-curve at a speed of forty or more miles an hour we hold our lives in our hands as well as the steering wheel
j. He looked through his pockets and found a comb two matchbooks four paper clips six pennies and a piece of bubble gum.

3. Punctuate, capitalize, and lowercase this paragraph.

for forty years they had come to this house by the lake and for twenty of those Years they had been as they thought a happy family but after Herbie died and Mary Lou went away to school and Joe jr married and started a family of his own it was different they were Strangers to each other and spent whole days staring at the lake stopping only for silent meals and sleepless Naps

_____

Semicolons

Semicolons between whole clauses. Semicolons separate whole clauses, making a pause longer or more emphatic than a comma, but shorter and less definite than a period. The semicolon shows that the clauses follow each other closely, are connected in idea or narrative. We may use the semicolon between two (or more) balanced and equal clauses.

> The sun rose; the sky lightened; day had come.

Or we may use it between clauses of unequal length and different construction.

> The sun rose; instantly, the air was alive with birds singing so happily that anyone who heard them could not help but smile.

These sentences are compound, the semicolon replacing a conjunction.

Semicolons with series. Sometimes, in a long sentence, semicolons separate series or divisions, making the divisions clearer than commas would, particularly if commas are already within the divisions.

> There were three sorts of students waiting on table at the Inn: fraternity boys who were dating expensive girls; girls from Detroit whose daddies cut off their allowances because they had moved in with their boyfriends; and street people, boys and girls, working for a week or two until they got tired of it.

Semicolons with conjunctions. A semicolon used with a conjunction shows more separation or pause between clauses than the comma would show.

> He flew to Denver that night; and we were glad he did.

Adverbs acting as conjunctions in compound sentences (*besides, nevertheless, also, however, indeed, furthermore, still, then*) take a semicolon, as do transitional phrases in the middle of compound sentences (*on the other hand, in fact, in other words, on the contrary*).

> Let us take the matter in hand; however, we must not be foolhardy.
> The sun rose in a clear sky; in fact, the sky was painfully bright.

Semicolons with incomplete clauses. Semicolons also separate incomplete clauses when a verb in one of the clauses is omitted but understood.

> Poetry is one thing; verse another.

Apostrophes

Possessives. We form the possessive by adding *'s* to singular nouns and most plural nouns (if the additional *s* makes pronunciation difficult, we add only the apostrophe).

> The bag was Sara's.
> It was the weather's fault.
> The technician's car was parked outside.
> the hens' feed
> Mr. and Mrs. Jones's automobile
> the women's club
> the Perkins' puppets

An apostrophe does not form part of the possessive of a pronoun. Pronouns have separate possessive forms: *my; your; his, her, its; our; your; their.*

Contractions. We also use the apostrophe to show contractions. Use an apostrophe to show that you have omitted one or more letters in a phrase, commonly a combination of a pronoun and a verb. *I'm, she's, he's, who's, we've, you've, they're,* etc; *we'd, you'd, he'd, she'd; he'll, she'll, who'll.* Three contractions become problems. *They're* (a contraction of *they are*) sounds like *their* and *there,* and we may spell one when we mean another. "*Their* out working" is as incorrect as "*there* work" and "working *their.*" (Correct: "*They're* out working"; "*their* work"; "working *there.*")

It's always means *it is.* It is *not* possessive, like "*its* shadow." Whenever you write or see the apostrophe with these letters—*it's*—remember that the *'s* must stand for *is.* Or memorize the phrase

> *It's* afraid of *its* shadow.

Who's is another common contraction and once again there is a confusion. *Whose* gets mixed up with *who's.* Again, the *'s* means *is,* and *who's* always stands for *who is,* where *whose* is a possessive pronoun.

> *Who's* drinking *whose* soup?

Other common contractions involve a verb and the negative: *isn't, aren't, doesn't, don't, can't, haven't, won't,* which are contractions of *is not, are not, does not, do not, cannot, have not,* and *will not.*

Plural of numbers. We use the apostrophe to form the plurals of typographic symbols, words referred to as words, letters, and figures.

> The 7's on the new office typewriter are black as *e*'s, 8's are unreadable, and half the time simple *the*'s are obscure.

Possessive pronouns used without a noun have no apostrophe: *mine; yours; his, hers, its; ours; yours; theirs.*

> *Her* book.
> The book was *hers.*

_____ **EXERCISES** _____

Cross out the incorrect apostrophes in these sentences. Add the missing ones.

   a. Poor dog! It's too late for it's supper.
   b. That Morocco-bound volume of Tolkien was supposed to be her's.
   c. Whose for tennis?
   d. Is'nt English spelling irrational?
   e. It's true he didn't know who's tax he had paid, his wifes or his own.

Quotation Marks and Punctuating Quotations

The exact words of a speaker or writer, included in a paragraph, are set off by quotation marks. Put a comma at the end of the quotation before the quotation mark, or a period if the quotation ends the sentence. If the quotation ends with a question mark or an exclamation point, these marks of punctuation take the place of the comma and occur inside the quotation marks.

Al asked Wayne, "Didn't you?"

On the other hand, sometimes we quote in order to exclaim or inquire about the quotation. In such a sentence, the exclamation point or question mark occurs after the quotation mark.

What did he mean when he said, "Good morning"?
She had the nerve to say "Hello"!

Notice that the first word of a quoted remark is capitalized. When we quote a passage longer than fifty words, in a research paper for instance, we can use a colon to introduce the quotation and detach the quotation from the text by indenting it. The quotation is not enclosed by quotation marks. Ellipses can help you avoid long, detached quotations.

We use quotation marks to indicate the exact repetition of words from speech or writing.

As Macbeth would say, "Tomorrow and tomorrow and tomorrow. . . ."

We use them when we cite words as words.

"Jazz" and "condo" are derogatory words.

In writing that uses many short quotations, as in *Writing Well*, an author may use italics instead of quotation marks: *mine, yours, his, hers, its, ours, yours, theirs.* In writing essays, use the traditional quotation marks.

We also use quotation marks to indicate the titles of songs, television shows, and short literary works, like essays and short stories and poems and chapters or other sections of a longer work. We speak of Tennyson's short poem "Tithonos"; when we refer to a book-length poem by the same author, we use italics instead: *In Memoriam.* We speak of Hemingway's story "A Clean Well-Lighted Place" and his novel *A Farewell to Arms.* "The Dead" is part of James Joyce's *Dubliners.* We use italics for the names of newspapers, magazines, and movies: *The New Haven Register, Blair and Ketcham's Country Journal, Animal House.*

When we quote *within* a quotation, we use single quotation marks: Molly said, "I'd like to read you Wallace Stevens's poem 'The Emperor of Ice Cream.' "

Other Marks of Punctuation

Brackets. Brackets are useful in prose especially in three places, all within or close to quotations. We use them when we add to a quotation material which was not in the original but which is needed for clarity. Sometimes a bracketed word supplies information lacking in the quotation but available in the context. The brackets can contain the antecedent to a pronoun:

"He [O'Toole] smashed his fist through the window of the bar."

or some important fact:

"It was mid-June [1986] that the storm began."

Sometimes, in quoting the spoken word, we use brackets to enclose an indication of action, like a stage direction.

" . . . and, finally, I want to ask you willingly and cheerfully to share the huge burden of responsibility which the age has thrust upon us all." [Boos.]

Sometimes we use brackets to correct a quotation.

"It all happened in the early hours of September 20 [actually September 21] when the sun began [to] rise over the boardwalk."

Colons. Colons direct our attention to what comes after them. Usually they follow an introductory statement that leads us to expect a follow-up, though sometimes the introduction is implicit, or the colon itself reveals that the clause preceding it was introductory. We use a colon when the second sentence fulfills a kind of promise made by the first. Here are some explicit introductions.

To a long quotation, either included in the text in quotation marks or indented without quotation marks:

> E. B. White wrote of his old professor: "In the days when I was sitting in his class he omitted so many needless words, and omitted them so forcibly and with such eagerness and obvious relish, that. . . . "

To an example:

> The results of the study were as follows: the closer subjects stood to the hoop, the more frequently they were able to make a basket.

To a list:

> Mona asked me to get a few things at the market: potatoes, carrots, and peas.

> When you pack your child's luggage for Camp Winnewaka, please include the following: towels, toiletries, and personal medications.

Less elegantly, to an appositive at the end of a sentence:

> Chosby took off his boots and looked at his toe: a swollen knob of pain.

A comma, here, would be just as correct and perhaps less prone to melodrama.

Sometimes we put a colon instead of a semicolon between two main clauses; it implies that the second clause is a result of the first.

> The hands of the clock seemed never to move: she had never been late before.

Here the colon adds a meaning that the semicolon would lack. The semicolon would present the two statements as closely connected, but without the implication that the second clause derived from the first.

Dashes. Use dashes with caution—but use them. Make them on your typed paper by putting two hyphens next to each other.

In the sentence above, the dash shows a hesitation in the voice, followed with a rush by something that seems almost an afterthought. Dashes are informal. For some careless writers, dashes become substitutes for all other forms of punctuation; they not only lose any special meaning dashes may contribute, they also rob other punctuation of its meaning. For instance:

> Yet many people use them too often—they become substitutes for all other forms of punctuation—and thus lose their special meaning—at the same time they rob other punctuation of its meaning—

Two legitimate uses for the dash are the implied afterthought, as in the first sentence of this section, and the informal parenthesis. Marks of parenthesis ( ) look more formal; dashes give a sense of speech. These two sentences illustrate a slight, characteristic difference:

> The myth of connotative and denotative meanings was destroyed by Carnap (the logician who taught at the University of Chicago) some twenty-five years ago.

> The myth of connotative and denotative meanings was destroyed by a logician and philosopher—I think it was Carnap—about twenty-five years ago.

Ellipses. Three dots in a row . . . indicate that you have omitted something from a quotation. Use four dots if the words left out were at the end of a sentence: three to indicate the omission, a fourth for the period.

Ellipses are useful in research papers or arguments using references. Much of a paragraph we want to quote may be irrelevant to our point. To include the whole paragraph in our text would slow the pace and violate the unity in our argument. Therefore we piece-cut the quotation and make it blend smoothly with our essay. Here is the long way to use a quotation:

> Marlowe was more direct than Shakespeare and more vigorous. As Professor William Wanger puts it:

>> If the *Jew of Malta* is Marlowe's *Merchant of Venice*, it is at the same time better and worse than Shakespeare's famous comedy. The lesser-known play has fewer quotable passages, perhaps, and certainly fewer that are quoted; but we must acknowledge that Marlowe's play has more energy than Shakespeare's. What it lacks in finesse it makes up in vigor, and the character of the Jew is surely more complex, and more thoughtfully observed, than the character of the Merchant.

> What Professor Wanger says of two plays, we can say of all. . . .

Instead, we can use ellipses and build the necessary quotations into our text:

> Marlowe was more direct than Shakespeare and more vigorous.
> Comparing comedies by the two men, Professor William Wanger found Marlowe "better and worse than Shakespeare . . . ," lacking "in finesse" but superior in "vigor" and "energy." He found Marlowe's characterization, in one comparison, "more complex, and more thoughtfully observed," than Shakespeare's.

When we are obviously making excerpts, as with single words like *energy* and detached phrases like the last quotation, we do not need ellipses, because ellipses provide information: if we already know that quotations are excerpted, we do not need rows of dots to tell us so. But after *Shakespeare,* earlier in the paragraph, when we cut between a noun and an apostrophe indicating possession, we need the ellipses. On the other hand, we need not use ellipses if we omit words at the beginning of a quote:

> Pelham told the conference, "Every day motorists kill one million animals on American highways."

Hyphens. We use hyphens to break a word at the right-hand margin. Dictionaries usually indicate the syllables that make up a word by placing a dot between them (com · pound · ed). Hyphenate only at the syllable break. Write com-/pounded, never comp-/ounded. When the syllable to be isolated is only one or two letters long, avoid division (a-long, man-y, compound-ed). Never hyphenate one-syllable words.

We use the hyphen on occasion to join two adjectives, or words serving as adjectives, modifying a noun. They make a temporary compound word.

> *blood-red* hair
> *mile-long* avenue

Avoid the temptation to multiply hyphenated phrases, which can become a virulent form of adjectivitis.

> The *purple-green cloud-forms sweep-crawl.* . . .

We use hyphens with some temporary compounds. Before *wheel* and *barrow* became the compound word *wheelbarrow*, there may have been a stage at which we wrote *wheel-barrow*. Consult your dictionary when you are in doubt. Hyphens in compounds are a matter of spelling.

We use hyphens in compound numbers from twenty-one through ninety-nine.

We hyphenate fractions.

> *a two-thirds* majority
> *three-quarters* of the population

We use the hyphen to avoid ambiguity. We must spell the word *re-creation* to avoid confusing it with *recreation*.

We use the hyphen with some prefixes and suffixes.

> governor-*elect*
> *ex*-wife
> *self*-determined

We use the hyphen as a typographic device to indicate a manner of speaking, when we indicate that someone is spelling a word by writing it *w-o-r-d,* or when we indicate a stammer, *w-w-word.*

Italics. When we type, or write by hand, we show italics by underlining the word: <u>italics</u>. It comes out in type, *italics.*

Use italics for the names of ships: the *Niña;* for the titles of books, films, and plays: *War and Peace;* for the titles of newspapers or magazines: *Sports Illustrated;* and for foreign expressions: *faute de mieux, in medias res.*

Also, we use italics to indicate a special use of a word.

> We might call the directory an *encyclopedia* of has-beens.

We use them, from time to time, to indicate emphasis.

> Do you really *mean* that?

Using italics for emphasis is tricky, however. Italics are a vague gesture, an attempt to register a tone of voice that often fails because it cannot indicate a *specific* tone of voice. A writer who relies on emphatic italics often is being lazy; a more careful choice of words, a more precise context, and the emphasis will be clear without italics.

Parentheses. Use parentheses to enclose material which digresses from or interrupts the main idea of the writing or which explains something but remains a detachable unit.

> The minister continued to pace up and down (though he normally slept through the night) and to stare out the window into the darkness.

> De Marque points out (not only in the *Treatise,* but in the *Harmonics* as well) that Jolnay was ignorant of Graf.

> Fred Papsdorf (Charles Laughton bought his paintings) lives on Jane Street, near East Detroit, in a small bungalow.

> She complained that she weighed ten stone (140 pounds; a stone, an English measure of avoirdupois, is fourteen pounds) and had been seven stone a year ago.

Also, use parentheses for numbers or letters that divide parts of a list.

> There are three reasons: (1) . . . , (2) . . . , and (3). . . .

___ EXERCISES ___

1. In these sentences, marks of punctuation are used incorrectly or loosely. Discover errors or places where exact punctuation would improve precision or clarity.

> **a.** Two thirds of the population is semi-literate, and has read nothing more complex than "Readers Digest."
>
> **b.** The triumvirate, a ruling-group of three, resembling a contemporary troika, took over from the dying emperor.
>
> **c.** The pumpkin stuffing October sun, as the poet (Rarity) called it in his sonnet, *Goose,* pumped calories into the uncoiling sausage of the valley.
>
> **d.** "Whatever you do", the potato farmer told me; "remember one thing; eat starch four times a day."
>
> **e.** The monk, with the Gucci shoes wearing the new tonsure, spoke, at last with a sigh, "Yes I am Ludwig Babo."

2. Punctuate and capitalize the following paragraph.

your grandfather a good man but not well educated came to this country when he was twenty two he worked in a dry goods store and then because he was industrious took a job with the greenwood star as a cub reporter he had a motto as he always told us work hard and keep your nose clean

---

KEEP MECHANICS CONVENTIONAL

Like punctuation marks, the mechanics of English prose are conventions that make life easier. We can argue that the rules of spelling or manuscript form are irrational, and we can make a good case. But if we all agree to abide by the same mechanical conventions—irrational or not—we can more easily understand each other. Here are some remarks about abbreviations, capital letters, manuscript form, numerals, and spelling.

Abbreviation

For the use of abbreviations in notes and list of works cited, see pages 334–335.

In formal writing, we abbreviate only some words that go with names, like *Mr., Mrs., Ms., Dr., St.* (for *Saint*, not *street*), *Jr., Sr.;* degrees, like *Ph.D.* or *M.A.;* and indications of era or time, like A.D., B.C., A.M., and P.M. (We use the latter two initials only when a specific time is indicated; we speak of "4 P.M.," not "it was the P.M.") We do not abbreviate *Monday* or *August* or *street* or *road* or *volume* or *chemistry* in ordinary writing.

Some writers use *no.* as an abbreviation for *number*, but it looks out of place in formal prose. So too does *U.S.A.* instead of United States and *Penna.* or *Pa.* instead of *Pennsylvania, lb.* instead of *pound*, and *oz.* instead of *ounce.*

Some institutions are so commonly called by their initials that it is overly formal to spell them out. The *Federal Bureau of Investigation* seems a pompous way to talk about the *FBI*. On the other hand, consider your audience; many people will need to be told the first time you mention it that *SEATO* is the *Southeast Asia Treaty Organization.*

In conjunction with a figure, *mph* and *rpm* are used in formal writing. We write *50 mph* and *1,000 rpm*. But if we write without figures, we spell them out.

It is difficult to assess the speed of a space capsule when it is told in *miles per hour.*

Titles like *Governor* can be spelled out or shortened. Frequently, we shorten a title when we give a whole name:

> *Gov.* William Milliken

and spell it out with a last name alone:

> *Governor* Milliken

Any abbreviation of titles is inappropriate to formal prose.

Capital Letters

Capitalize the names of people, cities, and countries; the titles of people, books, and plays; names of religious or national groups, languages, days of the week, months, holidays, and organizations and their abbreviations; the names of events or eras in history and important documents; and the names of specific structures, like buildings and airplanes and ships. In titles of books, plays, poems, songs, television shows, and movies, capitalize the first word and all subsequent words *except* articles and prepositions.

John Doe	June
Great Britain	Memorial Day
Berlin	General Motors or G.M.
Mayor David Dinkins	"Why Do Fools Fall in
Moby-Dick	Love?"
The Importance of Being	Declaration of
Earnest	Independence
Methodist	Empire State Building
Polish or European or	the *Winnie Mae*
Bostonian	the *Titanic*
Monday	*Play It Again, Sam*

Do not capitalize the seasons, or the names of college classes (freshman, senior), or general groups like *the lower classes* or *the jet set*. Do not capitalize school subjects or disciplines except languages:

> physics
> French

Adjectives are capitalized when they derive from proper nouns and still refer to them, like *Shakespearean*. Other nouns or adjectives which derive from names but no longer refer to the person lose their capitals:

> boycott
> quisling

The title that is capitalized before the proper noun, as

> *Mayor* Hermann Garsich

loses its capital when it is used outside of its titling function, as a descriptive word placed after the proper noun:

> Hermann Garsich, *mayor* of our town

Sections of a country may take capitals:

> the *West*
> the *South*

but the same words take lowercase when they are directions:

> Go *west,* young man.

Capitalize the first word of a quoted sentence:

> Mother said, "Come back soon."

> Sentences begin with capitals.

Manuscript Form

Type or word-process if you can.

Double-space on one side of white 8½-by-11-inch twenty-pound bond paper. Never use erasable paper; it won't take inked corrections, it smudges, it sticks together, and it is altogether unpleasant to read. (If you must use it, hand in a photocopy of the finished paper.) Use Ko-Rec-Type, Liquid Paper, or a similar easy device for corrections.

Always make a photocopy. The most careful graders occasionally lose a paper. The corporations providing stolen papers for rich students make off with manuscripts when they can. Keep a copy to protect yourself.

Make margins of 1 inch to 1½ inches at top, bottom, and sides.

Number pages consecutively, including notes, appendixes, and list of works cited.

Put your name in the upper left-hand corner of the first page.

Type the title, capitalizing the first letter of the first word and of all other words except articles and prepositions, 2 or 3 inches down from the top of the first page. Do not underline or add a period to your title.

If quoted material is short—up to fifty words of prose or two lines of poetry—place it within the paragraph, and use quotation marks. With lines of poetry, use a slash mark (/) to indicate line breaks, and follow the capitalization of the poem.

Of man's first disobedience, and the fruit / Of that forbidden tree. . . .

If quoted material is longer than fifty words or two lines of poetry, detach it from the text. Indent the quotation half an inch to the right of the place where you begin paragraphs, and double-space the quotation. Do not use quotation marks.

Numerals

In dealing with decimal points and highly precise or technical figures, it is wise to use numerals.

69.7 decibels

It is acceptable to type dates in numerals also.

June 14, 1971

The same goes for population figures and addresses.

104,000 inhabitants
1715 South University Avenue

Spell out figures, except when they are long to the point of being ridiculous. If you can write that a town has *one hundred four thousand inhabitants*, it is easy enough to write it out. If necessity requires precision, *104,627* will do; *one hundred four thousand, six hundred and twenty-seven* might look precious.

Never begin a sentence with a numeral.

97.6 mph showed on the speedometer.

Either spell out the number (*Ninety-seven and six-tenths*) or rewrite the sentence.

The speedometer showed 97.6 mph.

The sentence

30 people stood up.

should certainly be written

Thirty people stood up.

It is unnecessary, unless you are a lawyer, to include both spelled-out numbers and figures. Do not write,

The building was at least twenty (20) stories tall.

Either will do—preferably the written-out word—but both together belong only to legal or business documents.

Spelling

English spelling is irregular and irrational. There are a few rules of thumb, but the rules always have exceptions. We memorize to learn to spell. By memory we write *there* when it is fitting and *their* when it is fitting. By memory we spell *plough, although, enough,* and *slough.*

Here are some problems in spelling and some suggestions about overcoming them.

All of us have problems of our own, and sometimes we make up our own ways to remember the correct spelling. Suppose you have trouble with the *ite/ate* ending: *definate* is a common mistake for *definite.* Maybe you can remember that it resembles the word *finite:* or maybe the third *i* in *infinity* will help you. Or maybe you write *infinate* by mistake. Remember the antonym *finite* and remember *separate,* as in "*separate* rooms," and not *separite.* (Not *seperate* either, for that matter.)

I/e, e/i. People mistakenly write *concieve* instead of *conceive,* and *beleive* instead of *believe.* The old recipe

I before *E*
Except after *C*
And when sounded like *ay*
As in *neighbor* and *weigh.*

is useful. Examples, both ways: *achieve, niece, piece, receipt, ceiling, receive.* Exceptions: *either, seize, weird, leisure, species, foreign.*

Variant plurals. Some words change spelling in moving from singular to plural: *wife/wives* (like *knife, life, calf,* and *half*); *man/men* (like *woman, milkman,* etc.); *hero/heroes* (like tomato, potato).

Dropping a final -e before a vowel. Most words ending with a silent *-e* drop it when we change them to a participle or other form that begins with a vowel. We spell the verb *move,* and we spell the participle *moving.* The silent *-e* usually remains when the added form begins with a consonant. Exceptions to both generalizations occur (*argue/argument; mile/mileage*), but they are infrequent and the rule is an unusually safe one.

The final -y. When *-y* is a final vowel after a consonant (*dry*) it turns to *-ie* before *-s,* and *-i* before other letters, except when the ending is *-ing,* in which case the *-y* remains: *dries, drier, drying; beauty, beautiful.* When the *-y* follows another vowel, it generally remains *-y,* as in *joys* and *grayer,* with occasional exceptions, as in *lay/laid.*

Doubling consonants. We double a final consonant before *-ed, -ing, -er,* or *-est* when the original verb or noun ends with a short vowel followed by a single consonant. *Hop* becomes *hopping.* When the vowel is long or a diphthong, we usually show it by a silent -*e* after the single consonant, and a single consonant with the suffix. *Hope* becomes *hoping*. Notice the difference between *plan/planning, plane/planing, slip/slipping, sleep/sleeping.*

Homonyms. Words that are pronounced alike but spelled differently present an irritating problem to writers. We have already mentioned *their/there/they're* and *its/it's.* Here are a few more:

affect/effect
accept/except
capital/capitol
principle/principal
gorilla/guerrilla
stationery/stationary
illusion/allusion

Here are some words frequently misspelled.

accept	embarrass	professor
accommodate	exaggerate	precede
acknowledgment	existence	proceed
advice	explanation	quantity
advise	friend	quite
all right	fulfillment	receive
allusion	grammar	referred
a lot	height	separate
annual	hypocrisy	shining
argument	irritable	similar
arrangement	its	succeed
beginning	it's	surprise
believe	library	than
business	loneliness	then
capital	lonely	their
capitol	necessary	there
coming	nuclear	they're
committee	obstacle	to, two, too
complement	occurred	villain
compliment	piece	who's
decide	possession	whose
definite	principal	writing
desert	principle	written
dessert	privilege	
divide	probably	

———— **EXERCISES** ————————————————————————————————

1. In this paragraph, circle every mechanical error and correct it.
the space between the lines.

During the weeks that I have spent on campus I have learned to
except the principal that definate explinations are often to exagerated
to beleive in alot. 9 out of 10 students embarass their professers by not
realising the mayor of there towns name, or not being alright in gram-
mer, or not suceeding in reading books like "Moby Dick." Its a disgrase.

2. Correct, capitalize, and punctuate this paragraph:

look at that shot thats ridiculous Graebner tells himself he glances at
Carole who has both fists in the air pull yourself together Clark this is a
big point Graebner takes off his glasses and wipes them on his dental
towel stalling Ashe mumbles while he is waiting he raises his left index
finger and slowly pushes his glasses into place across the bridge of his
nose just one point Arthur Graebner misses his first serve again Ashe
moves in he hits sharply crosscourt Graebner dives for it catches it with
a volley then springs up ready at the net Ashe lobs into the sun thinking
that was a good get on that volley I didn't think hed get that Graebner
punches the ball away with a forehand volley deuce Ashe is rattling the
gates but Graebner will not let him in Carole has her hand on the top of
her head unbelievable

John McPhee, "Ashe and Graebner"

A Glossary of Usage and Grammatical Terms

The Glossary entries are of two kinds:

1. Words frequently misused—clichés, commonly confused pairs of words, and words or phrases that should be avoided.

2. Grammatical and rhetorical terms and the names of figures of speech. Each of these entries includes general comments and references to the pages in the text where the subject is discussed

A, an

See **Article.**

Abbreviation

See pages 400–401.

Absolute element

An absolute element is a word or a group of words which is grammatically independent of the rest of the sentence and which is not joined to it by a relative pronoun or a conjunction. It modifies the whole clause or sentence. Absolute phrases are often made up of a noun followed by a participle.

> *All things considered,* he recovered quickly from his injuries.
> *Her youth gone,* the old woman passed her days in remembering.

Many absolute constructions are common phrases.

> *Come hell or high water,* I'll get to Dallas by Thursday.
> Neither twin was there, *to tell the truth.*

Abstract, abstraction

An abstraction is a noun referring to the idea or quality of a thing and not to a thing itself: *redness, courage.*

We use the word *abstract* relatively, referring to more general and less particular words. *Enclosure* is more general, say, than *room* or *cage* or *zoo.*

For remarks on abstractions and prose style, see pages 115–117.

Accept, except

These words sound alike but mean different things. *Accept* means to receive something voluntarily.

> I *accept* the compliment.

Except as a verb means to exclude.

> I *excepted* Jones from the group I wished to congratulate.

Except as a preposition is more common.

> I congratulated everyone *except* Jones.

Acronym

An acronym is an abbreviation, pronounced as a word, which is composed of the first letters of the words in the title or phrase abbreviated.

> *SAC* (Strategic Air Command)
> *snafu* (situation normal, all fouled up)

Use with caution.

Active voice

Verbs are in the active voice when the subject of the sentence does the action the verb describes.

> Bob *hit* the spider.

When the subject is acted upon, the verb is passive.

> *The spider was hit* by Bob.

See **Passive voice.**

Adjective

Adjectives describe or limit a noun or a noun substitute. These adjectives describe:

> *green* onions
> *happiest* year
> The man was *old.*

Other adjectives limit in a variety of ways.
Indefinite:

> *Some* men walked in the road.

Demonstrative:

> *Those* men walked in the road.

Possessive:

> *Their* men walked in the road.

Numerical:

> *Twelve* men walked in the road.

Interrogative:

> *Which* men walked in the road?

Relative:

> Nouns can be used as adjectives.
>
> *university* professor

But the writer should beware of using several nouns in a row as adjectives.

For the formation of comparatives, see **Comparison of adjectives and adverbs.** For a stylistic approach to adjectives, see pages 122–129.

Adjective clause

An adjective clause is a dependent clause used as an adjective.

> The man *whose nose is purple* will stand out in a crowd.

Adjectives frequently misused

Try to avoid the adjective used vaguely. These words once meant specific things: *terror* once inhabited *terrific;* now *terrific* can mean "unusually pleasant."

> What a *terrific* summer day!

Some other adjectives are frequently used as vague praise, vague blame, or vague intensives.

terrible	nice	cute	real	unbelievable
funny	unique	wonderful	fantastic	wicked
awful	interesting	incredible	great	obvious

> That *terrible* man with the *cute* name was *awful* to the *nice* girl.

Adverb

Adverbs describe or limit any words except nouns, pronouns, prepositions, and articles. Adverbs work with verbs, adjectives, other adverbs, verbals, and entire clauses.

Adverbs commonly show degree:

> *extremely* hungry

Manner:

> ran *slowly*

Place:

> hurried *here*

Time:

> she *then* left

For stylistic advice on the adverb, see pages 122–129.

Adverb clause

An adverb clause is a dependent clause used as an adverb.

> I'll be gone *before she starts spraying.*

The adverb clause, *before she starts spraying,* modifies the verb *will be gone.*

Adverbs frequently misused

Most of the adjectives frequently misused become misused adverbs, with an *-ly* added. *Terrible* becomes *terribly,* as in "terribly comfortable." Strictly adverbial adjectives are misused also.

terrifically	actually	wonderfully	literally	incredibly
certainly	very	rather	hopefully	totally
absolutely	virtually	practically	really	obviously

> It *certainly* was a *very* hot day and I was *practically* done at the *absolutely* last minute when *actually* a *rather* large man *virtually* beheaded me.

Advice, advise

Advice is a noun; *advise* is a verb.

> I was *advised* to ignore your *advice.*

Affect, effect

The two words are commonly confused. These examples illustrate proper uses of them:

Bob *affected* (influenced) the writing of Wright.
Sarah *affected* (assumed) the manner of a Greek tragedian.
The harder spray was *effected* (brought about) by an adjustment of the hose's nozzle
The *effect* (result) of the new style was unpleasant.

Agreement

The correspondence in form, or the matching of one word with another. Sentence elements must correspond in number, person, and gender.

> *He is* so evil.
> *They are* so evil.
> *Tom* took *his* crocodile down to the river.
> *Tom* and *Maria* took *their* crocodiles down to the river.
> The *car* and *its* trailer rounded the corner.

See pages 375–383.

Agree to, agree with

One *agrees to* a proposal or an action; one *agrees with* a person.

All ready, already

The words differ in meaning. To say that someone is *all ready* is to say that he is prepared; the word *already* means beforehand in time, as in

> He was *already* there.

All right, alright

All right is the correct form. *Alright* means the same thing, but is a recent creation based on an analogy to the old word *already*. In formal writing, stay away from *alright*.

Allusion, illusion

An allusion is an indirect reference; an illusion is a false belief or perception or a deceptive appearance.

> Barnhouse bored us with his *allusions* to his illustrious family.

> Under the *illusion* that he was invited, Barnhouse appeared for dinner at seven o'clock.

Almost, most

Almost is an adverb meaning "nearly"; *most* is an adjective meaning "nearly all" or "the greater part of." Avoid using *most* as a shortened form of *almost*.

> *Almost* all of us lead lives of quiet desperation.
> *Most* men lead lives of quiet desperation.

Along with

Avoid this wordy and useless phrase, in sentences like

Along with tennis, big game hunting is my favorite sport.
MacDowell is my candidate for the presidency, *along with* Vander-schmidt and Creelman-Carr.

Instead, say something like

Big game hunting and tennis are my favorite sports.
For the presidency, I favor MacDowell, Vanderschmidt, or Creelman-Carr.

A lot

Many people have taken to spelling *a lot* as one word, *alot*. *A lot* is two words, like *all right*.

A lot of policemen showed up.

Although, though

Although is preferable in formal writing.

Altogether, all together

The two do not have the same meaning. *Altogether* means *wholly* or *entirely*. *All together* combines two commonly understood words.

Xavier, Abby, Frank, and Al were *all together* at the table.
Guy Woodhouse was *altogether* disgusting.

Ambiguity

Writing is ambiguous when it has more than one possible meaning or interpretation.

Amid, amidst

Avoid these words, which are not common to the American language and which sound stuffy and bookish.

Among, amongst

Among is preferable. *Amongst* is bookish.

Among, between

Use *between* when you are dealing with two things, *among* for more than two.

between you and me
among the three of us

In highly informal writing, this distinction is often ignored.

Amoral, immoral, unmoral

Amoral means outside morality, neither moral nor immoral.

Beauty is *amoral*.

Immoral is contrary to codes of morality.

Benedict Arnold was *immoral*.

Unmoral is a near-synonym for *amoral* and is seldom used. *Amoral* is often used when the assertion is argumentative, *unmoral* when the statement is merely factual.

Dogs and cats are *unmoral*.

Amount, number

Amount refers to a quantity of things viewed as a whole or to the quantity of one item; *number* describes the separate units of a group.

The *amount* of money in his bank account was staggering.
The *number* of dollar bills on the floor was small.
He took a large *amount* of salt a *number* of times.

Analogy

An analogy is an extended comparison, used for illustration and argument. For examples and stylistic uses, see pages 137–138. For use and abuse in argument, see pages 307–308.

And/or

This legalism frequently occurs in nonlegal prose where *or* would do just as well.

Cooking with pots *and/or* skillets requires nothing more than a hotplate.

Omit the unnecessary *and*.

Antecedent

An antecedent is a word or group of words to which a pronoun refers.

As *Kevin* and *Quentin* ran in, *they* dropped the gas pellets.

Kevin and *Quentin* are the antecedents of the personal pronoun *they*.

Antonym

An antonym means the opposite of another word. *Bad* is the antonym of *good*. As there are no exact synonyms, so we must not expect antonyms to be precisely opposite.

Any, any other

Be careful to use these words properly. If you say

> "*King Lear* is more moving than *any other* play in the English language."

you are probably saying what you intend. If you say, however, that

> "*King Lear* is more moving than *any* play in the English language."

you imply that *Lear* is not in English—or that *Lear* is better than itself, which would be nonsensical. If you say

> "Sophia is sexier than *any* woman in Italy."

you imply that she is not in Italy.

Anybody, anyone

The words are singular, not plural. They take singular pronouns, as do *every, everyone, everybody*.

> *Everyone* charges *his* meal at Alice's.

is formally correct, not

> *Everyone* charges *their* meal at Alice's.

But an exception to this rule could make the second example the preferable form of the sentence. When a pronoun has *anybody* as an antecedent, and the gender of the person being discussed is unknown, we may wish to use forms of the plural *they* to avoid deciding between *he* and *she*, because *they* does not indicate gender.

> Did *anybody* call? What did *they* say?

Anyways

This form of *anyway* belongs to informal speech, not to writing.

Apostrophe

See pages 392–393.

Appositive

An appositive is a noun, or a noun substitute, which is placed next to another noun and which explains or defines it.

> Peter, *the flying dwarf*, escorted Tarquina, his *good fairy*.

Flying dwarf is the appositive of *Peter*, and *good fairy* is the appositive of *Tarquina*.

Apt, liable, likely

> *Apt to* means "having a tendency to."

> > Sarah is *apt to* be discouraged if she doesn't win.

> *Likely to* implies "probably going to." Do not say "We will *likely* arrive . . . ," but

> > We are *likely* to arrive in Cincinnati by early afternoon if the radiator doesn't overheat.

> *Liable to* should be used only in situations that imply negative consequences.

> > That child is *liable* to fall if he leans too far out the window.

Argument

> Writing designed to convince or persuade.

Article

> The definite article is *the,* the indefinites are *a* and *an.* They are adjectives, always indicating that a noun or a noun substitute will follow.
> *The* names a particular:

> > *the* table
> > *the* abstraction

> *A* and *an* name a member of a class:

> > *a* table
> > *an* abstraction

> The difference in meaning is small but indispensable.
> The article *a* is used before words beginning with a consonant sound (even if the letter is a vowel):

> > *a* train
> > *a* unit

> *An* is used before words beginning with a vowel sound:

> > *an* imaginative idea
> > *an* herb

As, like

> *As* is a conjunction, *like* is a preposition. In speech we often find *like* used as a conjunction:

> > He smiles *like* he felt good.

But in writing, we should avoid using *like* as a conjunction. We should use *as* or *as if* instead. Instead of writing

I write *like* I talk.

we say

I write *as* I talk.
I write *as if* I talked like a Frenchman.

Like works as a preposition, in language written or spoken:

He talks *like* a Frenchman.

Aspect

This noun is commonly used as a blank. Avoid it.

We listened to a lecture on various *aspects* of fishing.

Usually if we remove the word we improve our sentence.

We listened to a lecture on fishing.

At

Don't use the redundancy "Where are you *at?*" *Where* means "at which place."

Auxiliaries

Auxiliaries in verb phrases indicate distinctions in tense and person. Common auxiliaries are *will, would, shall, should, be, have, do, can, could, may, might,* and *must.*

We *are* eating the chocolate.
You *would have* done the same.

Awful, awfully

Literally, if we were *awful,* we are "full of awe." We no longer use the word to mean what it means. It is a vague intensive like *terrific, wonderful,* and *horrible.*

Bad, badly

When we use the adjective *bad* after sensory verbs, in an expression like "I felt *bad* yesterday," we sometimes confuse it with the adverb *badly.* If you claim that you "felt *badly,*" your words mean that your sensory apparatus did not function correctly. This use of *bad* holds true for sensory verbs like *feel, taste,* or *sound,* and also for verbs like *seem, appear,* and *look.* In grammatical terms, *bad* in these circumstances is a predicate adjective.

Using *badly* instead of *bad* as a predicate adjective affects gentility but reveals ignorance. It is correct to say

> She looked *bad* when she came up to bat.

and incorrect to say

> She looked *badly* when she came up to bat.

The latter sentence denigrates her vision. It is correct to say

> They seemed *bad* this morning, after the ocean voyage.

referring to the appearance of illness. Do not say

> They seemed *badly* this morning after the ocean voyage.

Other constructions require the adverb *badly*.

> She played *badly* the first seven innings.

In

> She played *bad* the first seven innings.

bad is incorrect.

Badly has another sense, which is "very much." This sense is colloquial or informal.

> They wanted *badly* to be elected.
> She was *badly* in need of a drink.

If you mean to employ this colloquialism, be careful of your word order. If you say, "She needed to sing very *badly*," you say something quite different from "She needed very *badly* to sing." If in doubt, be more formal; say

> She needed *very much* to sing.

not

> She needed to sing *very much*.

Balanced sentences

See pages 177–187, where we discuss balance and parallelism.

Being as

A common illiteracy.

> Being as it was almost noon. . . .

Rewrite to eliminate. Usually we can substitute *because*.

> Because it was almost noon. . . .

Beside, besides

Each of these words has several meanings of its own.

She stood *beside* (by the side of) the bureau.
Matt was *beside* himself (almost overwhelmed) with anger.
It's *beside* (not connected with) the point.
No one was awake *besides* (other than) him.
Besides (furthermore), it's in questionable taste.

Between

See **Among, between.**

Bibliography

See pages 330–335.

Big words

Never use a big word where a little word will do. Never say *domicile* where you could say *house.* Never say *individual* where you could say *person.* Never say *utilize* where you could say *use.*
See **Genteel words** and **-ize verbs.**

Brackets

See page 395.

Bring, take

Bring (to) implies movement toward.

Bring me a cup of coffee.

Take (from) implies movement away from.

Take the memo to the secretary.

Can, may

Both words express possibility. *Can* (or *could*) expresses *physical* possibility.

He *can* go to market because he has the car.
She *could* eat the potato salad, but she doesn't want to.

May (or *might*) implies that something is a *chance*, and often implies *volition.*

He *may* go to Alaska (or he may not).
She *might* be the last of the clan (or she might not).

Often we can hesitate between the two, and choose the one over the other for the precise shade of meaning. "He *could* take the exam" and "He *might* take the exam" offer different possibilities.

In conversation, and in the most informal writing, *may* often disappears in favor of *can,* and a distinction disappears, which is a loss. Or instead of saying "She *may* read Shakespeare, or Julia Child, or *Young Lust*," we substitute the wordier "She *can* read Shakespeare, or Julia Child, or *Young Lust*, depending on what she feels like." The final clause supplies the chanciness and the volition implied in *may*.

In asking or granting permission, genteel prose uses *may*.

> *May* I enter?
> Randolph, you *may* not.

But *may* in this usage almost invariably sounds like an effort to be refined.

Cannot, can not
The spellings are equally acceptable. *Can not* looks more formal.

Can't hardly
Because *hardly*, as Bergen Evans says, "has the force of a negation," *can't hardly* functions as a double negative, or at least as an ambiguity. Does "I *can't hardly* hear you" mean "I *can't* hear you" or "I *can* hear you well" or "I *can hardly* hear you"? Logically, the double negative should make it mean the second, but the speaker probably meant the last. We should increase the clarity of our language by saying simply, "I *can hardly* hear you." The same advice applies to *can't scarcely*.
See **Double negative.**

Capital letters
See pages 101–102.

Case
See **Inflection.**

Cf.
We often find this abbreviation in footnotes and sometimes in parentheses. It tells us to "compare," as in

> This decision was an exception (*cf. Toothe v. Carey*).

Circumlocution
Circumlocution is taking the long way to say something, using clichés, verbs combined with other parts of speech instead of simple verbs, and filler words and phrases. In

> *Notwithstanding the case of* the seamstress, it is *going to be* obvious that *in general, in a manner of speaking, we do well to remember the observation that* a man who is always in a hurry will lose *something or other in the long run.*

the circumlocution occurs throughout, and phrases typical in circumlocution are in italic. Notice that the last seventeen words might be rendered

Haste makes waste.

Cite, sight, site

Cite means to quote or to refer to.

They *cited* the constructive things they'd done.

A *sight* is a view:

a moving *sight*

or vision itself.

A *site* is a location:

a building *site*

Clause

A clause is a part of a sentence with a subject and a predicate. It may be principal (or main or independent) or subordinate (dependent on a main clause).

The year ended and *the year began.*

In the sentence above, two whole clauses are made into a compound sentence by *and.*

The year ended *when it had just begun.*

In this sentence, the italic clause is subordinate.
See page 150.

Cliché

A cliché is a much used combination of words. *Writing Well* uses and defines this word several times. See pages 5–7, for instance.

Collective noun

See **Noun.**

Colon

See pages 395–396.

Comma

See pages 386–390.

Comma splice

See pages 371–374.

Common nouns
> See **Noun.**

Compare to, compare with
> To *compare to* shows similarities between things that are obviously different.

>> He *compared* the sparrow *to* a ten-ton truck.

> (Of course by showing similarity, it reveals difference as well.) To *compare with* shows differences between things that are obviously similar.

>> She *compared* lunch *with* dinner.

> (Of course it reveals similarities at the same time.)

Comparison of adjectives and adverbs
> The comparison of adjectives and adverbs indicates relative degree. The three degrees are positive, comparative, and superlative.

Positive	*Comparative*	*Superlative*
good	better	best
obnoxious	more obnoxious	most obnoxious
quick	quicker	quickest
quickly	more quickly	most quickly

Comparisons
> For a discussion of simile, metaphor, and analogy, see pages 134–138.

Complement
> As a grammatical term, a complement is one or more words that complete the meaning of a verb or an object. A subject complement:

>> Phyllis is a wicked *girl.*

> The predicate noun—*girl*—completes the sense of *Phyllis,* which it refers to. An object complement:

>> The dog chewed the bone *raw.*

> *Raw* modifies and completes *bone.*

Complement, compliment
> A *complement* makes something whole or complete.

>> Work is the *complement* of play.

A *compliment* is praise.

> I paid you a *compliment.*

There is also an archaic meaning in which *compliments* means something like formal politeness, and which survives in the phrase *compliments of the season.*

Complex sentence

A complex sentence contains a main clause and a subordinate clause. Here the subordinate (in italics) is a relative:

> I whistled at the boy *who hung from the cliff.*

See pages 152–153, 160–164, 202–205.

Compound sentence

A compound sentence includes two or more main clauses and no subordinate clauses.

> The moon rose at 10:35 P.M. and the stars appeared to recede into the darkness.

See pages 151–152, 164–167.

Compound-complex sentence

This sentence type combines, as you might expect, the complex and the compound sentence. It has two main clauses and at least one subordinate clause.

> The snow stopped falling when the sun rose, but the temperature stayed below 10°.

See page 153.

Compound word

A compound word contains two or more words that are commonly used together as a single word.

> president-elect
> brother-in-law
> blackbird
> wheelbarrow
> handwriting

See a dictionary for current spelling.
See page 398.

Conjugation

See **Inflection.**

Conjunction

Conjunctions connect or coordinate (*and, but, for, or,* and occasionally *yet* or *so*) or they subordinate (*after, because, while, when, where, since*). With coordinate conjunctions be careful to preserve unity by keeping the coordinate phrases or clauses parallel (see pages 177–182). With subordinate conjunctions, remain aware of the habits of complex sentences (pages 152–153, 160–164, 202–205). Contrary to the old rule, even the best contemporary writing uses conjunctions at the beginnings of sentences.

Conjunctive adverb

A conjunctive adverb can be used to connect main clauses: *then, besides, however, therefore, otherwise.* Use a semicolon between the main clauses (before the adverb) and a comma after the adverb. See pages 166–167.

Conscience, conscious

These words mean different things. *Conscience* is a noun meaning the human faculty that distinguishes right from wrong.

After he lied to his boss, his *conscience* would not let him sleep.

Conscious is an adjective describing a state of awareness or being awake.

Eleanor was *conscious* of a sharp pain behind her left eye.
The patient became *conscious* after spending a week in a coma.

Consider . . . as

Writers frequently misuse the verb *consider* by adding an unnecessary preposition, *as.* Say

She *considered* him handsome.

not

She *considered* him *as* handsome.

Another use of the verb takes *as* appropriately. In the preceding example, *consider* means "believe to be." In the following example, *consider* means "think about" or "talk about."

She *considered* him *as* an administrator and *as* a scholar.

Consist in, consist of

Consist of refers to the parts that make a whole.

The government *consists of* legislative, executive, and judicial divisions.

Consist in refers to inherent qualities:

> The value of democracy *consists in* the responsibility with which it endows the citizen.

Continual, continuous

The two words have slightly different meanings. *Continual* describes an action that is repeated frequently.

> He called her *continually* throughout the day.

Continuous describes an action done without stopping.

> The bleeding was *continuous* for three hours.

Coordinates

Coordinate means equal in rank. Two infinitives are coordinate, for instance, or two main clauses, as in a compound sentence.
See pages 152–153, 160–161, 164–167.

Correlative conjunctions

Both . . . and, either . . . or, neither . . . nor, and *not only . . . but also* are coordinating conjunctions and require parallel forms in the phrases or clauses they coordinate.

Could have, could of

The correct phrase is *could have. Could of* is a mistake. Don't say

> She *could of* been a great actress.

But say

> She *could have* been a great actress.

Counsel, council, consul

Counsel is advice, or a lawyer, or someone acting as a lawyer. Though it would be a confusing sentence, one could say

> The court-appointed *counsel* gave his client *counsel.*

A different spelling, with the same pronunciation, gives us the word *council,* which is a legislative group.

> Harris for City *Council!*

A *consul* represents his government in another country where he keeps residence.

> *The vice-consul* was out to lunch.

Couple

    In the idiomatic sense of *a few*, the word is extremely informal, and in your writing you ought to substitute *two*, or *a few*, or *several*.

Cutting words from quotations

    See pages 397–398.

Dangling constructions

    A phrase placed loosely in a sentence dangles. Modifiers dangle frequently and disastrously.

    See pages 381–383.

Dashes

    See pages 398–399.

Data

    In the most formal prose, we recognize the etymology of *data* as a Latin plural and therefore use the word with a plural verb form. It is correct—if highly formal or scientific—to say

    These data *convince* us.

rather than

    This data *convinces* us.

The singular, rarely used, is *datum*.

Declension

    See **Inflection.**

Deductive reasoning

    In this form of thinking, we apply a general truth to a specific instance. Thus, if it is true that going through a time warp causes pain, we may *deduce* that if Quasimodo goes through a time warp, he will feel pain.

Demonstratives

    Demonstratives are adjectives, like *this, that, these,* and *those*, used to point the finger.

    This is the man who took it; *that's* my basketball.

They can also be pronouns; when they are, they should have clear antecedents. Do not say

    You said that you couldn't read and that you had never learned how. I could not believe *that*.

See pages 379–380.

Diction
> The choice and use of words.

Different from, different than
> *Different from* is usually preferable, especially in formal prose.
> When a clause follows, *different than* is acceptable.

>> This place is *different than* I expected it to be.

Direct address
> A noun or pronoun used to direct a remark to a specific person,
> set off by commas.

>> I was thinking, *Ron,* that you'd like to go up in a balloon.
>> *Irving,* close that closet.
>> Hey, *you!*

Direct object
> See **Object.**

Direct quotation
> See pages 394–395.

Discreet, discrete
> The two words have different meanings. *Discreet* means
> "prudent in one's conduct or speech."

>> She would never reveal it; she was exceptionally *discreet.*

> Discrete means "distinct" or "separate."

>> The words are different; they have *discrete* meanings.

Disinterested, uninterested
> These words are frequently confused. To be *uninterested* is to
> lack fascination about something, even to be bored by it.

>> I tried to arouse his enthusiasm for a game of golf, but he was *uninterested* in such a pastime.

> *Disinterested* is the condition of being impartial or neutral, or of
> having no stake in an issue. Frequently the word is used positively
> as a precondition for fairness, as in the phrase *"disinterested
> party."*

>> The judge declared his *disinterest* in the matter.
>> This judge proclaims his ability to judge the case fairly.

Doesn't, don't
> *Don't* goes with *I, you, we,* and *they,* but not with *it, he,* or *she.*
> It contracts *do not.* It does not contract *does not; doesn't* does.

Double negative

A double negative occurs in a sentence that uses two negative terms when only one is needed.

> He *didn't* say *nothing.*
> You *shouldn't never* do that to a bird.

In earlier English such doubling was thought to give emphasis, as in "I never treacherously slew no man" (Bergen Evans's example). But today double negatives are regarded as unacceptable and illogical. If I should *not* never do something, then by implication I should (positively) do it sometime.

See **Can't hardly.**

Doubt but

Omit *but.* Also omit *but* in *help but.*

> They couldn't *doubt but* that the Racquet Club was best.

becomes

> They couldn't *doubt* that the Racquet Club was best.

and

> They couldn't *help but* know the worst.

becomes

> They couldn't *help* knowing the worst.

And always avoid "They couldn't *doubt but* what. . . ."

Due to

Never use *due to* for *because of* in adverb phrases. "She won the race *due to* her long legs" sounds unnatural. It is probably best to reserve the word for finance. Sometimes people multiply error by writing, "due to the fact that. . . ."

Each, every

Each is a pronoun:

> *Each* went his own way.

and an adjective:

> *Each* package of bubble gum has five pieces.

Each means the individual units of a conglomerate:

> *Each* of the Boy Scouts

but *every* means the conglomerate itself:

> *Every* Boy Scout

In the Boy Scout examples, *each* is a pronoun, *every* is an adjective.
   When the adjective *each* modifies a singular noun, the following verb and pronouns are singular.

> *Each* player *lifts his* bat.

When *each* modifies a plural noun or pronoun and comes before the verb, the verb and pronouns are plural.

> They *each go their* own way.

When *each* works as a pronoun, it is usually singular.

> *Each goes his* own way.

There are exceptions. In the preceding example, if the pronoun referred to men and women, we might have written

> *Each go their* own way.

When *each* refers to two or more singular words, or when a plural word comes between *each* and the verb, the number of the verb is optional. We may say

> *Each* of the players *is*

or

> *Each* of the players *are*

We may say

> When *Mark and Linda* speak, *each* of them *says*

or

> When *Mark and Linda* speak, *each* of them *say*

   The negative of *each* is *neither*. Do not write *each* with a negative:

> *Each* did not speak.

but write

> *Neither* spoke.

Effect, affect

See **Affect, effect.**

E.g.

This is the abbreviation for a Latin expression that means *for example.* It is usually best to use the English, but on occasion we will find these initials, often in scientific or legal prose.

The review board overlooked significant evidence, *e.g., Baxter v. Baxter.*

Egoism, egotism

Egoism has the connotation of a philosophy, *egotism* of a neurosis. *Egoism* is the other side of *altruism* and is a belief in the value of self-interest. *Egotism* is the necessity to use the word *I* all the time.

Either

Either, like *each*, can be pronoun or adjective.

Either path leads us home.
Either of the twins . . .

When *either* means one or the other, it takes the singular.

Either Rick or Chris *is* lying.

When it means both, it still takes a singular verb.

Either of you *is* qualified.

Sometimes *either/or* and *neither/nor* connect a singular and a plural subject. Then the verb agrees with the subject closest to it.

Either Peggotty *or* the Steerforths *are* coming to dinner tonight.

As a correlative conjunction, *either* takes *or* and does not take *nor. Nor* belongs to *neither.*

Elicit, illicit

Elicit means "to bring out."

We could *elicit* no further response from the members.

Illicit means "not permitted."

They were having an *illicit* love affair.

Ellipses

See page 397.

Eminent, immanent, imminent

> *Eminent* means outstanding.

>> The *eminent* philosopher . . .

> *Immanent* means inherent.

>> . . . will discuss *immanent* ideas . . .

> *Imminent* means impending.

>> . . . *imminently*.

Enormity, enormousness

> An *enormity* is a moral outrage. *Enormousness* is hugeness.

Etc.

> This abbreviation meaning "and so forth," from the Latin *et cetera*, is out of place in formal prose. In formal and informal prose, it often trails off the end of a sentence into vagueness and avoids extending the brain. Stay away from it in formal prose. Think before you use it in any context.
> See **Foreign words and phrases.**

Etymology

> *Etymology* is the study of the origins and histories of words.

Euphemism

> Euphemisms are fancy or abstract substitutes for plain words. We use them for social elevation, as when the *undertaker* becomes a *mortician*, or to avoid facing something frightening, as when we say that someone *passed away*, instead of saying that he *died*.
> See pages 94–96.

Everybody, everyone

> *Everybody* and *everyone* take a singular verb.

>> *Everybody goes* to church.

> The words can take a singular pronoun, especially in a formal context:

>> *Everyone* finds *his* seat and waits for the minister.

> or a plural pronoun, especially when it refers to men and women and we wish to avoid the prejudice of picking either *his* or *her*.

>> *Everybody* waited until *they* caught *their* breath.

> See pages 375–377.

Exclamation point
> See page 386.

Expletives
> When *it* and *there* fill space in a sentence without contributing to its meaning, we call them expletives.

>> *There are* thousands of people in the United States who cannot read.
>> *It is* understood that the rain was falling.

> These could be written:

>> Thousands of people in the United States cannot read.
>> Rain was falling.

Exposition
> Writing designed to explain or analyze.

Fact
> Avoid the phrase *the fact that*, which is wordy and unnecessary.

Famous, notorious, infamous
> To be *famous* is to be well known or celebrated. To be *notorious* is to be well known for something shady. To be *infamous* is to be well known for something detestable.

>> He was a *famous* movie star, musician, and second baseman.
>> He was a *notorious* pirate, extortionist, and linguist.
>> Bluebeard was an *infamous* character.

Farther, further
> As "distance to go" the two are interchangeable. Where *further* means "more," *farther* is not a possible alternative.

>> We have no *further* use for him.

Few
> See **Less.**

Field
> A field is a place for growing hay or daisies. Don't use it as a blank, or invisible noun, as in "the field of agriculture."

Figure
> See **Numeral.**

Fine
> This adjective is vague and overused.

Finite verb
> A finite verb is complete, a predicate in itself.

The house *collapses.*

Gerunds, infinitives, and participles are not finite verbs but *verbals.*

Footnote
See pages 333–335.

Foreign words and phrases
Foreign words and phrases often look pretentious in our writing. In dialogue, they can be useful to characterize someone as foreign or as pretentious. Occasionally nothing in English seems quite so apt as a foreign phrase. But look hard before you give up. If you must use one, italicize it by underlining it.

Foreword, forward
The two have different meanings. A *foreword* is a preface, the introductory statement at the beginning of a book. *Forward* is usually a direction. On occasion, *forward* means "bold" or "presumptuous."

> She leaned *forward* and stuck her tongue out at him; she was very *forward.*

Fused sentence
See **Run-on sentence.**

Gender
Gender is a grammatical indication of sex. English nouns lack gender except as their own sense indicates. That is, *sister* is feminine, *brother* masculine, and *sibling* can be either. Some pronouns have gender (*he, she*), but most do not (*I, they, you, we*). In some languages, all nouns are assigned a gender. In French, the word for *grass* (*herbe*) is feminine, and the word for *time* (*temps*) is masculine. In English both words are neuter.

Genteel words
Some words act as euphemisms by seeming socially preferable to plainer alternatives. People who use them seem to be *trying* to be genteel. Avoid them unless you are making a genuine distinction.

Genteel	Ordinary
perspire	sweat
wealthy	rich
home	house
luncheon	lunch

Gerund
>   See **Verbal.**

Get
>   We multiply this little word in our speech; it has small place in
our writing. "I went down to *get* some wallpaper" is passable but
often imprecise. In writing, it would be better to *choose* or *buy* the
wallpaper.

Good, well
>   It is common to use *good* as if it were an adverb, but it is
incorrect.

>>   He ran *good.*

>   When referring to an action, *well* is the right word.

>>   He ran *well.*

>   Be careful with the word *feels;* to say that a person *feels good* is to
say that he is in a pleasant frame of mind; to say that a person *feels
well* is to say either that he feels healthy or that his sense of touch
is functioning efficiently.

Grammar
>   Grammar describes how words function in a language.

Guerrilla, gorilla
>   A *guerrilla* is an irregular soldier. A *gorilla* is an animal. *Guer-
rilla* is also used as an adjective and has been used adjectivally to
indicate activity in the service of revolution: *guerrilla* theater,
guerrilla television.

Had ought
>   This combination is clumsy. Instead of writing

>>   We knew he *had ought* to come.

>   write

>>   We knew he *ought* to come.

Hanged, hung
>   *Hanged* pertains to the execution of human beings, *hung* to the
suspension of objects.

>>   Sam Hall was *hanged* in October.
>>   We *hung* the portraits in the hall.

He, him

> *He* is a subject, *him* an object.

Other pronoun pairs, subject and object, are *I/me, they/them, she/her, we/us,* and *who/whom.* (See **Who/whom.**)

> *He* walked to Joe's. *He* and Jane walked to Joe's.
> Joe saw *him.* Joe saw Jane and *him.*

A common error uses the subject when it ought to use the object.

> Joe saw Jane and *I.*

is wrong. You would not say "Joe saw *I*" and therefore you do not say "Joe saw Jane and *I.*" It is correct to say

> Joe saw Jane and *me.*

This error, like many errors, is a false correction. When we are children we may say

> *Me* and Jane went down to Joe's.

We learn to correct this to

> Jane and *I* went down to Joe's.

which is fine because *I* is a subject. Then by mistake we use *I* when we should use the objective *me,* as if we corrected the old error.

This error happens most often after a preposition like *across, at, behind, between, by, for, from, in, of, on, over, to, under,* and *with.* Prepositions take objects. Always say

> This happened to Jane and *me.*

Never say

> This happened to Jane and *I.*
> This happened to Jane and *he.*
> This happened to Jane and *we.*
> This happened to Jane and *they.*

All of these examples are incorrect.

The way to remember: if it sounds wrong when you use the preposition alone, as in

> This happened to *I/he/we/they* . . .

then it is wrong when a proper name comes between the preposition (or the verb) and the pronoun.

Also see **Pronoun.**

He or she

This locution is awkward and clumsy. Sometimes we use it to avoid sexism.

See pages 172–174.

Help but

See **Doubt but.**

Homonym

Homonyms are words that, although pronounced the same, are spelled differently and mean different things.

to, too, two	bare, bear	their, there, they're
through, threw	blew, blue	heir, air

Hopefully

Hopefully is an adverb meaning "full of hope" that frequently becomes a dangling modifier. We say

Hopefully, the plane will be on time.

when we do not mean to imply that the plane is full of hope. We could say

Hopefully, I awaited her arrival.

We come to use *hopefully* as if it meant "I hope." The first example is meant to say

I hope the plane will be on time.

Hyperbole

Hyperbole is extreme exaggeration to make a point.

That cat *weighs a ton.*

Use hyperbole with discretion; do not use it, like some writers, a thousand times on every page.

Hyphen

See page 398.

I, me

See **He/him.**

I.e.

I.e. abbreviates the Latin *id est,* meaning "that is." We use it sometimes to introduce an explanation or definition of a word or phrase.

She was nonessential, *i.e.,* they didn't need to employ her.

Usually, the expression seems overprecise and too much like legal or scientific writing. The sentence above can omit the Latinism and use instead a colon or a semicolon.

> She was nonessential: they didn't need to employ her.

Immigrant, emigrant

An *immigrant* is someone who enters a country; an *emigrant* leaves one. Our ancestors had to emigrate before they could immigrate.

Incredible, unbelievable

In theory, these words are synonymous. In practice, *unbelievable* holds up better.

> The charges were *unbelievable*.

statcs rather straightforwardly the disbelief.

> The charges were *incredible*.

suffers from the use of *incredible* as a vague intensive.

> Those hamburgers were *incredible*.

simply praises the hamburgers in hyperbole from which constant use has withdrawn the strength. *Unbelievable* undergoes some of the same diminishment:

> . . . *unbelievably* rare

and may also lose its utility in time.

Indefinite pronoun
See **Pronoun** and pages 378–380.

Independent clause
See **Clause.**

Indirect object
See **Object.**

Indirect quotation
We use indirect quotations when we attribute a remark without claiming to use exact words and without using quotation marks.

> The congressman from Ohio then claimed that he had heard enough.
> She said that Herbert was the nicest boy she had ever met.

When we indirectly quote information taken from a source, we should footnote it just as we would a direct quotation.

Inductive reasoning
This form of thought draws general conclusions from particular examples or evidence.

> As a result of these experiments we conclude that if water temperature falls below 32 degrees the water will freeze.

Infer, imply
We *infer* or understand from what a speaker or writer *implies* to us. *Infer* means "conclude"; *imply* means "suggest."

> From the tone of her voice on the telephone, I *inferred* her terror.
> She *implied* that she had seen a face at the window.

We cannot say that another person *inferred* something to us. He or she *implied* it, and we *inferred* a meaning in the implication.

Inferior to, inferior than
Inferior than is incorrect. Say either *inferior to* or *worse than.*

Infinitive
See **Verbal.**

Inflection
Inflection is the change in the form of a word to indicate a change in meaning or grammatical relationship. The inflection of nouns and pronouns is called *declension;* of verbs, *conjugation;* and of adjectives and adverbs, *comparison.*
Inflection of nouns indicates *number* and *case.*

> aardvark, aardvarks, aardvark's, aardvarks'; man, men, man's, men's

Inflection of pronouns indicates *case, person,* and *number.*

> she, her, hers; who, whom, whose; they, them, their

Inflection of verbs indicates *tense, person,* and *mood.*

> laugh, laughing, laughs, laughed
> spring, springing, springs, sprung

Inflection of modifiers indicates *comparison* and *number.*

> thin, thinner, thinnest
> this dog, that dog, these dogs, those dogs

In regard to, in regards to
In regard to is preferable. The good stylist rewrites to avoid either. Instead of

In regard to your letter of May 9 . . .

we might say

Answering your letter of May 9 . . .

Intensive pronoun
See **pronoun.**

Intransitive verb
An intransitive verb neither has an object nor is passive in form.

I *was* at Annette's house in Santa Fe at the time.
Quaker *has been waiting* on the flagpole for hours.

Irony
Intentional irony is a conscious statement intended to convey the opposite of what it seems to say. It can be used humorously; it can be gentle or sarcastic and biting. We can say that the weather is marvelous when we are standing in a downpour. Our irony is obvious. When Jonathan Swift wrote his satirical "Modest Proposal," he suggested that Irish babies be slaughtered and eaten, as a convenience to the English. He did not intend the suggestion literally. Most of his readers perceived his irony.

Irregardless
Use *regardless. Irregardless* is a redundancy, made in error on the model of *irrespective.*

Italics
See pages 398–399.

Its, it's
It's always stands for *it is. Its* is possessive.

It's eating *its* supper.

See pages 384–385.

-ize verbs
Avoid making new verbs ending in *-ize*, like "*tomato-ize* the spaghetti." Avoid using some recent coinages too: *utilize* (say "use"), *personalize, finalize, prioritize.*

Jargon
Jargon is the argot of a profession, or a peer group, like educationists' jargon, or astronauts', or rock musicians'. Businessmen fall into a jargon frequently. Sometimes they *firm up* a deal before

they *finalize* it. Sometimes two negotiators are not *in the same ballpark;* one of them, however, may *come out of left field.*

Slang makes jargon too, and every campus—every year, every term—invents a local dialect of student jargon.

Jargon is a language by which we attempt to prove that *we* are the initiated and to keep noninitiates in confusion and befuddlement. It is language not to communicate but to exclude.

Jargon has a real purpose when it is the precise shorthand of a science. But for most of us most of the time, jargon has a tendency to be considerably vaguer than the larger language we share.

Kind of

This phrase is misused, and even used properly is often not helpful. When we say *"kind of* big" we are qualifying *big,* as if we said *"rather* big." It is a misuse of the word *kind. Kind* means species.

> It is a *kind of* pine tree.

This usage works, but we often slide into vague species-making

> She is a *kind of* blonde I can't stand.

The sentence cannot be rewritten; it must be rethought. What exactly is it that you cannot stand? Name it.

> I do not like a blonde who has red eyebrows.

The same remarks apply to *sort of.*

Lay, lie

Lay/laid/laid, meaning to put or place, applies to the following uses: "she *lays* an egg"; "you *laid* the book on the table"; "I *laid* my pen on this pad." *Lay* takes a direct object. The past tense of *lie* is *lay,* which is a source of confusion. *Lie/lay/lain,* meaning to rest or recline, applies to these uses: I *lie* on the grass; she *lay* on the bed all day; we *had lain* in the sun. *Lie* never takes a direct object.

Lead, led

Lead is present tense, *led* is past, and *lead*—when pronounced like *led*—is the metal.

> Yesterday I *led* the class.
> Today I *lead* the escape.

Leave, let

Leave means "to go away"; *let* means "to allow."

> *Leave* me. (Go away from me.)
> *Let* me. (Allow me to.)
> *Leave* me out. (Don't include me.)
> *Let* me out. (Allow me to go.)

Less

This word is frequently misused where *fewer* would be correct.

> There are *less* flowers in the vase today.

should be

> There are *fewer* flowers in the vase today.

Fewer refers to actual numbers; *less* refers to quantity in general.

> The powerful nations are *fewer* than they used to be.
> Nations have *less* power.

Lie, lay

See **Lay, lie.**

Like, as

See **As, like.**

Likewise

This expression is a clumsy transition, almost always a piece of bone in the hamburger.

Linking verb

A linking verb expresses the relationship between the subject and the predicate noun or predicate adjective. The principal linking verbs are *appear, be, become, seem,* and verbs used for sensations (*feel, smell, sound, taste, look*).

> Lorca *is* magnificent.
> Rose *became* a mother.
> Joe *looks* sick.
> The steak *smells* rotten.

Literally

We often say *literally* when we mean the opposite: *figuratively.* We use a metaphor, but we realize that it is dead and we play Dr. Frankenstein to the monster by applying the cathodes of *literally* (or *literal*).

> She was *literally* as big as a house.
> He was a *literal* man of straw.
> He hit the ball *literally* a thousand miles.

The monster never walks. Use *literally* only to emphasize that you mean just what you say.

> When the police broke into the warehouse, they found the prime minister *literally* weeping tears of gratitude.

Literal means "according to the letter" or "as it actually appears." Never use it unless you mean it literally. When you find yourself misusing it for the purposes above, you can either omit it and settle for the corpse of your metaphor, or you can make a new metaphor, "She was as big as. . . ."

Litotes

Litotes is a figure of speech understating something by saying the negative of its opposite. Saying "It's not a beauty" may mean "It's ugly."

Little

Often we misuse this word—which is necessary to common speech in its literal meaning—as a vague qualifier.

> He's a *little* late.

We misuse *pretty* in the same way, without considering its meaning. James Thurber tormented his editor on *The New Yorker* by writing that something was "a little big" and "pretty ugly."

Logic

See **Deductive reasoning** and **Inductive reasoning.** Also see pages 287–316 for some remarks about persuasion and an account of some common errors in thinking.

For further reading, consult Manuel Bilsky's *Patterns of Argument.*

Loose, lose

Different spellings make different words.

> The dog is *loose.*
> I *lose* the dog.
> The *loose* rope *loses* the dog.

Lot, lots

These are informal substitutes for other quantitative words: *a great many, a number of.* Avoid in formal writing.

Mad, angry

Mad means "crazy" or "insane," but popular speech has made it synonymous with *angry:* "I'm *mad* at you" means "I'm *angry* with you." Use *angry* in formal writing.

Main clause

A *main clause* can stand by itself. It can be a whole, simple sentence.

> They built an armadillo.

Two *main clauses* can make a compound sentence.

> They built an armadillo and they traded it for a VW.

In a complex sentence, the main clause (in italics) governs a subordinate clause.

> When night fell, *they built an armadillo.*

Man who . . .

A common circumlocution uses a noun (like *man* or *woman* or *person* or *senator* or *typist*) in a relative clause when the extra words serve no function.

> He was *a man who* drank half a bottle of scotch before breakfast.
> She was *a woman who* knew better.
> She was *a senator who* always filibustered.

If this last sentence gave us the information that she was a senator, it would be justified.

> He was *a typist who* never typed more than twenty-seven words a minute.

These sentences can become

> *He drank* half a bottle of scotch before breakfast.
> *She knew* better.
> *She always* filibustered.
> *He never typed* more than twenty-seven words a minute.

Manuscript form

See pages 402–403.

May, can

See **Can, may.**

Metaphor

See pages 134–136.

Mixed constructions

Avoid sentences that begin as if they will follow one form, switch forms, and become mixed and confusing. Do not say

> Because the annual snowfall reaches eighty inches causes everybody to keep a supply of food.

This example uses a dependent clause as a subject. It could be repaired into

> Because the annual snowfall reaches eighty inches, everyone keeps a supply of food.

Here is a mixed construction in which an adverb clause is used as a noun.

> A Fourth of July celebration is when you have fireworks and picnics.

This can be changed to

> At a Fourth of July celebration, you have fireworks and picnics.

Modifier

Any word or group of words that describes or qualifies another word or group of words is a modifier.

For a general account of adjectives, adverbs, and other modifiers, see pages 122–129. For attention to some problems common in the use of modifiers, see pages 381–383.

Momentary, momentous

Momentary has to do with time. It refers to something that lasts only a moment or happens at any moment. *Momentous* means of extraordinary importance, as in the cliché "a *momentous* occasion."

> The affliction was *momentous*.
> She looked west, awaiting his *momentary* arrival.

Mood

The mood (or mode) of the verb indicates an attitude on the part of the writer. The mood may be indicative, imperative, or subjunctive. The *indicative* mood states a fact or asks a question.

> Jim Rice *is* here.
> *Was* Bill Walton there?

The *imperative* mood gives a command, gives directions, or makes a request.

> *Beware* of the darkness.
> *Turn* right at Golgotha.
> *Mend* my parachute, please.

The *subjunctive* mood expresses uncertainty, contradiction, wishfulness, regret, or speculation. It is the most common in contrary-to-fact clauses beginning with *if* ("If it *were* possible, I would fly") and after certain verbs such as *move* ("I move that the meeting *be* post-poned") and *demand* ("They demand that the bail *be* fixed").

Morale, moral

Moral is a matter of ethics, *morale* of high or low spirits.

> Their *morals* were low, but their *morale* was high.
> Murder is not a *moral* act, usually.

Ms.

A recently invented title, on the anology of *Mr., Mrs.,* and *Miss, Ms.* reveals female gender while it conceals marital status.

Myself

Do not use *myself* as a substitute for *I* or *me*. Do not say

> Richard and *myself* went to the circus.
> The elephant paused a few yards downwind from *myself*.

Do say

> Richard and *I* went to the circus.
> The elephant paused a few yards downwind from *me*.

Narration

Writing that tells a story in a connected series of events.

N.b.

This common abbreviation from the Latin means "Notice well!" and draws our attention to something.

Neither

See **Either.**

Neologism

A neologism is a made-up word, often used out of laziness or affectation when an old word would do. *Finalize* is a neologism; *end* or *finish* are the old words.

None

None can be either singular or plural, depending on context and intention.

> *None* of the other guys *were* going to the game.
> *None* of his fellow senators *was* likely to take so strong a stand on the war.

Nonrestrictive modifier

A nonrestrictive modifier is a parenthetical expression that does not limit the noun or pronoun modified. It can be a nonrestrictive clause:

> The Buick, *which was a car new to my neighborhood,* was the object of fascination.

or a phrase:

> The banana, *a fruit new to our taste,* was divided evenly.

See page 368.

No one, nobody

These words take a singular verb. Third-person pronouns, singular and plural, can refer to them: *he, his, him, she, hers, her, they, them.* We use *they* and *them* when we feel that the gender of the pronoun would be invidious.

Not un-

Eschew the habit of writing *not un-'s*

> A *not* undistinguished gentleman, in a *not* unelegant dinner jacket, *not* ungracefully strode past the *not* unchic lady.

Noun

There are several types of nouns. *Common* nouns belong to one of a class of people, places, or things (*woman, country, table*). *Proper* nouns are names of specific people, places, or things. (*Max von Sydow, Liv Ullmann, Casablanca, Ann Arbor, Statue of Liberty*). *Concrete* nouns name something that can be perceived by the senses (*acid, trees, eggs, horses*). *Abstract* nouns name a general idea or quality (*terror, love, harshness, agony*). *Collective* nouns refer to a group as a unit (*band, team, council, league*). These categories are not mutually exclusive; a word like *tree* is common and concrete.

Nouns, whatever their functions in a sentence, retain their basic form, varying it only in forming the plural and the possessive. The plural of most nouns is formed by adding *-s* to the singular, the possessive by adding an apostrophe and an *-s* to the singular or an apostrophe after the *-s* of the plural: *hen, hens, hen's, hens'; house, houses, house's, houses'.* Some nouns add *-es* for the plural: *hero, heroes, hero's, heroes'.* A few nouns change their internal spelling for the plural: *man, men; woman, women;* here, the possessive is formed by an apostrophe and an *-s,* in singular and in plural (*man's, men's*). Other nouns with an irregular plural are listed on page 404.

For stylistic advice about nouns, see pages 113–120.

Nouns commonly used as blanks

Many nouns, which are perfectly useful when spoken with care, are frequently used imprecisely, wordily, and without utility— nouns used as blanks: *aspect, case, character, factor, fact, field, element, effect, experience, nature, manner, respect, situation,* and *feature.*

> Some *aspects* in the *case* of Rumpelstiltskin have the *character* of *elements* that seem sinister in *nature.* The *fact* that the enraged dwarf was a *factor* in the *nature* of the King's *manner* is a *feature* with *respect* to which we can not distinguish the *effect.*

This paragraph has the consistency of mud or an annual report.

Noun substitute

A noun substitute, whether clause or phrase or pronoun, functions as a noun.

Number

See **Inflection.**

Numeral

See page 403.

Object

A complete sentence needs a subject and a verb; it need not have an object.

> The cat screeched.

is a complete sentence.

> The cat clawed *Herbert.*

includes an object. An object is something a verb acts upon.

Objects are direct and indirect. A *direct object* is any noun (or noun substitute) that answers the question "What?" or "Whom?" after a transitive verb. Direct objects are the objects of the verb's action.

> She toppled *the giant.*
> He knows *what she wants.*

An *indirect object* is a noun or noun substitute which is indirectly affected by the verb's action and which tells *to whom* or *for whom* the action is done.

> She gave *him* a karate chop.

Him is the indirect object, *karate chop* the direct object.

Object complement
> See **Complement**.

Of

> We often use *of* when we don't have to.

>> outside *of* the house
>> off *of* the ground
>> inside *of* the room

> The phrases read more stylishly as

>> outside the house
>> off the ground
>> inside the room

> Keep the *of* when the extra preposition changes meaning. *Outside of* can mean "to the exclusion *of*," and we are correct to say "Outside *of* scientific speculation, there is no use for such calibration." *Inside of* can mean "in less than." "*Inside of* an hour, he had finished the work."

One, you

> Be careful not to use *one* in place of *you* so much that it sounds awkward or pretentious.

>> Should *one* be careful to avoid the use of the word "one" when *one* is speaking to a woman whom *one* loves?

> As suggested by this example, context is important when you consider using *one*. It is useful at times, but it has a way of seeming affected. Never use it as an obvious disguise for *I*.

>> *One* took an amusing jaunt to Cedar Point last summer.

> Finally, be careful not to mix *one* and *you* or *I* in the same sentence.

One of the most . . .

> This cliché is drained of meaning.

>> She is *one of the most* lovable people in the world.
>> The rodeo was *one of the most* exciting experiences of my life.

> If you use this phrase, cross it out and consider the particulars to which you refer. One example, showing the character *being* lovable, is worth ten thousand assertions. An exciting anecdote from the rodeo makes assertion unnecessary.
> Show, don't tell.

Parallelism

See pages 177–181.

Parentheses

See page 399.

Participle

See **Verbal.**

Passive voice

A verb is in the passive voice when it *acts upon* the subject.

LeFlore *was hit* by the pitch.

See **Active voice.**

Period

See page 386.

Person

In grammar, the person of a verb or a pronoun shows that someone is speaking (in *first person*), or is spoken to (*second person*), or is spoken about (*third person*). In *I see, you see, he sees,* the person of the pronoun changes each time; the verb form of the first person and the second person happens to be the same, but the verb form changes to indicate the third person. With a few verbs, the form changes with each change of person (I *am,* you *are,* he *is*).

Phrase

Phrases function as a part of speech and do not have a subject and a predicate.

An *infinitive phrase:*

I studied *to learn Greek.*

A *prepositional* phrase:

The flower grows *in the mountain.*

A *verb* phrase:

The zebra *is catching up.*

A *participial* phrase:

Sliding into second, Zarido tore a ligament.

Plagiarism

Plagiarism is using other people's work, whether it is a published source used without acknowledgment or a friend's old paper or a term paper bought from an entrepreneur.

Possessive

For the possessive of nouns, see **Noun.** For the possessive of pronouns, see **Pronoun.**

Precede, proceed

To *precede* is to "go before" or "in front of."

The Pirates *preceded* the Reds onto the field.

To *proceed* is to "continue" or to "begin again."

After the game, they *proceeded* to the airport.

Predicate

A predicate is the part of the sentence *about* the subject. It includes verbs and, on occasion, adverbs, direct objects, indirect objects, and clauses attached to the predicate.

See page 148.

Predicate adjective

See **Complement.**

Predicate noun

See **Complement.**

Preposition

Prepositions show the relationship between a noun or noun equivalent and another word in the sentence. Some of the most commonly used prepositions are *across, after, at, behind, between, by, for, from, of, on, over, to, under,* and *with.*

Tom hid *in* the attic.

The preposition *in* relates the noun *attic* to the verb *hid.*

Presently

This word means "in a little while," not "now" or "currently." Say

He is *at present* a milkman.

not

He is *presently* a milkman.

But say

He will come back to Chicago *presently.*

Pretty
    See **Little.**

Principal, principle
    Principle is a noun meaning a general truth (the *principles* of physics) or moral ideas (she had the highest *principles*). The adjective *principal* means "the foremost." One could speak of the *principal principle* of a science or a philosophy. The noun *principal* means the chief officer.

    Alex Emerson is the *principal* of Bob's school.

Pronoun
    A pronoun is a word used in place of a noun.
    Personal pronouns:

    I, you, he, she, we, etc.

    Relative pronouns:

    who, which, that

    Demonstrative pronouns:

    this, that, these, those

    Indefinite pronouns:

    each, either, any, some, someone, all, etc.

    Reciprocal pronouns:

    each other, one another

    Reflexive, or *intensive,* pronouns:

    myself, yourself, etc.

    For pronoun usage, subject and object, see **He/him.**

Proper noun
    See **Noun.**

Prophesy, prophecy
    The word with the *s* is the verb, the word with the *c* the noun.

    The priest *prophesied* doom.
    It was an accurate *prophecy.*

Proved, proven

Proved is the regular past participle form of *prove* and is preferred in American usage. *Proven* is a Scottish version of the participle, sometimes found in current usage.

Punctuation

See pages 386–399.

Quotation marks

See pages 394–395.

Rational, rationale

Rational means "reasonable and sensible." It is an adjective. *Rationale* is a noun meaning "the whole system of reasons behind an idea, a position, or an action."

> His arguments were *rational.*
> Her *rationale* for the program was easy to discern.

Real, really

Conversational usage accepts *real* as an adverb, but it will not do in writing. Write

> The boat was *really* handsome!
> Josephine seemed to be a *really* happy girl.

Don't write

> The boat was *real* handsome.
> Josephine seemed to be a *real* happy girl

Real as an adjective survives.

> It was a *real* boat.

Frequently, we use *real* and *really* as weak intensifiers, but our sentences will be stronger without them.

Reason is because, reason why

Don't use these constructions. If you must use *reason is*, have it be "*reason is that.* . . ."

Relative clause

See **Subordinate clause.**

Relative pronoun

See **Pronoun.**

Respectfully, respectively

Respectfully is an adverb that modifies an action full of respect.

I remain, yours *respectfully,*

Respectively pertains to each of a number, in an order.

He swore that he saw Ted and Joan wearing a flower and a bowler, *respectively.*

Therefore to end a letter "Yours *respectively*" makes no sense.

Restrictive clause or modifier

A restrictive modifier is a clause or a phrase essential to the identity of what is modified.

Everybody *who wants* can get to the top.

See **Nonrestrictive modifier** for contrast.

Rhetoric

Rhetoric is the art of discourse, either spoken or written. The use of *rhetoric* to mean "inflated or exaggerated speech" is recent.

The politician's promises were mere *rhetoric.*

Rhetorical question

The rhetorical question is a frequent device of argument or persuasion. We ask a question, not to be answered, but to affect the listener or reader.

Are we born, to suffer and to die, only to satisfy the whims of rich warmongers?
Must we write themes forever?

Run-on sentence

A run-on sentence fuses two sentences.

I was eight my brother was ten.

is a run-on or fused sentence. It should read

I was eight. My brother was ten.

Satire

Satire is a form of literature, either prose or poetry, that uses ridicule to expose and to judge behavior or ideas that the satirist finds foolish, or wicked, or both.

Seldom ever

This phrase is redundant. *Seldom* will do. Instead of

He *seldom ever* brushed his hair.

say

He *seldom* brushed his hair.

Semantics

The study of the meanings and associations of words. A good book on semantics is S. I. Hayakawa, *Language in Thought and Action.*

Semicolon

See pages 391–392.

Sensual, sensuous

The two words have different meanings. *Sensual* has unfavorable connotations and means "preoccupied with or inclined to the gratification of the senses or appetites."

He was wholly *sensual* in his priorities; his gluttony came first.

Sensuous has complimentary connotations and describes things that give pleasure to the senses.

The passage is one of the most *sensuous* in all literature.

Sentence fragment

See pages 153–156, 368–371.

Sentence types

See **Compound-complex sentence, Compound sentence, Complex sentence,** and **Simple sentence.**

Shall, will

In common speech and most writing, we make small distinction between the words. Formally, *I shall* expresses a person's belief about his future.

I shall be twenty-one in December.

I will expresses his will power, his wish.

I will get to Japan before I die!

She/her

See **He/him.**

Should, would

> *Should* expresses obligation.

> > You *should* be ashamed.

> It is confused with *would* when it is used in other senses.

> > I *should* not have reached Chicago without your loan.

> When we use the past of *shall* in an indirect quotation, formal prose requires *should* instead of *would*.

> > I said that you *should* be ready before eight.

> *Would* commonly expresses habitual activities.

> > He *would* visit the lake and fish from dawn to dusk.

> When another phrase (like "every summer," if it were added to the last sentence) expresses habit, we can drop the *would* and use the past tense alone.

> > He visited the lake every summer and fished from dawn to dusk.

Should have, should of

> The words are *should have*, which can be pronounced *should've*. *Should of* does not make sense.

Sic

> Pronounced "sick," this Latin word appears in quotations, enclosed in brackets, to signify that an error was made in the source material, not by the writer copying the quotation.

> > Studebaker writes, "I would rather be Thoreu [sic] unhappy than a contented pig."

Simile

> A figure of speech in which comparison is openly made, usually by *like* or *as*.

> > He walks *like* a turkey.
> > The fabric was soft *as* a baby's bottom.

Simple sentence

> A simple sentence has one main clause and no subordinate clauses.

> > She barked at the full moon.

See pages 150–151.

Slang

The special, idiosyncratic vocabulary or jargon associated with a culture or subculture. Slang words have been absorbed into English from various ethnic groups ("Fred is such a *klutz,* his career is *kaput"*), from sports ("It's your *ballgame"*), and, most recently, from technology ("I asked him to give me some *input* on that"). Most slang is short-lived. Avoid using it in formal prose.

So

This word is a stylistic pitfall for many beginning writers. As a coordinating conjunction, *so* is often boring and repetitious, leading the writer into dull compound sentences.

> She was tall *so* he asked her how she liked the weather up there.
> She was tired of hearing that question *so* she knocked him flat.

As a vague intensive, *so* is as useless as *wonderful* and *terrible* though it occupies less space.

> The building was *so* tall.
> I am *so* glad to see you!

Sort of

See **Kind of.**

Spelling

See pages 404 405.

Split infinitive

An infinitive is the form of the verb that uses *to,* as in *to run, to think, to scratch.* When we place another word (commonly an adverb) in the middle of an infinitive, we are splitting the infinitive.

> to *quickly* run
> to *occasionally* think
> to *from time to time* scratch

Grammarians used to insist that the infinitive never be split. People split them anyway.

> Remember *to never split* the infinitive!

Now, most grammarians consider a prohibition against split infinitives fussy. But careful writers rarely split them.

Stationary, stationery

Stationary is an adjective that means "standing still." *Stationery* means "writing materials."

Style

See especially Chapters 4–6. See also William Strunk and E. B. White, *The Elements of Style;* Bergen Evans, *A Dictionary of Contemporary American Usage;* and *A Dictionary of Modern English Usage* by H. W. Fowler, rev. and ed. by Sir Ernest Gowers. See also *The Modern Stylists,* ed. by Donald Hall, a collection of essays and excerpts by George Orwell, Ernest Hemingway, Ezra Pound, Edmund Wilson, James Thurber, and others.

Subject

A subject is a noun, or a noun substitute, about which something is stated or questioned. The subject usually comes before the predicate. The complete subject is the subject and all the words (modifiers, etc.) that belong to it.

> *The grinning barbarian, his teeth clenched,* looked into the barnyard.

Barbarian is the simple subject; the first six words make the complete subject.

Subjunctive

See **Mood.**

Subordinate clause

A subordinate (or dependent) clause cannot stand by itself and make a whole sentence. It depends upon a main clause.

> I cannot see *who it is.*
> The claws are not lethal, *because he was de-clawed.*

Substantive

A *Substantive* is a word or group of words used as a noun; it may be a noun, pronoun, phrase, or noun clause.

Suppose, supposed

The past tense often disappears, and meaning disappears with it. See **Used to, use to.**

Syntax

Syntax is the way in which words are put together to form larger units, phrases, clauses, or sentences. It is also the part of grammar that describes this putting together.

Tense

The tense of a verb shows the time in which an action takes place. In the last sentence, *shows* is in the present tense. In

> I *showed* you.

showed is in the past tense.

> I *will show* you.

uses the future tense.

Than, then

These words are different in spelling, meaning, and function. *Then* refers to time, and *than* makes a comparison.

> We were nice *then*.
> She was taller *than* he was.

That, which, who

We use the word *that* in a number of ways.

It is a demonstrative, as in "*that* cat."

Many writers are confused about when to use *that* and when to use *which* in introducing clauses. Nonrestrictive (nondefining) clauses take *which*.

> The old car, *which* was struggling through the winter, seemed younger when spring arrived.

When the clause is restrictive or defining, we use *that* when it is possible, which is most of the time.

> The old car *that* Mr. Hornback owned was struggling up the hill.

Which is possible in this last sentence, but seems overprecise or rigid, and is stylistically inferior. However, when a sentence requires several restrictive clauses in a row, *that* can become confusing, and we had better revert to *which*.

> The old car *which* Mr. Hornback owned, *which* had one headlight dangling loose, and *which* smelled perpetually of gasoline chugged struggling up the hill.

Remember that *who* applies to people, whether the clause is restrictive or nonrestrictive, and *which* never applies to people.

> The folks *which* lived next door.

is incorrect. Some writers, informally, substitute *that* for *who* on occasions when the person is seen as if from a distance.

> The man *that* stood outside the door was tall and fortyish.

Then

In a familiar balance, within a sentence, we use *then* after *if*.

> *If* statistics imply the opposite, *then* the statistics are incorrect.

Their, there, they're
See pages 392–393.

They, them
See **He/him.**

Through, thru
Thru is incorrect, merely a labor-saving device, adopted by sign painters, advertisers, and the fabricators of headlines.

To, too, two
These homonyms are sometimes confused. *Two* is only a number. *Too* is only an excess: *too* much is *too* much. *To* is a preposition (I handed the book *to* Geronimo) or part of an infinitive (*to* be or not *to* be . . .).

Toward, towards
Either is possible. *Toward* is more American, *towards* more British.

Transitive verb
A transitive verb *must* have a direct object to fill out its meaning.

He *put the book* down.

Book is the direct object of the transitive verb *put.*

Try and

Try and see if she's home.

is a long way to say

See if she's home.

Type
Type is another word to stay away from. Even used grammatically, it is usually filler.

It was a strange *type* of animal.

boils down nicely to

It was a strange animal.

Occasionally, as with *sort* or *kind*, we actually mean something by the word.
Never use it next to a noun, without the preposition *of* coming between. It is useless to say:

> a new *type* soft drink   their *type* business
> a long *type* Buick   that *type* handsomeness

In all these examples, an *of* would make the phrases more acceptable; but in the first three, omission of *type* would be the better solution. We save a word. In the fourth example, the idea of *type* (or *sort* or *kind*) has more meaning, but could benefit from greater specificity.

Unthinkable, inconceivable

Something that is literally *unthinkable* is probably literally unmentionable. We use *unthinkable* as a hyperbole, usually to describe something that we deplore.

> His conduct was *unthinkable.*

Inconceivable means "impossible to imagine or explain."

> Her absence was *inconceivable.*

Until, till

We say *till*, but we write *until*. *Till* looks stilted and literary on the page.

Used to, use to

The correct form is *used to*.

> I *used to* see her every morning at nine o'clock.

Probably because of our slovenly pronunciation, we sometimes drift into

> I *use to* see her every morning at nine o'clock.

when we write it down. We should use the correct form to make temporal sense. The same is true of *supposed to*.

Verb

For advice on style and the verb, see pages 104–111. Also see **Active voice, Intransitive verb, Mood, Object, Passive voice, Predicate**, and **Transitive verb.**

Verbal

Verbals are words derived from verbs but used as nouns or adjectives and sometimes as adverbs. Verbals are *gerunds, participles*, and *infinitives*.

Gerunds always end in *-ing* and are used as nouns.

> *Flying* is fun.
> *Running* is good exercise.
> Neal and Liz have benefited from their *running*.

Participles (past and present) are used as adjectives.

> This *flying* manual is essential.
> His *shattered* hip was mending slowly.
> "The *rising* cost of living" is a common phrase.

Infinitives are used primarily as nouns, but sometimes as adjectives or adverbs. They are composed of *to* and a verb.

> We started *to run* from Godzilla.
> *To fail* is a pleasure he can't afford.
> He dropped out *to begin* his career as a clown.

Vocative
> See **Direct address.**

We/us
> See **He/him.**

When
> Don't use *when* as an introduction to definitions.

> > Loneliness is *when* you play the radio just to hear the announcer's voice.

> You could say instead

> > You are lonely *when* you play the radio just to hear the announcer's voice.

> or

> > It is a definition of loneliness to play the radio just to hear the announcer's voice.

Where
> See **When.** The same injunction applies.

Which, that
> See **That, which, who.**

While
> The word means "at the same time" or "during the time that." Sometimes writers use it in place of *although*, and it can work.

> > *While* John is large, his stomach is not excessive.

> But this usage is prone to ambiguity.

> > Winter is warm in the southern hemisphere, *while* summer is cold.

> Think about this sentence for a moment; it is absurd.

Who, whom

Who is a subject, *whom* an object.

> *Who's* on first?
> *To whom* should I deliver the testimony?

In the last sentence, *whom* is the object of the preposition *to*. In formal writing, always say *whom* when it is an object—of a verb or of a preposition.

Sometimes position leads us into error. When a pronoun precedes a verb, it sounds as if it were a subject; it isn't always. We may be tempted to write

> From *who* is the noise coming?

but the phrase is *from whom*, and *the noise* (not *who*) is the subject of *is*. We should write

> From *whom* is the noise coming?

Sometimes a clause separates the subject *who* from its verb, and we misuse *whom* for *who*. We write

> Herbert, *whom* she said would be here at 6:30, strolled in at 8.00.

In this sentence the three noun-verb combinations make a box within a box within a box. "Herbert . . . strolled" is the outside box, "who . . . would be here" is the middle box, and "she said" the in-side box.

When *whom* comes before a preposition of which it is the object, it is correct but highly formal.

> *Whom* am I looking at?

Here, we always write *who* in informal writing. Frequently, *whom* will sound too formal even in an essay that is mostly formal. Use your judgment. The position of the pronoun makes the problem, which comes up when it is the object of a verb as well as when it is the object of a preposition.

> *Whom* do I see?
> *Who* do I see?

The first is correct and the second incorrect—technically—but it would take a highly formal context to accept the "correct" form without creating a moment of stuffiness.

Whose, who's

See pages 393–394.

-wise

Stylewise, avoid this syllable in combination with words with which it has not been combined before. *Clockwise* and *otherwise* are parts of the language. Avoid *literarywise, poetrywise, intelligence quotientwise, Septemberwise, costwise, Sallywise, ecologywise*—and anything similar.

Woman, women

People sometimes forget that the two spellings show a difference in number. *Woman* is singular, *women* plural.

ACKNOWLEDGMENTS

Isaiah Berlin. Quotation from "Vico and the Ideal of the Enlightenment" in *Against the Current* (New York: Viking Penguin Inc.), page 120, by Isaiah Berlin.

Janet Burroway. Quotation from "Opening Nights: The Opening Days" in *The Writer on Her Work* (New York: W. W. Norton & Company, 1980), edited by Janet Sternburg.

Annie Dillard. Quotation from *Pilgrim at Tinker Creek,* pages 4–5, by Annie Dillard. Copyright © 1974 by Annie Dillard. Reprinted by permission of Harper & Row, Publishers, Inc., and Blanche C. Gregory, Inc.

Ralph Ellison. Quotation from "The Golden Age, Time Past" in *Shadow and Act* (New York: Random House, 1958), page 116.

M. F. K. Fisher. Quotation from "Once A Tramp, Always" in *With Bold Knife and Fork* (New York: Putnam Publishing Group, 1969).

George Garrett. Quotation from "My Two One-Eyed Coaches" in *The Virginia Quarterly Review,* 1987.

George Gilder. Quotation from "But What About Welfare's Grim Side?" *The New York Times,* April 22, 1984. Copyright © 1984 by The New York Times Company. Reprinted by permission.

Elizabeth Hardwick. Quotation from "Boston: The Lost Ideal" in *The Penguin Book of Contemporary American Essays* (New York: Viking Penguin, 1959).

Mary Harron. Quotation from "McRock: Pop as a Commodity" in *Facing the Music* (New York: Pantheon, 1988), pages 209–210, edited by Simon Frith.

Edward Hoagland. "Walking the Dog" from *The New York Times,* April 16, 1979. Copyright © 1979 by The New York Times Company. Quotation from "The Courage of Turtles" from *The Courage of Turtles,* by Edward Hoagland. Copyright © 1970 by Edward Hoagland. Reprinted by permission of Random House, Inc., and Harold Ober Associates.

Mary Hood. Quotation from "Why Stop?" in *The Gettysburg Review* and reprinted in *Best American Essays 1989,* edited by Geoffrey Wolff. Copyright © 1988 by Mary Hood. Reprinted by permission of the author.

John G. Ives. "Questionable Role of Law Review in Evaluating Young Lawyers," a letter to the editor of *The New York Times,* March 11, 1981. Copyright © 1981 by The New York Times Company. Reprinted by permission.

Randall Jarrell. Quotation from *A Sad Heart at the Supermarket: Essays and Fables* by Randall Jarrell. Copyright © 1962 by Randall Jarrell. Reprinted by permission.

Oliver Jensen. "The Gettysburg Address in Eisenhowese" by Oliver Jensen, previously published in *The Territorial Enterprise* and *The New Republic,* June 17, 1957. Reprinted by permission of the author.

Andrew Kopkind. Quotation excerpted from "U. S. to Critics: Keep Out!" *The Nation,* April 28, 1984. Copyright © 1984 The Nation Company, Inc. Reprinted by permission.

D. H. Lawrence. Quotation from *Pornography and Obscenity,* by D. H. Lawrence. Copyright © 1930 by Alfred A. Knopf, Inc. Reprinted by permission of Alfred A. Knopf, Inc., Laurence Pollinger Ltd., and the Estate of the late Mrs. Frieda Lawrence Ravagli.

Phillip Lopate. Quotation from "Modern Friendships" in *Against Joi de Vivre,* page 142. Copyright © 1989 by Phillip Lopate. Reprinted by permission of Poseidon Press, a division of Simon & Schuster, Inc.

Mary McCarthy. Quotations excerpted from "America the Beautiful" in *On the Contrary.* Copyright © 1957, 1961 by Mary McCarthy. Reprinted by permission.

Antonio Machado. Quotation from *The Sea and the Honeycomb* by Antonio Machado, translated by Robert Bly. Copyright © 1971 by Robert Bly. Reprinted by permission.

John McPhee. Quotations from *Coming into the Country* by John McPhee. Copyright © 1976, 1977 by John McPhee. Reprinted by permission of Farrar, Straus and Giroux, Inc.

Al Martinez. "Bad Luck Bob and His Dog" and "Heeding the Winds of Change" in *Ashes in the Rain.* Copyright © 1989 by TQS Publications, Berkeley, California. Reprinted by permission of the publisher.

Margaret Mead. Quotations from "Needed: Full Partnerships for Women" by Margaret Mead, *Saturday Review,* June 14, 1975. Copyright © 1975 by Saturday Review/World, Inc. Reprinted by permission of the Institute of Intercultural Studies.

H. L. Mencken. Quotation from *The American Language,* abridged ed., by H. L. Mencken. Copyright © 1936, 1963 by Alfred A. Knopf, Inc., and renewed 1964 by August Mencken and Mercantile-Safe Deposit and Trust Company. Reprinted by permission of the publisher.

Mark Crispin Miller. Quotation from "The Lives of the Stars" in *Boxed In: The Culture of TV,* pages 205–206. Copyright © 1988 by Mark Crispin Miller. Reprinted by permission of Northwestern University Press.

Susan Mitchell. Quotation from "Dreaming in Public: A Provincetown Memoir." Copyright © 1987 by Susan Mitchell. Reprinted by permission of the author.

V. S. Naipaul. Quotation from *The Return of Eva Perón with the Killings in Trinidad,* by V. S. Naipaul. Copyright © 1974, 1975, 1979, 1980 by V. S. Naipaul. Reprinted by permission of Alfred A. Knopf, Inc., and Aitken & Stone Ltd.

Michael Novak. Quotation from *Solzhenitsyn at Harvard: The Address, Twelve Early Responses, and Six Later Reflections,* edited by Ronald Berman, Ethics and Public Policy Center (1211 Connecticut Avenue, N.W., Washington, D.C. 20036), 1980. Reprinted by permission.

Joyce Carol Oates. Quotation from "On Boxing" from *The New York Times Magazine.*

John A. Parrish. Quotations from *12, 20 & 5: A Doctor's Year in Vietnam* by John A. Parrish, M.D. Copyright © 1974 by John A. Parrish, M.D. Reprinted by permission of E. P. Dutton, Inc., and Gerard McCauley Agency.

G. V. Perkins, Jr. Quotation from "What's New in Agriculture," *The New York Times,* March 25, 1984. Copyright © 1984 by The New York Times Company. Reprinted by permission.

Robert M. Pirsig. Quotations from *Zen and the Art of Motorcycle Maintenance* by Robert M. Pirsig. Copyright © 1974 by Robert M. Pirsig. By permission of William Morrow & Company and The Bodley Head Ltd.

William Raspberry. Quotation from ". . . and Men, Too." Copyright © 1989 The Washington Post Writers Group. Reprinted with permission.

Readers' Guide. Example of an entry in *Readers's Guide to Periodical Literature,* 1980. Copyright © 1980 by the H. W. Wilson Company. Reprinted by permission of H. W. Wilson Company.

Phyllis Rose. "Shopping and Other Spiritual Adventures" from *The New York Times* and reprinted in *The Norton Reader/7.* Copyright © by The New York Times Company. Reprinted by permission.

Antoine de Saint-Exupéry. Quotation from *Wind, Sand and Stars.* Copyright © 1939 by Antoine de Saint-Exupéry; renewed 1967 by Lewis Galantiere. Reprinted by permission of Harcourt Brace Jovanovich, Inc.

Mary Lee Settle. Quotation from "London—1944" in *The Virginia Quarterly Review.*

James Thurber. Quotation from *The Years with Ross* by James Thurber, published by Atlantic-Little, Brown. Copyright © 1959 by James Thurber, © 1987 by Rosemary A. Thurber. Reprinted by permission.

Anne Tyler. Quotation from "Still Just Writing" in *The Writer on Her Work* (New York: W. W. Norton & Company, 1980), edited by Janet Sternburg.

Margaret Walker. Quotation from "On Being Female, Black and Free" in *The Writer on Her Work* (New York: W. W. Norton & Company, 1980), edited by Janet Sternburg.

Diane White. Quotation from "The Noble Asparagus," the *Boston Globe,* May 26, 1977. Reprinted by permission.

E. B. White. Quotation from "Calculating Machine" in *Poems and Sketches of E. B. White.* New York: HarperCollins Publishers, 1951.

James Q. Wilson and John J. DiIulio, Jr. Quotation from "Crackdown" in *The New Republic,* July 10, 1989, pages 21–25. Copyright © 1989 by The New Republic, Inc. Reprinted by permission.

Author and Title Index

Subject Index